I0886506

HEALING AFFLUENZA AND RESISTING PLUTOCRACY

Praise for *Healing Affluenza and Resisting Plutocracy*

This book is for Christian revolutionary nerds—or, more precisely, for those who encounter God in the struggle for justice and in deep, searching engagement with the Bible. Myers's readable and learned account tracks close to the text, while setting it in the sort of wide-ranging conversation that illuminates its meaning for Jesus's time and our own. Strikingly, Myers uses movement wisdom to read the biblical text, and reads the biblical text for movement wisdom. He thus eschews easy answers (of the liberal or conservative kind), recovering instead Jesus's invitation to Sabbath Economics. I hope it will nourish and strengthen those seeking to accept it.

—Lucila Crena, assistant professor of Christian ethics and public theology, Wesley Theological Seminary

For more than a generation, Ched Myers has uniquely combined the tools of rigorous biblical and theological interpretation, critical social analysis, and movement-building for the sake of congregational renewal, social justice, and planetary healing. In this most recent book, Myers brings together themes that have marked his life's work—political economy, racial justice, decolonial discipleship, and ecological repair—in a clarion call for what King named "a radical revolution of values." The result is yet another brilliant and timely contribution from one of our most important scholar-activists: a summons to our seminaries and churches to follow Jesus by getting our hands in the soil and our feet on the ground, marching toward a freedom made possible only through shared abundance, generosity, and justice.

—Timothy R. Eberhart, Robert and Marilyn Degler McClean Associate Professor of Ecological Theology and Practice, and director of the Center for Ecological Regeneration, Garrett-Evangelical Theological Seminary

Ched Myers is the most astute and profound reader of the Scriptures of this generation! Again and again, he discerns previously unseen connections and implications. In his reading of Luke, he shows the way to practice Sabbath Economics in a world suffering from affluenza. This book is a continuous inspiration to reengage in personal and collective economic organization and action.

—Richard Horsley, Distinguished Professor Emeritus of Liberal Arts, University of Massachusetts Boston; author of *Jesus and Empire: The Kingdom of God and the New World Disorder*, *Jesus and the Politics of Roman Palestine*, and *You Shall Not Bow Down and Serve Them: The Political Economic Projects of Jesus and Paul*

Jesus gave his first sermon in Nazareth, calling for a revival of the Jubilee Year. Myers gives convincing scholarly evidence for making this passage in Luke 4 the centerpiece of Jesus's teaching. He describes the social context of Luke's gospel in a vivid and convincing way.

—Michael Hudson, author of . . . *and forgive them their debts: Lending, Foreclosure and Redemption from Bronze Age Finance to the Jubilee Year*

Reaching back into the storied roots of the Torah and Prophets, Myers's insightful and illuminating exegesis probes the oppressive and dehumanizing economic injustices of the first century alongside our own wealth-dominated social and political context. The result is a vibrant picture of Jesus's radical vision for a community shaped by Sabbath Economics. Written with Myers's characteristic quick wit and steeped in wisdom learned from his lifetime of activism, this compelling reading of Luke will resonate with all who long for the biblical vision of Sabbath to renew creation and our world.

—Sylvia C. Keesmaat, coauthor of *Romans Disarmed: Resisting Empire, Demanding Justice*

HEALING AFFLUENZA AND RESISTING PLUTOCRACY

LUKE'S JESUS AND SABBATH ECONOMICS

CHED MYERS

FOREWORD BY CHUCK COLLINS

FORTRESS PRESS
Minneapolis

HEALING AFFLUENZA AND RESISTING PLUTOCRACY
Luke's Jesus and Sabbath Economics

30 28 27 26 25 3 4 5 6 7 8 9

Library of Congress Cataloging-in-Publication Data

Names: Myers, Ched, author.
Title: Healing affluenza and resisting plutocracy : Luke's Jesus and Sabbath economics / Ched Myers ; foreword by Chuck Collins.
Description: Minneapolis : Fortress Press, [2025] | Includes bibliographical references.
Identifiers: LCCN 2024022642 (print) | LCCN 2024022643 (ebook) | ISBN 9798889834366 (print) | ISBN 9798889834373 (ebook)
Subjects: LCSH: Bible. Luke--Social scientific criticism. | Economics in the Bible. | Social justice--Biblical teaching. | Sociology, Biblical.
Classification: LCC BS2595.6.E35 M94 2025 (print) | LCC BS2595.6.E35 (ebook) | DDC 226.4/06--dc23/eng/20240906
LC record available at https://lccn.loc.gov/2024022642
LC ebook record available at https://lccn.loc.gov/2024022643

Cover art: Copyright Ted Lyddon Hatten; photography by Rick Lozier
Cover design: Kristin Miller

Print ISBN: 979-8-8898-3436-6
Ebook ISBN: 979-8-8898-3437-3

To twelve exemplary disciples:
Teachers and friends gone: Dorothea Bradley, Marty Coleman, Murphy Davis, Dan Erlander, Norman K. Gottwald, Michael Iafrate, James Lawson, Vern Ratzlaff, and Dale Stitt.
Mentors still: William J. Barber II, Marian Wright Edelman and Catherine Morris.

The great obstacle is simply this: the conviction that we cannot change because we are dependent upon what is wrong. But that is the addict's excuse, and we know that it will not do.

—Wendell Berry, "What Are People For?"

CONTENTS

Part II
Telling and Showing
Sabbath Economics in the First Half of Luke

Part III
Parables and Object Lessons
Sabbath Economics in the Second Half of Luke

ACKNOWLEDGMENTS

This book was curated and written at Bartimaeus Cooperative Ministries, where we live and work in the Ventura River Watershed, the heart of traditional, unceded, and untreatied Chumash territory in southern California. We are committed to learning the stories this land and people hold in order to face, and work toward repairing, the long history of disenfranchisement of Indigenous peoples here and elsewhere on Turtle Island. We thank the Barbareño-Ventureño Band for their hospitality, and for friendship and collaboration in the work of economic and social justice and decolonization in this place.

Throughout this book, I recognize many "inspirators" and partners, both intellectual and practical, in advancing the vision and practices of Sabbath Economics. It seemed good in my dedication to single out from among this wide, ecumenical, and beloved community the following twelve (a discipleship number). I wish to honor nine friends who have passed into the Cloud of Witnesses over the last four years, and three veterans still among us. Because it is important to acknowledge the genealogy of one's work, a brief word about each:

- **Dorothea Bradley** (d. 2020) was a giant of justice among and for marginalized communities in Pasadena, California, where I worked for a decade. As I note in my introduction, Dorothea modeled Baha'i principles of service and mutual aid, and resisted plutocracy with wry humor, truly embodying the spirit of Luke's "persistent woman" (18:1–8; see 12A).
- **Marty Coleman** (d. 2024) helped connect me with kindred spirits upon my return to Los Angeles in 1987. She was a peace and justice legend among Episcopalians in the region, ever hospitable to us and our Cooperative, loved biblical conversation, and brought joy to every collaboration.
- **Murphy Davis** (d. 2020), a Presbyterian minister, cofounded the Open Door Community in Atlanta, which for thirty years brought justice and compassion to homeless folk and those on death row. She battled cancer, denominational ambivalence, and the political powers of the prison industrial complex in Georgia.[1] As I was

completing this book, my partner Elaine Enns and I traveled to Jubilee Partners in Comer, Georgia, to join Murphy's family and many coconspirators to bury her ashes next to poor men who had been executed by the carceral state or died on the streets.

- **Dan Erlander** (d. 2022) was a beloved Lutheran artist and author. His remarkable translation of Norman Gottwald's work into the popular education resource *Manna and Mercy* mobilized a generation of church folk for social justice and helped rescue the Bible from both fundamentalist severity and Sunday School trivialization.[2] He personified the grace and faith reflected in his art and prose.
- **Norman K. Gottwald** (d. 2022) was a groundbreaking, Baptist Hebrew Bible professor, whose work on the origins of ancient Israel changed the academic field. It inspired my reading of Sabbath Economics and animated many other activists around the world. Norm was an exemplary "people's scholar," whose friendship graced our Word and World Schools, built the Center and Library for the Bible and Social Justice, and seeded a generation of innovators working to liberate biblical studies.[3]
- **Michael Iafrate** (d. 2021) was Co-Coordinator of the Catholic Committee of Appalachia and served as lead author of their groundbreaking "People's Pastoral: The Telling Takes Us Home: Taking Our Place in the Stories that Shape Us." A beloved singer-songwriter and promoter of old time music, he was completing a dissertation in theology at the University of Toronto when he was struck down at age forty-four. He left behind a spouse and three young girls, and a wide community of friends and colleagues who painfully miss his leadership in faith, activism, and culture.[4]
- The legendary **James Lawson** (d. 2024) passed as I was doing final edits on this manuscript. I met this giant of justice in the early nineties when we were forming Clergy and Laity United for Economic Justice in Los Angeles. Mentor to Martin Luther King Jr. and animator of nonviolent resistance to American apartheid, Lawson moved to Southern California in 1972 to resume his Methodist pastoring, and here similarly became a lynchpin of labor rights and social justice organizing. He continued up until his final days to act generously as a gracious "founding father" of the modern movement, tirelessly tutoring us younger activists.
- **Vern Ratzlaff** (d. 2024) was the pastor of Elaine's home church, Nutana Park in Saskatoon, SK; he baptized her, married us, buried

her parents, and welcomed me into the Mennonite fold. Vern curated wide ecumenical and interfaith relations, stemming from his service with Mennonite Central Committee in Manitoba and Egypt. He was, for us and many others, a trusted friend, confidant, and revered elder.

- **Dale Stitt** (d. 2022), a Disciples of Christ minister, was a strong partner in spreading the vision and practices articulated herein through his work with Ministry of Money at Church of the Savior, Journey into Freedom in Portland, Oregon, and our national Sabbath Economics Collaborative. Dale and his partner Esther Elizabeth helped midwife many into journeys of transformation.

I also dedicate this volume to three iconic mentors still among us, whose work and witness is a North Star for all those who struggle to heal affluenza and resist plutocracy today:

- It was through the agency of Gordon Cosby of Church of the Savior (see below) that I met revered mother in faith and justice **Marian Wright Edelman**, who celebrated her eighty-fifth birthday as I was writing this tribute. As Jim Lawson was, Marian is a living embodiment of the great Southern Freedom Struggle of the 1960s, who has also carried it on while pressing its spirit and tasks on to us. Having coffee with her in 2014 on my first day at Haley Farm—the amazing space of hospitality and movement-building Marian curated—was like touching the hem of Jesus's garment and began my regular pilgrimage to those sacred grounds.
- Since 1987, my spiritual home in Los Angeles has been the Catholic Worker community, shaped and led over a half century by **Catherine Morris** and her partner Jeff Dietrich. Catherine, ninety, embodies the spirit of movement founder Dorothy Day (with whom she was once arrested) and has for a half century exemplified the evangelical arts of service to the poor and speaking truth to the rich. I am grateful to be an extended part in this circle—with whom I still facilitate occasional Bible study, to Catherine's beatific smile![5]
- I first collaborated with **William J. Barber II** in 2006 at a Sabbath Economics seminar in Raleigh, North Carolina. This Disciples of Christ minister has since become arguably the most prominent faith leader in the US, particularly in his role reviving Dr. King's historic commitment to a Poor Peoples' Campaign. Whenever I've had the

> opportunity to work with either Lawson or Barber, they have taught me more about the origins of disparities under American "plantation capitalism" (as Lawson calls it) and about how to build a moral and spiritually grounded movement for radical change.

These three followers of Jesus and movement leaders are national treasures who we should continue to celebrate and learn from.

* * *

There are, of course, fingerprints of so many more on this project. I am grateful to all those who have worked through Sabbath Economics theology with me, contextualizing it and putting it into practice over the last two decades, especially those who have continued to work our BCM Household Covenant (see appendix II, i). This roll call is long, yet it is always good to celebrate one's community of conviction (list is alphabetical; those who have passed are asterisked):

> Lisa Bachman, Rob Baird, Eddie Beres, Mike and Lynn Boucher, Cheryl Broetje, Devorah Brous, Steve Borla and Kate Foran, Myra Brown, Jim Callan and Spiritus Christi Church, Jordan Cantwell and Laura Fouhse, Kevin Cashman, Paul Choi, Shane Claiborne and the Simple Way, Diane Clarke, Joe Collier, Marty Collier, Chuck Collins and United for a Fair Economy, Warren Cooper, Jonathan Cornford and Manna Gum, Jeff Cowmeadow, Paul and Irene Creasey, Art Cribbs, Fr. Gerry Curry* and the Scarborough Center, Nancy Davis, Russ Daye, Charles Demere*, Marie Dennis and Pax Christi, Leonard Doell, Paris Dunning, Tevyn East and Jay Beck and Dreaming Stone, Margaret Ernst, Greg Edwards, Tom Ewell, Judith Favor*[6], Rose Feerick and Wisdom and Money, David* and Susan* Fetcho, Michael Fiala and the Cleveland Catholic Worker, John Freesemann, Jacque French, Ray Funk, Jerome Garciano, Greg Garvan, Jamie Gates, Sharon and Bill Gerred, Elizabeth and Tim Gibbs-Zehnder, Wendy and David Gist, Stan Goff, Julie Graham and Jennifer Janzen-Ball, Darrel Grothaus, Barbara Haddon*, Eileen and Les Klassen Hamm, Andy Harris, Jonathan Wilson Hartgrove, Bill Heffernan, Steve Heinrichs, Jennifer Henry and Susie Henderson, Tensie Hernandez and Dennis Apel, Paul Hertig and Young Lee, Peter Hiltner, Carol and John Hirt, Eric Hodge, Walter Hudson, Bob Hulteen, Eileen Hurley, Benni Isaak-Krauß, Logan Janzen, Joyce and Nelson Johnson, George* and Vivian Johnson, Donna Jones, Jacqueline Camara Jones, Glenn Jordan*, Philip Kennedy, Jin Kim, Charlie King, Lindsay and Jason Kliewer, Doris Kung, Ellen Klyce, Diem Lafortune, Peter Laarman, Rich Lang, Eric LeCompte

and Jubilee USA, Taehoo Lee, Ted Lewis*, Mike Little, Frances Loberg, Lance Loberg, Grecia and Josh Lopez-Reyes, Eduard Loring and The Open Door, Lee and Juanita Mangan-Van Ham and One Earth Jubilee, Tina and Michael Mata, Ray and Rita McGovern, Andrew McLeod, Elizabeth McMeekin and Phil Moses, Kate McMichael and Theresa Hauser, Darrel Meyers, Rita and Jim Mize, Melanie Morrison, Otis Moss III, Gail and Peter Mott*, Bert and Gloria Newton, Solveig and Peter Nilsen-Goodin, Jeff Nelson, Sarah Nolan, Steve and Dawn Novak, Will O'Brien and Dee Risher, Mark Olson, Gordon Oyer, Sue Park and Hyun Hur, Ann Pettifor, Terry Provance and Oikocredit, Mary and Jim Ramerman, Merilee Robertson, Peg Rosenkrands, Mauricio and Cynthia Salgado, Jonathan Schorsch, Chad and Sheila Schwitters, Michael Schut, Kate and Charlie Segerstrom, Ken and Nancy Sehested, Richard Sewell, Barry Shelley, Amy Simes, Robyn Smith, T. Anthony Spearman*, Jenny Speice and Michael Fallat, Frank Stasio, Doug Stelling, Kate Stevens and John Hoffman, John Stoner, Nancy Sullivan, Paul and Cara Taylor, Stuart Taylor, Nancy Thurston, Geza Tokes, Sharon Tool, Richard Truitt, Rick and Kitty Ufford-Chase, Shawn and Justin Whelan, Stephanie and Jake Martin-White, Faith Wilder, Scott Wright, Bill Wylie-Kellermann, Todd Wynward, Kristy and Tyler Zabriskie, Barbara Zelter, and Rick Zemlin.

Apologies to those I missed! Two elders who supported the Sabbath Economics vision deserve special mention. Virgil Wood, another veteran of the civil rights struggle, helped curate the important Jubilee Legacy Bible Project, which was in inspiration and resource to me and many others.[7] The late Gordon Cosby, cofounder of Church of the Saviour in Washington, DC, the oldest continuing alternative ecclesial experiment in the US, affirmed and resourced our early efforts in Sabbath Economics education, and was my spiritual director and encourager during those years.[8]

I also am indebted to scholarly colleagues who have accompanied and deepened our Sabbath Economics work, including: George Armstrong, Scott Bartchy, Sandra Beardsall, Geoff Broughton, Pamela Brubaker, John Cobb, Matt Coomber, Lee Cormie, Lucila Crena, Gabriele Dietrich and Bas Wielenga*, Ulrich Duchrow, Laurel Dykstra, Tim Eberhart, John H. Elliott*, Neil Elliott, Pete Gathje, Obery Hendricks, Paul Hertig, William Herzog*, Richard Horsley, Wes Howard-Brook, Nick Johnson, Brigitte Kahl, Sylvia Keesmaat and Brian Walsh, Ross Kinsler*, Mark Lau Branson, Anthony Mansueto, Cynthia and Ron Moe-Lobeda, Rick Lowery, Doug Oakman, Hugh Page, Jim Perkinson and Lily Mendoza, Jorge Pixley*, Patrick Reyes, Anthony Ricciuti, Joerg Rieger and Rosemarie Henkel-Rieger, Sharon Ringe, Christopher Rowland, Rodney

Sadler, Alan Streett, Elsa Támez, Sam Thomas, Osvaldo Vena, Herman Waetjen, Arthur Waskow, Sam Wells, Gerald West, Ann Wire, and the inimitable Janet Wolf.

Matt and Jill Colwell, Marcia and Clancy Dunigan, Steve and Christine Clemens, C. John Hildebrand, Andy Loving, Steve and Sheryl Taylor, and Bob and Ritchie Two Bulls have been long and strong supporters of BCM's work. So have past and present members of our board and staff: Ann Coburn*, Carter Echols, Elaine Emily, Joe Franko*, Shady Hakim, Adrianne Hall, Karen and Brian Hooks, Jason Jenkins, Rick Kidd, Gloria Kinsler, Cassie Lewis, John Parker, Deb Pendrey, Joe Roos, and Susan Taylor. Our Cooperative is sustained by a "community-supported ministry" mutual aid model, and we are grateful for each of our partners who make our work possible—not least for me to set aside six months for full-time writing!

Chris Wight and Elaine Enns held everything down at BCM during that grueling stretch, and helped with many aspects of manuscript wrangling. Rose Marie Berger and Heidi Thompson were trusted advisors-editors in the process. New Testament scholar Bill Richards graciously checked my Greek, and I am grateful for his corrections and suggestions. Adella Barrett helped with wrangling the indices. And I am pleased to have Ted Lyddon Hatten's art grace the cover of this book. Thanks to Greg Jarrell for introducing me to Laura Gifford at Fortress Press; with a gracious hand, she and her colleagues guided the editorial course through a demanding deadline so that this book might be available for the next lectionary Year of Luke. Xuxa provided comfort and comic relief.

I leaned hard on Elaine's steadying encouragement and love through the arduous ordeal of writing this. We sent the manuscript off on our twenty-fifth anniversary, and I thank God for every year of her companionship in our life and work of Sabbath Economics.

LIST OF FIGURES

FOREWORD

A Dose of Ancient Medicine

Chuck Collins

For over four decades, US society has been steadily pulling apart. As we live through a period of extreme wealth inequality, we need healing from the culture of affluenza, the top-down disorder of disconnection, wealth hoarding, and excessive consumption. And we need to resist plutocracy, the harmful concentrations of wealth and power that are disrupting our workplaces, communities, and ecological viability.

We are fortunate that activist theologian Ched Myers offers signposts on the road to healing and resistance. His focus is how the biblical teachings of Sabbath Economics shaped the Gospel of Luke. As Ched reminds us, these inequality trends are not acts of nature, nor the work of divine will, but the result of a sin-sick, human-engineered system of laws, rules, and individualistic cultural norms.

What has gone wrong? The simple explanation is: *the rules governing the economy have been tipped in favor of wealthy investors, at the expense of wage earners.* This has activated a "wealth pump" that has extracted income and wealth from the bottom 90 percent of households and funneled it to the already-have-a-lots. As a result, the lion's share of income and wealth gains have flowed not just to the top 1 percent of households, but the richest 0.1 percent—those with assets north of $40 million.

In the thirty years after World War Two, between 1945 and 1974, real wages rose steadily for all income earners, including for women and people of color. This era—still in living memory—shows that we *can* rewire our economy for shared prosperity. But since the mid-1970s, real wages for low- and middle-income households have remained stagnant. Meanwhile, income and investment returns surged to the rich: during this same period, roughly *fifty trillion dollars* was transferred from bottom 90 percent to the top 1 percent.

Wealth is a critical multigenerational gauge of economic well-being. Wealth is what one owns minus what one owes: the measure of the financial cushion a family has to fall back on during hard times. Many have seen their wealth and savings decline over this period. Wealth disparity is also where the legacy of racism shows up: in people's bank accounts and in home ownership and equity. Median white household wealth is roughly ten times median Black wealth—and nine times Latino and Indigenous wealth. This present-day racial wealth divide is an economic archeological marker, embedded within the multigenerational story of land theft, slavery, racial plunder, and discrimination. It is where the past is present, where the wound at the center of US history going back four centuries is still open, waiting for repair. The surging wealth pump of the last few decades has supercharged these deeply rooted racial inequalities.

We see the results around us: rising numbers of unsheltered people alongside an increase in private jet ownership, diminished savings and economic precarity alongside ostentatious displays of wealth and profligate consumption. The huge US mortality rates from the COVID-19 pandemic, highest among Black and brown people, revealed extreme inequality as the preexisting condition that weakened our body politic as well as the immune responses of our bodies. Unequal societies have the worst health indicators, even among the affluent. During the pandemic, the combined wealth of the US billionaire class almost doubled, to $5.4 trillion, while most frontline workers were Black, brown, and low-income. The unequal rewards and sacrifices offered a crash course about the harms of disparity.

Myers describes our current political and governance system as a plutocracy: a society dominated by the power of the wealthy. The interpersonal manifestation of this is affluenza: the cultural disorders driven by excessive wealth concentrating in the hands of a few, along with the idolatry of excess. Affluenza dehumanizes everyone, starting with the wealthy. As he writes, "It is a pandemic that empowers the rich, endangers the middle class, taunts the poor, and ransacks the planet." It is an illness that must be addressed at its roots.

In a plutocracy, the wealthy deploy their wealth and power to warp our laws and culture to their own narrow interests. Tax, trade, and other government policies are altered to benefit investors over wage earners. In plutocratic societies, the wealthy lack the personal and political will to pay taxes, or to invest in greater access to health care, education, and a basic safety net.

These harms are widespread and touch every aspect of our lives. Myers warns that the "deepening crisis of persistent socioeconomic disparity threatens social coherence, democratic prospects, and ecological viability." Yet as the new physics of inequality accelerates advantages for the already wealthy and compounds disadvantages for low income people, we are witnessing advanced plutocratic plunder.

The wealthy own enterprises that hyper-extract wealth from renters, farmers, nature, small businesses, and people trying to meet their basic needs for health care, medicine, food, and housing. Billionaire-backed private equity firms acquire hospitals formerly owned by religious orders, cutting costs, selling off valuable assets, and squeezing nickels from patients for their already-wealthy investors.

At the top of the economic pile, affluenza is a "disconnection drug," walling off the hearts of the rich from the harms of the economic apartheid being constructed by their own actions. The solution is connection and healing, the spiritual and societal spark that faith communities can curate and disseminate. The way forward is not charity but change, especially as billionaires use philanthropy primarily to extend their power and influence. We hunger for justice, not charitable affirmations of the status quo and the distracting band-aids of incremental distributions.

The fundamental tenets of a Sabbath Economics remind us that there is abundance, enough for everyone's need but not everyone's greed, as Gandhi said. Inequality is a social sin, a disorder that Myers calls the community of faith to mitigate "through the regular practice of redistribution and reparation." Jubilee economics elevates to sacred status the "social duty of canceling debts, redistributing the land, and liberating debt servants." The prophets, then and now, call us to a discipleship of equality, working for a society that leaves no one behind, and where all can thrive.

There is good news: social movements resisting plutocracy are working to break up concentrations of wealth and power in order to save democracy and protect the earth from excessive consumption. There are workers taking back agency and power in their workplaces and communities. There are also some beneficiaries of wealth inequality who are healing affluenza by speaking out against the system that made them financially advantaged. These dissenters of the elite are working together with promising movements to address the harms of extreme inequality, racial capitalism, and for reparations and healing.

They include a veteran wealth advisor who leads a "progressive advisor's movement," helping clients entirely rethink their relationship to wealth and pressing for a higher purpose: aiding clients to deploy resources to *heal the harms caused by wealth extraction*. Some of these wealth managers are defecting, blowing the whistle on systemic abuses and helping craft laws to close tax loopholes they helped to create. And there are networks of wealth holders pledging to redistribute their wealth, share decision-making, and to "decolonize wealth." Others are calling for higher taxes on themselves, higher wages for workers, reduced money in politics, and reforms in the laws governing philanthropy. These trends are flickers of possibility, cracks in what often appears to be an omnipotent system.

The power of today's billionaires—and their enablers in the wealth defense industry—is formidable. They command huge pools of resources that have captured political systems, in oligarchic fashion, all over the world. Yet the defectors and imagineers represent a harbinger of new possibilities for building regenerative and just economies that serve social and ecological needs and flourishing.

In this book, the Gospel of Luke comes alive in a way that will inspire, empower, and nurture such efforts while recruiting people of faith and conscience to join the movement for repair and renewal. Ched offers us scripture as "ancient medicine" that can animate both ecclesial discipleship and wider social movements of economic justice. I commend it to you.

* * *

Chuck Collins is a researcher, storyteller, and campaigner based at the Institute for Policy Studies, where he directs the Program on Inequality and the Common Good and coedits Inequality.org. He is the author of over ten books on inequality, philanthropy, and environmental issues, including *The Wealth Hoarders: How Billionaires Pay Millions to Hide Trillions; Born on Third Base: A One Percenter Makes the Case for Tackling Inequality; Bringing Wealth Home and Committing to the Common Good*; and, with Bill Gates Sr., *Wealth and Our Commonwealth.* See www.chuckcollinswrites.com.

ARTIST'S STATEMENT

The iconography on the book's cover comes from the Third Gospel and conversations with Ched. I encountered his commentary on Mark in 1989 (ironically, in a class on Luke); we met a few years later at a snowy seminar in Minneapolis, and have been friends since. We collaborate whenever we can; Ched commissioned this piece during Lent, 2024.

The sycamore tree (*Ficus sycomorus*) on the cover of this book was rendered with pyrography (drawing with heat) and encaustic (painting with molten beeswax), on a forty-year-old slab of sycamore wood (a jubilee branch), quarter-sawn by Ryan Gay. It was produced at Dovecote Studio in Indianola, Iowa and photographed by Rick Lozier. I also work with words, photography, metalpoint, installation art, site-specific ephemeral art, wood carving, and dry painting. The materials I use—including myrrh, liquefaction, ash, soil, frass, coffee grounds, wax, dry pigment, grain, glass, sand, salt, and tea leaves—have two things in common: they are gratifying to touch and smell, and they hold compelling stories that add additional layers of meaning to the art.

This sycamore, a fixture in Jericho's landscape and local economy, is rooted firmly in the beginning of the end of Luke's story. Its trunk runs up the spine, its branches stretch from back cover to front. A raven (*Corvus corax*) rests on a limb at upper right (Luke 12:24), staring down an imperial tower in the distance (13:4; 14:28). When a wealthy, fraudulent baron climbs up this tree (19:4), it will give him a different outlook on his world—a bird's-eye view. Feet dangling between worlds, it becomes an *axis mundi* for him, a place where heaven and earth meet—like Jacob's ladder, or Mount Sinai, or the cross.

Luke, physician and artist, has a keen interest in how seeing can lead to healing—and vice versa. This is elegantly demonstrated in his twinned stories of a blind mendicant who is rich in faith, and a rich tax collector who is blind to affluenza (18:35–19:10). Both are healed: the former sees and follows Jesus, the latter glimpses a vision while perched in the raven's roost.

In my midrashic imagination, in that tree Zacchaeus experiences vertigo from three unsettling forces:

Beauty. The world looks different when seen from above: patterns, colors, symmetry. Philosopher Elaine Scarry asserts that "beautiful things give rise to the notion of distribution, to a lifesaving reciprocity, to fairness not just in the sense of loveliness of aspect but in the sense of 'a symmetry of everyone's relation to one another.'"[1] This helps us discover balance and equality as the hallmarks of justice.

The asymmetry of a world out of balance due to dehumanizing disparity. In the distance he recognizes a disabled and destitute neighbor who was relegated to begging, but who now leads Jesus's approaching entourage (18:43). He wonders about his own role in perpetuating a system in which haves take from the have-nots. It gnaws at him as he peers through newly greening sycamore leaves (it is springtime, just before Passover, the great feast of liberation). Because in this mystical tree, those six leaves represent each of the challenging object lessons in Luke's series of rich man stories, which form the spine of his Sabbath Economics narrative.

The raven singing her "beyond barns" catechism about God's Great Economy (see 8B). Zacchaeus realizes that the world doesn't have to be splayed across cruel disparities; a shared Commonwealth can be constructed around need, not greed.

Dizzy, he clambers *down*.

At the base of the tree he encounters a small cave. He senses the spirit of Elijah hovering there (1 Kg 19:9), a prophet similarly tutored and sustained by ravens (1 Kg 17:4–6). Zacchaeus peers inside, through roots and rhizomes, though it's too dark to see the graffiti on the wall, or the white linen cloth rolled up in the corner. Yet when he turns and his eyes adjust back to daylight, he beholds a lily of the field nearby (*Anemone coronaria*)—another catechist of both beauty and the Great Economy. She seems to tower over the imperial edifice in the distance; as Jesus put it, "Solomon in all his glory was not arrayed like one of these flowers" (Luke 12:27).

Luke, however, doesn't *tell* us what Zacchaeus saw up in that sycamore. Instead he *shows* us the result of the rich man's immersion into the arboreal *axis mundi*: soon after his feet hit the ground, this plutocrat surprises everyone by announcing a commitment to reparative justice (19:8). In this way, the healing of equity comes to the stratified House of Abraham (19:9). After all, the Great Ancestor was also a rich man who, way back at the roots of the sacred story, fled oppressive tower-culture (Gen 11:1–9; 12:4) and similarly encountered the Creator's vision under a Teaching Tree (Gen 12:6–7).

These are ways this cover image echoes the argument of this book. A second piece (also pyrography and encaustic on another cross section of sycamore wood) appears on the dedication page. It imagines the vista *from* that holy sycamore tree: a closer look at the raven, the six sycamore leaves, and a Trinity of lilies (Tyrian purple in the color original). These images all invite us to dance into the Great Economy.

—Ted Lyddon Hatten, Passover 2024

Find more of Ted's art at: https://www.tedlyddonhatten.com.[2]

Introduction

Four Stories

> So the people worked all day and night and all the next day, gathering the quails; the least anyone gathered was ten homers. . . . But while the meat was still between their teeth . . . God struck them with a very great plague. So that place was called *Kibroth-hattaavah* [graves of craving].
>
> —Numbers 11:32–34 NRSV

> I will tell you something about stories, [he said]
> They aren't just entertainment. Don't be fooled.
> They are all we have, you see,
> all we have to fight off illness and death.
> . . . .
> Their evil is mighty,
> but it can't stand up to our stories.
> So they try to destroy the stories,
> let the stories be confused or forgotten.
> . . . .
> Because we would be defenseless then.
>
> —Leslie Marmon Silko, *Ceremony*[1]

AT A KEY juncture in Luke's narrative of Jesus's public ministry, the Nazarene spins a short, foreboding cautionary tale. It is set in the afterlife, where a rich man who is a model of entitlement and denial encounters Abraham, the primal progenitor of his people. They have a tense and terse exchange, albeit at a distance. Abraham tries to explain to him two truths about the economic life and world the rich man has just left. The first is that his wealth was predicated upon a fatal sociological, moral and theological condition the patriarch calls a *chasma mega* (huge gulf). It separated and insulated him from people who were impoverished and dehumanized by the system that created and sustained his privilege, people whose pain can only be grasped from *their* side of that social chasm. The second truth is that in order to find the will and way to eradicate this cruel gulf, he must reread his sacred Scriptures (chapter 11).

This tale summarizes the thesis and purpose of Luke's story of Jesus—and of this book. In our historical moment, the deepening crisis of persistent socioeconomic disparity threatens social coherence, democratic prospects, and ecological viability both globally and in North America. I believe the biblical vision of Sabbath Economics as narrated by Luke represents ancient medicine, which can help us muster the moral and political imagination necessary to survive and heal this terminal disease. My reading of the Third Gospel arises from a half century of learning, teaching, writing, and organizing. I offer it to people of faith and conscience trying to respond to and transform this crisis under the gathering storm of authoritarian plutocracy, and amidst the latest wars of the rich on the poor in Ukraine and Gaza.

This project embraces the traditional wisdom of Laguna Pueblo novelist Leslie Marmon Silko. The opening lines of her acclaimed novel *Ceremony* place the above warning on the lips of an elder. It testifies to how ancestral sacred stories are key to Indigenous healing and survivance in the face of the "mighty evil" of a half-millennium-long European domination of native lands, bodies, and spirits.[2] In my opinion, Silko's words *also* articulate a parallel conviction found in the biblical prophetic tradition, and with a concise profundity I have rarely encountered in Western theology. I will invoke them repeatedly through this book. Like Silko's Pueblo elder, the Hebrew prophets (not least Jesus of Nazareth) engaged the perennial human struggle between memory and amnesia, responsibility and denial. They too understood that this struggle turns upon the stories that shape our convictions, interpret our past and present, and animate our practices. An example is a primordial biblical warning tale: the "graves of craving" story, also cited above. The lesson of *Kibroth-hattaavah* predates by over twenty-five hundred years contemporary diagnoses of the capitalist disease of affluenza; it also takes on a dreadful poignancy in light of the social and ecological endgame bearing down upon us.[3]

I am aware of how deeply counterintuitive it is for children of modernity to call upon old wisdom in pressing times. We reflexively assume that our technologies and managerial adjustments will somehow save us. Yet addressing symptoms, while relying on the very methods that spawned and deepen the crisis of disparity, will not do; we need to expose and treat this dis-ease at its roots. Luke's venerable old story of Jesus and Sabbath Economics can help us as we face the brimming apocalypse of economic dehumanization and ecocide today.

Allegedly a core sacred story for churches, the Gospel has too often been confused, forgotten, or used as mere religious entertainment. This has left too many contemporary Christians fooled by and defenseless against the enchanting mendacities of our capitalist cosmology, with its infinite tolerance of wealth, of poverty, and of the gulf between them. It is my conviction and experience, however, that Luke's accounts of Jesus's good news to the poor and warnings to the rich can inspire us to fight off the endemic illness of affluenza and stand up to the death sentence of plutocracy. If we have ears to hear (Luke 8:8).

That is the short version of this project. What follows is a more fulsome introduction, which outlines further details about its why, what, and how. If you wish to dive directly into my reading, you can orient yourself by consulting the introductions to each of the three sections, which offer brief summaries of their chapters. One important caveat: because this is a close study of Luke's story, it is essential that you have the biblical text at hand as you read this book; in most cases I have not reproduced it in my commentary.

i. The Practice of Contextual Biblical Interpretation

Without our sacred stories we are indeed defenseless. But as Paul Ricoeur liked to point out, the texts themselves are also defenseless against mishandling, to which the history of Christendom—from the medieval Doctrine of Discovery to current American Christian nationalism—attests.[4] In fact, the word "hermeneutics" is derived from the god Hermes, who in classical antiquity was the patron saint of interpreters—but also of thieves. The only remedy to burgled, dysfunctional, or toxic readings of the Bible are ones that are stronger, more coherent, textually faithful, and above all *contextual.*

Interpretation is not a simplistic proposition, however. This is not well grasped by ideologues (and some preachers), though it is perhaps *over*emphasized by many academics. The best way to summarize the hermeneutic challenge is to recognize that whenever we approach a biblical text, we are actually engaging, consciously or unconsciously, in *four* story-worlds, not just one.[5] Here are four vectors of text and context to which my reading of Luke attends:

1. the text (and world) of Luke's narrative;
2. the ancient social context of that text and its production—the historical story;
3. our current social and historical context (and ideological narratives) as readers—the story of now, including past and current interpretations of Luke's text that have shaped (and misshaped) us;
4. our resulting interpretation of Luke's text—the recontextualized story we tell in and for our personal and political moment.

Figure 1 illustrates this process in terms of working a jigsaw puzzle. While we can concentrate on any of its quadrants at any given moment, we must engage the whole puzzle.

This model acknowledges that there is no text without context (the quadrants separated by the vertical line), and that the art of interpretation must

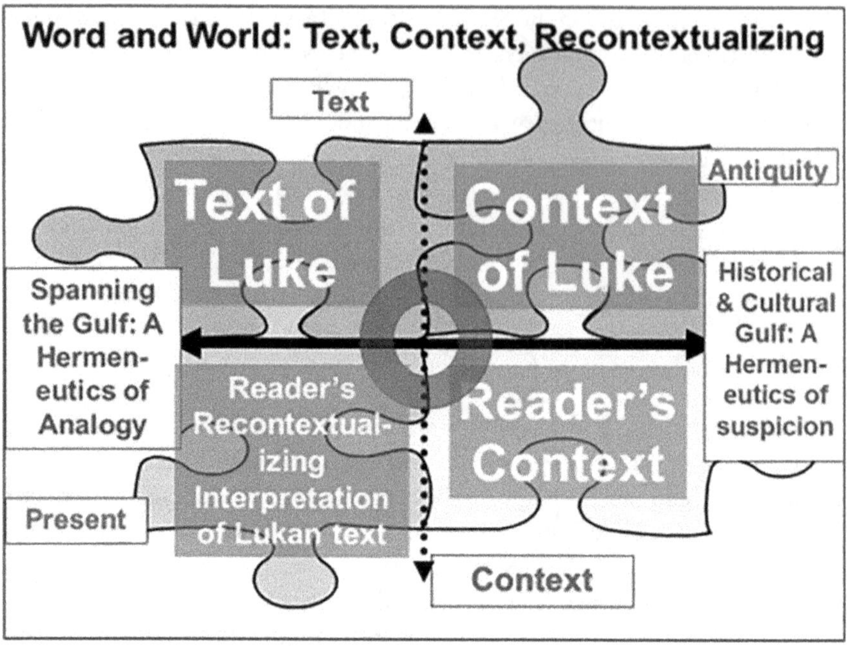

Figure 1. Word and World: Text, Context, Recontextualizing (Diagram by Ched Myers).

respect historical and sociocultural *gulfs* between ancient and modern texts and contexts and readings (the quadrants separated by the horizontal line). Thus, readers should exercise a certain "hermeneutics of suspicion" (as it is called in the academy) as a check on the preconceptions and presumptions we bring to the text. Yet the *goal* of interpretation is to span these gulfs, which requires finding appropriate *analogies* that help past text speak to present context (right and left boxes in Figure 1).

The bottom left quadrant seeks to interrelate all the pieces of the puzzle, resulting in an integral interpretation (inner circle). This process is never completed; our recontextualized readings are ever subject to revision by further work on the puzzle, our own or that of others (especially others in different contexts). I will briefly elaborate on all four quadrants for reading Luke as I explore them in this book. Let's start with what is most existential, addressing our collective social and historical context, as well as my personal one.

ii. Our Context

Dorothea Bradley, an African American elder in Pasadena, California, was a treasured friend. A longtime resident of a low-income neighborhood, she ran a food program out of the back of the community organizing office where I worked from 1987–1995. Distributing "Commodity Supplemental Food" was just one of her many acts of service to local poor and disabled folk. Dorothea had to sustain the food program on a shoestring budget, relying on a colorful cohort of volunteers and her own sheer determination. She had no patience for those who ignored or invisibilized poverty. Increasingly disabled herself, she eventually operated the program out of her own rented home, saved from eviction only by her widespread community reputation. A delightful conversation partner and exemplar of deep faith and humor, Dorothea taught me in countless ways the bootstrap art of practicing mutual aid in marginalized neighborhoods. In the early days of the recent pandemic, low-income people of color succumbed disproportionately. Dorothea was among them.[6]

Of all the perplexing and troubling characteristics of this third decade of the third millennium here in the US, this book tackles the crisis of economic disparity—the structures and policies that make and maintain both extreme poverty and wealth. Here are four understandings I have developed over a lifetime of working in the social justice field, mentored by beloveds like Dorothea:

- Economic disparity is a social and political pathology, not a condition of nature. The biblical narrative is clear that Creation is abundantly sufficient for the needs of living creatures—just not for human greed (as Gandhi paraphrased it; 2A).
- Socioeconomic disparity is *not* a lamentable-but-inevitable (or even a necessary!) by-product of economic progress, as asserted by capitalist apologia.
- The architects of inequality are the rich and powerful, who create, sustain, and benefit from its systems and ideological legitimations today, as in countless earlier chapters of civilizational history.
- Poor, oppressed, and marginalized people have no stake in this project, but are experts in its brutalizing impacts.[7]

I do not argue these perspectives in this volume, though I point to others who have.

Obviously, global economic realities are difficult and complex. The danger of *over*emphasizing this, however, is that regular folk in both church and society quickly become overwhelmed and disempowered, feeling like mere spectators in a cosmic drama we can neither comprehend nor control. In organizing for change, there is a time to make complicated things simpler. Not *simplistic*, as in the economic fairy tales we hear from politicians and the media, but *intelligible* enough to inspire cultural action for transformation. Amidst the economic obfuscations dispensed by the priests of capitalism, Christians need to practice the Quaker discipline of speaking plainly.

Consider two examples of such speech, ancient and modern. Two millennia ago, John the Revelator caricatured the domination of the poor by the rich under the Roman Empire through the image of four horsemen of apocalypse (Rev 6:6–6).[8] And just two generations ago, Martin Luther King Jr., our greatest American prophet, named poverty and extreme materialism—wherein "profit motives and property rights are considered more important than people"—as one of the "giant triplets" threatening the sustainability of the nation.[9]

Racial capitalism in the US is today ushering in a second Gilded Age, where wealth, as it did at the end of the nineteenth century, is steadily concentrating at the top, as outlined in Chuck Collins's foreword and depicted by the simple chart (see Figure 2).[10] The very rich are increasingly influential in affairs of state, in and out of office (more than half of the members of the 116th Congress were millionaires).[11] This trend, which is intensifying under the influence of wealthy autocrats like Donald Trump and Vladimir Putin, represents the single greatest force undermining the hope for political and economic democracy. The ascendant fusion between aristocracy and oligarchy persuades me to deploy in this book the term "plutocracy": the dominance of politics by the rich. As one reviewer said recently: "The notion of oligarchy has troubled thinkers since antiquity, but in the late 20th century we seemed less bothered about the class of the uber rich."[12]

Not only has the return of plutocracy strengthened current iterations of John's horsemen and King's triplets. It is also accelerating climate catastrophe, the preeminent threat to our history. George Monbiot summarizes:

> In front of every great fortune lies a great crime. Immense wealth translates automatically into immense environmental impacts, regardless of the intentions of those who possess it. The very wealthy, almost as a matter of definition, are committing ecocide . . . Surplus money allows some people to exercise inordinate power over others: in the workplace; in politics; and above all in the capture, use and destruction of the planet's natural wealth. If everyone is to flourish, we cannot afford the rich . . . Though they are disproportionately responsible for our environmental crises, the rich will be hurt least and last by planetary disaster, while the poor are hurt first and worst . . . The grim truth is that the rich are able to live as they do only because others are poor: there is neither the physical nor ecological space for everyone to pursue private luxury.[13]

"Life on Earth," Monbiot concludes, "depends on moderation." Moderation, however, is *anathema* to resurgent "plantation capitalism."[14]

If plutocracy is the political face of our national disease, "affluenza" is its interpersonal manifestation.[15] This term, popularized in a late 1990s Public

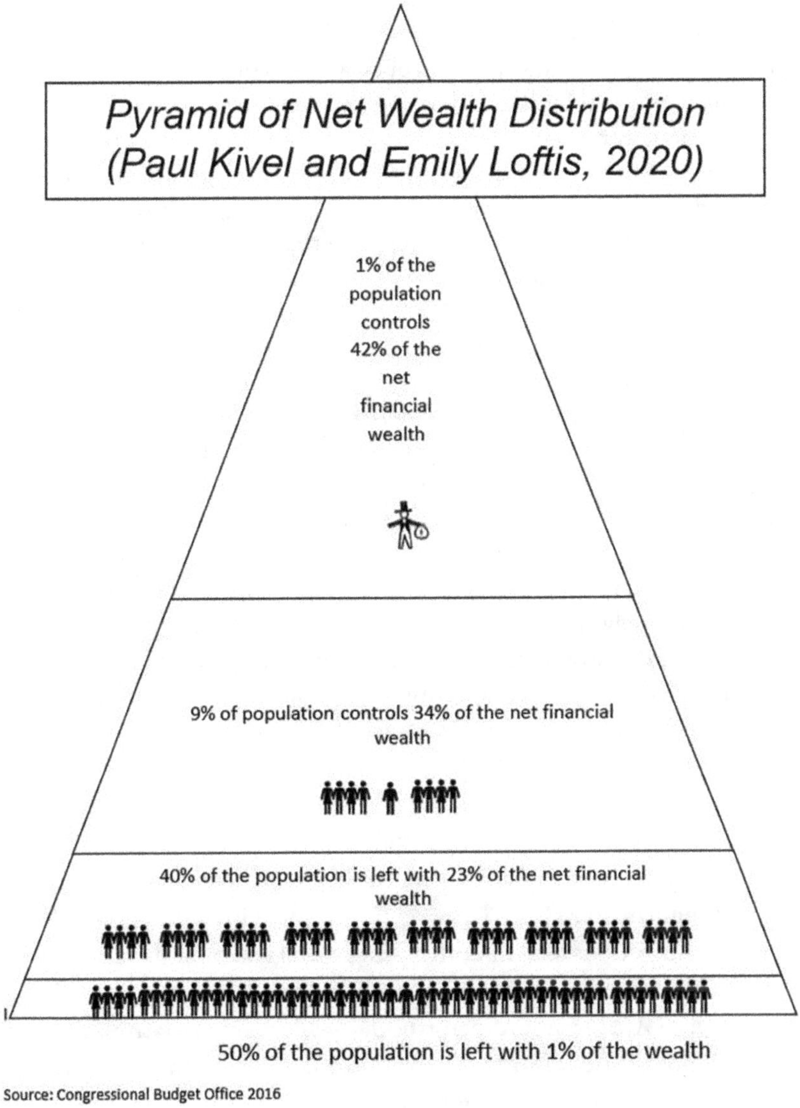

Figure 2. Pyramid of Net Wealth Distribution (reproduced by permission of Paul Kivel).

Broadcasting System series on consumerism, has become shorthand for the psychocultural pathology of having too much. Affluenza generates anxiety, addiction, and alienation around and within *all* of us, driving an insatiable pursuit of more money, things and mobility. It is a pandemic that empowers the rich, endangers the middle classes, taunts the poor, and ransacks the planet.

All of us in the middle classes of highly industrialized countries consume excessively, bearing a disproportionate responsibility for exhausting the earth's resources and concentrating wealth in fewer hands. Kentucky philosopher-farmer Wendell Berry defines our dilemma: "We all live by robbing nature, but our standard of living demands that the robbery shall continue. We must achieve the character and acquire the skills to live much poorer than we do."[16] Captive to our delusions and appetites, however, we are no longer able to imagine the world differently. The socialized paralysis we exhibit in the face of racial (think George Floyd's murder) and ecological (think shrinking ice caps) ultimatums is what Berry calls "the addict's excuse" (cited in the beginning epigraph).

It is not the purpose of this volume to analyze at length the contemporary crisis of disparity, nor to brandish a phalanx of statistics, nor to parse in detail the culture of affluenza or the political economy of plutocracy. Illuminating studies of all these matters are readily available.[17] For example, Eugene McCarraher's brilliant *The Enchantments of Mammon: How Capitalism Became the Religion of Modernity* would be an ideal companion to my study of Luke. This sweeping historical study examines how and why market economics came to dominate the spirituality and culture of the West over a half-millennium: "Avarice—once one of the seven deadly sins—morphed into the 'self-interest' or 'initiative' indispensable to wealth and innovation, while the inscrutable ways of Providence yielded to the laws of supply and demand."[18]

Analysis is important, but it is equally important to learn from the experiences of people like Dorothea and from the perspectives of activists. I warmly point readers to the work of two US organizations, cofounded respectively by Rev. William Barber and Chuck Collins:

- The Poor Peoples' Campaign (www.poorpeoplescampaign.org) generates intersectional analysis and data around domestic poverty and its human impacts, and its advocacy and activism earns its moniker as inheritor of Martin Luther King's last great project.[19]
- United for a Fair Economy (www.faireconomy.org) has since 1995 helped Americans to deconstruct fairy-tale policy narratives; understand realities of social disparity through the economic literacy tools of popular education; and resist the greed system through organizing.[20]

I've had the privilege of collaborating on Sabbath Economics education with both leaders over the last twenty years. Barber, a Disciples of Christ minister cut from the cloth of the Kingian tradition, is included in this book's dedication; Collins, whose work is deeply informed by Catholic faith, graciously offered the Foreword. Find more on their (and other) organizations in appendix II.

My purpose in this book is to challenge the widespread silence in our churches regarding the crisis of disparity. North American Christians, lamented Jesuit John Haughey, tend to "read the Gospel as if we had no money, and spend our money as if we know nothing of the Gospel."[21] Indeed, the topic of economics is exceedingly difficult to broach in most congregations, more taboo than sex. Yet no aspect of our individual and corporate lives is more defining—and few subjects are more frequently addressed in our scriptures. Tragically, our churchly attention span around economics tends to stop at Stewardship Sunday, while our discourse about wealth and poverty is generally timid, moralistic, strictly personalist, charity-oriented, and disengaged from the politics and human impacts of plutocracy and affluenza.

For over four decades, I have attempted to challenge these habits as part of a movement working to re-read the Bible economically and politically, so we might read the economy and body politic biblically (to paraphrase the great William Stringfellow). Since thankfully the older interpretive habits of hiding behind veils of anonymity or putative objectivity are no longer acceptable, a word about my personal social background and location is in order here.

I grew up in suburban Los Angeles in a middle class home, not raised in any church tradition. After a difficult year studying abroad, at age eighteen I was challenged by the Gospel. I began my journey of faith among conservative evangelicals, but soon found my spiritual home in the radical discipleship movement, mentored by exemplars such as Elizabeth McAlister, the Berrigan brothers, Ladon Sheats, and Athol Gill. In the first decade of this journey (1975–1985), I was part of an intentional Christian community in a low-income neighborhood in the San Francisco Bay area, while organizing to resist US militarism and support Indigenous sovereignty movements in the Pacific Basin. I also pursued graduate studies in New Testament, during a short window when political hermeneutics, sociological exegesis and liberation theology received significant airtime in North American theological schools.

Committed to the primacy of praxis, after the 1988 publication of *Binding the Strong Man: A Political Reading of Mark* I chose not to pursue either academic or pastoral vocations. As someone with race, class, and gender privilege, I felt my interpretive work—in order to be accountable to communities struggling for justice and peace—should be located within faith-rooted social movements. My second decade (1986–1996) was thus spent organizing around a wide range of justice issues with the American Friends Service Committee, writing and teaching avocationally in Los Angeles in a barrio not far from where I grew up. Overt and covert military adventurism in Central America, the first Gulf War, the Columbus Quincentenary, and the second Los Angeles uprising all made powerful imprints on my work and consciousness.[22]

Yet increasingly I felt that we activists needed to amplify our theological voices, so in 1997 I shifted my energy toward building experimental grassroots pedagogic spaces that sought to integrate the insights and capacities of "seminary, sanctuary and streets and soil."[23] With my life-partner Elaine Enns and others, I cofounded Bartimaeus Cooperative Ministries, which has been our platform over the last quarter century for advocacy and activism, popular education and publication, and intersectional movement building.

One of BCM's early commitments was involvement in the Jubilee 2000 international debt-relief movement—an extraordinary ecumenical campaign led by the global South to address extreme poverty.[24] At the request of that movement, I wrote *The Biblical Vision of Sabbath Economics*, a booklet sketching the scriptural roots and branches of Jubilee equity and sustainability.[25] BCM then co-curated a nationwide collaborative to build capacity for Sabbath Economics practices in the framework of our Sevenfold Household Covenant.[26] Elaine and I moved north in 2005 from Los Angeles to the Ventura River watershed, leading us to take up other issues as well: bioregional literacy and protection[27]; sustainable building, organic gardening and native plant cultivation; and restorative decolonization.[28]

We continue Sabbath Economics education with partners like Just Money Advisors and Faith and Money Network (see appendix II). Still, I have felt that a deeper dive into the biblical narrative of Sabbath Economics would be helpful. Luke's Gospel was the obvious choice, since over the last twenty years I've been exploring with groups, and through a few publications, many of the texts featured in this book. On one hand, the following pages represent a "report out" from that workshopping, which I hope might inspire and support communities of faith to embrace more deeply the urgent struggle for transformation and survival facing us. On the other hand, I also offer here a more detailed contextual exegesis and exposition of Luke's narrative. Admittedly, designing an approach that is equally helpful for the diverse contexts of seminary, sanctuary, streets, and soil has been a challenge!

iii. Luke's Text

The Luke-Acts corpus is formidable, representing more than 27 percent of the New Testament (based on Greek word counts). Few contemporary scholars, therefore, attempt a comprehensive commentary on *one* of these books, much less both. So unlike my study of Mark, this book is not a pericope-by-pericope treatment of the Third Gospel. Rather, I focus my efforts on Luke's "showing and telling" of Sabbath Economics threads, which constitute more than a third of his story. This book thus offers in-depth attention to 35 percent of Luke's total verses, and summary commentary on another 15 percent, not including the review in chapter 2 of Sabbath Economics in the Hebrew Bible and the epilogue's treatment of Acts 2.

In Luke, three basic sources are at play in any given passage (I accept the still-majority theory of synoptic gospel genealogy called the "Two Source Hypothesis"). Per custom, I call these "M" (Mark); the hypothetical "Q" source (parallels with Matthew that are not in Mark), and "L" (Luke's unique material).[29] My literary-critical approach analyzes four aspects that provide the most reliable windows into Luke's priorities and concerns:

1. *L material.* Obviously, this reflects issues and traditions Luke deemed important to supplement M and Q. Source-critical studies show that much of L is economic in theme; by the same token, Luke's economic argument is carried by L, particularly evident in his "Special Section" (see part III). Thus fully two-thirds of the texts I examine in this book are L material.
2. *Luke's editing of M's narrative.* His changes to the earliest Gospel's chronology and content often seem subtle, but closer looks reveal significant differences in emphasis. These contribute to Luke's overall narrative strategy (see for example Luke's changes to Mark's Strongman Parable, 7B).
3. *Luke's broad narrative patterns and overall structure.* Form is as important as content in understanding literary meaning. Luke gives a distinctive order and shape to his story that itself is part of his argument for Sabbath Economics; I have shaped this project around these patterns.
4. *Vocabulary.* In each passage, I point out key Greek words and phrases, paying particular attention to those unique to Luke, or to their distribution in the other Gospels, the rest of the New Testament, and when applicable, to the Greek version of the Hebrew Bible, or Septuagint (hereafter LXX). Obviously, vocabulary is key to advancing, or challenging, a perspective. See endnote for an explanation of how I show transliterated Greek words in this book.[30]

Tracing a narrative thread or theme through a longer work is a core discipline of literary-critical study. I give attention not only to setting, character, plot, and narrator, but also to rhetorical patterns, macro and micro literary structure, scenario interrelationships, transitions, repetitions, motif development, symbols, caricatures, metaphors, and voice.

My socio-literary methodology combines the tools of sociology of literature (examining the narrative in light of the socio-historical context in which it was produced) with those of literary sociology (studying the social world portrayed *in* the text). It parallels my approach to Mark, and I refer those who wish to understand this method in detail to my discussion there.[31] I have little interest in traditions that might lie *behind* the received text. Many scholars whose work I lean on—for example, friends Douglas Oakman and the late William Herzog—seek to reconstruct "what the historical Jesus might have said."[32] I prefer to concentrate on the canonical text in front of us—since that is what forms (and when "confused," deforms) our churches.

I focus on the historical context *of* and *in* the text . My goal is to show that the aggregate evidence (from more than thirty scenes and teaching sequences) offers sufficient breadth and depth to confirm Sabbath Economics as arguably Luke's *primary* theme, led by Jesus's critique of plutocracy and affluenza. I hope this is enough to both persuade and trouble fellow Christians who still look to the Gospel as a rule of faith and life.

The volume and spectrum of scholarly writing on Luke published over the last 50 years is wide! Thankfully, then-novel socio-literary tools used in *Binding the Strong Man* are now well-established in readings of Luke. Here are nine representative books that use a range of these methods spanning this period:

- Literary methods: Tannehill (1986); Talbert (1992); Dicken (2023);[33]
- Sociological methods: Neyrey (1991); Oakman (2008); Brawley (2020);[34]
- Economic hermeneutics: Pilgrim (1981); Moxnes (2004); King (2022).[35]

Richard Cassidy's *Jesus, Politics and Society* (1978) helped pioneer sociopolitical approaches to the Third Gospel in the US, as did Luise Schottroff and Wolfgang Stegemanns's *Jesus and the Hope of the Poor* (1986) in Europe.[36] Having drawn widely on these and related studies, my exegesis of Lukan passages is rarely wholly original. Often, however, academic treatments pull a text's punches by confining its meaning to the first century. I try to remedy this by connecting dots to the present.

During this same period, many books appeared that center the *theme* of wealth and poverty in Luke. In sharp contrast with the approaches of Latin American liberation theologians such as José Miranda and Elsa Támez (2006), writers in the Global North have tended to frame economic issues in terms of individualist middle-class social ethics, rather than the politics of deconstructing disparity.[37] Their conclusions are couched in platitudes about good stewardship, generosity and charity, or money for mission ("provision for your vision," as one evangelical put it). But they equivocate concerning structural inequality. This is perhaps not surprising, given that most theologians, ethicists, and pastors are dependent upon academic or denominational structures, which in turn depend upon donors who chafe at talk of Jubilee wealth redistribution! But these studies of Luke are also ambivalent about disparity because they fail to recognize how his narrative is grounded in the Hebrew Bible's Sabbath Economics cosmology—which is *unequivocally opposed to structural inequities.*

As I was finishing this manuscript, I came across David King's recent *Reclaiming the Radical Economic Message of Luke.*[38] I was delighted at the resonance between our approaches and perspectives. He begins by noting how the revolutionary vision of Dr. King has been neutered by official hagiographies, and compares that to how Luke's economic radicalism is domesticated by white scholars. He cites Philip Esler's 1987 indictment of how "the ingrained disregard among scholars for the social and economic setting of Luke-Acts . . . originate in a clear middle-class bias. Generations of scholars . . . have been so successful in making Luke's message on possessions palatable for bourgeois tastes that its genuinely radical nature has rarely been noted".[39] David King offers an overview and critical assessment of a dozen key recent monographs on Luke and wealth, happily saving me from having to undertake this formidable task.[40] I recommend his study to readers who wish to orient themselves to that wider conversation.

In sum, three commitments distinguish my project from more mainstream treatments:

- its intertextual Sabbath Economics framework;
- its detailed tracing and exposition of this thread through the Third Gospel; and
- its correlation of Luke's narrative argument to the crisis of disparity today.

I look dialectically at Luke through the lens of our struggle against plutocracy and affluenza, *and vice versa.* Though I do not explore here contemporary practices of Sabbath Economics, I do point readers toward trusted organizations doing advocacy, education, organizing and household covenant work, especially in appendix II.

As a nonprofessional scholar, I find it impossible to keep up with ever-expanding critical biblical and hermeneutic studies, but do my best to be representative here. Yet as a popular educator, I try to avoid scholarly debates, especially when they get lost in self-referential academic labyrinths. And I too often see how preoccupation with theory or critical conundrums can distract us from engaging the text *and its demands on our discipleship*—the latter being the goal of this project. I do, however, summarize key issues or terms, and refer readers to basic popular resources that explain and explore important questions or interpretive issues (as in the brief discussion of the two-source hypothesis above). I have relegated many details and references to the end notes to *enable*, without *requiring*, further investigation.

My intention is for this volume to be relevant to Lukan studies, but also accessible to those outside it, especially those involved in the work of faith-rooted economic justice.[41] For preachers and congregational study groups, appendix I correlates my exploration of passages to the Revised Common Lectionary, and suggests how to curate a Luke study group. I strongly believe that when tackling fraught (or silenced) issues in our churches, such as socio-economic disparity, we ought let the Word do the heavy lifting!

iv. Luke's Context

My colleague Matthew Coomber, in his recent introduction to *Economics and Empire in the Ancient Near East*, writes:

> Economics and economic concerns do not run parallel to the field of biblical studies: they run straight through it.... [R]ecognition of the Bible's economic backdrop reveals previously unnoticed levels of meaning in even the most familiar of texts.... Understanding the economic systems of the ancient world, which functioned differently than our own, better equips readers to recognize when modern paradigms—such as free-market or socialist ideologies—are imposed on biblical texts. Additionally, for scholars and non-scholars alike, paying attention to the Bible's recurring economic themes can help bring into view those texts that confronted ancient forms of exploitation that are also present today, such as political corruption, predatory resource extraction, and other financial abuses.[42]

This captures why an economic analysis of texts is not only justified but necessary.

Socioeconomic inequality was already a problem in ancient Israel. But as Hellenism and then the Roman Empire spread across the Mediterranean world, inequality became increasingly widespread—acutely in Jesus's Palestine. The estates of the rich portrayed in Luke's story grew in several ways. Assets were sometimes consolidated through the joining of households in marital or political alliances. At other times, militarily expropriated land was distributed through political patronage. But the primary mechanism was acquiring land through the debt-default of the poor. Small, traditional agriculturalists groaned under the burden of rent, tithes, taxes, tariffs, and operating expenses, not to mention natural disasters such as drought or pestilence. When they inevitably fell behind in payments, they were forced to take out loans secured by their land. When unable to service these loans, the land was lost to lenders—in most cases, large landowners who in the absence of banking institutions made available their surplus capital at a handsome profit.[43] This basic pattern is depicted or implied throughout Luke's narrative, as are portraits of those being crushed or cast off because of it.

Sociology, archeology, anthropology, and history shed light on relations of social power and economic production in Roman antiquity, and I have referenced key studies.[44] Two helpful compendiums on which I draw often here are Bruce Malina and Richard Rohrbaugh's *Social Science Commentary on the Synoptic Gospels* and K. C. Hanson and Douglas Oakman's *Palestine in the Time of Jesus*.[45] Especially important to my project, and to helping modern readers better understand Sabbath Economics, is economic anthropology.[46] Its classic three modes of exchange are market, redistribution (think tax systems), and reciprocity; the first two are familiar to the culture of capitalism, while the third is not.

Traditional reciprocity involves "the exchange of goods and services . . . rooted in a mutual sense of obligation and identity . . . and the role that gifts play in cultural systems around the world . . . [that] creates links between the people involved."[47] In Roman antiquity, "negative reciprocity" (getting more than one gives) characterized the strategies of elites toward peasants and clients, while "balanced reciprocity" describes how elites treated each other (giving with expectation of immediate return).[48] The mode of generalized reciprocity (gifting without calculation or expectation of return) is crucial to understanding Jesus's economic cosmology. In modern societies, this practice is considered foolish except inside the household; in antiquity, however, it was an ethos that held village and peasant economies together. What is *truly* foolish, according to Luke's Jesus, is a rich landowner's strategy of personal accumulation and consumption (Luke 12:20; 8A)—though that is the very definition of economic orthodoxy under capitalism.

Jerome Neyrey's comprehensive *The Social World of Luke-Acts* is an excellent handbook for social-scientific modeling. It offers two approaches that have particularly animated my reading of Luke's narratives of eating and healing. One is how the human body is a replica of the social body, a symbol and microcosm of it.[49] I explicate this here in terms of how political bodies mirror the body politic in Luke's characterizations (9A). The other is how meals function as social maps, which explains how and why Jesus's practices of inclusive table fellowship across purity and economic boundaries are so controversial (9B). Other social models of ancient Mediterranean life deployed by scholars help make sense of Gospel texts and their world, such as limited good, fictive kinship, purity boundaries, and the culture of patron-clientelism.[50] I will point out how these and other concepts illumine passages as we go along.

Luke's own social location requires not just extrapolation but speculation, which I leave to others. I accept Oakman's careful hypothesis as reliable:

> Luke stands sociologically somewhere between preindustrial city and peasant village, without endorsing unambiguously the interests and values of either one. Luke does not look to the countryside as one who labors on the land . . . [but] cannot ignore the countryside either, because of its prominence in the early Jesus traditions. Luke sees in certain aspects of the peasant moral economy a solution to difficulties within his own community . . . [which] probably resides in a large town or city somewhere in the Roman Empire. Luke's literary work . . . addresses primarily the landlords and creditors . . . [because] the behavior of the powerful and the rich that affects the quality of communal life for all.[51]

Nickolas Fox, using social identity methodology, concludes that Luke focused on forming Gentile converts in "cultural memory and prescribed group behavior . . . while redefining a number of core symbols of Judaism."[52] This coheres with my underscoring of Luke's emphasis upon literacy in "Moses and the prophets" (chapters 1 and 2, 11B).

To close this section, I invoke a monograph that got my attention some years ago, which extrapolated data from ancient sources to analyze disparity between rich and poor in the Roman Empire of the early second century CE. It seems profoundly telling that it determined economic inequality to be *greater in the US today than it was in Luke's time*![53] That stunning fact certainly lends relevance to my advocacy-oriented treatment of Luke and disparity, to which I now return.

v. My (Recon)text(ualization)

Paul Ricoeur reminds us that a text is without a voice until the interpreter restores one to it.[54] Literary and social analysis inform and empower my attempts herein to reread Luke's narrative in its context, but in a way that also speaks to our context of deepening disparity and skyrocketing "ecological debt" in the Anthropocene.[55] We, the privileged in a world of cruel inequalities, must guard against our tendency to use scripture to justify ourselves. Fowl and Jones, alluding to a famous exhortation of Dietrich Bonhoeffer, assert: "Christians will need to learn to read the Scriptures 'over against ourselves' rather than simply 'for ourselves.'"[56] I try to abide by Ricoeur's beautiful summary challenge: hermeneutics should "be animated by this double motivation: willingness to suspect, willingness to listen; vow of rigor, vow of obedience. In our time we have not finished doing away with idols and we have barely begun to listen to symbols."[57]

Still, biblical studies can sometimes feel like paleontology. But these old bones are not *fossils*; they have life in them (as famously articulated in Ezekiel 37). My thinking about this metaphor has been inspired by Indigenous efforts over the last half century to repatriate the bones of their ancestors, which are locked up in settler museums for "observation and analysis." While Westerners apprehend bones as inanimate objects for study of the past, Native peoples understand them as sacred and essential to the identity of the living.[58] This is a lesson for the vocation of scripture study: to liberate our texts *from* "museum curation" and *for* lived discipleship! Another analogy: Bible study can seem like abstract music theory—analyzing old scores from dead musicians with no intention or interest in playing them. Yet a musical score is only truly realized ("fulfilled," to use Luke's metaphor in Acts 2:1) through community performance. Similarly, only when we try to *embody* a scriptural text in our context are we truly interpreting it.

Here are some of the ways I employ contemporary economic frameworks and vocabulary in my interpretations. As mentioned, I use "affluenza" and "plutocracy" throughout this volume to describe lethal diseases that Luke's Jesus diagnoses and endeavors to heal—or resist. Another contemporary framing is my rephrasing of Jesus's primary metaphor: the kingdom of God. The symbolism and narrative of kingship is problematic as an anachronism that freights hierarchy and domination. This has led many activist colleagues to adopt "kindom of God" as an alternative. This is an attractive suggestion, especially given the rich thread of fictive kinship (or "family by conviction") discourse found throughout the New Testament. Unfortunately, it lacks the political bite of Jesus's *contrastive* trope (God versus kings) and its origins in the Hebrew Bible (see, e.g., the prophetic indictment of 1 Sam 8).

I follow, and hopefully build out, Halvor Moxnes's groundbreaking thesis in *The Economy of the Kingdom*: the archetypal spatial/temporal symbol of "God's Kingdom" envisions a social, economic and political rehabilitation of generalized reciprocity, which prioritizes the poor and advocates for redistributive justice.[59] This definition is captured by Wes Jackson's suggestion of the "Great Economy" as a helpful metaphorical synonym for the Kingdom, which Wendell Berry has adopted. "We seek the Kingdom of God, in part, by our economic behavior, and we fail to find it if that behavior is wrong," Berry writes in a seminal essay entitled "Two Economies" (see Figure 3). "The human economy, if it is to be a good economy, must fit harmoniously within and must correspond to the Great Economy."[60] He is referring to Creation: the integrated and functioning biosphere that operates according to "principles and patterns by which values or powers or necessities are parceled out and exchanged."[61]

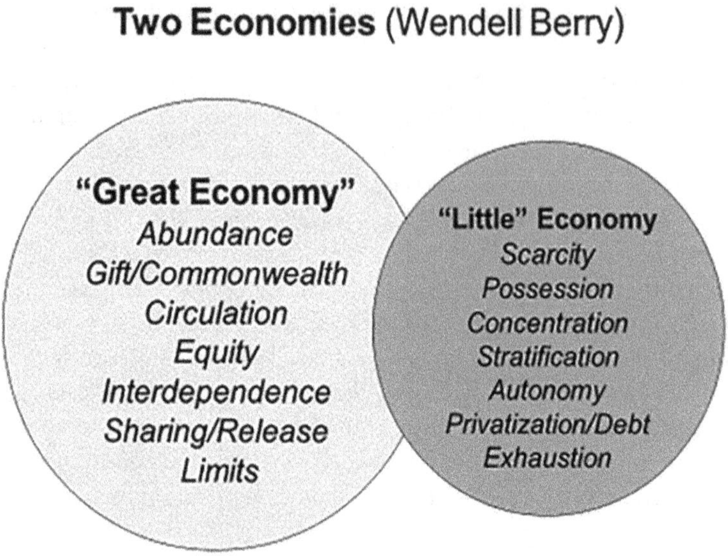

Figure 3. Two Economies (Diagram by Ched Myers).

Human systems are "little economies" that depend upon and operate within the Great Economy. The problem, however, Berry writes, is that our industrial economy, with its managerial penchant for control and lack of limits,

> does not see itself as a little economy; it sees itself as the *only* economy. It makes itself thus exclusive by the simple expedient of valuing only what it can use—that is, only what it can regard as "raw material" to be transformed mechanically into something else... Once we acknowledge the existence of the Great Economy, however, we are astonished and frightened to see how much modern enterprise is the work of hubris, occurring outside the human boundary established by ancient tradition. The industrial economy is based on invasion and pillage of the Great Economy.[62]

Jackson and Berry understand this metaphor to be theological, invoking the Gospel admonition to "seek first the kingdom of God, and God's justice" (see 8B). I thus adopt "Great Economy" as a re-metaphorizing of the Kingdom throughout this book. To paraphrase my teacher William Herzog, it is not an "earthly symbol with heavenly meaning," but an earthy symbol with heavy meaning.[63]

I draw on other economic models to aid interpretation of particular passages. Here are three examples:

- I reference the recent economic philosophy of "limitarianism" as a contemporary attempt to make sense of the Sabbath Economics core value of constraint (2A).
- My reading of Luke 12:13–34 deploys ecological and feminist economist Hazel Henderson's famous metaphor of the "economic cake" (8A), which resonates with Jesus's teaching. Private extraction, production, and accumulation all are actually predicated upon a "social cooperative economy of love," which in turn is predicated upon nature—despite the latter two being invisibilized (and thus mercilessly exploited) in capitalist economic valuations.
- My consideration of the "Defect-ive Manager" uses a different but equally instructive framing of "two economies" by German sociologist Ferdinand Tönnies a century earlier than Berry (10A).

These orientations from the modern history of economic philosophy help make complicated things simple enough to engage in order to struggle to change systems. They also provide useful analogies for connecting the crises that stalk us with Jesus's storytelling.

Luke's Gospel reminds us that the divergent economies of community and capital have been making competing claims on the earth and on human hearts, minds, and lives for a very long time. If at points you find any of my recontextualizing interpretations too generalizing, unrealistic, subversive, or theologically thin, I invite you to revisit these introductory reflections regarding the first and fourth quadrants of my hermeneutic model.

"We cannot afford maximum profit or power with minimum responsibility because, in the Great Economy, the loser's losses finally afflict the winner," writes Berry. "Now the ideal must be 'the maximum of well-being with the minimum of consumption,' which both defines and requires neighborly love."[64] For people of privilege, the bad news of Luke's story is Jesus's consistent diagnosis of personal affluenza and political plutocracy as terminal diseases. The good news (for those of us who are not poor) is Jesus's equally consistent invitation to the Way of healing (Luke 5:31–32; 4B and 7B). But he understands that only those who *know* they are dis-eased will seek this Way. His call is *not* directed to those who believe there is nothing fatally flawed about their personal or political worlds—denial being the enemy of discipleship (Luke 18:21–23; 12B). Healing requires *repentance*—that venerable, if sentimentalized, biblical verb connoting the hard work of *turning our personal and political histories around*. As the Disciples' Prayer stipulates, we can only be "released" as we "release" others (11:4; 7A).

So, I conclude with one more contemporary analogy: the Way of discipleship as recovery from addiction, especially as understood in the Twelve-Step movement.[65] Discipleship and recovery are both traditions of tough love, which press us to reckon with our private and public diseases and their consequences in ways that few other postmodern discourses dare. The point of radical diagnosis is *change*. Neither blaming nor shaming of ourselves or others will liberate us; nor will paralysis of analysis; nor dissociative, dogmatic, or dictatorial ideologies; nor denial of grace. Only a fierce hope for transformative justice will—and this is the whole plot of Luke's story of Jesus. To resolve Haughey's lament with which this section began, we Christians must no longer segregate economic disparity and the Gospel.

Luke's Emmaus Road epilogue, with which I start my reading (1A), offers a moving portrait of bewildered disciples struggling under the shadow of death. A stranger invites them to face the somatic traumas wrought by empire, so they might bear witness to resurrection as an insurrection for life and justice. He begins the process by rereading with them their scriptures *through the lens of prophetic faith*. I am hopeful that you will join me in doing exactly this: engaging Luke's sacred story through the prophetic tradition in order to encounter a Jesus who is not an authoritarian or magical "answer" to our personal and political confusion, denial, paralysis, and despair, but a compassionate yet resolute *Interrogator*, inviting us to discipleship.[66]

Our Christian faith has been colonized by supremacist heresies since Constantine. It is being seduced afresh by neoliberal economics and authoritarian Christian nationalism. The Creation is groaning (Rom 8:22–23), and the poor still await good news. The evil indeed is mighty. But it can't stand up to our stories.

Part I

Re-Orientation

Remembering Moses and the Prophets

Chapter 1 opens with reflections on Luke's *epi*logue as a *pro*logue to this project. It may seem a bit disorienting to begin at the end of a story, but I do so because it offers a crucial re-orientation for how to approach the Third Gospel as a whole. The famous Emmaus Road tale is read in churches every Easter Sunday evening. It depicts an unsettling conversation along a back road of occupied Palestine between two demoralized disciples and a mysterious Stranger, in the immediate wake of Jesus's execution by empire. At the outset I will deconstruct Docetic readings of this story in an exercise that clears the way for an economic interpretation of the whole Gospel. Then we'll explore this "Bible study of the Road" as the church's first catechism, urging us to reread the Jesus story, Christian faith, and our own histories through the lens of the prophetic tradition, a fitting entrée to this book.

Per these Emmaus Road instructions, I turn in chapter 2 to Moses and the prophets, offering a brief summary of their ancient vision of Sabbath Economics. Though a principal thread running throughout both Torah and Nevi'im (the Prophets), Sabbath Economics has been largely overlooked, misunderstood, or dismissed by our synagogues and churches. Israel's first "catechism" commences in Exodus 16. Contrary to the trivializing and domesticating treatment this text usually receives in our faith communities, the purpose of Moses's instructions to a people newly freed from empire is to prevent a return to slavery. This requires a return to the Great Economy of nature's sustenance and community constraint and cooperation.

Chapter 3 begins again at Luke's beginning, looking at three key theme-setting scenes from his prelude, full of song and fire. Mary's Magnificat recontextualizes the ancient Song of Hannah as a prophetic proclamation, "preparing the Way" for her son even before John the Baptist. It dreams of a radical restoration of equity from the bottom up. This vision will be narrated through the second half of Luke in stories that lift up the destitute poor and bring down the plutocratic rich (part III). John reiterates this revolutionary anticipation in the second scene, opening the thread of repentance so crucial to Luke's story. The third scene, Jesus's first temptation in the wilderness, mystically revisits the Exodus 16 crisis of hunger and provision, reminding us that the primal "test" of liberative faith is to resist extractive economics.

These opening exercises in "remembering as re-orientation" prepare us to read Luke through a Sabbath Economics lens, and introduce the reader to my expository approach.

CHAPTER ONE

The Church's First Catechism

Luke's Epilogue as Prologue (24:13–49)

"You are children of the prophets and of the covenant which God gave to your ancestors. . ."

—Peter's second sermon, Solomon's Portico (Acts 3:25a)

"The people and their rulers. . . did not recognize Jesus, nor understand the utterances of the prophets which are read every Sabbath. . ."

—Paul's first sermon, Antioch of Pisidia (Acts 13:27)

LUKE'S UNIQUE GOSPEL epilogue is the best antidote to Christian depictions of the Risen Jesus as ethereal spectacle. His account of the empty tomb (Luke 24:1–9) affirms the resurrection, echoing Mark's narrative (though with a characteristic addition highlighting the key role of women witnesses, despite their dismissal by the male disciples, 24:10–11). The Emmaus Road tale is not, however, mere embellishment, as historical-critical scholars often argue. It plays an integral role in Luke's overall narrative strategy, functioning in two crucial ways:

1. *to thwart interpretations of the resurrection as a "happily ever after ending."* Luke understood that triumphalist readings of the resurrection would function to eclipse all that preceded it: the story of Jesus's life; its roots in the traditions of his ancestors; and the historic contexts of both in the shadow of imperial oppression. Indeed, such readings across the history of the church have fueled the Docetic drift of both ancient Christendom and modern spiritualizing theologies.[1]
2. *to re-orient disciples to a "prophetic hermeneutic" for reading past, present and future.* To combat this drift, Luke's epilogue draws attention away from ontological questions about the resurrection, asserting instead that followers of Jesus then and now can rightly comprehend the fate of their leader and his movement *only* through the lens of "Moses and the prophets." Luke believed this prophetic orientation had atrophied in his time, as evidenced by the apostolic

> indictments from Acts cited above. Luke thus closes his Gospel by placing discipleship in the genealogy of prophetic literacy and practice. Jesus's movement for personal and political transformation can be sustained only if rooted in and guided by ancestral wisdom.

A. Re-Placing Resurrection in Political Time and Space

The fact that the Emmaus episode has been so thoroughly sentimentalized in contemporary middle class North American Christianity is perhaps the most telling indication of the continuing hegemony of triumphalist resurrection theologies and supremacist political ideologies. To be sure, resurrection is generally underemphasized in our churches, where it tends to be handled with either timidity or swagger. The idea of corpse resuscitation is embarrassing to theological modernists, while conservatives transform it into abstract dogma or heroic literalism. In either case, the Easter story often degenerates into a happily-ever-after fairy tale. Commercialized civil religion exhibits an evil genius for further domesticating Easter by "chocolate-coating" it (the Easter bunny industrial complex), or "whitewashing" it through artistic renderings that bleach the Risen Christ into an "unbearable whiteness of being."[2]

Such expressions of Euro-American religious imagination have been essential building blocks of supremacy since the Renaissance, making Western minds and hearts "sluggish," as Jesus puts it in 24:25. They portray the Risen Jesus floating above the world, offering the distraction of otherworldly fantasies. And for all the preoccupation in both Catholic and Protestant soteriology with being "saved by the blood," this Christ exhibits no trace of blood; only highly sanitized, virtually arthroscopic wounds. Such scrubbed images function to divorce private, spiritual matters from public, terrestrial ones. Salvation occurs outside of, or beyond, Creation, from which the body is removed. Docetic Christianity in North America today is thus unable and unwilling to challenge our carbon and capitalist status quo, functioning instead to numb us to the escalating horrors of both social and ecological violence, about which most of our churches are ambivalent.

Luke's epilogue has been particularly colonized by this theological drift. It is typified by the famous 1877 painting by Robert Zünd, a Swiss Pietist painter of the Hudson River School of romantic art.[3] "The Way to Emmaus" depicts a contemplative stroll along a shaded forest path beside a babbling brook, the travelers' tête-à-tête delightfully interrupted by a begowned-in-white risen Lord, who gestures toward the heavens. This warm and tranquil Disneyland-esque interpolation, however, completely overwrites the real world portrayed in Luke's Passion narrative.

In historical context, this moment would have been the furthest thing from leisurely or contemplative. According to Luke's narrative, only 48 hours earlier

Jesus of Nazareth had been summarily executed by the Roman military, in a fashion all too familiar to Palestinian Jews of the time: as a dissident crucified for resisting the occupying authority. A third-century CE centurion dedication plaque found in northern England—which, like Palestine, lay at the frontiers of the Pax Romana—portrays war god Mars brandishing a spear, and the mythological hero Hercules holding a club; at bottom is a running boar, symbol of the 20th Legion (which was also deployed in Palestine).[4] The intimidating propaganda of Roman dominion was a reality check in politically contested colonies like Jewish Palestine. Indeed, Luke 23 narrates painfully how these very forces decisively beat down Jesus's little grassroots movement.

Luke's Emmaus story opens with two unindicted coconspirators heading away from Jerusalem "that very day" (24:13), that is, the Sunday after Jesus's murder.[5] Common sense suggests these two would be trying to "melt into the countryside" (as the Pentagon says of grassroots insurgents today), hustling down a back road, dazed and confused, getting the hell out of Dodge so they won't meet the same fate as their leader.

Their destination is a village mentioned nowhere else in our scriptures. However, several generations before Jesus, Emmaus was a site where vastly outnumbered Jewish guerillas had heroically defeated Syrian invaders (see I Maccabees 3:40–4:15). And two generations after Jesus, the historian Josephus notes that Roman emperor Vespasian, after vanquishing the Judean revolt in 70 CE, made a political point by settling 800 Roman military veterans at "a place called Emmaus."[6] These two historical fragments suggest a hamlet with a reputation for homegrown resistance, which may well have offered refuge for our fugitives.

We would better reimagine Luke's Emmaus Road scene through the lens of an artist contemporaneous with Zünd, but decidedly non-romantic. Abolitionist Thomas Moran's 1862 "Slave Hunt in the Great Dismal Swamp" depicts people trying to escape slave-hunters.[7] (Harriet Tubman's famous "Wade in the Water" song advised those fleeing to walk through streams to mask their scent from tracking dogs.[8]) This swamp was a refuge for thousands of runaway slaves during this period, so Moran's painting uses it as a metaphor for an America mired in the Civil War. Moran and Tubman better capture the angst of Luke's disciples hightailing it to the margins in order to lay low for a while.

Luke tells us they were debriefing "all the things that had happened" (24:14), a phrase throughout the Gospels that specifically refers to the arrest, trial and execution of Jesus. These terrified movement members were likely blaming each other for the mess they'd gotten into, wondering what their next move might be, lamenting Roman kangaroo justice, cursing the colonizers—and maybe even cursing Jesus for failing to deliver on promises of a new social order. A couple of exegetical notes confirm that theirs was an animated exchange, carried out between labored breaths and anxious glances over the shoulder.

First, the distinctively Lukan verb for "discussion" in 24:14–15 (*hōmilein*, from which we get our term homiletics) appears twice more in Acts. It describes Paul's sobering farewell sermon at Troas, a serious through-the-night conversation about how the young movement was going to survive (Acts 20:11). It also pertains to the apostle's conversations with Roman governor Felix concerning "justice and coming judgment," which scared the ruler to death (Acts 24:26). *Homilein* thus refers to weighty matters, not pious banter (let our own preaching take note). And the companion verb *suzētein* (Luke 24:15) in the New Testament almost always connotes a passionate dispute.

Into this traumatized, grief-laden, contentious moment under the shadow of death steps a Stranger. The pair's preoccupation with their desperate situation may explain why "their eyes were kept" from recognizing their teacher (24:16). But it is just as plausible that Jesus was literally *unrecognizable* due to disfigurement by his torturers (as suggested by Isaiah 52:14, a text through which early Christians read the Jesus story). After all, Luke tells us later in this tale that Jesus's wounds were still visible—and they would have been considerably more gruesome than those tiny incisions of pious art.

I have elsewhere used as an analogy how the open casket funeral of Emmett Till in 1955, following his murder by White Supremacists, shocked viewers into recognizing the brutality of Southern Jim Crow.[9] Or perhaps, Luke is alluding here to the *midrashic* tradition of an "incognito Second Coming," in which rabbis speculated that the prophet Elijah would return anonymously to see if the world was ready to receive him. In either case, Luke's Risen Jesus appears first as a *stranger,* and the Emmaus narrative challenges disciples to reckon with the *traumatic somatic*—two desperately needed Christological lessons to the church. But we cannot make theological and political sense of them without the prophetic tradition.

The Stranger understands he has walked in on a heated debate. "'What words were you launching (*antiballō*, only here in the New Testament) at each other while you were making your way?' And they looked gloomy" (24:17). He sees that these disciples are struggling with each other under the weight of what they'd just witnessed in Jerusalem. The otherwise obscure figure of Cleopas now takes center stage (significantly, members of the Twelve are not featured in this important episode). His response betrays a distinct tone of impatience: "So are you the *only* one in Jerusalem who doesn't know," he asks incredulously, about "*all the things that have happened*?" (24:18). Perhaps he is just exhibiting wariness about the prying of an unknown interlocutor.

Having established sufficient angst in this unhappy scene, there is a grim irony in how the Stranger pleads ignorance: "Do tell!" (24:19a). Given what Jesus had just been through, this retort is unbearably sardonic. Passionately, if a bit recklessly, the two launch into the whole sordid affair: how Jesus of Nazareth had resuscitated the prophetic tradition in his ministry, igniting hope among people longing for liberation and *shalom*; and how their own leaders (bloody Quislings!) had railroaded him over to the imperial oppressors, who mercilessly strung him up (24:19b-20). Finally, their frustration boils over: "And we had counted [*ēlpizō*, the verb for expectant hope in the New Testament] on him being the One to liberate Israel" (24:21). Their bitter disappointment, sense of betrayal, and confusion over the crushing political events are palpable.

It isn't hard to feel empathy for these two. They had staked their life on the possibility that *this* messianic movement (unlike so many others in recent generations) would finally break the yoke of oppression that had strangled their people for centuries. They had committed themselves to the risky business of challenging the native aristocracy and their imperial overlords. Yet everything had gone wrong. Jesus's march on Jerusalem had sparked not a popular uprising, but a vicious counterinsurgency blow by the Romans. Their leader was publicly lynched, and their compatriots had fled for their lives under all-points bulletins. They conclude their miserable saga by relating (with apparent aggravation) a rumor circulating among some of their dispirited companions—*women's* tales mind you—about visions of angels and an empty tomb (24:22–24, echoing 24:10–11). Well, they weren't buying it: the authorities had probably confiscated Jesus's body, the fix was in, everything had fallen apart, they'd been arguing about it all day, and frankly they'd *had* it. No, Mr. Zünd, that Emmaus road conversation was definitely *not* a stroll in the park.

For contemporary Americans, a more fitting analogy for this scenario might be the days immediately following Martin Luther King's assassination at the Lorraine Motel in Memphis, Tennessee, on April 4, 1968.[10] An iconic photo shows Andrew Young and Jesse Jackson frantically gesturing toward the shooter from the balcony in front of King's room seconds after he was shot.[11] We know now that the man kneeling by the fallen leader was a government agent, and that King's assassination was choreographed by officials both local and national.[12] Luke's world was similarly one of covert ops and conspiracies, of "justice" meted out by good old boys who can hardly contain their glee at the prophet's demise, followed by stern calls for law and order in the wake of this "tragedy" broadcast by the system that engineered it.

Two days after King's murder, Memphis was on lockdown, and his lieutenants were going crazy trying to figure out what really had gone down: why and how their leader had been shot in broad daylight, who was behind it, what it meant for the movement, and whether any of *them* might be next on the hit list. I know this because one of those lieutenants was the late Tony Henry, who later became my mentor in community organizing with the American Friends Service Committee. Yet in all the years we worked together, Tony only spoke of that day once, when I pressed him hard. It was *that* traumatic.[13]

I will offer this kind of historical analogizing throughout my reading of Luke—because scripture scholarship is obliged to rescue texts from a sentimentality that insulates us from the possibility that we might be captive to the same Powers that got rid of Jesus—and King.

B. Re-Reading the World through the Prophets

The Stranger's response to his beleaguered companions is instructive (24:25–27). He doesn't scold them for mixing religion and politics, nor redirect them to turn inwards to a life of the spirit, nor console them with pat doctrines of history or theology. Instead, he walks with them for a few miles, listening to their pain. As civil rights movement elder Ruby Sales always asks when meeting with beat-down folk: "Tell me where it hurts."[14] Then, amidst all this Sturm und Drang, he offers, of all things, a *Bible study.* To be precise, the first recorded scripture lesson in the life of an Easter church that hasn't yet been empowered at Pentecost. "OK fellas," says the Stranger, "it's the worst of times, alright. So open your sacred texts, and let's re-read our history together under the shadow of death."

This turn in the narrative makes theological liberals blush, while busting the hermeneutic program of conservatives. What the Stranger offers here is neither the kind of high academic treatise loved by the former, nor the rigidly boundaried, pietistic preachments ubiquitous among the latter. He starts by addressing his fit-to-be-tied disciples as "fools" (24:25, *anontoi*). This term in the New Testament refers to the clueless (Rom 1:14), the seduced (Gal 3:1, 3), the envious (Titus 3:3) and "those who wish to be rich" (1 Tim 6:9). It functions here as a rhetorical slap upside the head: "Yo, wake up and smell the coffee!" The Stranger diagnoses their hearts as "sluggish" (*bradeis*), as indeed are ours, because we are similarly socialized to interpret the meaning of events through the dominant lens and logic of the status quo. We are neither literate in, nor trusting of, the counterintuitive wisdom of the Hebrew prophets.

Here we arrive at the reason I chose Luke's epilogue tutorial to launch this exploration of the Third Gospel. Prophets—then and now—tell us that horses and chariots cannot save us, whereas we are transfixed by the omnipotence of modern military technology. They tell us to defend the poor, but we lionize the rich; call for justice, while we complain of compassion fatigue. And prophets warn us that the way to peace in a world locked down by violence, to liberation in a world of enslaving addictions, to transformation in societies of deadened conscience and numbing conformity, is the way of militant yet nonviolent, creative yet sacrificial love. Which is why we balk at the Stranger's punchline, the key query upon which a truly *theological* reading of history hangs: "Was it not necessary (*dêi*) that Messiah should suffer?" (24:26).

Dêi (here in the imperfect form) is a technical apocalyptic term that appears throughout the New Testament. It refers here to the fact that a violent reaction by the Powers to prophetic witness is "inevitable," which is a better translation. This is not a prompt to reflect on cosmic propitiation or atonement, but rather a rhetorical question. The prophet's death is not *required*, given who God is; it is, however, *inevitable*, given what the State is, as history repeatedly reveals. This problematizes our deepest assumptions, and unmasks our profound captivity to conventional wisdom about rule from the top down, justice as retribution, and peace through military might. Nevertheless, the counter-vision of the prophets insists on revolution from the bottom up, the wisdom of outsiders, the power of the least.

We Christians today are just like the disciples in Luke's story: even if we understand enough to acknowledge that Jesus lived a prophet's *life*, we don't yet understand enough to recognize the historically redemptive power of his prophet's *death*. Because as the Apostle Paul famously put it, the cross—rightly understood as the *inevitable* consequence of nonviolently resisting oppression—is a stumbling block (1 Cor 1:23).

"Then beginning with Moses and all the prophets, he interpreted to them the scriptures" (Luke 24:27). The verb is *diērmēneuō*, and every other time it appears in the New Testament it means to translate from a foreign language into one's native tongue (e.g., Acts 9:36). In other words, the Stranger is patiently working to *decode* the old scriptural stories so his "sluggish" disciples can get it. The vocation of *un*domesticating Bible study is to render the texts intelligible, to engage them contextually, and to empower action for transformation.

The inconvenient conscience of prophets is forever silenced, jailed, exiled, or killed by both church and society. Once safely disposed of, the prophet might get a statue, a national holiday, or a street named after them, but once canonized, their life and message is either ignored or chocolate-coated by public officials. Jesus warns us about this very phenomenon earlier in Luke's story: "Woe to you! For you build the tombs of the prophets whom your ancestors killed . . . from the blood of Abel to that of Zechariah . . ." (11:47, 51). It is the prophets themselves, *not* their dubious hagiographers, who should orient us for how to read our collective story. Their witness is the hermeneutic key to our weary history, right up to the present. This is why, at the outset of the Easter movement, Luke insists that the work of building literacy in the prophetic tradition should stand at the center of discipleship communities.

Yet Luke also slipped this powerful proposition into an earlier story: the infamous tale of Lazarus and Dives, the archetypally disparate poor and rich man (16:19–31; chapter 11). This dark vision features a tragicomic conversation across the cruel gulf that separates haves and have-nots (16:27–28). As noted in the introduction, the exchange between Dives and Abraham culminates with the latter's stunning response to the former's presumptuous petition for amnesty from the wages of economic sin:

> Abraham said, "They have Moses and the prophets; let them hear them."
> And the rich man said, "No, father Abraham; but if someone goes to them from the dead, they will repent."
> Abraham said, "If they do not hear Moses and the prophets, neither will they be convinced if someone should rise from the dead" (16:29–31).

This remarkable prolepsis (a literary term for pointing forward in a narrative) anticipates our Emmaus epilogue, in which "someone risen from the dead" insists to his followers that they cannot make sense of life and death under empire except through tutelage by the prophetic tradition.

The Stranger exhibits classical "peripatetic philosophy" on the Emmaus Road (from *peripatētikos,* "walking up and down").[15] His catechism apparently took a while, for it grows dark. The two disciples compel (*parabiazomai,* implying coercion) this peculiar pedagogue to lodge with them, perhaps reminding him that once Roman curfew fell it would be particularly dangerous for the traveler (as if he doesn't know). What happens next is the part of Luke's epilogue that typically gets churchly attention: the Stranger is revealed in the breaking of the bread (24:283–2). I will revisit this moment in my own epilogue (ii).

As important as this eucharistic epiphany is, Luke immediately shifts our focus *back* to the conversation on the road about the prophetic tradition. The "sanctuary" moment is made possible only by a "seminary of the streets." The two exclaim: "Were not our hearts burning within us while he was talking to us on the road, while he was opening the scriptures to us?" (24:32). The verb *dianoigo* in every other appearance in the Gospels refers to the opening of deaf ears (e.g., Mark 7:34f), of a closed womb (e.g., Luke 2:23), of unseeing eyes (as in the immediately preceding verse here, 24:31) and of a hardened heart (Acts 16:14). Notably, the only other time it is employed in relation to the scriptures is when Paul tries to persuade his synagogue compatriots that "it was *inevitable* that Jesus had to suffer" (Acts 17:3). This underlines the point of the Emmaus catechism: navigating traumatic history is not ultimately a matter of rational persuasion, but of liberating locked-down minds, hearts and imaginations through the hermeneutic key of prophetic faith. *This* is what will make our hearts burn with renewed commitment to discipleship under the shadow of death.

In the second half of the Emmaus narrative, the action dramatically reverses directions. The two disciples who were fleeing Jerusalem after the execution of their leader now return to face its dangers (24:33a). There the fractured community regathers, presumably in another safe house, and the pair relates their experience to the other confused members of the movement. They describe the Stranger's pedagogy on the road, then how he was revealed in the breaking of bread (24:35). At this point, the Risen Jesus abruptly appears again, now to the whole group (24:36).

The disciples' reaction—surprised now for the second time in this story—is revealing. They are "terrified and awestruck" (24:37a). The first verb is entirely understandable: their leader had just been crucified, a gruesome form of execution reserved only for political dissidents. This spectacle had only one function in Roman Palestine: to intimidate subjects in the occupied territories, broadcasting the message *This is what happens to those who challenge the hegemony of Caesar.* The only other time *ptoeō* (terrified) appears in the New Testament is earlier in 21:9: "When you hear of wars and upheavals, do not be terrified; these things are *inevitable.*" Jesus's community lived under the shadow of inescapable imperial violence in the same way that Black and brown people do in America today, resulting in all-too-familiar, terrorizing images of police chokeholds or shootings.

But the disciples are also "awestruck" (*emphobos*), an adjective usually describing reaction to the presence of divine power. This strangely twinned vocabulary suggests that they are caught between two types of fear. On one hand, they cower before the handiwork of official terrorism imprinted on the body of Jesus. On the other, they reel before the prospect that somehow Rome has *not* had the last word, that the divine conspiracy for life has defied the straightjacket of Death. Jesus is *back*, and ready to continue organizing the movement. But this awe can quickly turn back to dread when the implications of resurrection become clear: *Are we now supposed to follow you back out into public to face again those who did this to you?*

The disciples retreat, wondering if they are hallucinating (24:37b). While the Risen One may be *elusive*, however, he is not *illusive*. Having gone unrecognized once on the road, Jesus now shows his "hands and feet," which bear all the marks of being nailed to a cross. He invites the disciples to touch them (24:39; *psēlaphaō*, which can mean to "grope"). Jesus's invitation is also a challenge: if they do not believe his executed body is now *redivivus*, they will render themselves supremely unclean by touching a corpse. These mangled extremities offer a second crucial Christological lesson: the Risen One *is* the Crucified One. The former neither negates nor eclipses the latter: the Resurrected Christ is not unscathed by the violence of empire. His traumatic somatic presence now becomes the central object lesson of both lynching and liberation.[16]

While they try to sort out their confusion, an exhausted Jesus asks, almost whimsically: "It's been a long couple of days, and I've been through, you know, a *lot*; anybody got a sandwich for a brother?" (24:41b). Here again, Luke radically centers the somatic: just as Jesus's body still bears the scars of his showdown with the world-rulers, he continues to feel hunger. Disciples are summoned not only to touch violated flesh, but also to attend to its needs.

Upon finishing his "Easter dinner," Luke's Jesus resumes the Bible study in "Moses and the prophets," begun with those forlorn disciples on the road (24:44). "He opened their minds that they might understand the scriptures," says Luke for a second time (24:45), unlocking faculties of perception that have been shut down by empire. The verb "to understand" (*suniemi*) could be paraphrased as "connecting the dots"—though it is more often employed in the New Testament to describe the many situations in which disciples are *unable* to do this (e.g., 2:50; 18:34; Acts 7:25). He reiterates the inconvenient part about the inevitability of suffering (24:46). The epilogue concludes with Jesus commissioning his community to take up this prophetic struggle to "turn history around" (the meaning of repentance) as the core practice of restorative healing (the meaning of forgiveness; 24:47a). This mission is not just to individual hearts; it is also to nations and systems, starting at the centers of power: for Luke, Jerusalem (24:47b), for our world, Washington, DC.

The Emmaus narrative, when re-placed in the real time and space of first-century occupied Palestine under the Roman boot, is a far cry from the whitewashing sentimentality of happy-ending theologies, or dogmas that posit resurrection as a cosmic trump card removing Jesus (and us) from the world. Quite the contrary: it offers the church's first catechism in the deep and continuing story of those who struggle against empire and for the Great Economy. Jesus's resurrection animates and empowers our *insurrection* against the powers of oppression and death. And to explain himself to his movement, the Risen Christ does not employ legal, poetic, royal, or sapiential strands of his scriptural tradition, but the enduring testimony of Moses and the prophets.

Such a radical re-orientation to Jewish literature and practice is all the more remarkable if Luke's Gospel was, as is widely believed, written by and for Gentile audiences. The prophetic traditions open the "sluggish" minds and hearts of Jew and Gentile alike to God's dream of justice and empower us to challenge imperial historiography with the alternative story of transformation from the margins and the revolutionary power of costly, nonviolent love. As beautifully expressed in a sixth century Georgian fresco of a Black Jesus teaching from the scriptures, Luke's Risen One is neither white nor triumphant, but a persistent *pedagogue* of the ancient liberation story that animated him.[17]

CHAPTER TWO

Israel's First Catechism

Sabbath Economics

> Israel's history begins in the household of slavery . . . in Pharaoh's economy. Israel comes to know God through its history of struggling to conform to God's economy, which is a household of freedom.
>
> —M. Douglas Meeks, *God the Economist*[1]

IN THE SPIRIT of Jesus's first catechism for his movement, I turn to a summary review of what I am calling "Israel's first catechism."[2] I focus first on the primal instructions of Exodus 16, then their footprints through various traditions attributed to Moses and the prophets. I read these Hebrew Bible texts narratively and in canonical sequence in order to emphasize the broad sweep of story and theme; I point readers to scholarly introductions to get a sense of the many historical-critical issues at play in this ancient literature.[3]

The principles of economic and social justice are woven into the warp and weft of Tanakh, an acronym referring to the traditional Jewish division of the Bible into Torah (or Teaching), Nevi'im (or Prophets), and Ketuvim (or Writings). Pull this strand and the whole fabric unravels (the same is true for Luke's Gospel). One of the main threads that runs through this corpus is the theme of Sabbath Economics: a cosmology of gift and limits, instructions for sharing equitably what the Creator gives, and warnings not to mistake gift for possession.

The economic implications of the Sabbath can be summarized in three axioms:

- The world as created by God is abundant, supplying enough for all living things—provided that human communities restrain our appetites and live within sustainable limits.
- Social disparities in wealth and power are *not* part of the order of Creation, but the result of human sin, and must be mitigated by the community of faith through the regular practice of redistribution and reparation.

- The prophetic message—characterized in both Testaments as "good news" to the poor—calls all peoples to construct and maintain social equity.

This ethical vision, which according to the biblical narrative arose out of an ancient experience of enslavement under imperial Egypt—howsoever that might be construed historically—is meant to be both *corrective* and *preventive*. It continues to offer communities of faith today hope for a Way out of our captivity to the systemic social inequality and alienation of plantation capitalism, its ideology of supremacist hierarchy, and its patterns of concentrating wealth and power and exhausting earth's resources for the benefit of a minority.[4]

A. Torah

"Keep a jar of manna throughout your generations . . ."

Given the long distinction (and even dissociation) between "Law and Prophets" in both Jewish and Christian traditions, it is important to begin this review by acknowledging that Moses is presented in the Exodus story first as a *wilderness prophet*. The adjective is key: he is shaped by, and apprentices to, places beyond the control of civilization and its empires. The Exodus narrative establishes the archetype of such formation: Moses is born in a river, instructed on a mountain, and tested in the desert. This will also be the case for Jesus of Nazareth.

Moses is birthed at the margins of a world under the imperial shadow of death (as is Jesus in the nativity stories of Matt 1–3 and Luke 1–3). Moses's mother entrusts him to a river, and a conspiracy of women watch over him, even in the house of the oppressor (Exod 2:1–10). These extraordinary roots lead an adult Moses to defect from his "insider" privileges in Pharaoh's regime: first skirmishing with street-level injustices, then fleeing to the wilderness, where he encounters the God of his ancestors (Exod 2:11–25).

Twice in Exodus, Moses is tutored on a mountain. On Mount Horeb, through the enchanted medium of a burning bush, a Voice from the fire reveals two characteristics of One-who-refuses-domestication, which rightly represent pillars of biblical theology (Exod 3:1–6).[5]

1. This deity is not an "alternative lord" to Pharaoh but rather dwells apart from civilization altogether. Though not immured in human systems, this One is nevertheless engaged with and attentive to them—especially to the groan of suffering under empire—and responds by animating and empowering movements for liberation (Exod 3:7–10).
2. This deity cannot be named—which is to say, drafted into (or branded for) any of civilization's theological, economic, or political

> ideologies. The moniker introduced here is "YHWH," meaning "I will be who I will be" (Exod 3:11–15).[6] The other mountain of instruction is Sinai. These highlands spaces function as both spiritual founts and geopolitical counterpoints to empire.

Spiritual leaders ascended these "holy heights" not only to commune with the Divine but in pilgrimage to the origins of all natural fertility, as Evan Eisenberg writes in *The Ecology of Eden*:

> The World Mountain is mythic shorthand for an ecological fact. There are certain places on earth that play a central role in the flow of energy and the cycling of water and nutrients, as well as in the maintenance of genetic diversity and its spread by means of gene flow. Such places provide many of the services that keep the ecosystems around them (and the biosphere as a whole) more or less healthy for humans and other life forms. They help control flooding and soil erosion. They provide fresh infusions of pollinating birds and insects. . . . They regulate the mix of oxygen, carbon dioxide, water vapor, and other ingredients in the air and keep its temperature within bounds. They are spigots for the circulation of wildness through places made hard and almost impermeable by long human use. All such places are more or less wild; many are forested . . . and from them great rivers flow.[7]

Here Moses receives Commandments for how the people should live; here Elijah (1 Kg 19, at Horeb) and Jesus (Luke 9:28–36, with Moses and Elijah) encounter assurances of divine accompaniment on their journey of speaking truth to power.

Eisenberg argues that the imperial urban civilizations of Mesopotamia attempted to reproduce, and thus domesticate, the peaks "where the gods dwelled":

> At the heart of every Mesopotamian city was a sacred precinct, and at the heart of every sacred precinct was a ziggurat, a stepped pyramid of mud brick . . . [which] seem to have imitated mountains in a fairly literal way. . . It is a sign of the Mesopotamians' pride that they drew the gods—and paradise itself—down from the mountains and into their own cities.[8]

That Moses meets YHWH on the *wild* mountain, then, is a pointed rejection of the artificially engineered mountains where rulers looked down upon their realm with managerial authoritarianism while communing with gods who were the patrons of empire. Moreover, the mountain epiphanies of Moses, Elijah and Jesus propel them into freedom struggles against these oppressive regimes.

Moses is commissioned to set his people free from Pharaoh's slave-economy (Exod 3:10), but given the mismatch in power, is promised the assistance of Creation (Exod 4–14). The forces of nature in turn generate an escalating campaign to pressure the autocrat to relent and ultimately usher the Hebrews out of empire through cloud and sea into unconquered wilderness.[9] Moses leads the escaping slaves into a hardscrabble wilderness freedom school, beginning with a "test" of hunger followed by a catechism concerning true economic liberation (Exod 15). Jesus faces this defining desert crossroads twice in Luke's story (3B and 6B).

On mystical Mount Sinai, YHWH issues the catechism in another form: the famous Decalogue (Exod 20). It is worth noting that two of the ten commandments receive particular elaboration. One is about keeping Sabbath (Exod 20:8–11, introduced in Exod 16:23–26). The other is the prohibition of idolatry (20:4–6), which is reiterated in a warning not to build altars of hewn stone" (20:23–26). Here is another rejection of ancient Near Eastern ziggurat/pyramid culture. The ironic exception is that this catechism is itself etched in stone (Exod 31:18). In ancient wilderness spirituality, sacred stone is alive, able to hear and "bear witness to covenants made between people, land, and the Creator (see, e.g., the listening cairns" of Joshua 24:24–27).

The lengthy elaboration on Sinai's Covenant Code (Exod 21–30) concludes as it began: with a focus on Sabbath fidelity (Exod 31:12–18). Yet Moses must do fierce battle with his people over their internalized seduction by imperial idols (Exod 32)—because it's easier to get the people out of Egypt than to get Egypt out of the people! This establishes another pattern for Israel's later prophets: calling out the injustices and toxic habits of one's own community. In short, Moses is entrusted with stewarding a covenant and leading a people not (as in other ancient Middle Eastern traditions) as a royal lawgiver, court attorney, or warrior-prince, *but as a "rewilded" prophet*. His own first wilderness test reveals Sabbath Economics as the core of that covenant.

The ideas constellated in Sabbath Economics are unfamiliar to our Global North churches in large part because they have long been marginalized by modern Western biblical interpreters, whose theological imaginations are captive to market-driven orthodoxies. Nowhere is this clearer than in the case of the weekly, annual, and cyclical Sabbath mandates of personal and political wealth and power recalibration. North American Christianity has consequently had too little to say or do concerning wealth disparity, from the last Gilded Age to our present one. This silence has helped legitimate the very systems of inequality that the Bible denounces.[10] I believe the roots of this failure lie in how we have ignored or trivialized the meaning and practice of Sabbath.

The divine command to keep Sabbath lies at the root of every principle of social and economic justice in Torah. It first appears as a verb at the culmination of the story of Creation (Gen 2:2). Notably the Hebrew verb *shavat* means "to cease working" four times more often than to "rest" in the Hebrew scriptures, suggesting the polemical tone of a "labor strike"—precisely what Pharaoh objects to in Exodus 5:5! But this call to "be" rather than to "do" is grounded in the primeval Genesis narrative that the Creator made a world that *cannot be improved upon by human work*. The adjective translated as "good" in the Genesis 1 litany is hardly an adequate rendering of the Hebrew *tov.* Hebrew Bible scholar and social justice activist Richard Lowery—whose brilliant *Sabbath and Jubilee* I recommend to those who want deeper exegesis of these biblical foundations—argues that better synonyms would be "delightful," or "God's cosmic Wow."[11] Think of adjectives you might utter while gazing upon a magnificent sunset, or majestic mountains, or a wild ocean. Creation is abundant, satisfying, indeed magical—and in need of no human reengineering.

The Creator models this: "On the seventh day, God ceased from all God's work" (Gen 2:2 and 3). Lowery notes: "In a delightful twist, 'rest' is signified as a verb in this passage and 'work' as a noun."[12] This establishes a redemptive pattern: good work is "completed" by Sabbath stoppage. For us children of the Protestant work ethic, it is important to recognize that Sabbath is *not* for the purpose of resting in order to work more. There is no "back-to-work Monday" in this Creation narrative. This is why Sabbath is "blessed" (2:3), just like the creation itself (1:22, 28). God's cosmic Sabbath introduces a prototype that human beings are to imitate: enjoying, sharing, and self-limiting are the three appropriate responses to divine gifts of sustenance.

We do not encounter *shabbāth* as a noun (which is to say, as an institution) until the remarkable Exodus tale of hunger in the wilderness (Exod 16), sandwiched between survival stories about thirst (15:22–27) and water (17:1–7). Having been sprung from slavery, the fugitive Hebrews now face the harsh realities of life outside the imperial system. Their first test of character is *economic*: how will they sustain themselves? They complain to Moses that they would have preferred to die "in the land of Egypt, where we . . . ate our fill of bread" rather than being led "into this desert to die of famine" (Exod 16:3). The ancient Israelites could not imagine an economic system apart from the Egyptian political-military-technological complex that enslaved them (this is even more the case with North Americans today). Moses thus has to practice shuttle diplomacy between YHWH and his own recalcitrant kin (Exod 16:6–12)—another pattern for the prophetic tradition.

Here we arrive at the root catechism of Sabbath Economics. The *manna* story is not a feeding miracle or a morality tale about "trusting God's provision," as typically taught in Sunday Schools. It is a didactic tale about the importance of "following instructions" (16:4). "Bread raining from heaven" symbolizes natural fertility as a divine gift, a process that begins with rain and ends with bread (as described in Isa 55:10, and alluded to in Josh 5:12, which compares the *manna* to the produce of a settled land). This moment represents a "test" to see if Israel will learn *how* to gather this gift, what Ellen Davis calls "the establishment of a new food economy, an economy of sufficiency."[13]

Or better, an old economy. We would do well to learn from the cooperative, egalitarian lifeways that sustained human beings for tens of thousands of years prior to the rise of agriculture, cities, and eventually imperial economies based on slavery.[14] After all, at this rate our industrial economies will not last more than a few hundred years! Yet it is little wonder that the Hebrews can't recognize it, having been socialized at the bottom of the social pyramid of empire (16:15, 31). The narrative captures the confusion in what Lowery calls a hilarious Hebrew play on words, in which "the answer is embedded in their question: 'What's that?' (*man hû*). 'That's *manna*!' (*hû man*)."[15]

Moses's ensuing instructions give three defining characteristics of Sabbath Economics.

1. Every family is told to gather only what they need (16:16–18). In contrast to Israel's Egyptian condition of deprivation, here everyone has enough: "Those who gathered more had no surplus, and those who gathered less had no shortage." In the Great Economy there *is* such a thing as too much and too little—which contrasts radically with modern capitalism's infinite tolerance for wealth and poverty, underlined as a disease by another version of the *manna* story found in Numbers 11 (cited in my introduction).
2. The *manna* should not be "stored up" (Exod 16:19–20). Wealth and power in Egypt was defined by surplus accumulation: indeed, Israel's forced labor built "store-cities" (Exod 1:11) into which the empire's plunder and the tribute of subject peoples was gathered. This instruction, too, contradicts capitalism, whose central principle Marx defined sardonically as: "Accumulate, accumulate! *That* is Moses and the prophets!"[16] The Bible understands that dominant civilizations exert centripetal force, drawing labor, resources, and wealth into city-states of idolatrous power (an archetypal description of this is found in the ancient judgment story against Babel's imperial ambitions in Gen 11:1–9). So, the Hebrews are enjoined to keep wealth circulating through strategies of redistribution, not concentrating through strategies of accumulation.
3. The third instruction introduces Sabbath discipline (Exod 16:22–30): "Six days you shall gather; but on the seventh, which is a Sabbath, there will be none." Lowery writes that such self-restraint

> "requires a leap of faith, a firm confidence that the world will continue to operate benevolently for a day without human labor, that God is willing and able to provide enough for the good life. Sabbath promises seven days of prosperity for six days of work. It operates on the assumption that human life and prosperity exceed human productivity."[17] It is important to recognize that the Sabbath "discipline of delight" is instituted here *before* the covenant at Sinai, then reiterated at the conclusion of the Covenant Code as a solemn warning: those who do not practice Sabbath will die (Exod 31:12–17). Not only is Sabbath the crowning blessing of creation; it is also the "beginning and end of Torah."

When the church became predominately Gentile, it adopted Sunday as a replacement of, rather than addition to, the Jewish Sabbath; beginning with Constantine, Christendom's states established public prohibitions on work.[18] But these have almost entirely atrophied in the modern urban West, as capitalist consumerism (and now online work- and shop-aholism) has overwhelmed the old "blue law" restrictions on commerce. Today many Christians trivialize the Sabbath as "merely" one of the Ten Commandments, or worse, profane it as an antiquated, legalistic Jewish code that churches rightly shed. We thereby miss its profound cosmological and ethical power as the Creator's strategy for teaching humans about dependence upon a divine economy of grace, instead of upon our own labor, technology, or social organization.

Because the *manna* story is such a foundational catechesis, it stipulates one exception to the prohibition of storage: the community must keep a jarful of *manna*, to be displayed in front of the covenant in perpetuity (Exod 16:32–34; see Heb 9:4). Clearly that jar was lost! The primary purpose of Sabbath observation is to remember weekly two economic principles: the goal of "enough" for everyone, and the prohibition of accumulation—or as Gandhi famously said, "The earth has enough for everyone's need, but not their greed."[19] This ethos is, of course, utterly contrary to economics as we know it. But as noted, Sabbath Economics is neither novel nor utopian but simply reiterates what anthropologists call "generalized reciprocity": a culture of cooperation and sharing that has characterized traditional societies for 99 percent of human history.[20]

Throughout the rest of Torah, the Sabbath Economics vision is developed and applied. Weekly Sabbath observation is first among the appointed feasts. It also defines the rhythm of the Levitical calendar of festivals (Lev 23:3ff), including Passover (vv. 6–7); Shavuot (v. 21); Feast of Atonement (vv. 24,31); and Sukkot (vv. 35f). The social justice code of Exodus 23 then extends the annual Sabbath cycle to every seventh year: "You shall let the land rest and lie fallow, so that the poor of your people may eat; and what they leave the wild animals may eat" (Exod 23:10–11). This pause means to restore ecological and social equilibrium by restraining the activity of producers, while re-enfranchising the marginalized and the undomesticated who the economy has shut out. Prescribing periodic rest for the land and human labor goes beyond the agricultural good sense of fallowing land. It functions to disrupt human attempts to control nature and maximize extraction. Because the earth belongs to God, who offers its bounty as a gift, people should distribute those fruits justly instead of seeking to own or hoard them.

The Deuteronomist goes further, interpreting the Sabbath year to include debt release (Deut 15:1–81). This was a hedge against the inevitable tendency of centralized societies to create hierarchical classes with the poor at the bottom. As summarized in my introduction, in agrarian Israel (or many parts of the two-thirds world today), the cycle of poverty began when a family fell into debt, deepened when they had to sell off their land in order to service the debt, and reached its nadir when landless peasants had only their labor to sell, becoming bond-slaves. Large landowners acted as creditors—and foreclosures added to their holdings.

Sabbath year debt release intends to safeguard both social justice ("there will be no one in need among you") and sound fiscal policy ("creditor nations will not rule over you," Deut 15:4–6). But anticipating the ubiquity of greed, the practical Deuteronomist specifically forbids people from tightening credit in the years immediately prior to the Sabbath remission (15:7–11)! The remission applies to debt-slaves as well, not only freeing them but also requiring that they be empowered to take with them sufficient resources to make it on their own, a principle grounded in Israel's memory of liberation from enslavement (15:12–17). Whether or not the community will enjoy the blessing of the land is contingent on its fidelity to this Sabbath discipline.

The fullest expression of Sabbath logic is the Levitical "Jubilee": a comprehensive remission to take place every "Sabbath's Sabbath," or forty-ninth/fiftieth year (Lev 25). The Jubilee (named after the *jovel*, a ram's horn sounded to herald the remission) aimed to dismantle structures of socioeconomic inequality by:

- releasing each community member from debt (25:35–42);
- returning encumbered or forfeited land to its original owners (25:13, 25–28);
- freeing slaves (25:47–55);

The rationale for this restructuring of the community's assets was to remind Israel that the land belongs to God (25:23) and that they are an Exodus people who must never return to an economy based on slavery (25:42). And as Rabbi Arthur Waskow points out, this tradition is rooted in Sinai.[21]

Jubilee is prefigured in the Feast of Weeks (*Shavuot*), a celebration of first fruits of harvest (Exod 23:16; Lev 23:15–25; Deut 16:9–12). Note the resonance in language and calculations:

> *Shavuot*: From the day after the sabbath, from the day on which you bring the sheaf of the elevation offering, *you shall count off seven weeks*. . . . You shall count until the day after the seventh sabbath, *fifty days*; then you shall present an offering of new grain to the Lord (Lev 23:15; see Deut 14:9).
>
> Jubilee: *You shall count off seven weeks of years*, seven times seven years, so that the period . . . gives forty-nine years. . . . And you shall hallow the *fiftieth year* and you shall proclaim liberty throughout the land to all its inhabitants (25:8,10).

This suggests that Sabbath Economics applied at *each* harvest, not just every other generation.

I am painfully aware of the many ways the Jubilee tradition has been, and still is, shrugged off as either utopian or fictional. On one hand, conservative church leaders dismiss it as irrelevant or unrealistic *because they are deeply committed to capitalist cosmology*. On the other, liberal academics skeptical of the Jubilee's historicity have not found sufficient evidence in either Testament—*because they have not been looking for it*.[22] Economist Michael Hudson has taken on both objections in his important work on the origins and practice of debt release in antiquity, concluding: "Viewed in its broadest ancient Near Eastern context, the Jubilee turns out not to be so utopian or impractical after all."[23]

Hudson points out that in fact, the Levitical Jubilee debt release program has antecedents dating some two thousand years earlier, beginning with Sumer in the twenty-fourth century BCE.[24] Throughout the ancient Middle East, kings periodically declared a "clean slate" for those in debt in order to stabilize the economy. Because interest rates were typically 20 percent or more, usury weakened society from within, as absentee owners monopolized the land, drove off its inhabitants, and reduced many to bondage. This undermined the ability of the peasantry to serve in the military, threatening security. Debt amnesty preserved widespread self-sufficiency on the land for its customary holders, and thus a free and economically independent fighting force. Hudson notes that clean slate legislation was enforced, and worked to stabilize the agricultural economy.

He also recognizes that "although the Jubilee shares the basic idea of a clean slate proclamation, it also has fundamental differences. Instead of a ruler declaring a clean slate on a whim, the principle was enshrined in Jewish law . . . of economic equity [that] would be periodic and automatic. . . . What was made sacred was no longer the king, as in Bronze Age Mesopotamia, but the law."[25] The rationale was also distinct. In Leviticus, YHWH, not the king, is the true landowner, and *all* human beings are only tenants (Lev 25:23). Nor is there any allusion to propping up the state or military; rather, the purpose of the Jubilee (and the prohibition of usury) is to regularly deconstruct the conditions of debt-servitude, because the God of Exodus *continues* to lead people out of slavery (25:35–42). This elevated to a sacred status the social duties of canceling debts, redistributing the land, and liberating debt servants.

Finally, Hudson argues that if, as the scholarly consensus holds, the Levitical codes were compiled in the sixth century BCE, it was largely as a reaction against a trend toward economic individualism and wealth-seeking that was emerging, from classical Greece to India.[26] Neither Israelite nor Babylonian kings had offered clean slate legislation for centuries (see, e.g., 1 Kg 12, Jer 34), and emerging imperial economies were intensifying usury and the commodification of land, resulting in growing latifundialization (concentration of more land in fewer hands). These are the very conditions that provoked protests from Israel's prophets from the eighth century onward. No longer, then, can the tradition of Jubilee release be dismissed as ahistorical idealism.

James Watts raises an equally important "objection to objections" to the relevance of the ancient Jubilee ethos. He argues that even as the exact historical character of the Jubilee is debated, "the meaning of a text cannot be restricted to just its literary context and ancient historical context."[27] Scholars have ignored how Leviticus 25 has "been cited prominently in political conflicts over such issues in Jewish and Christian societies, especially in the last 500 years"[28]:

> The contrast between scholarly assessments of the chapter's meaning... and its proven power to inspire movements for freedom . . . poses a moral challenge to the conventional methods of biblical scholarship.... [D]ismissing revolutionary appeals to Jubilee as misreading the biblical text prevents interpreters from wrestling with the literary and cultural specifics of how communities actually employ scriptures.... Biblical interpreters should not get in the way of this text's rhetoric by deciding what is or is not "real," much less by pretending to know what is or is not economically and socially possible.... Morally preferable, by far, are interpretations that... take the proclamations of Lev. 25:10, 23, and 55 as a license to dream creatively about better futures and take action to bring them about.[29]

I concur with this thesis, which parallels the earlier work of Michael Walzer on how the Exodus story has been used for two millennia to inspire social struggle and reform.[30] The subversive memory of Jubilee justice surfaced in Hebrew prophets, in the witness of Jesus of Nazareth and has kept erupting throughout Jewish and Christian history. This gives ample evidence of the ancient vision's meaning that is empirical—and infinitely more compelling than scholarly equivocation!

Jubilee imagination animated early monastic experiments, medieval communitarians, and radical Reformers. Even the rise of modern capitalism, with its fierce antipathy toward Sabbath Economics, could not extinguish this vision. Seventeenth and eighteenth century Levelers and Diggers drew on it for popular struggles in England against the privatization of the Commons and early industrial worker exploitation. As a Tommy Spence song put it:

> Since then this Jubilee
> Sets all at Liberty
> Let us be glad
> Behold each man return to his possession![31]

Or consider the prayer of the nineteenth-century abolitionist William Lloyd Garrison:

> God speed the year of jubilee, the wide world o'er!
> When from their galling chains set free,
> Th' oppressed shall vilely bend the knee,
> and wear the yoke of tyranny, like brutes, no more—
> That year will come, and Freedom's reign,
> to all their plundered rights again, restore.[32]

"The idea of Jubilee suffused the culture of American abolitionism," writes Bennett Parten, "because it offered something that all great social movements need—a collective means of imaging profound political change."[33]

The Jubilee imaginary was best captured and reanimated through nineteenth-century spirituals sung by African slaves in American fields.

> Linebaugh traces the first known African American usage of the concept of Jubilee to an 1834 edition of a children's magazine called *The Southern Rose Bud.* The description of slave children singing a hymn reads: "Don't you hear the Gospel trumpet sound Jubilee?" From this we know that by 1834 the idea of Jubilee was well known to the slaves—even children.[34]

Spirituals such as "The African Hymn" fired Nat Turner's rebellion and guided Harriet Tubman and Sojourner Truth along the underground railroad:

> Good Lord, O when shall slavery cease, And these poor souls enjoy their peace...
> O! come, ye Africans, be wise, We'll join the armies in the skies!
> We'll ruin Satan's Kingdom, Come and go, along with me—Go sound the Jubilee.[35]

Coded songs of resistance and escape, including "Go Down Moses," "Steal Away," "Wade in the Water," and "Swing Low Sweet Chariot," were later introduced to white America through the amazing Fisk Jubilee Singers.[36]

Not only did Jubilee dreams of liberation help Black Americans preserve their dignity and struggle for justice; the Black church, in turn, has helped rescue the biblical Jubilee tradition from attempts (theological and otherwise) by white supremacy to disappear these texts altogether.[37] Without the witness of Tubman and Truth, would any of us be writing about these things today? If they could stake their lives on this vision, so can we. It lives as long as there are people willing to advocate for and embody it.

At the turning of the millennium, the vision of "release from the bondage of debt" again mobilized faith-based activists around the world in the remarkable Jubilee 2000 movement, which successfully advocated for relief for heavily indebted poor countries and seeded a wide variety of economic justice work.[38] Such movements in turn produce fresh readings of both the Bible and the economy, which are helping to animate new movements for justice, as well as small-scale experiments here and around the world with more equitable business practices, sustainable technologies, cooperative land uses, fair trade, and reduced consumption.

B. Nevi'im

"The spoil of the poor is in your houses!"

Israel's prophets were first in this genealogy of re-membering the Sabbath Economics vision. Whenever the nation's leaders sought to marginalize, compromise, or spiritualize the divine vision of enough for *everyone*, the prophets invoked and recontextualized the old stories and songs—and often paid a price. Conversely, the fact that Israel's prophets repeatedly criticized the nation's leadership for betraying poor and vulnerable members of the community is the strongest evidence that Sabbath Economics was an older measuring stick to which they could appeal.

Early on, Samuel warned that a monarchy would gear the economy to the elite through ruthless policies of surplus-extraction and militarism (1 Sam 8:11–17a). If Israel's leaders recreated an "Egyptian condition" among their own people, Samuel lamented, God would no longer hear their cries (1 Sam 8:17b–18). Indeed, the historical narratives of the Hebrew Bible show how, as the old ethos of a tribal confederacy was eclipsed by centralized political power under the Davidic dynasty, economic stratification and political oppression followed inexorably. This abandonment of Sabbath Economics become a central complaint of the prophets.

Elijah returns from exile in 1 Kgs 21 to pronounce doom on King Ahab's murderous plot to assert eminent domain over traditional farmer Naboth's land. Hebrew Bible scholar Ellen Davis calls this story an expression of "two economic systems or cultures in conflict, each with a different principle of land tenure."[39] Naboth resists by invoking "ancestral rights" to his vineyard, using the Hebrew term *nahala* (1 Kg 21:3). It connotes neither possession nor inheritance, but stewardship of land that is understood as a gift from the Creator, contingent upon an intergenerationally enduring covenant relationship. Tellingly, there is no appropriate word in English that expresses such a meaning, since our language developed alongside the rise of capitalism and its presumptions of ownership and extraction. Naboth's objection is predicated on a theological notion of impurity (*halila*): to sell the land would defile him. The only line he speaks in the entire drama articulates concisely an Indigenous cosmology: the land does not belong to him; he belongs to the land. In this tale, the biblical storyteller captures the incommensurability of two conflicting ways of life that have defined the history of civilization: an aggressive political-legal culture based upon an ideology of land possession and a Sabbath Economics ethos in which there *are no words* for land ownership or commodification.[40]

Isaiah's "Song of the Vineyard" charges the nation's leadership with robbery: "The spoil of the poor is in your houses; what do you mean by crushing my people, by grinding the face of the poor?" (Isa 3:14f). This echoes the *manna* tradition's censure of stored wealth in the face of community need (see similarly Mal 3:5–12). In this parable, Isaiah uses the metaphor of a mismanaged vineyard to attack the ruling classes for how they exploit mechanisms of debt and foreclosure to consolidate their holdings while the poor become landless: "Woe to you who join house to house and field to field until no space is left and you live alone in the land!" (Isa 5:8). The prophet sees this as a betrayal of Israel's vocation to be "God's pleasant planting; God expected justice, but saw bloodshed" (Isa 5:7). This bitter denunciation makes little sense if Sabbath strictures on accumulation were not part of the people's cultural consciousness. Centuries later, Jesus of Nazareth remembered and recontextualized Isaiah's parable in a similar warning to elites.[41]

Amos accuses the commercial classes of regarding Sabbath disciplines as an obstacle to market profiteering: "When will the new moon be over, that we may sell grain? And the sabbath, that we may offer wheat for sale, that we may make the *ephah* small and the *shekel* great, and practice deceit with false balances?" (Amos 8:5). Land barons treat the poor as an exploitable class instead of guaranteeing their gleaning rights (see Exod 23:10f; Lev 19:9; Mic 7:1), "buying the poor for silver and the needy for a pair of sandals, and selling sweepings of the wheat" (Amos 8:6). And Hosea laments that fidelity to international markets has replaced Israel's allegiance to God's economy of grace: "I will go after my lovers; *they* give me my bread and my water, my wool and my flax, my oil and my drink" (Hos 2:5).

It should not surprise us, then, that the most concrete literary evidence that periodic debt release *was* practiced in ancient Israel is found in the prophetic writings. Jeremiah blasts King Zedekiah when he reneges on his declaration of Sabbath year manumission:

> Thus says the Lord: "I myself made a covenant with your ancestors when I brought them out of the land of Egypt . . . saying, 'Every seventh year each of you must set free any Hebrews. . .' But your ancestors did not listen to me. . . . You yourselves recently repented and did what was right in my sight by proclaiming liberty to one another . . . but then you turned around and profaned my name when each of you took back your slaves" (Jer 34:13–16).

That this is understood by Jeremiah as the main reason for Judah's defeat and exile suggests the seriousness of such a breach of the Sabbath year. Lowery comments: "Zedekiah's decree is the kind of thing kings did in the ancient Near East. And the creditors' heartless enslavement of those they had promised to free is all too familiar."[42] Israel's ancient historians chronicled Jeremiah's judgment: "God took into exile in Babylon those who had escaped the sword . . . to fulfill the word of the Lord by the mouth of Jeremiah, until the land *had made up for its Sabbaths*. All the days that it lay desolate it kept Sabbath, to fulfill seventy years" (2 Chr 36:20f; see Lev 26:34f).

Later, the reformer Nehemiah resurrects the Levitical prohibition of interest (Neh 5:6–13), as well as Sabbath strictures on commercial production, transaction and finance. "If the peoples of the land bring in merchandise or any grain on the Sabbath day to sell, we will not buy it . . . and we will forego the crops on the seventh year and the exaction of every debt" (Neh 10:31). Even in late Second Temple Judaism we find allusion to the Sabbath Year in the Book of Jubilees and in the writings of the Jewish historian Josephus.

The Sabbath also functioned symbolically: the number seven, for example, is archetypal throughout the Hebrew Bible, prominent in the stories of Noah

(Gen 7–8), Samson (Judg 14, 16), Elijah (1 Kg 18:43f), Elisha (2 Kg 4:35; 5:10–14), and Esther (Esth 1–2). Most famous is the old story of an assault on the Canaanite fortress of Jericho led by Joshua (who, like Moses, is considered a prophet). God instructs the Israelite rebels to march around the city for seven days, then on the last day, march around it seven times while trumpeting the *jovel*, after which the walls come a'tumblin' down (Josh 6). Not only is this tale a hilarious parody of ancient military tactics of laying siege; its Jubilee symbolism could not be clearer. The city represented Canaanite political and economic hegemony over the hinterlands; Joshua's Jubilee circle dance represented a vision of liberation from its oppressive system of tribute and violence.

Finally, there are eschatological visions of Jubilee. Land redistribution is forecast by Ezekiel: "My princes shall no longer oppress my people; but shall let the house of Israel have the land according to their tribes" (Ezek 45:8; see 46:17–18; 47:13ff). And the Jubilee commission of Isaiah 61:1–2 begins with a call to "bring good news to the oppressed poor," and ends with a proclamation of "the year of the Lord's favor." Of all the possibilities in his scriptures, it is *this* text that Jesus of Nazareth chooses to define and inaugurate his mission (Luke 4:18–19; 4A).

I conclude this brief review of the Sabbath Economics tradition of the Hebrew Bible with two poignant stories that are germane to its prophetic transmission. One is from 2 Kings 22, where King Josiah of Judah is told that an old "book of the Law" has been discovered in the basement of the Temple. When it is read to him, it's clear that it is an oracle of judgment, so Josiah does what any self-respecting ruler would do: he asks for a second opinion (2 Kg 22:11–13). All his court advisors are summoned to interpret the meaning of this scroll, but these luminaries turn immediately for help from an obscure figure: Huldah, the wife of a "keeper of the wardrobe" (22:14). Mentioned only here in the Bible, this working-class seamstress is a prophet—one of only seven females so designated in the Hebrew scriptures. Yet it is she, not the royal scribes, who interprets the meaning of the lost book to the king.

In a decidedly disrespectful allusion to his royal highness, Huldah begins: "Thus says the God of Israel: Tell that man who sent you to me" (22:15)! She proceeds to relay the bad news: the fall of his regime is coming; the good news is only that it won't happen in his lifetime (an echo of Elijah's indictment of Ahab in 1 Kgs 21:29). And that's the last we hear of this mysterious truth-telling woman. Scholars believe this story refers to the appearance of the book of Deuteronomy, which launched the most significant reform in the history of Judah. At a critical turning point in the life of the nation, it is the prophet who interprets Torah. This reflects the fact that, although Torah appears canonically before the prophets and is set in an earlier historical world, it was Israel's prophets who preserved and interpreted older Sabbath Economics traditions.[43]

The second story is connected to the Huldah tale and similarly speaks to prophetic commitment to passing on scriptural witness and wisdom. Josiah launched a reform but died in a battle with Pharaoh (2 Kg 23). His son Jehoiakim, ruling as a vassal of Egypt (and then Babylon), bleeds his country dry with tribute, having returned to the decadent and oppressive royal ways his father had sought to halt. Thus, God instructs Jeremiah to chronicle "all the words that I have spoken to you against Israel and Judah and all the nations, from the days of Josiah until today" (Jer 36:2). This is a quite a project, since Jeremiah had been active for twenty years opposing official policies of the nation, leading to the crisis of 604 BCE. That year Babylonian King Nebuchadnezzar defeated Jehoiakim's suzerain Pharaoh Necho at Carchemish (Jer 46:2), after which Jerusalem came under attack, submitting to Babylonian control after a brief siege (Dan 1:1). The entire region was shaped by the imperial struggle between Egypt and Babylon, which as usual blew right through Palestine. Jeremiah sets about compiling his oracles, recruiting Baruch, one of his disciples, as his secretary (Jer 36:4).

But the prophet has been banned from the Temple (36:5)—unsurprising given his fierce public critique of the ruling class! Jeremiah gets around this by commissioning Baruch to read his manifesto to the people at a "town meeting," in the desperate hope that the truth might turn around Israel's leaders and people (36:6–7). He is drawing on the Deuteronomist's decree that Moses's instructions be read publicly "at the end of every seven years, at the set time of the year of release, at the feast of booths, when all Israel comes to appear before the Lord at the place which God will choose" (Deut 31:10–11, see 15:1). Baruch's reading goes forward (Jer 36:10–11)—followed by official backlash. Mid-level officials report to royal officers, who summon Baruch to verify that these oracles are really from the notorious Jeremiah. Significantly, this cabinet includes both the son and grandson of Shaphan, the court scribe who had sought out Huldah (2 Kg 22:14)! Knowing they will have to report to the king that the banished prophet's words are again loose, they counsel both Baruch and Jeremiah to lie low (Jer 36:11–19).

What happens next is one of the most extraordinary moments in all of scripture. The scroll wends its way up the political ladder, finally reaching the king himself:

> Sitting in his winter apartment . . . there was a fire burning in the brazier before him. As Jehudi read three or four columns, the king would cut them off with a penknife and throw them into the brazier, until the entire scroll was consumed in the fire (36:22–23).

Then the king issues an order for the arrest of both prophet and amanuensis, who go underground (36:26). A king of Israel using a prophetic text as kindling! We might imagine that Jeremiah, upon hearing of such official contempt, might go deeper into hiding, despairing of any possibility for change. Instead, however, he instructs Baruch to "take another scroll and write on it all the former words that were in the first scroll, which King Jehoiakim of Judah has burned" (36:28). Not only is the prophetic vocation about speaking truth to power, in season and out; it also is about rescuing, preserving, and reasserting texts of truth-telling—as many times as it takes.

The stories of Huldah and Jeremiah encourage efforts to rehabilitate the biblical vision of Sabbath Economics in our time. It is indeed like an old scroll that for too long has been gathering dust in our churches, or worse, has been pared into the royal barbecue by the powerful. The instructions of Sabbath and Jubilee are strange and troubling to the children of modernity, and many of our interpreters relegate them to the margins or delegitimize them altogether. We once again need the wise but unsettling voice of prophets—whether they reside in sweatshops or in exile—to help these ancient traditions of justice live again.

The biblical vision is diametrically opposed to our modern assumptions about economics. Capitalism's primary axioms of scarcity as a natural condition, and of unlimited human appetite, breed resignation to unequal systems of distribution and ideologies of unlimited economic growth. Indeed, it is a cruel parody of Sabbath Economics, creating artificial scarcity by relentless plundering of the earth's resources while demonstrating incredible ingenuity at manufacturing artificial abundance—think of the unlimited kinds of cereal or toothpaste at your local supermarket—for those who can afford it! The gifts of creation have been transformed into commodities, which by definition do not circulate equitably to everyone. We have reengineered God's world, and our economists, politicians and captains of industry have pronounced it good.

Yet our interlocking ecological and social crises are forcing many to reconsider this assessment and to defect from capitalist orthodoxy to holistic notions, such as Berry's call for humans to readapt to the "Great Economy." Some economic theorists are even proposing models that echo principles of Sabbath Economics. For example, Belgian philosopher Ingrid Robeyns writes and advocates for "limitarianism":

> There should be upper limits to the amount of income and wealth a person can hold. One argument for limitarianism is that superriches can undermine political equality. The other reason is that it would be better if the surplus money that superrich households have were to be used to meet unmet urgent needs and local and global collective action problems. A particular urgent case of the latter is climate change. . . . Limitarianism as an ethical or political view is, in a certain sense,

> symmetrical to the view that there is a poverty line and that no one should fall below this line. Limitarianism claims that one can theoretically construct a riches line and that a world in which no one would be above the riches line would be a better world.[44]

"This call for a levelling down is perhaps the most blasphemous idea in contemporary discourse," writes George Monbiot, "but her arguments are sound."[45]

Brian Czech, author of *Supply Shock: Economic Growth at the Crossroads and the Steady State Solution*, directs the US Center for the Advancement of Steady State Economics.[46] According to their website, they educate and train leaders to realize that economic "growth is causing more problems than it solves at this point in history," and to transition to a steady state model in which economic systems are in balance with environmental integrity. Economic thinkers like this are often called "midwives of a new economic world"—even if they are applying ancient wisdom to our modern crisis.

Israel's first catechism in Sabbath Economics, seeded in her earliest tribal stories, was repeatedly re-visioned by her prophets over many centuries and under differing circumstances. This catechism was fully rehabilitated in Luke's Gospel story of the latter-day prophet Jesus, and recited in the church's first catechism on the Emmaus Road. For two millennia, this legacy has continued to seed hope among justice-seeking Jews and Christians. It is up to us, as Luke put it, to be "witnesses to these things" in our weary world (Luke 24:48). To his story we now turn.

CHAPTER THREE

Luke's Prelude

Prophets Preparing for the Great Economy

> While shepherds kept their watching, O'er silent flocks by night. . .
> Down in a lowly manger, Our humble Christ was born. . .
> Go, tell it on the mountain, Over the hills and everywhere.
> —African American spiritual, preserved and popularized by John Wesley Work and the Fisk Jubilee Singers[1]

I OPENED THIS study of Luke's Gospel with a reflection on its epilogue, problematizing how we read this notoriously sentimentalized text, and reorienting us toward its strong prophetic hermeneutic. I now return to the beginning of Luke's story, to commence our exploration of its narration of Sabbath Economics.

The double theme of this chapter is beautifully reflected in the old African American spiritual "Go Tell It on the Mountain," which combines wilderness spirituality with a scenario of social marginality (a baby born in a barn surrounded by poor folk). I call Luke 1–3 a prelude instead of a prologue because of how the Nativity drama is composed around three canticles: Mary's "Magnificat" (1:46–55); Zechariah's "Benedictus" (1:68–79); and Simeon's "Nunc Dimittis" (2:29–32).[2] The long tradition of singing carols during Advent and Christmas (the season in which I drafted these pages) is rooted singularly in Luke's narrative.

I focus here on three core samples from Luke's Prelude, each of which inaugurates a key theme in the Gospel as a whole. The Magnificat is the first articulation of the divine intention to turn the world upside down. John the Baptist's message initiates the call to turn history around. And Luke opens the story of Jesus's ministry with his "vision quest" into the wilderness to trace the ancestral memory of Sabbath Economics.

A. Mary's Magnificat, John's Jeremiad (1:46–55, 3:1–22)

The prolegomenon to Jesus's nativity is structured around stories of two women for whom conception is problematic. Elizabeth is too old, and Mary is unwed. The narrative of their surprising pregnancies unfolds in back-and-forth parallel:

Annunciation to Elizabeth (1:5–25)	→	Annunciation to Mary (1:26–38)	→
Elizabeth's Response (1:41–45)	→	Mary's Response (1:46–56)	→
John's birth (1:57–66)	→	Jesus's birth (2:1–20)	

The distinctly *un*-patriarchal gender dynamics in this sequence foreshadow the Magnificat's vision of a world overturned.

The Zechariah and Elizabeth vignette is patterned after the Abram and Sarai tale (Gen 18:12–15), but in Luke it is the man (a priest no less!) who is upbraided by a heavenly messenger for incredulity at the promise of a child (Luke 1:13–20). Moreover, while Zechariah is struck mute, Elizabeth issues a spirit-filled proclamation (1:42–45)! Similarly, Joseph appears in just three brief cameos (1:27; 2:4, 16), while Luke's lengthy drama centers Mary. The men are silent; the pregnant women find their voices. They also discover common cause as mothers of sons who, as Gabriel announces, will become prophets tasked with changing the course of the nation. The last word in Luke's Christmas story also belongs to a woman: the prophet Anna (2:36–38). The Simeon/Anna dyad concludes a birth narrative that opened with Zechariah and Elizabeth. Like Zechariah, Simeon has an epiphany in the Temple; like Elizabeth, Anna is elderly. All four are portrayed as patiently waiting for divine intervention, listening for signs of change—a posture Luke commends to his audience.

At the midpoint of their parallel narrative, the old woman and the peasant girl, pregnant with prophets, greet each other—as do their fetuses! It is an enchanted moment, embodying what C.S. Song called a "theology of the womb."[3] This is underlined by Elizabeth's triple blessing upon womanhood (1:42-45). In all these ways at the outset of Luke's story, women take center stage, vessels for transformation who recognize the blessing, mystery, and sacredness of life.[4] This literary strategy represents a profound break from patriarchal mores and androcentric narratives.

All three canticles are prophetic oracles, anticipating social upheaval and the liberation of an oppressed Israel. When Zechariah (1:79) and Simeon (2:29) sing of peace, it does not refer to the Pax Romana, under which Jewish Palestine suffered military occupation, but the subversive mission of a marginalized Messiah. The birth of this "Savior and Lord" (2:11) is accompanied by an angelic host chanting "Glory to God in the highest and on earth peace" (2:14)—phrases that normally applied exclusively to Caesar Augustus in Luke's world.[5] No wonder Luke's nativity story ends with Simeon's reality check: this anti-imperial gospel will be opposed by many, and carry a cost (2:34–35).

This subversive tone is most evident in Mary's Magnificat, a revolutionary song which ironically is still chanted at high Mass and sung in high society by professional choirs.[6] The first part of her song is deeply intimate: She is astonished that she has been "seen" (1:48), being invisible as a peasant woman to all whose gaze fixed upon the Caesar, Herod, and high priests. Her state as a pregnant and unwed peasant girl "would have brought untold social stigma and ostracism in first-century Palestine," writes Frank Dicken.[7] Yet essential to Luke's perspective is the conviction that history is transformed not at its center but at its margins.

The Magnificat's second half sings about God's extraordinary strength (1:51), ironic given who has been chosen as protagonist. Mary is recontextualizing one of the primal texts of the prophetic tradition: the Song of Hannah (1 Sam 2:1–10).[8] Luke uses this old tradition to shape his whole nativity story. The prophet Samuel is born to a woman unable to get pregnant (1 Sam 1), and grows up to warn Israel against adopting a monarchic model (1 Sam 8)—as will John and Jesus. God's power, ignored by the "proud," is mysteriously lodged in poor women giving birth in the teeth of domination, echoing the conspiracy of midwives who nurtured life in defiance of Pharaoh's war on Hebrew firstborn (Exod 1–2). The same notion is reiterated at the end of the first century CE, not long after Luke wrote, by political prisoner and apocalyptic seer John the Revelator. He envisions a woman struggling to protect life in the face of a Beast (a coded moniker for the lethal violence of empire; Rev 12).[9]

At the conclusion of the Magnificat is this incendiary stanza about threefold divine action (1:52–55):

> God has shown strength, has scattered the proud in the imagination of their hearts;
> God has brought down the powerful from their thrones, and lifted up the lowly;
> filled the hungry with good things, and sent the rich away empty.
> God has helped servant Israel, in remembrance of mercy, according to the promise made to our ancestors, to Abraham and descendants forever.

This remarkable string of indicative verbs, each in what Alan Streett calls "the elusive aorist tense,"[10] simultaneously refers to past (remembering covenant), present (feeding the hungry), and future (bringing down plutocracy). He points out that the simple past tense would connote "God's mighty acts in Israel's history," while the "prophetic perfect tense" would speak "imaginatively as if they have occurred already" for Mary and/or Luke's audience.[11] Streett then compares it, using the power of interpretive analogy, to the civil rights movement's famous hymn "We Shall Overcome," a song which assured both victims of white supremacy, and activists struggling to end it, that "universal freedom was on the horizon, but not yet achieved."[12]

This is both a *social* vision of justice for the poor that critiques the affluenza of the rich, and a *political* one, asserting that YHWH's ancient covenant with Mary's people will eclipse Roman occupation. And it is the first time "the rich" are named in Luke, introducing the central theme of Sabbath Economics redistribution that will thread throughout Luke's story.[13] Provisioning the poor and/or restoring the surpluses of the rich back to the Commonwealth will be tropes that characterize every object lesson narrated in Luke 12–19 (part III)—especially the final one (13A).

The Magnificat establishes two other key thematic patterns: alerting us to Luke's narrative strategy of prophetic memory and resurgence, and articulating Jesus's mission statement. Frank Dicken contends that is as much a "programmatic passage" for the Gospel as is Jesus's Nazareth sermon (4A), anticipating the "Great Reversal . . . Luke's vision of God working to overturn the social norms."[14]

The geographic, sociopolitical, and somatic landscapes of this Prelude are all key to its meaning. The biographical literature of Roman antiquity, much like the "infotainment" media of our culture, focused exclusively on subjects and settings belonging to the rich and famous. In contrast, Luke features poor folk as the true protagonists of history, often in jarring juxtaposition to the elites of first-century Roman Palestine. Mary and Joseph are rural people displaced by the demands of Quirinius's census, a tool for managing the colonial occupation (2:1–7). Sylvia Keesmaat writes:

> Joseph, who was from the house and lineage of David, was no longer in the town of his people, but rather Nazareth (2:4). Is it possible that he had joined the ranks of young men whose land had been taken by a wealthy landowner? Had he left his hometown in order to escape the scrutiny of the tax collectors? This was the exact scenario that the census was intended to address. Caesar was attempting to get a handle on all of those shifting people in the empire, recently displaced, and no longer paying into the tax base.[15]

The holy couple could not have understood the powerful political, economic, and military forces at play in this moment. Luke's historiographic prefaces to each of his first three chapters (1:5; 2:1–2; 3:1–2), however, take pains to point out the rulers who *did*. Luke wants his readers to be clear that this story is not a fairy tale but a gritty tale unfolding in real political time and space. This is lost on modern North American readers who read the Gospel as a cosmic drama with no real terrestrial tether. Yet every time Luke names imperial officials who *think* they are in charge of history, he immediately swings the story back to the poor people who will change it. For example, in a "context snapshot" in 3:1–3, Luke introduces Caesar, Procurator Pilate, the Herodian Tetrarchs of Palestine, and high priests—a genealogy of palatial power. But the list ends pointedly with *John in the wilderness, to whom divine revelation comes.*

Underlining the Holy Family's marginality in Luke's narrative is the fact that, having completed the long trek on foot back to Bethlehem, they cannot even find lodging in Joseph's hometown. This implies two possible things. Did Joseph's kin reject him because of the scandal of Mary's pregnancy under a cloud of illegitimacy (see the parenthetical comment in Luke's genealogy, 3:23)? Or had these relatives also been displaced by the political and economic forces of empire?[16] Whatever the reason, the couple must deliver their baby outside in a feed trough, surrounded by herdsmen, a class of outdoor workers marginalized due to their "unclean" contact with animals (2:8, 15–18). Precisely because they are able to endure harsh conditions and make hard choices, all these characters are spiritually powerful, sensitive to visions of mysterious messengers who implausibly suggest that somehow this back-alley birth will challenge the dominating colonial rule of Caesar (2:9–14)!

The family's low social status is further reflected in how their infant is presented in the sanctuary: they make a purity offering of two doves (2:24), the minimum requirement used by the poor. It is hardly surprising, then, that Jesus would later emphasize in his teaching the very thing he was denied at birth—hospitality—which he insists should be extended to all people, even one's enemies (see 7:19; 23:42–43). Both poverty and the powerful faith of the holy family would have impacted Jesus's formation as a child—especially if songs like the Magnificat were sung to him as lullabies!

Luke appends to his nativity tale a unique "lost in the Temple epilogue," in which Jesus, just prior to his coming-of-age at twelve, engages rabbis in give-and-take. This means to signal that from an early age, Jesus took a keen interest in his tradition (2:41–52)—and so should we.[17] From that point on in Luke's story, however, Joseph disappears, whether by early death or imprisonment we are not told (though in 4:22 Jesus is still called "Joseph's son"). It appears that Jesus journeyed through puberty in a single parent home, steadily "increasing in wisdom" (*sophia*, 2:40, 52; see 7:35).

* * *

At this point Luke turns abruptly to the work of Jesus's "relative," John, a character who is presented as even more marginal.[18] As noted, the narrative is grounded in its historico-political era, while also contrasting the obscure wilderness prophet John with named and notorious personalities: imperial (Tiberius and Pilate), local (Herod Antipas, Philip, and Lysanias), and religious (Annas and Caiaphas; 3:1–2).[19] Through the first seven decades of the century, tensions in occupied Palestine over Roman political domination and economic "globalization" gave rise to multiple Jewish prophets calling for radical change. This included armed insurrectionist streams which converged into the Judean revolt, and Roman counterinsurgency, of 66–70 CE.[20] But Luke's recitation of the political geography of this fraught historical moment also alludes to the beginning of the book of Jeremiah (Jer 1:1–3), implying that John is taking his cue more from the prophetic legacy of nonviolent resistance than the Maccabean tradition of revolt. Jesus will also take this road less traveled.

Luke 3:3 draws on Mark's narrative for the first time, portraying John in the wilderness at the Jordan river calling for a baptism of repentance (Luke 3:2b–4, 7 // Mark 1:2–5). John invites his people into sacred waters of renewal far from the domesticated ritual baths of city and village—and from the attention of urban-based elites. The Jordan was, and remains, the spine of the land of Israel, the only truly perennial stream in Palestine. It runs some 156 miles north to south, from Mount Hermon in southern Lebanon into the Sea of Galilee, then on down the rift valley, eventually emptying into the Dead Sea. Its name (*nehar hayarden* in Hebrew) means "descender," as it plummets from mountainous heights to four hundred meters *below* sea level. The river features both dramatic gorges and rapids as well as meandering bends and quiet pools, ranging from trickles in dry season to floods in wet. It only averages ninety feet in width and three to ten feet in depth, and certainly wasn't navigable, though was often uncrossable during the rainy season (there were some sixty fords along its length in antiquity). Yet archaeological evidence suggests human habitation along the Jordan for more than a hundred thousand years. It was and is a deep ancestral place.

While the Jordan may not have been so "deep and wide," as the old spiritual imagined, it represented the watery soul of that arid land. For John, it offered a holy immersion into the origin stories of his people. Mentioned 180 times in the Hebrew Bible, the Jordan coursed through the heart of Israel's narrative: from Jacob's wrestling match with an angel (Gen 32:22–32; Hos 12:3–5) to Joshua's ceremonial crossing into the Promised Land (replete with the symbolism of twelve sacred stones, Josh 3–4), and from Elijah's fiery departure (2 Kg 2:1–15) to Elisha's healing bath for an enemy general (2 Kg 5, to which Jesus will allude in Luke 4:27). John's prophetic renewal movement commences in this primal space, proclaiming Isaiah's "way in the wilderness" (3:4). This trope refers back to the Exodus way of liberation (Exod 13:17–18), reiterates Zechariah's dream of the way of peace in the Nativity story (1:79), and anticipates Jesus's way of discipleship (Luke 9:3).

Luke's portrait of John differs from Mark's in some notable ways. He lengthens the citation of Isaiah 40 (3:4–6), underlining the prophetic genealogy, a pattern Jesus will reproduce in his invocation of Isaiah 61 at his "coming out sermon" (4:17–19). Having already established that John will operate "in the spirit and power of Elijah" (1:17), Luke doesn't include Mark's allusion to that prophet's "costume" (Mark 1:6). And Luke adds some Q material: a warning

(Luke 3:7–9 // Matt 3:7–10) and a promise about the coming apocalyptic harvest (Luke 3:17–19 // Matt 3:12). Prophetic themes pile up in these additions, while Luke's unique exhortation to practical repentance (3:10–14) anticipates Jesus's insistence on concrete practices of Sabbath Economics.

John's language of "repentance for the release from sin" (3:3) has long been domesticated by the modern Western church's preoccupation with private spirituality. To repent means to change direction, personally *and politically*; it is within its semantic field to render it "turning history around."[21] And as we shall see time and again in Luke, the verb "release" (*aphiemi*) anticipates the Jubilee semantics of Jesus.[22] John's radical mission statement explains the edge he exhibits in 3:7–14.

He addresses the "crowd" (*ochlos,* 3:7, 10, the first time it appears in Luke) coming for baptism harshly: "You offspring of vipers!" (3:7a). The metaphor of snakes slithering away from agricultural fields set aflame after harvest underlines the jolt of this "greeting."[23] Malina and Rohrbaugh call it "as insulting a label as one could imagine in a society in which honor is fundamentally a function of birth."[24] John knows the nation is in crisis, and half-hearted or merely pietistic expressions of remorse will hardly do: repentance must be *shown* (3:8a).

The notion of trees being "judged for their fruits" (3:9b) clearly arises from an agrarian cosmology and will appear in several of Jesus's teachings (6:43–44; 8:8; 12:17; and especially 13:6–9). For marginal farmers, fruit bearing is the difference between life and death. This emphasis on *demonstrating* repentance extends through Luke's Gospel (e.g., Luke 6:43–49, again the fruit metaphor) and second volume (Acts 26:20). This is *radical* analysis: the "axe" of divine judgment is "laid at the root" of the status quo (Luke 3:9), another agrarian metaphor.[25] This includes a warning against reflexive appeals to patrimony: "Do not start telling yourselves 'We have Abraham as our ancestor'" (3:8a). Assertions of ethnic entitlement must have been the first objections John encountered, and he rebukes them sharply with one of the most evocative images in the Gospel: the Creator can "awaken (*egeirō*) children of Abraham from these stones" (3:8).

Connection to Abraham will be a central concern of Luke's:

- The Abrahamic Covenant is invoked three times in his Gospel (1:55, 73, 13:28), and in Acts speeches by Peter (Acts 3:13, 25), Stephen (7:2, 8, 16, 17, 32), and Paul (13:27).
- Being restored to Abraham's family is a key theme in two healings that we'll look at later: Luke 13:16 (9A); and 19:9 (13A).
- The Great Patriarch will have hard news for the presumptive rich in the eschatological parable of Lazarus (16:23–30, chapter 11).

Exonerating oneself by heritage represents a denial of responsibility, a "move to innocence," as we call it in our decolonization work.[26] John challenges his people to awaken *from* their nationalist egoism (something all too characteristic of modern Americans) and *to* their prophetic heritage. Luke also thereby opens the door of discipleship to those outside of the history and traditions of Israel.

The next, uniquely Lukan, scene has the crowd inquiring as to the practical implications of this radical analysis (3:10–14). John's instructions are uncomfortably specific and strategic—but by no means simple or cosmetic. Those who have the means of daily sustenance *must* share with those who don't, not as a matter of charity, but of justice (3:11).[27]

> Clothing was a valuable possession that one either always wore (those who had two tunics wore one over the other) or even stored in a vault. It seems that the possession of two tunics distinguished the better situated of the little people from the poorer. . . An outer garment was such a valuable possession of the poor that it could serve as security (Matt 5:40) or could be stolen (Luke 6:29).[28]

This ethos of mutual aid is grounded in older village ways (6B). In Luke's narrative, these will be fully restored through Spirit-empowered communities of goods, in which no one remains poor (Acts 4:34; epilogue, iii).

When turning to the extractive economy of the Roman occupation, however, John's imperatives grow more subversive. Tax collectors are told to collect "no more than the amount prescribed (*diatassō*) for you" (Luke 3:13; in Acts, *diatassō* connotes an order by a Roman official, [Acts 18:2; 24:23]). Yet such a constraint would contradict the very architecture of tax farming in antiquity, since the middle-man collector only profited by charging people *more* than he had to turn over to Rome, resulting in widespread graft.[29] Such a profession-undermining prohibition is then extended to soldiers (Luke 3:14), whom John boldly calls out for practices of oppressive policing that his hearers knew all too well. In order to supplement their meager wages, soldiers routinely used extortion (*diaseiō*) and false accusation (*sukophanteō*).[30] John insists they must stop using armed authority to shake down vulnerable people—a request equally unlikely to be met. It is no wonder that his audience wondered whether John's fiery critique signaled that he was a Messiah (Luke 3:15)!

John now changes his focus, if not his tone, and points toward a successor who will "baptize with the Holy Spirit and with fire" (3:16b, see 12:49; Luke again follows Mark here). This, too, will be realized at Pentecost (Acts 2:3).[31] Then comes another warning, an agrarian image from Q that echoes the apocalyptic tenor of 3:9: "His winnowing fork is in his hand, to clear his threshing floor, and to gather the wheat into his granary, but the chaff he will burn with unquenchable fire" (3:17). Again John draws on the prophetic imaginary of harvest as metaphor for judgment (see, e.g., Isa 18:5; Jer 12:13, 51:33; Joel 3:13; Hos 6:11).

Yet John's judgment oracle is characterized as "good news" (Luke 3:18)! Jesus will shortly clarify: this is good news *to the poor* (4:18). For those continually dehumanized under the status quo, divine justice can only bring improvement.[32] But it certainly was not so perceived by those in power; consequently, John would soon land in jail (3:19–20). The Jewish historian Josephus, a contemporary of Luke, corroborates the Gospel witnesses about John's fate, writing that Herod Antipas, tetrarch of Galilee and Perea from 4 BCE–39 CE, executed him for plainly political reasons: the Baptist's preaching was stirring up a popular insurrection.[33]

Of all the contemporaries Jesus might have chosen to initiate him, why does he make his way to *this* politically notorious prophet, whose days were numbered (3:21–22)? After all, such an association would implicate the Nazarene in John's rebel movement. The answer, borne out by Luke's subsequent narrative (7:25–26), is that John embodied the radical tradition of the wilderness prophets: animating public conscience, standing with the least, and speaking truth to power. There is an interesting dialectic in their relationship in Luke's telling (following Mark). On one hand, John recognizes that he will soon pass on the mantle, shades of Elijah and Elisha; true mentoring in the prophetic tradition is about movement building. On the other, Jesus is consciously apprenticing to John by submitting to baptism in Jordan's wilderness waters.

Unfortunately, later churchly Christology played down Jesus's discipleship to John, to the point of disappearing it altogether, a theological suppression that continues to depoliticize the gospel narrative. Clearly, however, Luke's Jesus shapes his ministry after his mentor:

- taking up the call to repentance after John is arrested (Luke 13:3,5);
- publicly patterning his ministry after Isaiah (4:18–19);
- talking of roots (8:13) and fire (12:49);
- bidding village folk to share clothing (6:29–30) and food (9:13);
- challenging tax collectors to abandon their ways (5:27–32; 19:1–10);
- defending John fiercely (7:24–27);
- and above all, sharing his fate at the hands of the authorities.

Mary taught Jesus the song; John showed him the Way.[34]

B. Mimesis or Mimosis? The Primal Temptation (4:1–4)

Catholic and mainstream Protestant churches inaugurate Lent by reflecting on Jesus's famous wilderness temptations, despite the fact that this tradition is largely opaque to modern readers. The temptation narrative tends to be ignored by liberals or spiritualized by conservatives, like the *manna* tale it draws upon, consumed as mere religious "entertainment" (Silko). It is an example of how sacred scriptural stories have been *dis*-membered by abuse, misrepresentation, dismissal, and manipulation over the history of Christendom, rendering us defenseless against the powerful myths of empire. Such tendencies were already at play in the biblical period, which is why the Deuteronomist commands: "*Re*member the way which YHWH has led you these forty years in the wilderness . . . testing you . . . whether you keep the commandments" (Deut 8:2).

Modern cultural theorists use the term "mimesis" to describe how *imitation* is shaped by *representation*, particularly in our storytelling and aesthetics.[35] For the Deuteronomist, recalling ancestral liberation stories means to recontextualize them in the community's current situation. Conversely, if the people "forget," they become like "the nations around them," destined to perish (Deut 8:19–20). Significantly, Deuteronomy 8 names affluenza and plutocracy as inevitable plagues if the Sabbath Economics instructions are forgotten or ignored:

> Beware . . . lest, when you have eaten and are full, and have built goodly houses and live in them, and when your herds and flocks multiply, and your silver and gold is multiplied . . . then you forget YHWH who brought you out of the land of Egypt, out of the house of bondage . . . who fed you with manna which your ancestors did not know, in order to test you (Deut 8:12–14, 16).

We might call this condition "mimosis": the pathological deformation of mimesis, defined as the simulation of symptoms of a disease.

Luke's temptations account follows hard on the heels of his distinctive genealogy of Jesus (Luke 3:23–38), as if to suggest that the whole history of Israel is encapsulated in this archetypal test.[36] In preparation for his mission, Jesus follows a mysterious yet compelling calling to desert solitude. He fasts, lives in the wild, wrestles with spirits (4:1). While this liminal sojourn may seem strange to modern ears, it is quite intelligible to Indigenous peoples the world over wherever different versions of a "vision quest" tradition survive.

For example, among Aboriginal and Torres Strait Islander people it is referred to as "renewal of the Dreaming"; the Sioux call it *hanbleceya*.[37] A ritual passage into selfhood, it lies somewhere between what Joseph Campbell called initiation ceremony and hero's journey. Shamans, writes Christopher Vecsey, "with the help of guardian spirits, travel to the land of the dead in order to restore the lost or stolen or diseased souls . . . out of love for their community."[38] This is both a very real *exterior* adventure beyond the margins of society and an *interior* passage of self-discovery and purification. Yet this journey to/in the spirit world is also a sojourn through mythic time to encounter the story and destiny of one's people.

That Jesus's journey lasted "forty days" (4:2) is clearly intended to invoke Israel's forty-year wanderings in the wilderness after liberation from Egypt. But what exactly is the connection? He is somehow interiorizing the experience of his people, though not in the sense that modern religious existentialists understand it. Rather, Jesus mystically retraces the footsteps of his ancestors to discover the root causes of his people's historical crisis. Course correction could only come through a kind of "re-visioning" of the fateful choices that led them back into captivity. To begin this formidable task, Jesus must return to his tradition's "myth of origins": the Exodus wilderness.

- Israel's distinctive identity commenced with its liberation by YHWH from Pharaoh's imperial straitjacket: "I will bring My people out of Egypt" (Exod 3:10).
- Similarly, in the Gospel, Jesus's distinctive identity has just been confirmed at his baptism by John: "You are My child, the Beloved" (Luke 3:22).

Jesus is then driven by the Spirit deeper into the wilderness where, like his ancestors, he must discover what this vocation means.

"*If* you are the child of God..." taunts the Devil in refrain (Luke 4:3, 7, 9). This is the question that Jesus—and disciples seeking to follow his Way—must answer: Are we still defined by the Exodus journey? Is God still known as the One "who brought you up out of Egypt" (some twenty-five times in Deuteronomy alone) among us? If so, we must give up the former lifeways of imperial captivity (Lev 18:2–3), and "never return that way again" (Deut 17:16). Thus, each of the three temptation illustrates a pillar of empire: the economics of exploitation, the politics of domination, and the theological presumption of omnipotence. These have not changed in our time.[39]

The wilderness is the best mirror in which to examine how we are socialized into mimosis. The un-reengineered spaces of nature reveal how domesticated we have become; as Eisenberg puts it, "Without wildness, civilization could not survive. The converse does not hold."[40] We can see more clearly how we have been lured into the seductive imperial narratives of Pharaoh and Caesar, of the National Security Council and the television news, of Wall Street and Hollywood. They promise prosperity, power, and prestige—but deliver only enslavement. Jesus knows he can resist these delusions only by staying grounded in the sacred Story; hence his counter-refrain, "It is written/said..." (Luke 4:4, 8, 12).

Luke's version (4:1–13) of this Q tradition narrates the second two temptations in different order than Matthew (Matt 4:1–11). But both agree on the first: the test that revisits the catechism of Sabbath Economics. In our world, wherever churches have forgotten or become confused about sacred prophetic stories, we end up simulating the "enchantments of mammon."[41] This explains why Jesus's primal test after his commissioning at baptism concerns *bread in the wilderness.*[42]

Surrounded only by sand and rock in deep Judean desert, Jesus hungers as his ancestors did (4:2b; Exod 16:1–2, 2A). Satan challenges Jesus to turn stones into bread (Luke 4:3), invoking the ambitions of imperial civilization to reengineer Creation by extracting resources, controlling the forces of production, and ridiculing the divine economy of grace as foolishness. But this temptation also reflected the felt crisis of hunger among the peasant majority as a result of land alienation and crushing tax-and-tithe burdens imposed by elites in Roman-occupied Palestine. The Tempter challenges Jesus to prove himself a hero by feeding the poor, *and* enrich himself at the same time by exploiting the land for profit in a bull market of desert stone! Jesus instead reboots the Exodus journey at this archetypal crossroad. He counters with the first of three citations from Deuteronomy, the book of remembering. It recalls the lessons of the *manna*: "God humbled you by letting you hunger, then by feeding you with *manna* . . . in order to make you understand that *one does not live by bread alone*, but by every word that comes from the mouth of YHWH" (Deut 8:3 = Luke 4:4).

This is the briefest of the three temptations, sufficing as shorthand for Israel's first catechism. Jesus will continually reassert its lessons throughout his ministry:

- reenacting this very scene in his feeding of the poor in the wilderness (9:10–17). While his disciples cannot see past market constraints (9:12–13), he demonstrates the economics of mutual aid so that "all ate and were satisfied" (9:17; 6B);
- repeatedly teaching Sabbath Economics at harvest (5:4–10; 6:1–5; 8:4–8; 13:6–9) and at table (5:29–32; 7:40–47; 14:1–24; 15:25–32; 16:19–21; 19:1–10);
- counseling disciples to be dependent on the gift economy of hospitality in their mission travels by not carrying their own bread (9:3; 6A);
- placing the petition "Give us enough bread for today" at the heart of the Disciples' Prayer (11:3; 7A); and
- offering a ritual of bread to symbolize his own somatic sacrifice, the ultimate gift of gratitude and memory (22:19). This ritual that will then be identified with economic sharing in the Pentecost community (epilogue, iii).

Jesus remembers the primal catechism, and chooses mimesis, standing firm against the seduction of mimosis. He thereby renews the Dreaming—because "stories are all we have to fight illness and death."[43]

Part II

Telling and Showing

Sabbath Economics in the First Half of Luke

THE FOUR CHAPTERS of part II examine key teachings about Sabbath Economics: Jesus's inaugural sermon at Nazareth; the Beatitudes; his instructions for how movement ambassadors should behave on the road; and the Lord's Prayer as another catechism. Each of these *tellings* is followed by demonstration projects in various settings, which *show* how Sabbath Economics is embodied through eating, healing and praying.

Chapter 4 examines Jesus's "coming out" *drash* at a Nazareth synagogue, which proclaims that the Jubilee tradition is being re-visioned here and now—if not in ways his audience expects. It is met with both delight and rage, which will continue throughout the story. We then look at three demonstration projects that follow his proclamation of release: the miraculous catch of fish call story; the disciples' gleaning of grain; and a party at a tax collector's house. Each is a subversive expression of what it means to bring good news to the marginalized.

Chapter 5 focuses on Luke's Sermon on the Plain, which first pronounces Beatitudes on the poor, then immediately prophetic woes on the rich. The crucial issue of socioeconomic indebtedness is just under the surface here. We then look at how the healings that follow again show what the Nazareth sermon told. I touch upon Jesus's assessment of John the Baptist, then focus on a major thematic healing at a Pharisee's house. Jesus centers the intimate grief of a marginalized woman as an object lesson to his host about the necessity of *seeing* the poor and enacting Jubilee release to liberate them from indebtedness.

Jesus's loaves and fishes meal in the wilderness was such a key demonstration project of Sabbath Economics that Mark narrated it twice. Luke, however, relates only one account—yet gives us *two* versions of Jesus's missionary instructions (the other synoptics just one). Chapter 6 explores how these differences reveal Luke's conviction that those two traditions illuminate each other. The instructions tell, and the feeding shows, how discipleship communities can practice economic interdependence and mutual aid as the art of giving and receiving hospitality.

Chapter 7 takes us well into Luke's Special Section. I examine the Lord's Prayer (which I prefer to call the Disciples' Prayer), at the heart of which is an invocation of Sabbath Economics: "Give us today enough bread" (11:3). Luke's shorter version of the Prayer represents a concise catechism on three crucial challenges to the Way, patterned after the Wilderness Temptations. I then look at Jesus's analogy of prayer as stubborn commitment to the old village ethos of mutual aid in light of the divine economy of gift and grace. This grounding enables disciples to engage in personal and political struggles for transformation in a world ruled by powerful plutocrats—which will be the focus of part III.

CHAPTER FOUR

Restoring Commonwealth

> Jesus . . . deliberately chooses the most powerful, most political bombshell he could have dropped in the middle of Roman domination: the very people that you have used your governmental power to exploit now have the assistance of a higher authority! He says, "The Spirit of God is upon me," and that Spirit chooses people to be dissenters, to bring good news to the poor over against the bad news of domination. Moral dissent, my friends, is not just . . . the stance of Jesus 2,000 years ago. . . . It is still our calling today.
>
> —Rev. William J. Barber II, 2013[1]

ON THE HEELS of the Temptation narrative, Jesus returns to Galilee "in the power of the Spirit," a phrase that may explain the notoriety that immediately follows him (4:14–15). This introduction to his public ministry emphasizes that he seeks out synagogues on the Sabbath—in other words, he is engaging the spiritual heart of his place and people. Preaching matters!

This chapter examines Jesus's "coming out performance" at a Nazareth synagogue, proclaiming that the ancient Jubilee vision is being resuscitated here and now—but not in ways his audience expects. His telling elicits a dialectic of delight and rage, which will characterize responses to his ministry through the rest of the story. I then focus on a sequence of food stories: an unlicensed fishing expedition, an unauthorized gleaning of grain, and an unseemly party at a tax collector's house. Each is a subversive showing of Sabbath Economics as good news to the marginalized.

A. Telling

Jubilee beyond Borders (4:14–30)

The camera quickly zooms in on how Jesus's Sabbath proclamation fared in his hometown of Nazareth, a keystone episode in Luke's plot, and another "programmatic passage" for his theme.[2] The village of Nazareth has already been established in Luke's Prelude as the place of Jesus's childhood, from Gabriel's annunciation (1:26) to the Holy Family's movements (2:4, 39, 51). Here it is simply named as "where Jesus had been brought up" (4:16a; *trephō,* "to be fed or nourished"). Yet the village is not mentioned outside the New Testament. Its significance lay chiefly in its proximity to Sepphoris (also called *Zippori*), the largest and most strategic *polis* in Galilee, located a mere three miles to the northeast.

Built in the first century BCE according to a Greek city planning template (including a theater), Sepphoris was Herod the Great's fortified capital of Lower Galilee. After Herod's death in 4 BCE, Judean nationalist rebels attacked Sepphoris, sacking the royal armory. Varus, the Roman legate of Syria, retaliated by razing the city and selling Jewish survivors into slavery. Such violence and trauma at his doorstep would have made a deep impression on Jesus, infusing in him a keen sense of the travails of empire—and perhaps inspiring his mother's revolutionary lullaby (3A)!

After the sacking of Sepphoris, Herod's son Antipas, a Tetrarch, moved to impose Roman Style order on the region:

> Among his first acts was the establishment of a modern administrative center from which security forces, market inspectors, and tax collectors could be easily dispatched. . . Antipas ordered that [Sepphoris] be reconstructed as a modern Roman city with a palace, treasury, archives, and forum. When it was completed, he brought in a new population of loyal functionaries and workers to replace the former inhabitants who had been killed by Varus's legions or sold off into slavery. He named the new city Autocratoris—literally . . . "belonging to the Emperor."[3]

If both Jesus and his father labored as construction workers (*tektōn*) in Nazareth, an hour's walk away, it is likely they would have gotten work rebuilding Sepphoris. Colonized people are forever forced to build the infrastructure of their oppressors, a phenomenon that remains in our time.[4]

Into this context of empire's tightening grip, Jesus delivers his inaugural public sermon, or *drash,* on the evocative text of Isaiah 61:1–2.[5] "As was his custom," Jesus enters the synagogue (Luke 4:16b). The carefully choreographed dramatic gestures that follow communicate high drama:

A Jesus *stands* to read.
    B The scroll is *given* to him.
        C Jesus *opens* and *finds* the text. (4:16–17)
            D Jesus's *drash.* (4:18–19)
        C′ Jesus *closes* the scroll.
    B′ *gives* it back.
A′ and *sits* down. (4:20)

"The eyes of all in the synagogue were fixed on him" (the narrative invites readers to do the same). The chiastic "text-ure," meanwhile, draws attention to Jesus's interpretation of the scroll.

Luke's scene also focuses on *perception,* as mediated by three somatic portals, each of which figure prominently in the rest of the gospel narrative:

- 4:20: "*Eyes* (*ophthalmos*) were fixed. . ." Eyes are referenced in 2:30; 6:20, 41f; 10:23; 11:34; 16:23; 18:13; 19:42; and 24:16, 31, not to mention the multiple stories about seeing literally and metaphorically—including here the phrase "recovery of sight to the blind," which Jesus adds to Isaiah 61.
- 4:21: "Today scripture is fulfilled in your *ears*" (*ous*). See 1:44; 8:8; 9:44; 12:3; 14:35; and 22:50.
- 4:22: "And all were astonished at the words of grace from his *mouth*" (*stoma). S*ee 1:64,70; 6:45; 11:54; 19:22; 21:15; 21:24; and 22:71.

The struggle for hearts and minds happens through these portals; as Jesus's mouth later declares, "Many prophets and kings desired to see what you are looking at, and did not see it; to hear what you hear, but did not hear it" (10:24).

There is some debate regarding whether the Isaiah text would have been Jesus's choice, or the *haftorah* portion designated by a lectionary (scholars aren't sure whether lectionaries were in use yet, but see, e.g., Acts 13:14f). In either case, it is significant that Jesus keys on the prophetic text and not the Torah portion. Isaiah is cited some 590 times in the New Testament (seventy-eight times in Luke alone), far more than any other Hebrew Bible text, drawing from sixty-three of canonical Isaiah's sixty-six chapters. Obviously, this prophet was important for both Jesus and the early Christians. Jesus sits down (as preachers still do for synagogue *drashes* today), and after a pregnant pause, delivers one of history's shortest homilies! Yet in our longest Gospel, it serves as *the* programmatic teaching, often called a "manifesto" by commentators.

Michael Prior, who devotes an entire book to this one scene, points out that Jesus's *drash,* like its setup, is also a chiasm, focalizing the middle:[6]

D The Spirit *of the Lord* is upon me, because God anointed me
  E *to proclaim* good news to the poor
    F God has sent me to proclaim *release* to the captives
      G *and recovery of sight to the blind*
    F′ to set at *liberty* those who are oppressed (from Isa 58:6)
  E′ *to proclaim*
D′ the acceptable year *of the Lord* (Luke 4:18–19).

Luke follows the LXX text of Isaiah 61:1, with a few important exceptions:

- the phrase "soothe the broken-hearted" is omitted;
- "recovery of sight to the blind" not in the Hebrew text;
- "liberating the oppressed" is patched in from Isaiah 58:6;
- the invocation of a "day of vengeance" is omitted.

More than half a millennium earlier, Third Isaiah had sought to offer comfort and vindication for returning exiles from Babylon. In Jesus's day, it had become a popular text, typically read as asserting God's care for Israel alone but judgment on her enemies. Jesus's *drash* will challenge this presumption sharply, just as toward the end of Luke's story he will instead anticipate a day of judgment *on his own people* (21:22).

There has been much scholarly discussion regarding whether Isaiah's use of "acceptable year" refers to the Levitical Jubilee (Lev 25; see 2A). Over the last half century, André Trocmé, John Howard Yoder, Robert Sloan, and Michael Prior all made affirmative cases, challenging the skeptical consensus among modern scholars.[7] The fact that Jesus twice invokes "release" (*aphesis*) in 4:18—one of which is his addition of the LXX version of Isaiah 58:6—certainly lends a strong verbal resonance.[8] The burden of evidence should not however be laid upon this one citation but determined by Luke's overall story. I will argue that Jesus's teachings, demonstration projects, and object lessons about wealth redistribution and social equity throughout Luke's narrative show that Jesus could only have been recontextualizing the Jubilee tradition in this sermon. But he also *de-nationalizes* it in his addendum, as we'll see.

The phrase "*today* this scripture has been fulfilled" (*sēmeron,* Luke 4:21) is an existential notion that runs throughout Luke's story:

- 2:11: born this day;
- 5:26: we've seen strange things today;
- 13:32–33: I heal today, and tomorrow . . . I go my way today, and tomorrow . . .
- 19:5, 9: today I must come to your house; today salvation has come to this house
- 23:43: today you will be with me in paradise
- 24:21: today is the third day since this happened

Jesus thus does with Third Isaiah what that prophet did with the Jubilee tradition: calls for an *embodiment* of this text in his own context. He invokes the dangerous hermeneutic of a living tradition—an approach that will prove to be controversial in Luke's story, and remains so today.

The initial audience reaction to Jesus's initial *drash* is ambiguous, judging by the three verbs Luke employs. On one hand, the community appears to approve of his words (4:22a; *emarturoun*, especially with the dative, consistently connotes a positive response in the New Testament.). However, they are also "amazed" (4:22b; *ethaumazon* can connote delight, but also skepticism in Luke, as in 11:38, Acts 2:7). And they voice incredulity over such eloquence coming from a humble construction worker's son, further indicating ambivalence (4:22c). Picking up on this, Jesus proceeds to raise the stakes by citing the famous "hometown prophet is not honored" proverb (4:23–24, significantly recorded in all four Gospels: Matt 13:57 // Mark 6:4 // John 4:44).

Jesus now moves from a defensive to an offensive posture with his emphatic and cautionary phrase "But I tell you in truth" (Luke 4:25–27). He extends his *midrash* (reflection), invoking two great wilderness prophets: Elijah (1 Kg 17:8–16) and Elisha (2 Kg 5). The tales to which he alludes center social and ethnic outsiders—which quickly turns his neighbors against him. The literary and social contexts of these two stories are important and worth reviewing.

Elijah was an egalitarian Yahwist, probably a peasant revolt leader or dissident headman associated with local ceremony sites rather than the central Israelite cult. He was from Gilead (1 Kg 17:1), a wilder, fringe area of ancient Israel which often played a swing role in debates over who ruled the confederacy. The episode Jesus cites comes from the literary cycle of Elijah's struggle with Ahab, who was widely considered the most apostate of Israelite kings (1 Kg 21:25f). Ahab's Phoenician wife Jezebel worshipped Baal, so Elijah pronounced drought, launching a war of myths against this imperial god known as "rider of clouds" and "lord of rainstorms." The prophet is reenacting the ancient tradition of nature versus empire articulated in the old story of Moses's struggle with Pharaoh.[9]

Ahab puts out an APB on the prophet, whom the Spirit directs to take refuge in the wilderness (1 Kg 17:1–7)—as do both John the Baptist and Jesus in Luke's story! "Drink from the *wadi;* I have commanded the ravens to feed you there" says the divine voice (17:4). This bird's resourceful intelligence is shared with the prophet (17:5–6)—a remarkable instance of interspecies symbiosis that is worth "paying attention to," as Jesus exhorts his disciples in a later Lukan teaching moment (see 8B). But Elijah is hoisted on his own petard: his *wadi*—the last place a seasonal stream would have water—dries up from the drought he invoked (1 Kg 17:7)! So, God dispatches him to Zarephath, a Phoenician town on the coast between Tyre and Sidon (17:8–10). This time, he is told to seek a widow's aid, which requires a scandalous overture from a Judean male to a woman of an enemy group. Yet she is desperately poor, on the verge of starvation (17:11–12), and the prophet conjures meal and oil "until the God of Israel [*not* Baal] sends rain on the earth" (17:14), and heals her son to boot (17:17–24). Jesus's first point of clarification in this "epilogue" to his *drash*, then, is how two unlikely allies help each other through the famine: a "beyond borders" demonstration of Sabbath Economics mutual aid.

Jesus then turns to the example of Elijah's disciple, Elisha, in his encounter with the powerful Aramean general Naaman. Naaman had been prevailing in military skirmishes with Israel but suffered from leprosy (in the Bible an omnibus term for a wide variety of skin diseases; 2 Kg 5:1). A captured Israelite slave girl boasts to him about Elisha the healer, and what unfolds is high political parody (5:2–4). Naaman seeks an audience with the prophet through diplomatic channels; this agitates the unnamed Israelite king in the story, who assumes this must be some sort of trick or provocation by his enemy (5:5–7). Elisha in turn scorns his king: "Let the general come that he may learn that there is a prophet in Israel" (5:8).

More burlesque follows. Naaman gallops up to the prophet's home accompanied by his militia, no doubt an intimidation tactic. Elisha responds by declining to receive him, instead sending instructions through a messenger for the heavily armed general to go wash in the Jordan River seven times (a shamanic ritual full of Sabbatarian symbolism; 5:9–10). This breakdown of protocol angers the Syrian, who snorts that "Damascus has better rivers!" (5:11–12). Once again it is the general's servants who persuade him to take the prophet's advice, and upon his healing he returns to reward Elisha handsomely. But the prophet rebuffs him once more, refusing to accept his payment (5:13–16). Elisha has kept this adversary at bay through compassion *and* resistance—which will also be Jesus's strategy! Indeed, Jesus's *drash* offers his community hope but also critiques their assumptions of exclusive entitlement to divine care. This sermon thus models the art of homiletics discussed in my introduction: Jesus identifies a text, reads it, and then offers an interpretation recontextualized for the listener's world.

Now comes a second "audience reaction," this time decidedly hostile (Luke 4:28–30). In a US context, it is hard not to draw an analogy to Martin Luther King's "Beyond Vietnam: A Time to Break the Silence" speech at Riverside Church in 1967.[10] Americans who loved the Nobel Peace Prize winner's "quality of character, not color of skin" eloquence bristled when he turned a searing critique on the Indochina war, prophetically questioning the nation's integrity.[11] King's meddling in foreign policy matters was perceived by most as "going too far," and his affront to national innocence similarly provoked a conspiracy to silence him (noted in my introduction, v).

The riled group's intent to throw Jesus off a cliff implies a punishment for false prophecy. However, Jesus "passes through them," suggesting he was already practiced in the art of evasive maneuvering. We see this again later when he is being pursued for publicly criticizing the Herodian regime; his keen sense that a "prophet can't perish away from Jerusalem" seems to drive his strategic dodges (13:31–33). Luke reports that, undeterred by this near fatal skirmish in Nazareth, Jesus immediately reemerges, teaching at a Capernaum synagogue thirty miles east (4:31), a village he alluded to in his sermon (4:23). The audience there is similarly astonished, remarking about his authority (or power; *exousia,* 4:32). He then performs his inaugural exorcism and healing in the story (4:33–39).

Here Luke for the first time adopts Mark's narrative order (Luke 4:31–44 // Mark 1:21–39). It is also the point at which Jesus inherits John's "crowd" (3:7,10; the word appears twenty-five times between 4:42 and 11:27 alone). This crowd—a mix of the poor and the sick, the curious and skeptical, and of course disciples and opponents—must be considered a character in the story.[12] It accompanies the narrative and often reflects the emotional landscape. In 11:29 the crowd "increases" (*epathroizō*); in 12:1 it becomes a "myriad" (*murias* = "tens of thousands"). The triptych of 18:36–19:3 is Luke's last mention of the crowd *following Jesus*; after that, it refers to the fickle observers of the Passion story.

Interestingly, the next time Jesus shows up in Capernaum he will "enact" his Nazarene sermon (7:1–16). That sequence consists of two unique healing episodes and a Q tradition discourse about "good news to the poor," which mirror the themes of his inaugural *drash* in inverse order (5A). Such literary parallelism functions to persuade the reader that Jesus's Nazareth sermon is indeed "being fulfilled" (Luke 4:21). By citing the dissident Tishbite and his won't-be-bought protégé, Jesus signals at the outset of his mission that he will be, as they were, embattled because of his solidarity with outsiders and opposition to elites. He has already apprenticed to the tradition of wilderness prophecy with the Elijah-figure John (Luke 1:17); will replicate a food-sharing miracle of Elisha (9:10–17, 6B); and will carry on the healing work of both prophets. Jesus has *told* his people that the old Jubilee vision is being revived; Luke now proceeds to *show* it through three demonstration projects concerning food justice.

B. Showing

Subversive Abundance from Lake, Land, and Table (5:1–39)

Luke now reaches backwards (relative to Mark's storyline) to introduce an expanded version of the call of the first disciples (5:1–11).[13] Luke's account is unique in the gospel tradition in how it stitches together two traditions of memory: the call of fishermen at the beginning of Mark (Mark 1:16–20), and a miraculous catch of fish found at the end of John's Gospel (John 21:1–14). Unfortunately, Jesus's encounter with fishermen at their work is typically romanticized in our suburban churches. This trivializes a powerful scenario that communicates defiance and delight, resistance and renewal. When contextualized in the real world of first-century Roman Palestine, this story reveals the political, economic and social character of the Great Economy as the first demonstration project of Jubilee.

Luke sets the episode at the "Lake of Gennesaret," an older name for Mark's Sea of Galilee, which eschews the imperially renamed "Sea of Tiberius." The lowest freshwater lake in the world, it was ground zero for Rome's efforts to exploit and extract resources in occupied Palestine. When Jesus was a young adult, Tiberius ascended to Emperor after the death of Caesar Augustus. Local ruler Herod Antipas commenced building a city on the southwest shore of the lake, naming it Tiberius in order to curry imperial favor. A key function of this new administrative center was to regulate the fishing industry around the lake, the most prosperous segment of ancient Galilee's economy. Scholars have drawn a compelling portrait of the colonization of the regional political economy emerging during this historical moment.[14] As John Dominic Crossan put it: "It was precisely and specifically by the shores of the Sea of Galilee that the radicality of Israel's God confronted the normalcy of Rome's civilization under Herod Antipas in the 20s of the first century CE."[15]

All fishing became state-regulated for the benefit of the urban elite—either Romans who settled in Palestine following military conquest or Jews connected with the Herodian family, now centered in Tiberius. They profited from the fishing industry in two ways. First, they controlled the sale of fishing leases, without which locals could not fish. Such leases were normally awarded not to individuals but to local kinship-based "cooperatives" (*koinōnoi*) such as the brothers Simon and Andrew or the Zebedee family depicted in this story. Second, local toll collectors taxed fish products and their processing and levied duties on product transport. Fish traditionally harvested in a sustainable fashion for local consumption by peasant cooperatives were now increasingly processed into salt preserve or fish sauce for export. Imperial interests, made possible by infrastructural improvements carried out by the Herodians (roads, harbors and processing factories), were structurally adjusting the traditional subsistence economy (see figure 4).[16] These new regulations benefited the wealthy managerial class while disenfranchising peasant boatmen. The former looked down on the latter even as they depended upon their labor; one ancient papyrus called fishing "the most miserable of professions." So when Jesus of Nazareth showed up at the lake, as is narrated in all four of our Gospels, he was walking right into a distressed economic landscape—boom for a few, bust for most. Top-down economic and infrastructure development inevitably enriches the few and impoverishes the many, as we still see everywhere in our world.

In 1986, a small boat dating to Jesus's time was found well-preserved at Kinnereth. Constructed originally of cedar, it had been repaired with no less than five other types of wood over a century. As a carpenter, Jesus may have gotten work as an itinerant laborer repairing boats, moving from harbor to harbor (see figure 4 showing locations of first-century CE harbors).[17] The fishing village of Capernaum, founded several centuries earlier and with a population of around fifteen hundred, was up the coast from Magdala and Tiberias. This was a reasonable place for Jesus to start building a movement of dissent and renewal, keying on

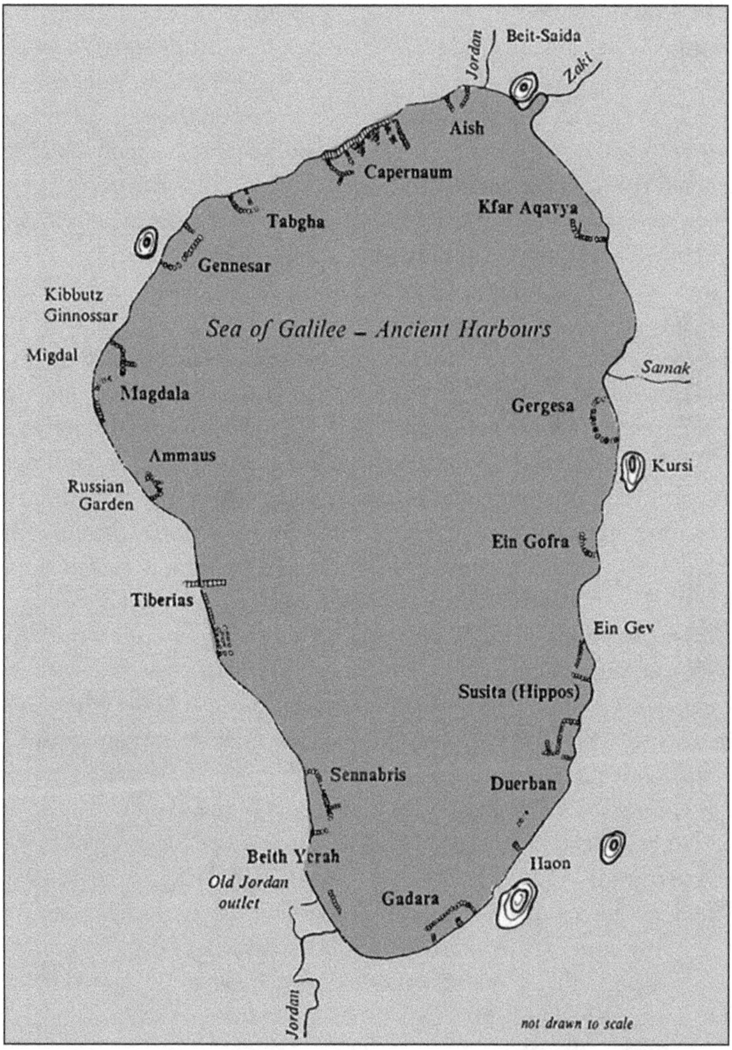

Figure 4. Map of Sea of Galilee and Harbors (Map reproduced with permission of Ritmeyer Archeological Design).

restless workers, who would have been particularly responsive to Jesus's vision of a Sabbath Economics alternative. As Oakman puts it: "If Tiberius was founded in 20 CE, then Jesus was already addressing the concerns of peasant fishermen within a few short years afterward."[18] Jesus's strategy was not unlike Gandhi's mobilization of the lowest *harijan* classes in India in his 1930 Salt March to the sea or Martin Luther King's fateful decision to stand with the Memphis sanitation workers' strike in 1968. True change can only come from below.

Luke depicts Jesus organizing a "teach-in" among these disgruntled workers. Borrowing a boat from a certain Simon, he pushes just offshore so he can use the water and beach as a natural amphitheater (5:3). He concludes his analysis of their plight with an object lesson, instructing Simon to shove off into deeper water and cast his nets one more time (5:4). The boatman's response is poignant: "We worked through the night, but caught nothing," he laments bitterly (5:5). Local waters were becoming fished-out, depleted by extractive colonization—like diamond mines in Africa today, rainforest logging in Latin America, or tar sands removal in Canada. It is testimony to Simon's desperation that he follows the prophet's advice anyway.

Then comes the moment of revelatory reversal: suddenly there were "so many fish that their nets begin to break," and when hauled in (the verb *sugkleiō* implies either a seine or trammel net operation), they "filled both boats so that they began to sink" (5:6–7). This mystical yet material moment symbolizes the abundance of creation restored, a glimpse of how their waters *used* to be before the artificial scarcity wrought by empire. It also portends a double disaster: the potential loss of nets and boat. Yet if this overwhelming catch tears their nets, it also smashes the cycle of their poverty! As in Luke's later story of multitudes sharing bread (and fish!) in the wilderness (6B), this prophetic sign is a reminder that Creation, rightly shared, can sustain everyone—starting with the poorest.

What do we make of Simon's response, confessing to his "sinfulness" (5:8)? Perhaps he is fearful that if his boat sinks, so will his economic prospects (in Luke, "sin" and "debt" are often interchangeable; see 7A). Perhaps his visceral reaction is one of shame about how entangled he is (like each of us) in an imperial system that exploits and pillages Creation. Or perhaps his astonishment (5:9; *thambos*, used only by Luke in the New Testament, also connotes fear) signals a wary realism; he and his companions know that danger lurks in any form of "wildcat" community resource redistribution (5:10). Their copious catch would certainly be criminalized by the authorities as contraband, inspired by an itinerant preacher without a fishing license! So should these hard-pressed peasants joyfully gather the illegal windfall—or run for the hills?

Jesus understands their anxiety and compassionately invites Simon to let go of his fear (5:10b). Then he offers them something even more powerful than a bumper harvest: a paradigm shift toward a radically alternative vocation. "From now on you will be catching *people*!"[19] One of the most famous lines in gospel literature, it is beloved to evangelicals, who have traditionally interpreted it to mean that Jesus was calling them to save souls. But, if we only hear it as a sort of Billy Graham-like summons, we miss the point of this recruiting slogan. In fact, Jesus is alluding to no less than four prophetic oracles about justice:

- Jer 16:16: Jeremiah envisions the Creator "sending for many fishermen" in order to *catch* leaders of Israel "who have polluted the land";
- Amos 4:2: Amos warns elites of his society who oppress the poor that God will "take them away with fishhooks," hauling them like sardines to judgment;
- Ezek 29:3–4: Ezekiel rants against Egypt's Pharaoh: "God will put hooks in your jaws, and . . . pull you up from your rivers," along with the fish to which *they* claimed exclusive rights; and
- Hab 1:14–17: Habakkuk laments how the emperor of Babylon "overfishes," feeding on conquered peoples, cannibalizing the nations in the interests of empire.

For Jesus, who both knew the prophetic literature and sought to embody it anew in his context, this "fishers of people" idiom was a divine invitation to join him in overturning structures of power and privilege in the world to restore both Creation *and* equity.

In modern parlance, the rabbi was challenging these peasants to help him "catch some Big Fish." And why wouldn't they, having so little to lose? Unlike John's account of this remarkable episode, there is no epilogue here about counting fish or feasting on them (John 21:9–11). Luke's "good news to the poor" results in the immediate mobilization of fishermen to join the movement (Luke 5:11). Breaking with business as usual, they "release" *everything* (*aphentes panta*)—that Jubilee verb! This same invitation is given later in Luke's story to a rich man, whose refusal is as immediate as the fishermen's embrace (18:22, chapter 12). In the epilogue to that story, release of home, family, and work specifically alludes to the discipleship community's alternative practice of redistribution and mutual aid (18:28). Following this Way entails specific social, political, and economic recommunitization, as we shall see repeatedly—but only when Luke's story is properly relocated in the real terrain of first-century Palestine.

* * *

Luke picks up Mark's plot again with a twinned sequence: Jesus declares a leper clean (despite not being a priest! 5:12–15), followed by "releasing" a paralytic from sin/debt (despite not being a scribe! 5:17–26).[20] The latter encounter becomes a debate with the Pharisees—think of them as local authorities trying to enforce law and order, propriety and social boundaries—who challenge Jesus's "authority/power" (*exousia*, 5:24; see 4:32, 36). Jesus's "unlicensed" Jubilee practice of somatic restoration is controversial enough to earn official concern, which will now hover over the rest of Luke's narrative.

The theme of economic sustenance returns in the next sequence, a series of food conflict stories between Jesus and Pharisees regarding *who* disciples eat with; *when* not to eat (i.e., fasting); and *how* and *where* they should eat (Luke 5:27–6:5 // Mark 2:13–28). As a Jewish renewal movement, Pharisees were rapidly gaining social power and influence. They sought to apply purity and debt regulations to all people in daily life, in contrast to an educated and affluent Judean clerical aristocracy that did not expect the masses to be observant. Pharisees focused on agricultural and household practices relevant to village life more than on Temple-centered obligations, and they represented real competition with the Jesus movement for the hearts and minds of the disaffected. They also employed "oral Torah" to either work around or counteract older Torah principles.[21] These tensions are reflected in all three episodes in which Jesus defends his disciples' practices regarding issues important to the Pharisaic program: restrictive table fellowship, public piety, and Sabbath observance. The settings of these stories symbolize the economic sphere in a traditional agricultural society: the table as the primary site of consumption, and the field (like the sea) as primary site of production.

A second discipleship call story then pointedly involves a seller of fishing leases, the tax (or toll) collector Levi (Luke 5:27–31 // Mark 2:13–17). This is the first direct appearance of a *telōnēs* in the narrative, and there is some debate about whether this term connotes a tax farmer or a street-level toll collector.[22] Levi was probably a local Jew employed by a tax-farmer who held contracts to collect local tariffs and levies (plus a profit). Native *telōnēs* were hated reminders of how the Judean nation was in debt-servitude to the Roman colonial system, but they were also despised as instruments of extortion. "As an astonishing number of materials indicate, the tax collectors stood at the center of exploitation in the empire," writes Pyung Soo Seo.[23] John's warning to them (3:14; 3A) struck at the very heart of their trade, founded as it was upon exacting from payees who had no recourse.

In his capacity as a local publican, Levi likely also sold or leased fishing rights, perhaps even loaning fishermen capital (at exorbitant interest) to build or repair boats. In approaching him, therefore, Jesus challenges both sides of the debt system: both indebted peasant fishermen *and* their broker/creditor are invited to radical change. Seo thinks that two Lukan additions to Mark's account indicate that Levi was a particularly well-off local bureaucrat, since he throws a "great feast" at "his *own* house" (5:29).[24] This banquet includes "fellow publicans and others," who are labeled by the authorities as "sinners," doubtless including the newly minted fishermen disciples (5:30). As the next meal story—at a Pharisee's home (7:39–50; 5B)—will show, Luke recognizes a close correlation between social outcasts considered unclean because of sin and those made poor by debt.

In ancient Mediterranean culture, the shared meal was the heart of social intercourse and thus a primary determiner of social relations. Pharisees object here because they were deeply concerned about the dietary, ritual, and legal issues surrounding table fellowship in their endeavor to keep clean and unclean separate. Since dramatic boundary-crossing at table would threaten the status quo, the only plausible explanation for this subversive meal would be Levi's decision to embrace Jesus's Jubilee call by redistributing his wealth and social power. We are told that he, like the fishermen, "left *everything* and followed" (5:29), prompting some commentators to consider this to be Levi's "farewell meal."[25] This, Luke's first banquet episode, foreshadows his last: the capstone demonstration of repentant hospitality by a *chief* tax collector (19:1–10; 13A). These two Jubilee meals bookend an amazing arc of showing and telling the "Year of God's favor" here and now.

That culminating Zacchaeus story is ultimately about healing and restoration, a matter to which Jesus now turns in response to those objecting to Levi's class-mixing. His famous adage that the healthy have no need for physicians (5:31) could well be paraphrased: "Only those who experience the system as broken will have any interest in changing it"; or "You can't heal people who don't know they are dis-eased." As noted in my introduction, this ancient insight has driven the modern Twelve-Step Recovery movement, and is equally germane to antiracism and decolonization work today. Jesus can't do much for those who are content with the status quo, but he can build a movement with those who contest it. The path of healing is the demanding, lifelong work of repentance as turning personal and political history around (5:32).

In the next vignette, Jesus cops more criticism for excusing his disciples from a recognized fast day (5:33–39 // Mark 12:13–17). Some early Jesus followers may have been impressed by the rigor of Pharisaic religious discipline, so here he cuts to a deeper issue: a society in which some can afford to fast ritually while others truly go hungry is "tearing the fabric" of the proverbial wineskin (5:36–39). In contrast to the cosmetic symbolics of deprivation, Jesus likens the Great Economy to a wedding party in which all experience shared abundance. There will be a time for fasting, however: when the "bridegroom" is silenced for his Jubilee advocacy (5:35).

Culminating this sequence, the disciples cut through a field and strip grain to eat, drawing fire from Pharisees because of Sabbath rules prohibiting "work" (6:1–5 // Mark 2:23–28). There was resentment among Galilean peasants about the legal control exercised by the Pharisaic establishment over the sowing, harvesting, and marketing of produce. Most poor peasants and sharecroppers simply could not afford to conform to regulations about tithing, leave their fields fallow during the Sabbath year, refrain from planting or eating certain things. From their point of view, the Pharisees were adjudicating the economy to their own benefit. This grainfield action demonstrates a rehabilitation of Sabbath *redistribution* in contrast to the Pharisees' proprietary ethic of Sabbath *restriction*.

Jesus appeals to a (somewhat loosely rendered) scriptural story about David (6:3–4; see 1 Sam 21:1–6). As a guerilla fighter on campaign, David commandeered the Bread of the Presence for his soldiers—a much more serious "transgression" than merely eating from a field. But Jesus's midrash clarifies that David and his followers were "hungry" (5:3), suggesting that in a Jubilee cosmology, hungry people have a right to food despite laws that might control such access. Jesus is merely following the Torah of Sabbath Economics: "When you gather the harvest in your country, you are not to gather the gleanings. . . . Leave them to the poor and the stranger" (Lev 23:22). This grainfield gleaning is nonviolent action at its best, transgressing a statute in service of a greater principle: in this case, the law of gleaning, which prioritizes Commonwealth availability to those in need over commodity ownership. Jesus's invocation of the Human One as Sovereign over the Sabbath" is thus not a negation of the tradition (as too many Christians have assumed) but precisely a restoration of Sabbath Economics![26]

This series of eating controversies represents a strong protest over the politics of food in Jewish Palestine. At Levi's house, haves and "have-nots share transgressive table fellowship. In the fasting debate, Jesus argues that the poor need shared abundance, not religious abstinence. And the grainfield "direct action" dramatizes the Jubilee ethic through an object lesson. These demonstrations on land and at table confirm what the "Great Catch" illustrated at Lake Gennesaret: the fruits of the earth are for people, not for profit. The Nazareth sermon is indeed being realized "in our eyes and ears."

CHAPTER FIVE

Centering the Marginalized

> Luke contains curses which parallel the beatitudes in the Sermon on the Plain. "Damn you rich! You already have your consolation. Damn you who are well-fed now! You will know hunger" . . . It is part of the standard theme of reversal, but it is also an acknowledgement of God's disdain for wealth.
>
> —David King, *Reclaiming the Radical Economic Message of Luke*[1]

THIS CHAPTER BEGINS by tackling the first half of Jesus's Sermon on the Plain, showing how it tells Sabbath Economics, particularly in its advocacy for relief from the acute socioeconomic problem of indebtedness.[2] I then note Luke's deft reiteration of the Nazareth sermon in two healings (7:1–22), and examine how Jesus interacts with John's movement (7:17–35). Finally I take a deep dive into the poignant story of the anointing woman (7:36–50), followed by the "coming out" party for women embracing Jubilee (8:1–3).

A. Telling

Blessing the Poor, Lamenting the Rich (6:20–26)

Luke's Sermon (6:17–49) is briefer than Matthew's more well-known Sermon on the Mount (Matt 5–7).[3] Luke 6:6–16 followed Mark's narrative, but now veers away to make room for this, Jesus's longest discourse, which is Q-heavy material.[4] I won't tackle the whole Sermon on the Plain, but will focus on its first half, which contains unique L material (6:20–36).

Luke's three opening Beatitudes—the Latin *beatus* and Greek *makarios* mean "happy"—are in the second person, Matthew's first eight in the third person. The latter's "Blessed are the poor in spirit" (Matt 5:3) is preferred by affluent readers, who take it to be a metaphorizing of poverty. "Blessed are you poor," on the other hand, leaves little wiggle room (Luke 6:20b). Luke uses *ptōchos* (from *ptōsso*, "to cower") as both noun and adjective, and twice as frequently as the other synoptics combined. At no point does it connote anything other than economic destitution.[5] The phrase ". . .for the Great Economy is *yours*" (6:20c) employs the possessive pronoun *humetera*, with the verb in present tense, giving a sense of immediacy. From this point onward in his narrative, "poor" is often a specific counterpoint to "rich" (here with 6:24; 16:20 with 22; 18:22; 19:8; and 21:23). This functions rhetorically to focus attention on the injustice of disparity. Jesus's good news is for the poor (4:18; 7:22); conversely, he later makes it clear that the Great Economy is *not* hospitable to those with wealth (18:24–25; below 12B).

Similar difference in tone is reflected between Matthew's "hunger and thirst for righteousness" (Matt 5:6) and Luke's second Beatitude ("you that hunger *now*," Luke 6:21a). Luke's third Beatitude, meanwhile, is unique (6:21b), introducing the poignant theme of "weeping" (*klaiō*), which recurs six times in the narrative, including the episode we'll look at in the next section.[6] Luke's "short list" of Beatitudes thus centers those who suffer existentially from poverty and trauma. For them, the Great Economy can be realized *here and now—if* they are joined by the non-poor in the struggle to end the pangs and the pain. The latter who do live in solidarity, however, will inevitably share the exclusion and suffering of the marginalized, because that is the vocation of prophets (6:22–23; see 1B).

These Beatitude reversals are then reversed again in a correlated list of "Woes" (6:24–26). This Lukan addition to the Q Sermon tradition further underlines tensions arising from disparity. The exclamatory particle (Hebrew *hoy*, Greek *ouai*) is ubiquitous in both Testaments. Originally associated with lament at funerals (e.g., 1 Kg 13:30; Jer 22:18; 34:5), in the prophets it often takes on a "damning" tone (as in David King's paraphrase above). Isaiah directs it toward a whole complex of pathologies characterizing the rich: latifundial monopolization of land (Isa 5:9); addictions (Isa 5:11, 22); justice subverted in the courts (Isa 5:23; 29:15); political oppression of the poor (Isa 10:1–2); and militarism (Isa 31:1).

Luke specifically echoes here the vocabulary of Mary's Magnificat:

Woe to you that are rich (*plousiois*, 6:24)...
Woe to you who are full (*empeplēsmenoi*) now, for you shall hunger (*peinasete*, 6:25)

God has filled (*eneplēsen*) the hungry (*peinōntas*) with good things,
and has sent the rich (*ploutountas*) empty away (1:53).

The Woes conclude with a jab at religious leaders who "talk prophetic talk" but do not walk its Way so they can flourish in the status quo; these are implicated as "pseudo prophets" (6:22–23).[7]

To the comfortable, Jesus seems polarizing, stirring up class enmities. But he is simply naming the existing architecture of social division in a world ruled by the rich. Luke's discursive strategy holds up a mirror to both sides: the exploited are assured that mercy and liberation *can* be realized, while exploiters are put on notice that justice and reckoning *will* come. This is a pedagogical technique similar to apocalyptic literature's rhetoric of "unmasking," which in Luke will reach a zenith in the warning tale of Lazarus and Dives (chapter 11).[8]

These harsh words are qualified, however, by the teaching that immediately follows (6:27–31). Those who are "hearing" Jesus's Woes must not weaponize them, try to solve the problem of disparity by dehumanizing the rich, or inflict violence against them. "But I say to you that hear, Love your enemies, do good to those who hate you" (6:27). Oppressors are to be met with nonviolent resistance (6:29–30) and treated according to the "Golden Rule" (6:31).[9]

Next comes another triplet that continues this Sabbath Economics tone:

> If you love those who love you, what credit (*charis*) is that to you?
> For even sinners love those who love them.
> If you do good to those who do good to you, what credit is that to you?
> For even sinners do the same.
> If you lend to those from whom you hope to receive, what credit is that to you?
> Even sinners lend to sinners, to receive as much again.
> (Luke 6:32–34; compare to Matt 5:42, 46–47)

Notably, only here in the New Testament do some modern translations render the noun *charis* as "credit"![10] We would do better to translate it, as in most other places, as "favor," "gift," or best of all, "grace."

The purpose of this teaching is to push listeners beyond the conventional ethos of balanced reciprocity to a cosmology of grace. To underscore this, Luke adds the summary exhortation: "But love your enemies, and do good, and lend, expecting nothing in return" (6:35a). This economic imperative is specifically couched in the language of generalized reciprocity. The version of this found in the Gospel of Thomas specifically indicts the system of usury: "If you have money, do not lend it at interest, but give [it] to one from whom you will not get it back" (Thomas, 95). This is how the mercy and generosity of the Creator can be replicated by the "children of the most High" (6:35b–36).[11] Luke's blending here of economic (lending) and moral language (sinners) is similarly woven into the story of the "anointing woman" that we shall look at shortly.

The Sermon on the Plain moves toward conclusion with another agricultural analogy about knowing trees by their fruit (6:43–44), shades of the Baptist's preaching (3:8–9). The closing warning to those who "hear but don't do" is illustrated by an all-too-familiar scenario: village homes wiped away in flash floods (6:48–49). Luke follows this long teaching sequence with more L material: two "bringing back to life" stories and a report to the jailed Baptist (7:18–23).

As noted, these episodes inversely mirror the themes of Jesus's Nazareth *drash* (4A):

Luke 4:18–27 (Nazareth)	Luke 7:1–22 (Capernaum)
a. proclaim good news to the poor, sight to blind	c' Jesus heals a servant of a foreign military officer (2–10)[12]
b. Elijah heals the son of a widow	b' Jesus heals the son of a widow (11–17)
c. Elisha heals Naaman, a foreign military officer	a' Tell John: "the poor have good news proclaimed, the blind see" (18–22)

This correlation again exhibits the elegance of Luke's narrative weaving: here Jesus embodies his *midrash*, showing his inaugural telling.

The subjects of the twinned healings in both sequences span vast social disparity: destitute widows on one hand, powerful officers of an enemy military on the other. This pattern recurs elsewhere in Luke's narrative:

- peasant fishermen and a broker of fishing leases in Luke 5 (4B);
- the daughter of a synagogue ruler and an impoverished and impure "daughter" in 8:40–56; and
- a woman bent over by debt and a wealthy man suffering from bloating (9A).

Such scenarios that contrast-yet-connect the respective illnesses of poor and rich set the stage for Luke's most dramatic healing dyad: the blind beggar and Zacchaeus (13A). These object lessons are central to Luke's case for Sabbath Economics redistribution.

Jesus's exchange with disciples of the imprisoned John the Baptist and the crowds (7:17–34), which is mostly Q material, functions in the narrative to reiterate key themes of Luke's Prelude while setting the scene for the next key episode of healing. John, having received word of Jesus's public ministry in jail, inquires anxiously whether Messianic liberation is near (7:17–20)—understandable given his own dire prospects! Jesus sends assurance to John that he is busy realizing the Isaian Jubilee vision he proclaimed in Nazareth. His adding here that "the dead are raised up" (7:22) functions to keep the controversial aspect (i.e., the resuscitation of a Gentile widow's son) of his *drash* in view, underlined by another beatitude: "Blessed is the one who is not scandalized by me" (7:23).

Jesus next addresses followers of the Baptist anxious about their leader's incarceration (7:24–30), defending him in language that turns tough—not unlike that of the John himself (3A). Jesus draws a stark contrast between the wilderness revolutionary John and the plutocrat Herod Antipas, representing opposite poles of national identity. His interrogative triplet unfolds like a three-part joke about "the king and the prophet":

i) What did you go out into the wilderness to behold? A reed shaken by the wind?
ii) What then did you go out to see? A man clothed in soft clothing? Nope, those who are gorgeously appareled and live in luxury are in kings' courts.
iii) What then *did* you go out to see? A prophet? Yes! (7:24b–26a)

The reed reference is likely "a title of ridicule and recognition for Herod Antipas, who had a reputation as a waverer."[13] Jesus's second "dig" is clearly a derogatory comment on the royal regime's insular plutocracy, remaining in palatial luxury dressed in finery. In leaving Herod's political space for that of a prophet the crowd encountered more than they bargained for: Malachi's forerunner of Messiah (7:26b–27; see Mark 1:2). John is the greatest among human beings (7:28a), opines Jesus; the king only *imagines* he's great! Yet from the perspective of the Great Economy, more paramount are those "of least importance" in the Herodian economy (7:28b).[14]

The parenthetical comment in 7:29–30 recognizes that John's baptism was politically polarizing. Yet Jesus understands that public opinion is fickle and expresses exasperation (or is it bemusement?) that prophets are dismissed: John is too austere, Jesus celebrates too much and with the wrong kind of people (7:31–34). Jesus here underlines the conflict brewing since 5:29–30 about how "eating and drinking" in contested space rouses the ire of the authorities—the very issue that will intensify in the next episode.

B. Showing

Women Embracing Jubilee (7:35–8:4)

The widow of Nain vignette reintroduced subversive gender dynamics to the narrative, largely absent since Luke 2. She was likely leading the funeral procession out of the village for her son, who contrary to patriarchal norms is described as "the only son of his mother" (7:12). Feeling compassion for her plight (the wonderfully onomatopoetic verb *splangchnizomai*), Jesus tells her not to weep, offering the consolation promised in the third Beatitude (7:13, see 6:21b). But when he touches the "coffin" (*soros*, only here in the New Testament, probably a pallet of some sort), Jesus renders himself unclean, which stops the procession (7:14). After the resuscitation, Luke tells us that "he gave him to his mother" (7:15). This is the identical phrase to the LXX of 1 Kgs 17:23 in the widow of

Zarephath story, confirming the link to Jesus's earlier *drash* (4:25) and thus identifying this too as a Jubilee moment. This readies us for how women will take center stage in another extraordinary showing of Jubilee reversals at another contested dinner party.

At the close of Jesus's rant regarding how prophets are perceived is what seems to be a rather strange non sequitur: "Yet Wisdom (*sophia*) is justified by all her children" (7:35). But this invocation of a venerable Hebrew Bible trope is in fact a bridge to the next episode—and to reversals of gendered power. Sophia appears far more often in Luke-Acts than the other Gospels because she is the spirit that animates the prophets (11:49; see Jer 7:25). Her personification in 7:35 invokes Proverbs 8–9: the portrait of Lady Wisdom as such a prophet, trying to get the attention of her village (the Hebrew *chokhmah* and Greek *sophia* are both feminine). She urgently "takes her stand, crying out on the heights, beside the way, at the crossroads, in front of the gates, at the entrance of the portals" (Prov 8:2). In the patriarchal culture of antiquity, a woman would not typically be seen in such prominent public places, being largely sequestered at home. Sophia's message of justice (Prov 8:15–16) breaks gender taboos through both insistence and persistence. She then sets a table for a feast to which those "without understanding" are invited (Prov 9:1–5). Both images are profoundly maternal: the wise old crone demanding a hearing and the householder offering hospitality for the purpose of both nurturing *and correcting* the community. The question is, Who will come to this table, and how will they behave? This is precisely what Luke's narrative takes up in the next scene, in which a woman inconveniently embodies insistence and persistence at a table of powerful men who are "without understanding"!

The "anointing woman" (Luke 7:36–50) is one of the very few scenes to appear in all four Gospels. Mark emphatically concludes his version with a remarkable use of a eucharistic formula: "Wherever the gospel is preached in the whole world, what she has done will be told *in memory of her*" (Mark 14:9). Obviously, this story was extremely important to the early church—and should be for us. Still, it exhibits a complicated tradition-history:[15]

- Matthew's version (Matt 26:6–13) follows Mark's (Mark 14:3–9) in opening the Passion narrative; Luke's and John's accounts (John 12:1–8) occur earlier in their stories.
- Matthew, Mark, and John (but not Luke) associate the setting with Bethany. Matthew and Mark locate it at the home of Simon the leper, Luke at Simon the Pharisee's, and John in a space identified with Martha and Lazarus.
- Only John names the anointing woman Mary.

- In Luke and John, she does not anoint Jesus's *head* (as in Matthew and Mark), but his *feet*, using her hair.
- The focus of the scene's conflict in Matthew, Mark, and John is whether her ointment was too precious to waste; Luke shifts it to the politics of table fellowship.

Anni Pesonen argues that Luke's account can be seen as a standalone "short story."[16] Here Luke builds on the banquet as a central metaphor for realizing the Great Economy, whose ethos of a reciprocity *should* disrupt social hierarchies, as will be fully articulated in 14:7–24 (9B). Let's look closely at how this carefully choreographed drama unfolds.

Scene I. Jesus receives a formal invitation from a Pharisee (*erōtaō*, as in 7:3; 11:37; 14:18); this is surprising, given his clashes with them in 5:30 and 6:2. He accepts without hesitation, and "reclines" at the table (7:36; as per ancient Mediterranean custom, not sitting but lying). The fact that the host *had* a table means he was an elite, as peasants would sit on the ground. As Jesus takes his place, we readers assume it is one of honor, though the end of the story reveals otherwise.

The plot immediately thickens with the appearance of a woman "sinner of the kind as was in the city" (7:37a; *hētis* is a classical Greek idiom). There is little doubt this is a euphemism for prostitution (a trade we still euphemize today). "Sinner" adds to the pejorative social labeling, which has already been used by Jesus's opponents to criticize those with whom he dines (5:30 and 7:34); this label is assumed by the host in 7:39. This setup invites readers to reflect on how *we* routinely distance ourselves from persons and groups by the way we either engage or ignore them (out loud or in our heads, consciously or unconsciously) through the lens of negative stereotypes and name-calling. Luke, however, immediately begins deconstructing this label, and the objectifying gaze that accompanies it, through the uninvited woman's bold agency.

"Having ascertained that he was eating in the Pharisee's house, she brought an alabaster jar of myrrh" (7:37b). Apparently, she felt she already had a substantial enough relationship with Jesus to feel she could join him wherever he might be. But the two delicious subtexts here are:

- How did she find out—was it "word on the street" or Jesus's own invitation?
- How did she know where Simon lived and how to get past the door—a former client perhaps?

She brings with her a precious gift, which may have been a tool of her trade. In John's version, the room fills with its aroma (John 12:3)—making this a story for *all* the senses. She "stations herself" behind Jesus at his feet, suddenly and importunately taking center stage. While the other three versions of this tale focus on the scandalous cost of this balm, here our attention is drawn to the embarrassingly intimate string of active verbs, each one worth lingering over (Luke 7:38).

The poignancy of this scene is better shown than told, and I encourage readers to act it out:

- *Wailing*. . . Women took on the role of public displays of personal and political grief in first-century Palestinian honor culture (as we saw above with the widow of Nain; see also 23:28, Acts 9:39). Jesus commends this "blessed" behavior (Luke 6:21b) and apprentices to it by weeping publicly (19:41; also *klaiō*); this latter scene is found *only* in Luke, portraying Jesus in the tradition of weeping prophets such as Elisha (2 Kg 8:7–12) or Jeremiah (Jer 9:1). Yet insofar as women "weep too much" because they suffer disproportionately from society's violence and poverty, Jesus also seeks to attenuate their grief (Luke 7:13, 8:52). We should not imagine this woman is quietly whimpering; the wailing would have been loud and disruptive, characteristic of traditional mourning culture, which of itself would have been enough to "create a scene" at this banquet.[17]
- *She began wetting his feet with her tears*. . . The verb tense here moves from aorist to present active. Poetically, the Greek verb *brexo* in every other use in the New Testament describes rainfall! "Tears" are ascribed only a half dozen other times in the New Testament, two of which are Luke describing the apostle Paul (Acts 20:19, 31; see 2 Cor 2:4). They are signs of pain that "will be wiped away from every eye" in the beautiful vision of John the Revelator (Rev 7:17; 21:4).
- . . .*and drying them with the hairs of her head*. . . This implies that she has unbound her hair, something a "proper" woman would never do in public, much less in the company of unrelated men (all women wore headscarves in this culture). Such a gesture is almost painfully intimate, even erotic, a connotation strengthened by the final two verbs in the string.
- . . .*and she continued kissing his feet and anointing them with myrrh.* So we don't miss the awkwardness of this moment, Luke uses a narrator's power to slow down time. These verbs, like the previous one, are all imperfect, implying that this "inappropriate" behavior

> is going on for a while, as the tension builds in the room. She is "kissing affectionately" Jesus's feet (*kataphileō* later in Luke's story describes what the father does to the prodigal son, 15:20).[18]

From the perspective of first-century propriety, this is truly a spectacle: a socially outcast, unclean, and uninvited woman with her hair unbound in public engages in intimate touching of a purported male prophet in the exclusive company of elite males. Whatever else this is, it is a train wreck of etiquette! Nothing about it, however, seems to bother Jesus.

Scene II. Suddenly the camera swings around to the host: "Now when the Pharisee who invited him saw it, he said to himself. . ." (7:39a). His internal dialogue—one of several such moments in Luke's narrative, usually revealing the thoughts of a powerful male (e.g., 12:17–19, 16:3–4)—is a hilarious understatement. From the moment she entered, this woman's improprieties had ushered an elephant into the room, bringing civil conversation to a grinding halt and charging the atmosphere with anger, perhaps even violence. One cannot overestimate the social disaster unfolding here. In the honor culture of elites, guests were invited to increase the prestige of the host; in turn, the host's hospitality, meal, and conversation would increase the cache of the guest—a social game of *quid pro quo*. Conversely, for either host or guest to act dishonorably would ignite a downward spiral for all. In other words, we can be *sure* that this host is muttering to himself!

At the center of his distress, however, are Jesus's putative prophetic credentials: "He should have known what kind of woman this is who is touching him" (7:39b).[19] The social label of "sinner" is all this powerful man can "see" in the woman who is wrecking his dinner party, and the fact that Jesus apparently does *not* see this disqualifies him as a prophet in the host's eyes. Simon is only concerned with male honor: Jesus's, his own, and that of his guests. To have them shamed by her behavior could mean political ruin for him.

Luke portrays a room thick with the toxic smoke of class and gender disparity as the awkward silence builds. On one pole are astonishingly inappropriate displays of affection; on the other, the weaponized, objectifying thoughts of the host (and doubtless others!), so loud you can hear them. *Finally,* Jesus breaks the tension, addressing the host by name—perhaps an effort to humanize beyond stereotypes the deteriorating situation. "Simon, I have something to say to you," he offers, ever ready to interrogate difficult realities (7:40). We can imagine the desperate host exploding into his first verbalization—"Teacher, *speak*!"—though he does not return the personal address. Simon is furious, desperately hoping for some explanation, some rationale that will rescue him from social disaster. This is another moment to stay with, feeling the social rage alongside the pathos.

How does Jesus respond, having been given the floor? He changes the subject entirely, calmly proceeding to tell a story. It is a parable—the preferred discourse of Jewish prophets speaking truth to power—though not labeled explicitly as such.[20] Parables use language an audience can hear, only to turn the story in a way that subverts their assumptions—or outright implicates them, as did Nathan's parable indicting King David in murder (2 Sam 12:1–12). The scenario Jesus poses is about calling in loans, and Simon and/or his guests certainly belonged to the moneylending class. It is a straightforward tale about "a certain creditor" and two "debtors" who default (7:41).[21] When it is revealed that "they could not pay it back" (7:42a, *apodidōmi*; see 12:59), the listeners wait for Jesus's righteous judgment.[22]

But Luke has other fish to fry. For a second time he signals the relative equivalence between two pejorative social labels: "sinner" and "debtor" (see 6:34 above). Jesus's little parable thus functions to illuminate the human backstory behind the "sinner" who has crashed the party: she was probably forced onto the street because of desperate poverty bred by indebtedness. Had Simon been around for Jesus's *midrash* on the ethics of lending during his Sermon on the Plain, he wouldn't be frozen by the curveball Jesus throws next: the lender in the story, without explanation or justification, "gifted them both with loan forgiveness" (7:42b).[23] It's a happy ending to the tale for debtors like the woman; not so much for Jesus's privileged male audience.

Simon's nightmare just got worse: first his home is invaded by a sinner whose shenanigans shame his guests; now Jesus presumes to declare a Jubilee for debtors! Yet Jesus keeps the focus on them, not the creditor, querying Simon concerning who would have been more grateful. It is a rhetorical question, of course, and the exasperated host's answer is equally so, reflecting either resignation or sarcasm: "I suppose the one who forgave *more*" (7:42b–43). He has been backed into a rhetorical corner, forced to acknowledge the alternative world of grace and reciprocity. A cosmology of gratitude mirrors the economics of gift—the very argument the apostle Paul makes in his advocacy for international church solidarity through practices of mutual aid.[24]

Scene III. In the final act of this drama, Jesus turns from comforting the afflicted woman to afflicting the comfortable man in a way that radically subverts social power. The heart—and punchline—of the whole episode is another rhetorical question: "Then turning toward the woman Jesus said to Simon, 'Do you see this woman?'" (7:44). Let us not miss the politics of gesture here: Jesus is *looking at the woman while talking to the host* (again, acting this out helps reveal its power). Of *course* Simon has seen her—but only as stereotype and social disaster, and not as a person yearning for dignity, freedom, and love, which was the moral of the parable. Her humanity is invisible in this company of elite males.

Jesus now "rereads" this scenario, revealing damning information, underlined by a string of emphatic contrasts through indirect ("she did this...") and direct address ("but you did not..."):

Simon	Woman
You gave me no water	She wet my feet with her tears
You gave me no kiss	She hasn't ceased kissing my feet
You did not anoint my head	She anointed my feet with myrrh (7:44b–46)

Not only does this overturn the reader's assumption that Jesus was a guest of honor, it also insists that the disrespect he endured was only rectified by the party crasher! This is an extraordinary shaming of the host in front of all his guests for failure to observe the most basic Middle Eastern customs of hospitality: neglecting to wash a guest's feet, make a formal greeting, or allow a freshening up. With each iteration, Simon's stature plummets, while that of the woman rises. In Luke's narrative, this is the first object lesson of Jubilee leveling—with many more to come (part III). Jesus's *denuncia* enacts his mama's Magnificat, pulling no punches in its critique of the presumption of an elite male. But Luke isn't done.

"*This* is why I tell you" indicates solemn emphasis. Jesus doesn't deny that this woman has been involved in "questionable transactions." Yet he continues to recognize her agency as someone trying to heal. Verse 47 is usually translated as "because her sins are forgiven, she loves much." But the Greek reads "she loved much—thus her sins, which are many, are forgiven."[25] Her proactive compassion has actually *animated* grace, and he affirms that she is forgiven (7:48). Though *aphiemi* is often used by Luke to describe forgiveness of sins (e.g., 5:24; 12:10; 17:3f; 23:24), it also describes healing illness (4:39), release from debt (11:4), and leaving one's status quo in order to follow in discipleship (5:11; 18:28). It is, in other words, a Jubilee verb.

This "good news to the poor" only deepens the conflict with the powerful. Jesus's pardon further rankles religious leaders at the table who were in charge of the "mercy business" (as it did earlier in 5:20–24). Now all the "fellow diners" get into the act (7:49), directing theological outrage at Jesus's bold usurpation of their authority—in their space, no less! They *still have not seen the woman*. Yet in the eye of this hurricane, Jesus retains his singular focus on the woman, unnamed perhaps to function as a cipher for every female who endures the violations of patriarchy. He offers her a customary Hebrew benediction, adding a final acknowledgment of her dignity: *her* faith has liberated her. His powerful commendations of initiative by marginalized characters will appear several more times in Luke's narrative (8:48; 17:19; 18:42). This episode thus establishes another key pattern: the agency of poor and sick people.[26]

So concludes this contentious tale. Party over.[27] We don't know its aftermath for Simon, but Luke's plot will continue to thicken going forward. The next time Jesus has a meal with a Pharisee he is immediately embroiled in a conflict that provokes his full-blown diatribe (11:39–52). He pronounces another series of Woes, a remarkable rant that includes another invocation of Sophia, who reveals the prophet's *inevitable* fate at the hands of the powerful (11:49–51; 1B). Thereafter Luke comments darkly that Jesus's adversaries "began to be very hostile toward him . . . and to lie in wait" (11:53–54). He will be summoned to dine with Pharisees one more time in the narrative, where they "watch him closely" (14:1). There Jesus launches his most elaborate teaching on justice at table, which again does not go well for the host (9B).

Scene IV. There is an instructive epilogue to this episode, which notes for the first time the appearance of women traveling with Jesus. In a brief but telling updated snapshot of the discipleship community (8:1–3), Luke emphasizes that the Twelve are now also accompanied by female disciples. Three are named, and the two who are described represent, unsurprisingly, opposite ends of the socio-economic spectrum. On one hand, the "liberated demoniac" Mary of Magdala could well have been a refugee from the fish-processing factories there.[28] On the other is Joanna, a courtier in the royal house of Herod, who appears only in Luke.[29] These two show up again at the end of the Gospel narrative (along with "Mary the mother of James and the other women") as witnesses of the resurrection—though their testimony is ignored by the male disciples (24:10–11)!

Luke is making two points through this epilogue to deepen the impact of his "short story." One is that the discipleship community, by its inclusive nature across class and gender lines, will appear socially suspect to the prevailing culture.

> Women leaving behind family responsibilities would have been considered seriously deviant, arousing suspicions of illicit sexual conduct. . . . The fact that they travel with Jesus and provide support implies reciprocity: Paying off the debt incurred when they were healed. It may also imply that they were widows who now see the surrogate family as taking precedence over biological family.[30]

The other point is that the discipleship community is explicitly embracing Sabbath Economics. Just as Jesus's parable about debt-forgiveness turned the *social* focus of the "scene" at Simon's table into an *economic* polemic, these women make their material means available—the very service (*diakoneō*) to which Jesus calls disciples (22:26–27).

To shrug this off as merely an expression of "women's charity," as many commentators do, misses how this vignette introduces two more key strands in Luke's narrative. One is the "eruption" of women into movement leadership, directly on the heels of the dramatic empowerment of the weeping woman. Equally significant is the inauguration of another major Lukan theme. The verb *huparchō* ("to be"), often in participial form as a substantive (e.g., *huparchontōn,* "being"), appears over forty times in Luke-Acts, more than twice as often as the rest of the New Testament combined. More than a third of the time the participle is translated as possessions or property (similar to our English "be-longings"). Luke first employs that semantic field in Jesus's caricature of those who "live in palatial luxury" (7:25; *truphē huparchontes*). In 8:3, it seems to imply a story of conversion: Joanna, who hails from just such a space, now appears to be "spoiling the Egyptians" by redistributing her wealth among the discipleship community. *We might well consider her the first person to be healed of affluenza in Luke's narrative.*

For Luke, possessions are what the proverbial strongman seeks to protect (11:21), and typically characterize large landowners (12:44; 16:1), including Pharisees (16:14). Conversely, Jesus warns that because they cannot substitute for life (12:15; see 8A), they should be gifted regularly (12:33) and ultimately "given up" (14:33). Most importantly for the narrative logic of Luke, a chief tax collector will distribute half of his *huparchontōn* as restitution to the defrauded poor in the final object lesson (19:8)—and *huparchontōn* is redistributed among the Pentecost Acts community (Acts 4:32, 34, 37; epilogue iii). Sabbath Economics heals us from being possessed by our possessions, and empowers us to redeploy assets to build community (10A).

Luke's "matrons of the movement" embody the Sabbath Economics lessons from the confrontation at Simon's house, showing what the Beatitudes told. It signals a return to the old ways: a community operating as an alternative, extended household economy (*oikonomia*)—which traditionally in the village was managed by women! This ethos is based on the "fictive kinship" of those following the Way—a teaching Jesus will shortly give (8:19–21).[31] And what of the "weeping woman"? We can presume she is now a sister (and perhaps leader!) in this newly organized female cohort, having found a home in the House of Sophia.

CHAPTER SIX

Practicing Mutual Aid

Ho, everyone who thirsts, come to the waters;
and you that have no money, come, buy and eat!
Come, buy wine and milk, without money or price.

—Isaiah 55:1

THE LOAVES AND fishes story was such a keystone scenario that Mark narrated two versions, and Matthew followed: the feeding of the 5,000 (Mark 6:30–44 // Matt 14:13–21) and the feeding of the 4,000 (Mark 8:1–10 // Matt 15:32–39). Luke, however, relates only the first account (Luke 9:10–17), which may seem odd, given the thesis of this book. On the other hand, he gives us two versions of Jesus's "missionary instructions" (9:1–10; 10:1–12), while the other synoptics provide just one (Mark 6:7–11 // Matt 9:35–10:16). Indeed, Luke's desert feeding story follows immediately upon Jesus's first set of travel directives. This chapter explores how these two traditions illuminate each other.

A. Telling

How (Not) to Build a Movement (9:1–6, 10:1–12)

Following his "women embracing Jubilee" sequence (7:35–8:3, 5B), Luke turns back in 8:4–56 to following Mark's narrative. Before turning to our focal texts, I will note briefly some passages that reflect footprints of Sabbath Economics:

i) 8:4–15: The Parable of the Sower portrays the hard realities facing peasants free-casting seed in their dry farming of marginal lands. Yet it concludes with a surprising, poverty-busting harvest of abundance—the triumph of the economy of grace represented by "good earth" (8:8). The parable is then reread as an allegory of movement building: three quarters of the "seeds of the Word" sown fail to germinate because of opposition, rootlessness, and the choking effect of "anxieties, wealth and hedonism" (8:14). Luke illustrates this precisely in his first "object lesson" about a rich landowner and greed (9A). But the seed-tenders who "persevere with patience" bear enough fruit to sustain the movement (8:15). Luke includes Mark's stern warning *not* to believe economic narratives that rationalize the polarization of wealth, an enduring caution to our own world (8:18).[1]

ii) 8:19–21: Luke's abbreviated version of Mark's story about Jesus's conflict over household and family reflects how fictive kinship was a fundamental aspect of the early movement, shaping a new social ecology of inclusion.[2]

iii) 8:26–39: The Gerasene demoniac's captivity/oppression under Legion articulates the political consciousness of a Galilean Jewish community under Roman imperialism. Another "political cartoon," the pigs drowning in the sea (8:33) alludes to the fate of Pharaoh's army in the Exodus story. On the material level the story also suggests that the economic value of an animal husbandry operation is subordinate to human liberation.[3]

iv) 8:40–56: The last episode in this sequence is the "tale of two daughters." As I noted in the previous chapter, it is one of many Lukan scenarios featuring twinned but socioeconomically disparate characters whose healings are interdependent. This episode again prioritizes females over males and poor and destitute persons over affluent and powerful ones. The symbolic number twelve connects the two intercalated women's political bodies to the body politic of Israel (see 8A).[4]

This takes us to 9:1–6, the commissioning of the Twelve (reiterated in greater detail in the sending of the Seventy, 10:1–20). Having located these missionary instructions in their narrative context, I will read them here not only in terms of Luke's social setting but also through the lens of the long and often lamentable history of Christian colonizing, which unfolded as a result of the church *ignoring* this teaching's straightforward counsel!

The instructions in 9:1–6 are constructed as a chiasm:

> [A] Jesus called the twelve together and gave them power and authority over all demons and to cure diseases, and sent them out to proclaim the kingdom of God and to heal.
>
> > [B] He said to them, "Take nothing for your journey, no staff, nor bag, nor bread, nor money—not even an extra tunic.
> >
> > > [C] Whatever house you enter, stay there, and leave from there.
> >
> > [B′] Wherever they do not welcome you, as you are leaving that town shake the dust off your feet as a testimony against them."
>
> [A′] They departed and went through the villages, bringing the good news and curing diseases everywhere.

The mission is defined as twofold: proclaiming the alternative sociopolitical order of the Great Economy, and healing (*therapeuein*) people oppressed by demons and diseases. These core practices are repeated in verses 1 and 6, framing the passage. Since every human society contains elements of both political oppression and personal illness, a mission that organizes and advocates for freedom, justice, and health would seem to have universal relevance as "good news."

Because hospitality to strangers was (and is) endemic to traditional cultures, first-century organizers could count on initial welcome. Jesus's instructions thus focus on constraining abuse. The significance of the first instruction (9:3) cannot be overstated: "Don't carry your baggage into your host community." This is not just about traveling light; it is about going *vulnerably*. The missionary is not in control. Jesus's rhetoric alludes (by way of contrast) to the old story of David, who famously approached the foreigner Goliath with a staff and a bag full of five stones—in other words, to do battle (1 Sam 17:40). Too often in the Western history of colonization, missionary baggage was weaponized because the ultimate goal was not liberation, but domination, not to heal, but to usurp. Jesus's directive to travel without bread and money similarly stipulates that missionaries should *not* be self-sufficient, but dependent upon hosts—who thus retain the upper hand.

What of the counsel to possess only one tunic? A change of clothes was a luxury among peasant Middle Easterners. Early in Luke's story John the Baptist exhorted, "If you have two coats, give one to the poor" (3:11). Early missionaries were expected to already have distributed their surplus. We might further extrapolate that a limited wardrobe means that over time the missionary will eventually adopt the local style of dress! Clothes are a way of either fitting in or remaining apart, of cultural imposition or adaptation. Tragically, European Christian missionaries almost always brought trunks full of their own culture to North America and imposed it (including their costumes) on native hosts.

The middle instruction concerns the missionary's navigation of welcoming spaces (9:4). The phrase "whichever house you might enter" (*eis hēn an oikian eiselthēte*) connotes a conditional or contingent prospect—hospitality cannot be assumed, much less demanded. Jesus then underlines two crucial imperatives regarding the guest's positionality:

- ". . . stay there. . ." (*ekei menete*: "remain or abide");
- ". . . and leave from there" (*exerchesthe*, which could be translated "then be gone").

The missionary remains a guest: doesn't move around, abides long enough to understand the new place and people, but ultimately leaves. The more the organizer lives into the local way of life (which, as anyone who has lived cross-culturally knows, can take a long time), the more their message can indigenize. But Jesus does not include the prospect of permanent settlement, nor does Luke's narrative of Paul's itineration in Acts. This is the *opposite* of colonizing settlement, in both demeanor and duration. And even if missionaries should be invited to stay, their tenure is still on the terms of the host community.

All of this is predicated on finding locals willing to provide more than "passing through" hospitality, and Jesus realistically assumes there will be places where this is *not* the case (9:5). So he gives one more simple instruction: If you are unwelcome, *move on*! Don't retaliate, don't force yourself on the locals, and don't take over their country! Shaking off the dust from one's feet is a symbolic gesture important to Luke, appearing also several times in Acts (13:51, 18:6, 21:3). Inhospitality is a serious problem, especially for traveling "movement emissaries." But all one can do is point it out. If local people don't have ears to hear good news—providing of course that the missionary's telling and showing of the Gospel is credible and respectful—then try elsewhere. Done and dusted.

Movements for social change arise and grow out of the hard work of building common cause, conviction and community across political and geographical landscapes. This requires approaches that are culturally appropriate, politically nonviolent, and predicated on an ethos of hospitality given and received—principles that were important to organizers of the early church.[5] However, after the consolidation of Christianity under Constantine, this became the road *not* taken. With the spread of European conquest and hegemony across the globe from the sixteenth century onward, Christian missionaries increasingly acted in the ways Jesus had specifically anathematized, often operating as handmaidens of colonization.[6]

Had Christians observed Jesus's straightforward guidelines for how to be among other peoples and places, the history of the world would be profoundly different. But for the most part, our ancestors in the faith ignored them. European missionaries in the Americas initially survived because of native sharing "almost unimaginable in its generosity—not only land but food, agricultural techniques, practical knowledge, and trade routes."[7] This hospitality was soon abused by missionaries, who often acted (consciously or unconsciously) as double agents of church and colonial powers, pursuing objectives more suited to conquest than community. Consequently, a bitter legacy of domination and genocide was visited upon every corner of the globe. The perverted gospel of colonization was (and still is) predicated upon *colonization of the gospel*: the theologically elaborate ways by which churches ignore, suppress, or rationalize away Jesus's clear directives. This text rightly haunts the conscience of Christendom, and it is crucial for today's mobile, globalized world that we recover "unsettling" styles of mission that embody good news of healing and liberation without taking over.[8]

Perhaps anticipating such apostasy, and repetition being the key to pedagogy, Jesus reiterates his instructions in 10:1–16. Let's first take a quick glance at the intervening narrative. After abbreviating Mark's longer flashback account of the murder of John the Baptist (Mark 6:17–29 // Luke 9:7–9; see 3:19–20), Luke resumes following Mark:[9]

- Luke 9:18–27: Peter's "confession" and Jesus's call to the cross;
- 9:28–36: The Transfiguration, where Jesus mystically communes with "Moses and the prophets" who represent the hermeneutic key to the whole gospel narrative (24:27, 44; as discussed 1B);
- 9:37–43: The healing of a "silenced" child (see 7B, fn. 14);
- 9:44–45: Another prediction of Jesus's passion;
- 9:46–48: Learning about true "greatness" from a child; and
- 9:49–50: Jesus prohibits disciples from "franchising" the work of liberation.

In 9:51, we arrive at a watershed moment in Luke's plot: Jesus "sets his face to go to Jerusalem." Scholars identify this as the opening scene of the Special Section (9:51–18:14), which as noted contains the majority of unique Lukan material, very few synoptic parallels, and leads us into the heart of this book project.

Pointedly, given the teaching just studied, the first leg of Jesus's long march to Jerusalem does not go well. Jesus and his disciples visit a Samaritan village (9:52–55), admittedly a controversial choice in light of historic tensions between his people and Samaritans (alienated cousins who descended from the northern Kingdom). Sure enough, they are *not* received there. The verb *dechomai* was the pivot point of the first set of missionary instructions (9:5) and also forms the backbone of the second set (10:8, 10). It will similarly shape Luke's second rich man story about the struggle to defect from the cosmology of mammon (*dechomai* appears in 16:4, 6, 7, 9; chapter 10). Though Jesus himself demonstrates hospitality along his way (9:11, 48; 18:17; 22:17), he also experiences the pain of its absence, which he warned would happen to movement organizers. Yet he firmly "rebukes" his disciples' desire to retaliate against inhospitable Samaritans (9:55), and "moves on."[10] This is followed by a series of exchanges with potential recruits along the way which stress the liminality with which disciples must reckon (9:57–62).[11]

This brings us to the expanded version of the missionary instructions. It begins with two more metaphors reflecting hardships of agrarian life: a harvest needing laborers, and lambs stalked by wolves (10:2–3). Then Jesus picks up the theme of 9:3, which he intensifies by adding a prohibition against taking "purse and sandals" (10:4).[12] The traveler is, upon entering a hospitable home, to pronounce a blessing of peace and discern from the host's response whether "that peace will return to you" (10:5–6). Jesus also expands the instruction of

9:4: "Remain in the same house, eating and drinking whatever they provide. . . Do not move about from house to house. Whenever you enter a town and its people welcome you, eat what is set before you" (10:7–8). In other words, don't move around looking for a better deal, don't demand special treatment, and eat locally and gratefully (stated twice).

In villages where the missionary is received (*dechomai*), healing and proclamation of the Great Economy should ensue, as befits the ethos of reciprocity (10:9; see 7B). But where there is no welcome, Jesus repeats that disciples may express protest upon departure by shaking dust off their feet (9:5 = 10:10–12). Malina and Rohrbaugh write:

> The Greek word here is better translated "squares" than "streets." These squares, usually at the intersection of internal city walls, were used for public ceremonies and communication with the non-elite of the city. . . The insult here is thus a very public act. When Israelites returned to the holy land from foreign lands, they shook the dust from their feet.[13]

This symbolic ritual, accompanied by a solemn "I tell you" (10:12), is associated with the story of Sodom (Gen 19). There, locals refused hospitality to, and then abused, the same angelic strangers whom Abraham and Sarah had welcomed (Gen 18). Jesus then invokes more Woes, extending them to well-known local cities who he accuses of demonstrating greater hard-heartedness than *enemy* cities such as Tyre and Sidon (Luke 10:13–15)!

These instructions conclude with the powerful warning: "Whoever rejects you rejects me, and whoever rejects me rejects the One who sent me" (10:16). The two verbs tell the story: *atheteō* is a strong repudiation, like nullifying or violating a covenant, and is used no fewer than four times in this sentence; *apostello* (from whence our word "apostle" comes) means "to send." These represent the two poles of the mission vocation: going out and being welcomed in—or not! Both sets of instructions include one-sentence epilogues that report on the return of those sent out (9:10; 10:17).

This double tradition is an interesting artifact of the ancient Jesus movement, which has become poignant by its subsequent wholesale dismissal by Christian missions. But what does it have to do with Sabbath Economics? As the primal catechism of Exodus 16 outlines (2A), a sharing-based ethos of community economics rooted in a cosmology of grace can be subverted (and ultimately destroyed) by two kinds of selfish behavior:

1. *Taking too much of the gift* (Exod 16:16–18). Luke's missionary instructions articulate a model for *receiving* hospitality with an eye toward problems of overreaching (or overstaying). Jesus understood that practicing intentional vulnerability and dependence are the

best hedges against presumptions of entitlement or pathologies of greed that turn *guest* into *conquest*. I have invoked the extractive and exploitive history of colonizing missions because it so painfully reveals the genocidal consequences of ignoring Jesus's instructions about self-limitation and replacing them with ideologies of superiority and domination. As Patrick Wolfe put it succinctly, "settler colonizers come to stay" on an "expropriated land base."[14] Needless to say, this is the *opposite* of bringing good news.

2. *Not sharing Commonwealth resources to which one has access* (Exod 16:19). Implied in the missionary instructions is the conviction that hospitality will be extended in traditional village networks, and an itinerant organizer for the Great Economy actually strengthens this ethos by calling on it. As long as missionaries reciprocate with the gifts of healing, mutual aid, and solidarity, and do not stay too long or consume inappropriately, they are encouraging the settled to keep circulating sustenance.

Receiving and giving material hospitality are intrinsic to community economics. This resonates with Indigenous practices of gift exchange, summed up by Lewis Hyde: "A cardinal property of the gift [is]: whatever we have been given is supposed to be given away again, not kept. . . . The only essential is this: the gift must always move. . . . 'One man's gift . . . must not be another man's capital.'"[15] In his instructions for how to build a movement, and how *not* to, Jesus tells the two pillars of Sabbath Economics, though one wouldn't see them in this section of Luke unless looking through this lens. Luke's wilderness feeding, in turn, shows hospitality to vulnerable people in hard times through the practice of mutual aid. I turn now to explore this venerable tale of "enough for all," as well as the equally well-known parable of the Good Samaritan—a related illustration of sustenance in the desert not usually read as a Sabbath Economics lesson.

B. Showing

Wilderness Provision (9:10–17, 10:25–37)

One of the final oracles of Second Isaiah is the beautiful, if ironic, phrase "you that have no money, buy without money or price" (Isa 55:1, cited at the top of this chapter). It was likely written shortly after the return of the Babylonian exiles to Jerusalem after 536 BCE, a time of widespread deprivation. Christopher B. Hays writes: "The city had not been rebuilt since its destruction by the Babylonians fifty years earlier, social and economic structures were weak, and there were struggles for the most desirable land between the returnees and those who had remained in the land."[16] Poor subsistence farmers who had stayed in Palestine while the elites were deported to Babylon had likely never seen money, since barter, honor, and generalized reciprocity sufficed in their hyper-local world. Yet currency and market-based economies were beginning to colonize the Mediterranean world, undermining the older village ethos of mutual aid. The prophet invites them to an old-school feast in which everyone is satisfied without cost.

In a Sabbath Economics cosmology, surplus belongs to those who are lacking basics, and abundance is to be enjoyed equitably in community. This idea shows up in Luke repeatedly, nowhere more prominently than in the story of loaves and fish. Modern readers tend to approach this "miracle" story with suspicion; shaped by a modern scientific worldview, we distance ourselves from stories of the "supernatural" in one of two ways. Liberals, in order to preserve rationalist assumptions, shrug off the idea of magically multiplying bread as primitive legend, then proceed to rescue the story through moralizing interpretations. In order to preserve the authority of the text, conservatives affirm a miracle, but discount our capacity to reproduce such abundance; amazing things like that happened back then, but not in our world, and not by *our* agency. Both approaches ignore the fact that Jesus's exhortation at the heart of the story—"*You* give them something to eat" (Luke 9:13)—is directed at *us*. These misinterpretations are reinforced by the way(s) in which this famous gospel story has already been interpreted to us through neatly packaged spiritual lessons from Global North pulpits or in church doctrines. Many Christians understand this story as a foreshadowing of the Last Supper: the eucharistic mystery thus eclipses any concern about realities of hunger or economic justice then or now.

This text is better understood through its own intertextuality—that is, its referencing and re-narrating of older biblical stories. As noted, Luke's account generally follows Mark's first wilderness feeding (Mark 6:31–44), which is already tied to the return of the Twelve from their inaugural mission (Mark 6:30 // Luke 9:10a). Mark portrays it as a retreat from the press of the crowd, emphasizing the setting as a "deserted place" twice.[17] Dusk falls upon the crowd that has followed him into the wilderness (Luke 9:11–12a).[18] The disciples urge Jesus to dispatch people to neighboring villages and fields to find lodging and provisions (9:12b)—ignoring his ethos of hospitality just articulated.[19] Jesus responds bluntly to this attempt to solve the problem of scarcity by relying on market economics: "*You* give them something to eat" (9:13a). The disciples are incredulous, indignant at the prospect of having to meet the crowd's needs by having to "buy food for all these people" (9:13b).[20]

While they agonize, Jesus organizes—and the numbers noted in 9:14 tell an important tale. First, we are told that "there were about five thousand men" present—meaning many more if counting women and children (see Matt 14:21). Such a crowd would have been larger than all but the three largest cities in Roman

Palestine, and up to fifty times that of a typical village—thus attracting the attention of the authorities.[21] Little wonder that following this episode, Jesus inquires about public perceptions of his work; the disciples answer that he has earned the reputation of a prophet (9:18–20), to which Jesus reveals that he will indeed face a prophet's fate—as will they (9:21–27).

Jesus delegates his disciples to arrange the people into "groups of about fifty."[22] This would approximate the size of a small Palestinian hamlet, which is where most of the crowd would have originated. Jesus's strategy seems to be to deconstruct the crowd into a smaller, more familiar social ecology in order to draw on their native peasant competence for shared consumption at such an intimate community scale. He then proceeds to bless and distribute the loaves and fish (9:14–16). The only miracle reported is that "all ate and were satisfied" (9:17).

It has often been noted—fueling traditional eucharistic readings of this moment—that the formula in 9:16 is nearly identical with the Last Supper: "Took . . . blessed . . . broke . . . gave . . ."[23] Narrative common sense, however, would assume that we should read the *later* episode in light of the *earlier* one, not vice versa (see epilogue, i). In fact, the allusions in this wilderness meal point back, not forward, to several stories from the Hebrew Bible, which provide a better lens through which to interpret this episode.

The wilderness setting and hunger-and-bread plot obviously invoke Luke's account of Jesus's temptations. Those who insist on a supernatural multiplication of loaves are unwittingly echoing Satan's logic there: turn stones into bread! Jesus, however, directed our attention instead to the *manna* story and Sabbath Economics in his response to the Devil (4:4; 2A). In the Bethsaida desert, as in Exodus 16, the focus is not upon miracles, but on instructions for gathering and distributing to ensure community sufficiency. But there is another old tradition upon which this gospel story also draws: the "food signs" of the prophet Elisha (2 Kg 4:38–44).

The scenario is a time of famine (2 Kg 4:38), which the Bible understood as both a natural and social disaster resulting from human economic systems of greed.[24] Elisha encounters a scene in which local people, driven to desperation by hunger, must return to ancient ways of foraging to survive (4:39). However, they are no longer competent in these traditional practices, which have atrophied due to forced integration into the command economies of empire. So here, desperate peasants unwittingly gather poisonous gourds: "There is death in the pot!" (4:40). Elisha first "heals" the soup pot (4:41), then turns his attention to bread. The loaves brought to him are from new grain (4:42), inferring that they are first fruits offerings appropriate to the early harvest feast of Shavuot (see Lev 23:15–21). While normally these would be offered back to God by priests, in this crisis Elisha redirects them toward those in need. In a line to which Luke's Jesus has alluded, Elisha instructs: "Give it to the people to eat" (4:42). Here, as in the Gospel story, this is met with incredulity (4:43). But the "Word of the Lord" prevails, transforming a situation of artificial scarcity into a celebration of God's natural abundance: "And they ate and had some left over" (4:44). This is precisely the conclusion of Jesus's re-enactment in the wilderness (Luke 9:17).

By following intertextual paths back into Moses and the prophets, we see that Jesus's feeding of multitudes is *economic* before it is *eucharistic*. Jesus is remembering Sabbath Economics, asserting that the divine economy of grace, not imperial markets, is the way to address problems of deprivation. This tradition teaches sharing of available resources in cooperative consumption. The real worlds of both Elisha and Jesus (and indeed of our own global economy) were characterized by widespread hunger and poverty that resulted from feudal systems of land ownership and extractive economic systems that benefited the urban elite while disenfranchising the rural poor. In such an economy, practices of enough-and-then-some for *everyone* were, and are, miraculous indeed.

The first Christians appear to have understood these connections. Luke's account of the church's inaugural breaking of bread—on the Feast of Shavuot!—animates a thoroughgoing communal redistribution of wealth (Acts 2:42–47; epilogue, iii). Eucharist rightly stands at the center of the church's life as an invitation to re-member—hyphenated because it is about metabolizing in our ecclesial body—not only Jesus's death but also the economy of grace practiced by our ancestors in the faith. Unfortunately, just as the disciples wanted to send the hungry crowds away to the villages in the gospel story, so do we today harbor too much faith in the ability of the market to meet peoples' needs in a world deeply divided between haves and have-nots. In the epilogue, I will argue that Christians need to re-anchor our celebration of Eucharist in biblical traditions of Sabbath Economics.

* * *

In Luke, the wilderness feeding follows closely upon Jesus's first set of missionary instructions. A second, more controversial showing similarly follows the second set. Jesus first takes a moment to celebrate that the revelation of the Great Economy has been embraced by his "lowly" followers, if not by the "wise and intelligent" (10:18–22). Countering his "Woe" on the cities (10:13), he pronounces another blessing (*makarios*) upon those given "eyes to see and ears to hear" what so many have missed (10:23–24).

This affirmation of his community is abruptly interrupted, however, by a member of the educated elite: "Just then a certain lawyer stood up to test Jesus" (10:25a). That his intent was hostile is indicated by the verb *ekpeirazō*, which appears elsewhere in Luke only at the conclusion of the wilderness temptations, in Jesus's final rebuke of Satan: "You shall *not* test the Lord your God!" (4:12). It is also indicated by the question itself, which Luke changes from Mark's debate over "which is the greatest commandment" (Mark 12:28) to the challenge posed again later by a rich landowner: "What must I do to inherit (*klēronomeō*) the Great Economy?" (Luke 10:25b = 18:18; see 12A). As there, this changes the issue from theological to *economic*, since the verb connotes material inheritance. This reflects a conceit typical of the elite, who presume salvation to be like the intergenerational transfers of wealth they enjoy. We will see this also in a question about inheritance (*klēronomian*) in 12:13, which provokes Jesus's diatribe on greed (8A).

Jesus will respond here with an economic parable, but first he engages his challenger in the expected verbal riposte. His double counter-question is telling: "What is written in the law? How do you read it?" (10:26).[25] This reflects the discipline of hermeneutics discussed in the introduction. It is not enough simply to cite a passage; we must also examine the way in which we read. As Fowl and Jones put it: "As a social activity, interpretation is confirmed, constrained and determined by the political constitution of those contexts in which interpretation takes place."[26] Jesus simplifies the hermeneutic issue in his response to the lawyer's answer (10:27). The best interpretation is embodied practice: "Do this and live" (10:28).[27] To do is to know in Hebrew epistemology.

How the lawyer reads is immediately revealed by his "self-justifying" claim of ignorance. He presses his interrogation (as lawyers do), offering a kind of courtroom objection: "But who is my neighbor?" (10:29). Problematizing straightforward texts in a way that renders practice impossible or ambiguous is a classic intellectual dodge. This occasions perhaps Jesus's most well-known, if widely decontextualized, parable: the Good Samaritan (10:30–36).

It is only the second full-blown parable so far in Luke's narrative, and the first that is completely Lukan material, so this is a good time to pause and consider this literary form. The parables preserved in the Synoptic Gospels likely represent the very oldest traditions in the New Testament. Despite this (or perhaps because of it), our North American churches still handle these stories timidly, and often not at all. Perhaps we intuit that there is something so wild and subversive about these tales that they are better kept at a safe distance from our consciousness. Many Christians simply ignore parables, believing that Jesus's teaching was eclipsed by later theological developments: his work on the Cross (evangelicals); Pauline doctrine as read through the Enlightenment (mainstream Protestants); or the Church and its Magisterium (Catholics and Orthodox). Parables are thus apprehended as quaint, or poetic, or theologically figurative—but hardly relevant for Christian discipleship. They are relentlessly spiritualized, such that stories about landless peasants and rich landowners, or lords and slaves, or lepers and lawyers are lifted out of their social and historical context and reshaped into theological or moralistic fables bereft of any political or economic edge—or consequence.

When the sociocultural context of a parable is ignored or suppressed, however, we inevitably recontextualize the story in terms of our own unconscious political assumptions. While our imposed schemas often defy the coherence of the text itself, this interpretive strategy functions to thoroughly domesticate the parable under *our* status quo. Stories meant to challenge our preconceptions are ironically used to legitimate them. This is how we disarm the Gospel's most powerful rhetorical weapons, whose purpose is to rescue us from our domestication by that same status quo.

"Let the wise hear and gain in learning, and the discerning acquire skill to understand *mashal* and figure, the words of the wise and their riddles" (Prov 1:5–6). Parables are by design irresistibly allegorical; the Hebrew word *mashal* comes from the root *m-sh-l*, meaning "to be like."[28] The most generic definition of allegory is the figurative treatment of one subject under the guise of another. The question becomes, then, what are the subjects being treated? This is where the church has too often jumped from trying to understand Jesus's allegory to ourselves *allegorizing* the *allegory*. Hence the tired old trope that parables are "earthly stories with heavenly meanings."

Jesus, however, was on a mission to get us to see the world differently. His pedagogic purpose was twofold: 1) to unmask our illusions about the status quo and our place in it, and then to 2) open our hearts and minds to the Great Economy (itself a metaphor). Today this is called deconstructing and reconstructing consciousness. Jesus thus employs two kinds of parables: those that attempt to unmask and critique the way the world *really is* (e.g., "there was a certain rich man. . .and a certain beggar. . ." 16:19f), and those that offer a vision of the way the world *could be* (e.g., the Parable of Prodigal Son, 15:11–32). The genius of these stories was that they narrated recognizable scenarios in plain language that any illiterate peasant could understand: farming and shepherding, being in debt and doing hard labor, exclusion from banquets and from the houses of the rich. These familiar vignettes draw the listener in, only to throw a surprise twist that challenges popular assumptions about what is proprietary and what is possible: a miraculous harvest, an enemy as a friend, unexpected vindication. In fact, then, parables were "earthy stories with heavy meanings," as my teacher William Herzog put it.[29]

This is certainly the case with the parable of the Samaritan. Oakman has done a careful social-scientific reading of this text from the perspective of Jesus's peasant consciousness, as "a careful observer of agrarian life" and "rural artisan working often within typical peasant contexts."[30] Oakman identifies several aspects of this perspective that challenge a simple moralizing reading of this parable,[31] which I summarize here:

- As an opponent of Roman occupation, and of domination by the Judean elite, Jesus would likely have shared peasant sympathies with the social banditry portrayed in the parable (if not with its violence) as a form of popular economic resistance.

- Though they might have criticized the clerical aloofness of the priest and Levite, peasants would have understood why they needed, for purity reasons, to avoid the scene of the crime. They were merely practicing the expected negative reciprocity with people outside their ethnic and family circles.
- Peasants would have shared Jewish suspicion of the Samaritan, not only because of their longstanding ethnic rivalry, but because the man is characterized as a traveling commercial agent (carrying luxury goods like oil and wine on a beast of burden, 10:34), which identified him as an extractive trader operating in Judean territory against the interests of local agrarians.
- Finally, the "inn" to which the Samaritan takes the victim was a space regarded by peasants as unsavory, violent, and unclean; they would have seen his "blank check" commitment (10:35b) as a hilariously ignorant invitation for the innkeeper to take advantage of the whole situation.

But Oakman contends that Jesus would have "counted on this kind of response" to the story.[32]

The parable's surprise is precisely the unexpectedness of the Samaritan's action. It is a sign of the Great Economy: a reversal not of fortune but of character. This resonates with Jesus's Nazareth *drash*, which reminded his people that outsiders could be subjects of God's Jubilee (4A). Here the social other is the animator of "imprudent" generosity. Oakman has carefully calculated the buying power of the two *denarii* the man leaves with the innkeeper (10:35a). He concludes that they "represent around three weeks' worth of food for one person, or about 1 percent of an ancient Palestinian family's annual budget," which "might feed the wounded man for around 24 days (two meals a day 'board')."[33] This and the Samaritan's commitment to make up for any additional expenses symbolize an almost unimaginable act of sharing—all on behalf of a stranger in need.

Like the feeding of the five thousand, this scene takes place in a marginal space, the desert between Jerusalem and Jericho; it, too, shows Sabbath Economics through a different kind of radical hospitality in the wilderness. The village ethos of mutual aid shown by sharing bread and fish here extends well beyond ethnicity or kinship to an enemy helping an enemy. As he did with Simon in his first mini-parable (7:42), Jesus here poses a rhetorical query in his closing exchange, circling back to the lawyer's dodge:

Jesus: "Which of these three, do you think, was a neighbor to the man who fell into the hands of the robbers?" (10:36).

Lawyer: "The one doing mercy to him" (*poiēsas to eleos*).[34]

Jesus: "Go and do likewise" (*poie homoiōs*).

Note the refrain of the verb "to do": hermeneutics is ultimately defined by praxis. In a Sabbath Economics cosmology, to love God is to act as neighbor in compassionate solidarity with human suffering, *no matter how deep into our own pocket we must go*. Mercy is shown through the redistribution of private wealth.[35]

CHAPTER SEVEN

Praying for Transformation

> Professor Very Pius, if Jesus's paradigmatic prayer (called the Lord's Prayer) has as its paramount concerns bread for subsistence in a time of hunger, relief from debt when an unjust debt structure crushed the people underfoot, and the establishment of God's sole sovereignty when the peoples' misery was largely the by-product of Caesar's imperial control, then why is the Lord's Prayer not also called the Lord's Paradigmatic Critique of Political Economy? The Lord's Model of Social Analysis?
>
> —Obery Hendricks, "Guerilla Exegesis"[1]

THE PRACTICE OF prayer weaves through Luke's narrative from beginning (1:10) to end (22:40–46). It lies at the core of Jesus's consciousness and mission. He maintains a contemplative discipline seeking God in the wilderness (5:16; 6:12; 11:1), and exhibits both self-reflection (9:18) and inner struggle (22:41–42). When he prays, sometimes the Voice speaks back: hovering above a magical bird at river baptism (3:21), joining his consultation with Moses and Elijah on the mountain of Transfiguration (9:28–29). Jesus speaks of wrong ways to pray, such as "those who devour widows' houses and for a pretense make long prayers" (20:47), and right ways, such as interceding for one's enemies (6:28) or resisting temptation (22:40, 46). He tells back-to-back parables later in the narrative to illustrate the difference between genuine and performative prayer (18:1–14; 12A), and draws parallels between prayerful and political tenacity, which we'll explore in section B. At only one point, however, does Jesus specifically instruct his disciples *how*, and for *what*, to pray. That is there we begin this chapter.

A. Telling

The Disciples' Prayer and Israel's First Catechism (11:1–4)

The Lord's Prayer is the most public prayer in North American culture—typically recited out loud in church and known to many beyond its walls. Yet ironically was a secret among the first Christians, revealed only after baptismal initiation. Christians imagine we know this prayer by heart; but while this may technically be true, we rarely read, hear or pray it as Jesus's urgent marching orders.

Luke's version is, again, shorter than Matthew's more familiar form.[2] Its composition means to link to Jesus's three temptations in his wilderness (3B), which correspond to Jesus's first three petitions in reverse order:

Disciples' Prayer Petition	Wilderness Temptation
May Your Name be held holy	Turn stones into bread
May Your Kingdom come	Rule all the Kingdoms of the Earth
Give us each day enough bread	Throw yourself from the Temple pinnacle

The Prayer thus begins by reiterating Jesus's resistance to the archetypal characteristics of the Devil's Domination System: extractive economics, imperial politics, and theological presumptions of omnipotence. This is why these two Lukan stories should be read synoptically. In taking a closer look at the first three petitions, I will proceed in reverse order (that is, according to their order in the Temptations narrative).

The third (and fourth) petition of Luke's Prayer summarizes the central concerns of Sabbath Economics: material sustenance and release from debt. Oakman translates the adjective *epiousios* in 11:3 as "give us today bread in *abundance*," echoing the *manna* story.[3] This is followed with an echo of the Jubilee (11:4): "Release [*aphes,* aorist imperative] our sins [*hamartias*]; for we ourselves are releasing [*aphiomen*] everyone indebted to us [*opheilonti,* present active participle)." It is important to recognize two aspects of Luke's construction:

1. The verbal tenses turn Jubilee from a periodic redistribution to a *standing practice*; and
2. For Luke, the nouns "debt" and "sin" are again essentially equivalent, as we saw in 7:39–43 (5B). Oakman further points out that in Aramaic, the oral language of Jesus, "the same word means sin or debt (*hôbâ*)."[4] Moreover, in the Greek New Testament, debt and sin are controlled by the same verb (*aphiemi*).

The third petition is a succinct telling of Sabbath Economics, just like the First Temptation.

Just as we traced that theme through Torah and the Prophets (chapter 2), we can do the same for the first two petitions/Temptations. The Prayer calls for a full realization of God's Kingdom (11:2c). In the second wilderness temptation, Satan parades "all the kingdoms of the world" (*pasas tas basileias tēs oikoumenēs*, 4:5) before Jesus. Matthew's version uses *kosmos,* but Luke uses *oikoumenēs*, a common reference in Roman discourse to the "civilized world," because he understands the Roman *imperium* as the essence of "all kingdoms."[5] This scenario articulates concisely the pathological nature of centralized and hierarchical politics: the pantheon of history's empires can be viewed "in a moment," because to see one is to see them all. And they all are administered by Satan, who generously offers to share his rule with Jesus—as his vassal! Our churches long ago abandoned such a clear perspective on the State.

Though Israel was birthed as a people sprung from oppression in Egypt, they were constantly tempted to go back. In the story of Gideon, a hero of the Israelite confederacy's liberation struggle, the people want to make him king; he however defers to YHWH's kingship (Jd 8:22–23). This exemplary moment is immediately followed by a warning tale about Abimelech's murderous grab for power, which is denounced in Jotham's wry parable about the olive, fig and vine, each of whom refuse to abandon their productive vocations to become "king" over all the other plants (Jd 9:1–21).

Another fateful turning point is narrated in 1 Samuel 8. The community, now settled, again gathers in complaint, this time demanding "a king to govern us" (1 Sam 8:5). Samuel, representing the old wilderness confederacy's polity of Judges (see Jd 1:16), warns of dire consequences from such a political project. In its wake will rise militarism and compulsory conscription (Jd 8:11–13) and state expropriation through eminent domain and oppressive taxation (Jd 8:14–18). But Israel was losing its vision of "holiness"—that is, its distinct identity—and was "determined to have a king over us so that we also may be like other nations" (Jd 8:19). Soon enough a monarchy indeed established its hegemony, making Israel indistinguishable from other regional powers. This drift was, of course, contested by the prophets (most famously by Nathan in his confrontation with David, 2 Sam 12). But court chroniclers lamented it too; Jacques Ellul has shown how they systematically *reproached* rather than eulogized the "great" kings of Israel, defying the historiographic conventions of antiquity.[6]

Following in this tradition, Jesus upholds the *exclusive* sovereignty of YHWH (Deut 6:13 = Luke 4:8), undermining all human claims to hegemony. Luke shows this conviction in a variety of ways in his narrative:

- through Jesus's proclamation of the "Kingdom of God" (Luke 4:43; 10:9);[7]
- in Jesus's delegitimization of the Davidic dynasty (11:31; 12:27; 20:41–44), as well as that of the Herodians (13:32);
- by choosing twelve apostles, invoking the symbol of the old Israelite tribal confederacy (6:13–16); and
- by subverting conventional expectations of political leadership through his own messianic practice, all the way to the cross (19:38; 23:1–3).

The first-century authorities understood clearly that Jesus's proclamation of God's Sovereignty was treasonous; it is *we* who have lost that plot.

The lead petition of the Disciples' Prayer invokes the holiness of God's name (11:2). YHWH (the "I AM") is no empire's patron, but the animator of the only truly sacred historical project: human liberation (Exod 3:14). This petition corresponds with the third and final wilderness test: the Devil transports Jesus to Jerusalem and sets him "on the pinnacle of the Temple" (Luke 4:9). It is a remarkable scenario: Satan with Jesus in tow, Satan with access to the Holiest place, Satan quoting scripture! It ought to give us pause about every religious claim. Satan knows that behind every dominant political-economic regime is a theological claim to divine patronage, and thus an entitlement to historical success by any means necessary. So, he thumps his Bible, choosing his text carefully: Psalm 91:11–12, a powerful statement of God's protection of those who "abide."

The Devil seems to know how this psalm, when read through the hermeneutics of power and privilege, can become a tune of national prerogative and invulnerability, and eventually an ode to empire. Witness how the Lutheran hymn "A Mighty Fortress Is Our God" (Ps 91:2) became a song of the Reich, or the fact that "though a thousand fall at your side" (Ps 91:7) remains a favorite verse of US military chaplains. Drafting God into *our* historical project, in order to presume God's blessing, is at the heart of the current resurgence of Christian nationalism in the US—not to mention modern Israel's continuing war on Palestinians.

The setting of this temptation is the highest precipice of the "dwelling place of the Most High" (Ps 91:9): the Herodian Second Temple, rising above the gleaming capital city, center of ancient Israel's universe. How radically different this space was from the earthy holy places of Hebrew origins. Abram needed only a "teaching oak" to build the Bible's first altar (Gen 12:6–7), Jacob only a "dreaming stone" to find the "gate of heaven" (Gen 28:10–19). Joshua erected a simple cairn from river rock to announce Israel's uprising against their Canaanite overlords (Josh 4:1–10) and drafted a single standing stone to bear witness to the people's covenant with YHWH (Josh 24:25–28). Above all, YHWH's final commandment on Sinai specifically prohibited building shrines made of hewn stone (Exod 20:22–26)—which is to say, *temples.*[8]

This is why the original cultic "center" of early Israel was a hand-carried mobile shrine called an Ark. This tabernacle carried the covenant, and on top of it stood a crucial symbol: an *empty* throne (Exod 25). Once an Israelite monarchic formation arose and consolidated power, however, it required a Temple. This is reflected in King David's anxieties about the asymmetry between his "dwelling in a house of cedar," while "the ark of God dwells in a tent" (2 Sam 7:2). The prophet Nathan mediated God's sharp rejoinder:

> Would you build *Me* a house to dwell in? I have not dwelt in a house since the day I brought up the people of Israel from Egypt to this day,

> but I have been moving about in a tent for my dwelling. In all places where I have moved with all the people of Israel, did I speak a word with any of the judges of Israel, whom I commanded to shepherd my people Israel, saying, "Why have you not built me a house of cedar?" (2 Sam 7:5–7)

In a concession, YHWH does however agree to build *David's* House (that is, his familial dynasty), and it is David's son Solomon who is allowed to construct a "house for my name" (2 Sam 7:12–13). But from the start, this project becomes a reification of Israel's imperial ambitions.

As bluntly narrated in 1 Kgs 5–7, lowlights of this building project included:

- foreign alliances to secure resource-extraction (1 Kg 5:7–12);
- construction using forcibly conscripted labor (5:13–16);
- the "side project" of Solomon's own grandiose "trophy home" (7:1–12); and
- in language dripping with irony: "at the king's command they quarried out great, costly stones in order to lay the foundation of the house with dressed stones" (5:17)—in specific violation of YHWH's "eleventh" commandment.

The concentration of wealth necessitates a hierarchy of political power, which in turn relies inevitably on a centralized cult for its ideological legitimation.

Local shrines were originally envisioned as storehouses for centrifugal redistribution of community surplus; a Temple-State, however, exerted *centripetal* force, drawing resources to the center. Instead of a place where sacrifices were offered on behalf of the people, it became a place where the people were offered in sacrifice to the regime. Do not trust in these deceptive words: "This is the Temple of the Lord," railed Jeremiah; "has this house, which is called by my name, become a den of robbery?" (Jer 7:4, 11). Jesus will remember these very words in his "exorcism" of that Temple (Luke 19:45–46) and will specifically repudiate the exploitation of the poor by the demands of the Temple cultus (21:1–6).

Teetering on the Temple pinnacle in the third temptation, Jesus clings to the Deuteronomist one final time: "You shall not test the Lord" (Luke 4:12 = Deut 6:16). The argument comes full circle: the Deuteronomist remembers Massah ("place of testing"), where wilderness Israel again despaired and began pining for Egypt (see Exod 17:7). Jesus for a third time chooses the road less traveled, insisting upon the radical Yahwist principle of divine non-identity and choosing the "unhoused God." Neither institutions nor edifices can keep God's name holy.

Having failed to seduce Jesus to take the fall, the Devil departs, seeking a more "opportune time" (Luke 4:13). The word here, remarkably, is *kairos*. It is Luke's pointed reminder that every moment of critical choice to embrace the Way of discipleship has the potential to be a moment of capitulation to empire. This is why Luke's Disciples' Prayer revisits this terrain, and petition by petition teaches us to "know by heart" our vocation: to keep YHWH's name undomesticated; to insist on God's Sovereignty over the empires of our moment; and to embrace Sabbath Economics by ensuring that enough bread is on everyone's table and committing to deconstruct debt-poverty *every day*. It is Jesus's most concise catechism.

Fittingly, the Prayer's final petition, "Lead us not into temptation," resonates with Jesus's final rebuke of Satan in the wilderness (4:12). Every time we recite this Prayer, then, is a *kairos* moment to remember and reenact this vision-quest, to examine the choices of *our* ancestors and lay bare the roots of *our* national pathologies. The three archetypal crossroads that faced Israel and Jesus also haunt our history, as we are inheritors of the profoundly flawed legacy of "progress" and children of empire. But we have been taught how and what to pray, so as to remain disciples.

B. Showing

Prayer as Personal and Political Tenacity (11:5–26)

The sequence that flows directly from the Prayer functions to de-sentimentalize our notions of both personal and political spirituality. Jesus spins the first of three stories unique to Luke that portray the practice of prayer as dogged, even desperate tenacity in petitioning for justice and mercy. The first story, which we'll look at here, is set in a peasant hamlet and narrates the ethos of economic reciprocity between village "friends." This is a plumbline of Sabbath Economics, but it requires stubborn insistence to resist the corrosive patronage culture of the rich (11:5–8). Later in Luke, we'll see the same principle affirmed in a more political context in the two other related episodes of persistent petitioning (18:1–14; 12A).

Jesus concludes the Prayer rather abruptly and proceeds to spin an illustrative story. It is not a parable but a real-life hypothetical. A neighbor needs help to fulfill the village obligation to show hospitality to an unexpected traveler who has arrived "at midnight" (11:5–6). Since traversing the desert after dark was highly unusual (and dangerous), it may be that this is a distressed sojourner, or even the kind of itinerant missionary instructed in 9:1–6.[9] If the traveler is a "friend" (*philos* is used four times in this passage) or otherwise known, the relationship requires the village to receive him. If he is an immigrant or resident alien, Torah obligates both hospitality (Lev 19:34; Deut 10:17–19) and sustenance (Lev 19:10, Deut 14:28–29). Either way, the unexpected guest is the responsibility of the whole village.

Herzog sketches the scenario more fully.[10] Village women would have baked only "bread for the day's needs" (as in the Prayer!), often in communal ovens. This meant the protagonist of the story would have known who in the village had the most recently baked loaves, appropriate for hospitality. His ask is thus not unreasonable: though bread was central to the meal, and thus the first order of business (three loaves were the minimum required for the guest), other neighbors would be expected to community-source the meal as well. Most likely the persistent knocking at a door at this hour would have awakened much of the small village. Moreover, the one being solicited is called a friend, so this request is based on an expectation of reciprocity. The twist in the story is his refusal (11:7), which would have been not only uncharacteristic but shameful. This request for help appeals not to charity or friendship but to a fellow villager to uphold collective honor. Malina and Rohrbaugh add: "The petitioner threatens to expose the potential shamelessness of the sleeper. By morning the entire village would know of his refusal to provide hospitality. He thus gives in to avoid public exposure as a shameless person."[11]

Herzog, however, emphasizes another factor that could explain the refuser's reluctance: the way in which patronage pressure from urban elites was undermining the "moral economy of the peasant." To counteract the inevitably extractive nature of their "client" relationships with landowners and commodity traders, peasants clung fiercely to

> the norm of reciprocity, which was the primary form of risk insurance associated with the village. Reciprocity meant that every peasant family was guaranteed a minimal subsistence from the resources of the village and could press a claim to the village's resources to the degree that its reserves could cover those needs. This expectation governed family relations in the village and provided "something of a living normative model of equity and justice" [James C. Scott]... If a village neighbor asked for help, one always agreed to help because, by doing so, one obligated the neighbor to reciprocate when the situation was reversed... The importance of this claim can hardly be overstated during a period when elites were become more predatory toward peasants and effecting changes in the social stratification of rural life in Palestine by forcing more and more smallholders into increasing forms of dependency as tenants and day laborers.[12]

The atrophy of reciprocity habits in stressed peasant villages dominated by patronage demands perhaps better accounts for the "closed door" response in the story.

Jesus commends the protagonist's shameless persistence in the traditional ways, enabling the village ethos of mutual aid to keep functioning as a strategy of resistance (11:8).[13] To modern middle class sensibilities, his strategy seems overly coercive or even manipulative, given our socialization into the individualist culture of "polite autonomy." But this assertive villager is showing the necessary commitment required to uphold a community covenant of reciprocity that, in turn, upholds collective justice. We'll see resonances of this in the later story of the tenacious widow and the unjust judge (18:1–8, 12A).

In his next teaching, Jesus grounds this ethos of reciprocity in God's radical generosity (11:9–13), a Q tradition that also appears in Matthew's Sermon on the Mount (Matt 7:7–11). He invokes contrast in the "open door" policy of a cosmology of grace, in which we only need to ask a willing Giver (Luke 11:9–10). This alternative social framework posits a universal fictive kinship under the loving parenting of a benevolent Creator (11:13b). If the previous strategy of persistent petitioning seems too socially aggressive to modern Westerners, we shrug this one off as unrealistic, having been enculturated into an "everyone for themselves" social Darwinism.

Yet Jesus's two extreme examples demonstrate polemically how in fact this ethos operates in daily life everywhere at the level of the kinship group, even among the most selfish (11:11–12). All we have to do is extend the ethos of the household! The radically hospitable character of the One being approached (unlike the closed door villager of the previous story) encourages and empowers us to press not only for daily bread, but for the big, world-transforming vision of the Prayer. Jesus will illustrate this again in his advocacy for table fellowship *beyond* one's circle of friends (14:12; 9B).

Jesus understands, however, the dialectical truth of a world ruled by the *opposite* of a benevolent ethos. So, he turns to reflect on prayer as struggle with the Powers, a reality check about the spiritual and political forces around and within us that seek to suppress our imaginary and discourage practices of an open door society of solidarity. Luke here circles back to pick up an important Markan sequence, in which the Galilean authorities launch their counterinsurgency campaign to delegitimize Jesus. To this the Nazarene responds with quilled queries and militant metaphors (11:15–23 // Mark 3:22–27).

The occasion is Jesus's healing of a man who has been silenced by a demonic spirit (11:14a). At the outset of Luke's narrative, Zechariah was muted by his skepticism about the good news of a radically different possibility (1:19–20). Here this man is liberated to speak (11:14b), as was Zechariah (1:63–64); both stories use the verbs *laleō* (to talk) and *thaumazō* (to marvel). In light of the sequence to follow, it is not a stretch to suggest that this "mute spirit" represents for Luke a symptom of our domestication under empire, which "dumbs down" our imaginations and silences our dissent.[14]

Jesus is accused of collaborating with Beelzebul in his exorcising, while others demand a "sign from heaven" (11:15–16). In other words, his liberating work is dismissed as either suspicious or just not spectacular enough! Interestingly, Luke does not specify that those accusing him are local authorities, as do both Mark (Mark 3:22, scribes) and Matthew (Matt 12:24, Pharisees). Perhaps this implies that *all* of us harbor doubts about, or hostilities toward, the prospects of radical liberation. "Knowing their thoughts" (Luke 11:17a, as in 6:8), Jesus offers a terse lesson on the fragility of a regime that can only respond to a rising social movement of difference, dissent, or deviation by denouncing it as heretical (in our day, race-baiting, red-scaring, or accusations of terrorism). Such a "divided House" will inevitably collapse from internal contradictions (11:17b).[15]

He then proceeds to probe the absurdity of their assertion that one can "cast out demons by the prince of demons" by posing a string of three conditional conundrums:

- 11:18: "If Satan also is divided against himself, how will his kingdom stand?" This political language implies an indictment of the Herodians.
- 11:19: "If I cast out demons by Beelzebul, by whom do your children cast them out?" This second query wonders whether these critics disapprove of *all* exorcists (since Jesus was not alone in this restorative/liberative practice).
- 11:20: "But if it is by the finger of God that I cast out demons, then the kingdom of God has come upon you!" This reference (unique to Luke) alludes to the old story of Pharaoh's magicians, who unsuccessfully competed with Moses's plagues, conceding that the Hebrews were empowered by "the finger of God" (Exod 8:15).[16] This concluding query implies that those who accuse him of siding with Beelzebul are agents of Pharaoh, trying to keep the people silent about an oppressive system! And they are on notice that an alternative "kingdom" is contesting their regime, just as in the old Exodus story.

Jesus now switches to the offensive, intensifying his metaphor of a house-in-danger in what is my favorite New Testament passage.

Luke offers a revealing *midrash* on Mark's remarkable image of the strongman's house (Luke's changes are underlined:

As long as a strongman, fully armed,
guards his own palace,
his goods are in peace;
but as soon as someone stronger than he
attacks and overpowers him,
he takes away from him all his armor on which he had relied, and redistributes his booty. (Luke 11:21–22)

But no one can enter a strongman's house and plunder his goods, unless he first binds the strongman; then indeed he may plunder his house. (Mark 3:27)

Let's examine how Luke reworks the scenario from Mark's burgling metaphor to one of taking back stolen wealth—from "binding" to "disarming and redistributing" the strongman's power.[17]

Luke expands Mark's single sentence into two contrasting conditional statements, best rendered: "As long as. . ." (*hotan,* 11:21a), ". . .but as soon as" (*epan,* 11:22a). He then layers in numerous differences and unique additions (underlined here):

- Mark's "house" becomes the man's "own palace" (*heautou aulēn*), a change with both economic and political overtones.
- Its owner "heavily arms himself"(*kathoplizō*; only here in the New Testament), still characteristic of the fortressed compounds of the rich today.[18]
- The purpose is to "guard"(*phulasso*) his "possessions" (*huparchontōn*; see discussion 5B). In stark contrast, Jesus will shortly issue a stern warning to "guard *against* all forms of greed"—especially the "abundance of possessions" (12:15; 8A).
- In a world of disparity, only *huparchonta* under armed guard will "be at peace"! Until this point in Luke's narrative, peace has connoted either divine or human greeting or blessing (*eirēnē,* seven times)—in other words, it is always *relational.* These first four bullet points all strongly suggest that the "palace" described here is a metaphor for the Roman Empire: Jesus has come to disturb the Pax Romana and divide the spoils of the armed rich (see 12:51).[19]
- "When one stronger than he appears" (*ho ischuroteros*) makes explicit what is implied by Mark, namely that Jesus is the "stronger one," which is how he was introduced by John (Mark 1:7 // Matt 3:11 // Luke 3:16). This is the "punchline" of this quasi-parable.[20]
- "He vanquishes him" (*nikaō*) borrows from the Greco-Roman military lexicon, part of Luke's anti-imperial spin (Nike was the Roman goddess of victory).[21]
- "Takes away his armor on which he relied" is a unique Lukan turn of phrase, poignantly describing the formidable nonviolent work of disarming the deepest layers of our personal and political trust in military security.[22]
- "Redistributes his *booty*": Luke deploys one more distinctive term to clinch his spin on the story: *skûlon* (only here in the New Testament). The man's barricaded wealth is the result of piracy, and must be redistributed (*diadidomi*) back to those who were looted. Fittingly, that compound verb appears only three other times: in Luke's call of the

> rich man (18:22; 12A); the Pentecost community of goods (Acts 4:35; epilogue, iii); and the Johannine distribution of loaves and fish (John 6:11).

Paying close attention to redactional details reveals how Luke shapes a received tradition in order to deepen his through-line theme of Sabbath Economics. His strongman account clearly anticipates his final object lesson: Jesus's "invasion and liberation" of Zacchaeus' "palace" (13A).

This sequence articulates a daunting imaginary of struggle. It invites us to recite daily the profound vision of personal and political transformation that is the Disciples' Prayer (11:1–4). It assures us that it is not futile to petition persistently for what we need (11:5–8) because the divine gift is free for the asking (11:9–13). On the other hand, the Prayer drafts us into the task of exorcising spirits that silence this vision, even in the teeth of those who would demonize us for so doing (11:14–20). This, in turn, takes us into battle with a fortressed ruling class, as Luke's Jesus fully politicizes what is at stake (11:21–22). It is little wonder that Jesus emphasizes the necessity of "gathering with the Stronger One," so that empire cannot "scatter" us further into isolation and alienation, despair and defeat (11:23)—perhaps the most concise rationale for coming together as church in the New Testament.

Demonic imagery and the exorcism practice of Jesus is uncannily revealing of our civilizational crisis. Tragically, these notions are either unwelcome or unintelligible to modernists. In contemporary Christianity, theological liberals shrink from its putatively "primitive" cosmology, while conservatives literalize Jesus's deep symbolism into a hyper-spiritualized kind of warfare that seems inspired more by militarism than by healing. Meanwhile, popular culture pathologizes or trivializes exorcism through zombie caricatures.

Yet exorcism is an intrinsic strand of Jesus's work in Luke (4:41; 6:18; 9:1, 49; 10:17; 13:32; similarly in the other synoptics). He engages demonic oppression afflicting persons (9:37–42), communities (4:33–36), and the political landscape (8:26–39). As agents of liberation, John (7:33) and Jesus are themselves demonized by the authorities, as we've just seen (11:14–20). But Luke's sequence here shows that fidelity to the catechism of the Prayer requires the inward and outward work of mapping and engaging our spiritual, psychological, social, economic, and political captivity under empire. The next teaching addresses exactly this, in arguably one of Jesus's strangest images (a Q tradition: Luke 11:24–26 // Matt 12:43–45).

This story is unique in being narrated from the point of view of the "unclean spirit" (used interchangeably with "demon" in Luke). It emphasizes the resiliency of pathological forces that *seem* to be resolved or healed, only to return more powerfully (or in greater multiplicity, 11:26).[23] The personification of a "stalking spirit" is strange to modern ears *until* we reconsider it through contemporary psychological lenses such as traumatic wounds and PTSD, cycles of dysfunctional behavior, or spiraling addictions. The intrapsychic experience of struggling for health and wholeness can feel like peeling an onion, each layer revealing another.

Just as illuminating is the social phenomenon of "hauntings." Sociologist Avery Gordon, in her important 1997 book *Ghostly Matters*, argues that "haunting is a constituent element of modern social life through which repressed or unresolved social violence makes itself known in everyday life, especially when supposedly over and done with (slavery, for instance) or when its oppressive nature is continuously denied."[24] Importantly, she emphasizes how reckoning with these ghosts *can* mobilize "individual, social, or political movements and change"—but *only* if they are faced. Indigenous scholar Eve Tuck names the oldest haunted history in North America:

> Genocide, desecration, poxed-blankets, rape, humiliation. . . . Settler colonialism is the management of those who have been made killable, once and future ghosts—those that had been destroyed, but also those that are generated in every generation. . . . Social life, settler colonialism, and haunting are inextricably bound; each ensures are always be more ghosts to return.[25]

A half-millennium of colonization has left no corner of the world untouched, and it is deeply woven into the fabric of our personal and political lives.

Martin Luther King voiced similar analysis: "For too long the depth of racism in American life has been underestimated. The surgery necessary to extract it is complex and detailed. As a beginning, we must X-ray our history and reveal the full extent of the disease."[26] It turns out, then, that this weirdest of Jesus's parable-like stories offers an uncanny description of the complex journey required to heal individual and collective hauntings. The unclean spirits of mammon, Moloch, and Mars, which possess our political bodies and occupy our body politic, inevitably come back seven times stronger when we try to change.[27] Anyone who has labored to overcome personal addiction, for example, or to free their community from systemic oppression, can attest to constantly having to confront the layers of control and conformity within them and around them.

As I have noted several times, Jesus was not a socializing physician, patching people up to resume business as usual. He was a *radical* healer, excavating beneath facades, seeking the *roots* of our personal and political pathologies. He had only one requirement: we must admit that we are sick (5:31). As he points out in a later parable about prayer, Jesus can't do much for us if we fancy ourselves pious, or successful, or "politically correct" (18:9–14). He can, however, build a movement with those who commit to the hard, lifelong work of delving "seven layers deep," and of turning their personal and political histories around (5:32).

Part III

Parables and Object Lessons

Sabbath Economics in the Second Half of Luke

IN THE FIRST half of Luke's Gospel, the vocabulary of wealth (adjective *plousios*, verb *plouteo*, noun *ploutos*) appears just three times, each in the context of censure (1:53, 6:24, 8:14). In the second half of the narrative, it is ubiquitous, raising it to a dominant theme of the Third Gospel. Jesus engages rich persons (in story or encounter) no less than seven times. The first four of these scenes—all unique Lukan material that form the backbone of his special section (9:51–18:14)—are parables that cast profoundly negative light on the wealthy:

i. *12:16: "The land of a rich man produced abundantly. . ."*
   Jesus's polemical portrait of bad behavior (12:13–21) and corrective teaching about the Great Economy (12: 22–34) are the focus of chapter 8.

ii. *14:12: "When you give a banquet, do not invite your. . .rich neighbors. . ."*
   Chapter 9 examines two interrelated healings (13:11–17 and 14:1–6) as examples of Luke's somatic symbolism, then continues with Luke's most extended symposium, at which Jesus diagnoses and disrupts systems of power and privilege as they are mirrored in the protocols of elite table fellowship (14:7–21).

iii. *16:1: "There was a certain rich man who had a manager. . ."*
   Chapter 10 looks at what I call the "Story of the Defect-ive Manager," who monkey wrenches the economy of a great

household to try to build social relations (16:1–8a). This is followed by Jesus's trenchant teaching about practical discipleship in the context of an uncompromising mammon system (16:8b–14).

iv. *16:19: "Now there was a certain rich man . . ."*
Jesus's apocalyptic story about living and dying astride an uncrossable socioeconomic divide (16:19–22) ends with Father Abraham pointing the tale's antagonist—and the reader!—to learn the antidote of Sabbath Economics by listening to Moses and the prophets (16:23–31). This is the focus of chapter 11.

These four story-worlds are complemented by three real-life encounters with rich persons as object lessons:

v. *18:23: "But when the young ruler heard this, he became sad; for he was very rich. . ."*
Chapter 12 begins with a consideration of two uniquely Lukan stories about prayer, in which marginalized petitioners are ignored by, and contrasted with, persons of entitlement (18:1–14). These lead up to the notorious non-discipleship of a rich ruler and a reiteration of Jesus's call to the Great Economy (18:18–30).

vi. *19:2: "Zacchaeus was a chief tax collector and was rich. . ."*
In Jericho, the last stop on Jesus's long march to Jerusalem, a diptych binds together the fate of a poor beggar and a rich bureaucrat. In Luke's capstone object lesson, the latter embraces what the ruler could not: reparative redistribution (18:35–19:10). To preclude fantasies of a Hollywood-style happy ending to the story, Jesus follows with a frank recognition of the fate awaiting those who resist (19:11–28). Chapter 13 tackles these two deeply related scenarios.

vii. *21:1: "Jesus looked up and saw rich people putting their gifts into the treasury. . ."*
If the Zacchaeus story is comic (in the sense of a happy outcome), the story of the widow's mite is tragic, portraying how a woman is made destitute by exploitive lawyers and the tithing demands of the Temple system (20:45–21:4). This seventh and final scenario in Luke's series about the rich concludes Luke's critique of disparity. Jesus summarily exits the Temple and pronounces doom on its economic structures (21:5–7). Though a close look at this sequence is beyond the scope of this book, I do touch upon it in 12B.

Most of the above portraits place the rich in uncomfortable proximity to no-longer-invisible poor people. This is most dramatically illustrated in the fourth scene, which lies in the middle of this series. Its dark tale of Lazarus and Dives is the stark fulcrum on which Luke's whole narrative balances—and the hermeneutic key to Luke's overall vision of Sabbath Economics.

These sequences, which take us up to the beginning of Luke's Jerusalem and Passion narrative, are the focus of part III. Together they represent the heart of Luke's Sabbath Economics argument. The tone of Jesus's encounters steadily escalates, as each scenario makes it increasingly clear that the Great Economy is incompatible with poverty and wealth, both of which dehumanize, if in contrasting ways. The good news is that radical personal and political change is possible, though costly.

My epilogue traces Luke's Sabbath Economics thread through three sacred meals—which bridge the end of his Gospel and the beginning of his second volume—teaching memory and animating practice.

CHAPTER EIGHT

Lessons from Latifundia and Lilies

First Rich Man Sequence

> The way of life which the Great Spirit has given to all the people of the world, whatever your original instructions, are not being honored. It is because of this great sickness called greed, which infects every land and country. Now we are at the very end of our trail. . . . Many people no longer recognize the true path of the Great Spirit . . . or respect for our precious Mother Earth, who gives us all life.
>
> —Dan Evehema, Hopi Elder[1]

WE NOW BEGIN our journey into the heart of Luke's special section. From 11:23 onward, the narrative consists almost exclusively of Q and L material; it doesn't pick up Mark's storyline again until 18:15.[2] Two series of Q sayings (11:29–36 and 12:1–12) bracket Jesus's long tirade of prophetic woes aimed at Pharisees and lawyers (11:42–54).[3] This outburst arises at yet another meal at a Pharisee's house, where conflict immediately breaks out over purity practices (11:37–41). As soon as Jesus leaves the home, scribal and Pharisaic leaders intensify their plotting against Jesus (11:53–12:1)—understandably, one could suppose, given his unrelenting criticisms.

I pick up the narrative at 12:13, a setup scene for the first of Luke's rich man stories, followed by a profound teaching about the Great Economy and Sabbath Economics cosmology. The first part of the sequence consists of two *negative* object lessons:

1. a dispute over inheritance (13–14)
2. the solipsistic world of a rich farmer (16–20)

These bracket Jesus's double warning against greed (12:15). The parable ends with a moral: "So it is with those who "treasure up" (*thēsaurizōn*) for themselves but are not "enriched" (*ploutōn*) in God" (21), both present active participial verbs, connoting habitual practices!

The second part of the sequence consists of two *positive* object lessons, which illustrate Jesus's command not to worry about material sustenance (22–23):

1. Pay attention to the raven; assurance of God's care (24); exhortation not to worry (25).
2. Pay attention to the lilies; assurance of God's care (27–28); exhortation not to worry; seek the Great Economy (29–31).

It concludes with one more exhortation not to fear and a direct call to redistribute wealth to the poor (32–33). The initial moral is then reiterated: "For where your treasure (*thēsaurōs*) is, there your heart will be also" (34).

We will look closely at both parts of this sequence as a unified thematic unit, which asserts the Great Economy as the only antidote to predatory greed.[4] It is bookended by two episodes that include "Human One" sayings and exhort vigilance (12:8–12 and 12:35–40), which suggests that there are powerful political and ideological forces that oppose this teaching on resisting greed. This is confirmed by how our churches have either trivialized or ignored it!

A. Greed

An Archetype of Solipsistic Wealth (12:13–21)

The unit begins with a dispute over inheritance (*klēronomia*, literally a "distribution of properties," 12:13). Israelite custom stipulated that an estate could be divided on the demand of a single son. The scenario implied here is a younger brother demanding to share the "double portion" portion designated for the firstborn male (see Deut 21:17).[5] Jesus's reputation as champion of underdogs may have motivated the man's approach for help with a just settlement of what had become a family conflict. Rabbis often took the role of legal arbiter, which is why Jesus is addressed here as "Teacher." However, because inheritance laws in antiquity (and still today) functioned to pass on material wealth from generation to generation, Jesus refuses to engage the dispute, instead taking the opportunity to address the deeper issue (12:14).

He issues two strong verbs of caution: "Watch out for" and "be on your guard against" (12:15a).[6] The latter is a pointed counter to the Strongman's "guarding of wealth" (11:21; *phulassō*); rather, we must avoid "every form of greed" (*pasēs pleonexias*). Jesus perceived *pleonexia* (avarice) not as a moral category but as a lethal, predatory force. It comes from the Greek root *ple*, used in words such as "multitude," "filled," and "flood," and is related to the verbs *pleonazō* (intransitive, "to have too much" or "grow too big") and *pleonekteō* ("to take advantage of or defraud," see 2 Cor 2:11, 7:2; 12:17–18; 1 Thes 4:6).

Greed was universally condemned throughout antiquity as one of the three greatest sins and routinely appears in New Testament vice lists (e.g., Mark 7:22; Rom 1:29; Eph 4:19). It is several times equated with idolatry (1 Cor 5:10–11; Col 3:5; Eph 5:5). It represents a violation of Exodus 16's first instruction: not to collect too much of the gift. As Paul reiterates in his mutual aid project: "As it is written, 'The one who gathered much did not take too much (*pleonazō*), and the one who gathered little had no lack'" (2 Cor 8:15). Jesus's grave double warning launches the second half of Luke's Sabbath Economics argument.

The proverb Jesus cites next reads, literally, "Not even when it abounds to them is a person's life made up of that which they possess" (12:15b). In a more contemporary idiom: We are *not* what we own. The Greek noun here and in 12:33 is *huparchonton* (I refer the reader to the brief discussion of its importance in Luke toward the end of 5B). Rather than being possessed by our possessions, we should deploy them to build community, as we will explore in the Parable of the Defect-ive Manager (10A).

To illustrate this point, Jesus offers a parable about a wealthy landowner presiding over his *latifundium,* defined by Webster as "a great landed estate with primitive agriculture and labor often in a state of partial servitude." The purpose of his caricature is not to personalize the issue of land and wealth inequity, but to offer it as a kind of political cartoon (12:16–21). Because it is such a key concept for reading the Gospels in historical context, let's take a moment to understand latifundialization—the process by which large landowners increased their holdings by foreclosing on indebted small farmers.

Ulrich Duchrow and Franz Hinkelammert sketch how this phenomenon had been steadily reshaping the Palestinian landscape since history's first wave of economic privatization spread throughout the Mediterranean world in the eighth century BCE:

> A new form of property economy with its credit mechanism seeped into the monarchic, feudal system. . . . It led to a concentration of land in the hands of large landowners, and drove smallholders into debt . . . The nouveaux riches were able to achieve their property concentration quite legally by means of creditor-debtor contracts. But they formed an upper class . . . that could manipulate the very law that, according to Israelite understanding, was supposed to protect the vulnerable and the poor. It was precisely this unfortunate development in public and social life, caused by the new property economy, which called forth the protest of the great prophets in the last third of the eighth and seventh centuries.[7]

Herman Waetjen rounds out the thumbnail historical overview:

> Large segments of the population had been dispossessed and reduced to unemployment and impoverishment as a result of Emperor Pompey's reorganization of the territory soon after the Roman annexation of Palestine in 63 BCE. The victimization of the peasantry continued under the rule of Herod the Great and his dynastic heirs, not

> only by the exaction of heavy taxes but also through the intensification of latifundialization. Herod had expropriated large tracts of farmland and granted them as allotments to his veterans, distributed them to officials of his court, and sold them to wealthy retainers of the Jerusalem aristocracy. Consequently, destitution continued to be widespread, as peasants and artisans who inhabited the villages of Galilee were forced into subsistence tenant farming or worse, day labor. According to the social stratification of agrarian society, those who sell their physical labor in order to make a living are identifiable with the degraded and the unclean, and represent the bottom of the sociological ladder.[8]

Luke earlier gave us a glimpse of reality for peasant workers on such estates in the parable of the Sower (8:4–8). The story of the rich farmer now articulates a "view from the manor."

Probably a well-known folktale, similar versions appear in the second-century BCE Wisdom of Sirach, as well as in the Gospel of Thomas:

> Whoever is greedy for wealth will not be blameless. . . . Some become rich through a miser's life, and this is their allotted reward: When they say: "I have found rest, now I will feast on my goods," they do not know how long it will be till they die and leave them to others (Sir 11:10, 18–19).

> Jesus said: "There was a rich man who had many possessions. He said: 'I will use my possessions to sow and reap and plant, to fill my barns with fruit, that I may have need of nothing.' Those were his thoughts in his heart; and that night he died. He who has ears, let him hear" (Thm 63).

Jesus's version opens by setting the story in the cosmology of grace: "The land of a rich man brought forth great fruit." The verb is *euphoreō* (whence comes our "euphoria"); in antiquity, it connoted not a psychological mood but a state of material well-being. Jesus makes it clear that the abundance resulted from the *earth's* work, not the landowner's (see Mark 4:26–28)!

The parable centers on the wealthy landowner's internal dialogue as a parody of wrong thinking (Luke 12:17–19)—despite the fact that it sounds exactly like most financial counseling today. He talks to his soul/life (*psuchē*), and indeed it is the soul's health that is at issue throughout Jesus's subsequent teaching. First-person pronouns proliferate in this rhetorical triplet:

What shall I do?
    I have nowhere to store my crops
I shall do this:
    I will pull down my barns and build larger ones;
    and there I will store all my grain and my goods;
And I will say to my soul,
    "Soul, you have many goods laid up for many years;
    take it easy, eat, drink and enjoy yourself!"

It suggests a solipsistic existence; even the second-person pronoun in the last two lines is the man addressing himself!

This is precisely the point of the caricature: a wealthy person who does not share abundance is devoid of genuine social relationship, isolated by his primary rapport with possessions. Indeed, this man's singular objective for agricultural surplus is how to store it (intoned twice) privately in his barns (*apothēkē*, from whence our apothecary). Hanson and Oakman point out how ancient elites favored "production of crops that replenish the estate storehouse or have commercial value," in contrast to peasant subsistence strategies.[9] This farmer purposes to lay up his surplus "for many years" (v. 19), suggesting that he may be stockpiling commodities against future lean times, when prices would be driven up and profits greater. Meanwhile, he will enjoy the bounty. The last verb in his monologue (*euphrainou*, to make merry in a feast) will appear again in a parallel parable describing the decadent Dives, who "feasted every day" while Lazarus starved at his gate (16:19; see 11A).

Though this landowner sees his prosperity as a private entitlement, it was widely understood in antiquity that latifundia were built on the backs of the poor. From Jesus's point of view, his bumper crop should have occasioned redistribution to those in need as reparation—something he will expect from the last two rich men in Luke's narrative. The landowner's "bigger barns" strategy is clearly suspect in light of Exodus 16's second instruction not to "store up" the gift but to keep it circulating. This political cartoon is an archetypical illustration of *pleonexia*. The punch line is sharp and unequivocal: the Creator demands back the landowner's *psuchē*, cutting short his long-term investment (12:20a).[10] As in the Lazarus parable, death—the only thing peasants could point to as a social equalizer—represents the true reckoning for hard-hearted rich people. The farmer is named a "fool" (12:20f), a *midrash* on two Hebrew Bible texts. The Psalmist speaks of the practical atheism of those who live in contempt of both the Creator and the poor: "Fools say in their hearts, 'There is no God.' They are corrupt, they do abominable deeds; there is no one who does good. . . . Have they no knowledge, all the evildoers who eat up my people as they eat bread. . .?" (Ps

14:1, 4). The prophet Jeremiah adds: "Like the partridge hatching what it did not lay, so are all who amass wealth unjustly; in mid-life it will leave them, and at their end they will prove to be fools" (Jer 17:11).

The parable ends ironically with the very question with which this sequence began: the dispute over inheritance. "These things you have prepared, whose will they be?" (12:20b). Jesus's proverbial conclusion clarifies the real point of the story: "So it is with those who 'treasure up' (*thēsaurizōn*) for themselves, and consequently are not 'enriching' (*ploutōn*) in God" (12:21; 1 Tim 6:17–19 is a later articulation of this same conviction).

This contrast between what Berry and Tönnies called the "Two Economies" introduces the focus of the rest of this section: nature as the embodiment of the Great Economy. This reversal of the rich man's paradigm is similar to "last shall be first" rhetoric. Creation precedes our "little" economic systems and will survive them. Private accumulation arises from delusions of immortality but is just a desperate, short-term hedge against the inevitable economic levelling that comes with death. The divine Commonwealth is the *only* thing that truly endures, the only treasure of actual value. Jesus offers both negative object lessons to argue that ownership paradigms must therefore be shifted from "mine" to "ours."

The point of this opening scenario in Luke's series of rich man stories isn't just that selfish wealth is morally problematic. It is that the virus of affluenza upholds an economic system of disparity and oppression and represents a terminal disease threatening all personal and political futures.[11] And it can infect *any* of us: shaping the appetites of the wealthy, but also the desires of the nonwealthy. This pandemic requires radical solutions, beginning with a recovery of our symbiosis with nature's Commonwealth, to which Jesus now turns.

B. Gift

Apprenticing to the Great Economy (12:22–34)

For his positive object lessons, Jesus pointedly turns to the nonhuman world.[12] Of course, his meditation about birds and flowers often strikes modern North Americans as simplistic, extreme, and naive. This is because it cuts diametrically across our most sacred anthropocentric assumptions about our entitlement to reengineer nature and secure economic security through extraction and accumulation. This may explain why the lectionary omits this second part of Luke's sequence! Yet what if Jesus means exactly what he says here? To take him seriously means we must confront the three primary pathologies of modern economic culture: anxiety, addiction, and alienation. This teaching may seem bizarre, but is essential to our liberation.

"For *this* reason I tell you, do not be anxious," says Jesus (12:22a; *merimnaō*). The imperative mood signals a prohibition, not a suggestion, the first of several that function as a refrain in the teaching that follows (12:25–26). The contrast between Jesus's counsel here and the rich landowner's self-referential strategy is striking:

Rich man: I will say to my soul (*psuchē*)... take it easy, eat, drink and enjoy yourself! (12:19).

Jesus: Do not be anxious for your life (*psuchē*), what you will eat, or about your body, what you will wear (12:22).

He then appears to take an ascetic turn: "For soul/life is greater than nourishment (*trophēs*), and the body more than clothing" (12:23).[13] Jesus, however, is interested not in self-denial but in reconnecting with the Great Economy.

"Turn your mind instead to this" (*katanoeō*, used fourteen times in the New Testament, here an aorist imperative) commands action, lost in the NRSV's "consider." It is better rendered "Pay attention!" In a parallel doublet, each example is followed by an assurance about God's cares for us, and reiteration not to be anxious:

> 24 Pay attention to the ravens: they neither sow nor reap, they have neither storehouse nor barn, yet God feeds them. Of how much more value are you than birds!
> 25 And can any of you by being anxious add a single hour to your span of life?
> 26 If then you are not able to do so small a thing as that, why do you worry about the rest?
> 27 Pay attention to the lilies, how they grow: they neither toil nor spin; yet I tell you, even Solomon in all his glory was not clothed like one of these.
> 28 But if God so clothes the grass of the field... how much more will God clothe you, you of little faith!
> 29 And do not keep striving for what you are to eat and what you are to drink, and do not keep being anxious. (12:24–29)

Jesus is likely pointing out these object lessons as he walks through a field with his disciples. The truth is close at hand, if we pause long enough from our civilizational preoccupations to encounter what Aquinas famously called "the book of nature."[14]

But paying careful attention to birds and flowers is exactly what most modern folk have no intention of doing (much less competence in). "Isn't that quaint," we muse, "Jesus as a plant geek and birdwatcher. All very sweet, but it has nothing to do with real economics!" This is *not* utopian ranting, however.[15] Jesus is talking about the very real biosphere—sensuous, embodied, alive, mystical—right in front of us. He understands that we do not have eyes to see it because we are wholly distracted by the works of our hands and our built environments (as later illustrated by the disciples' fascination with the Jerusalem Temple, 21:5).

We, children of industrial capitalism, are much further down the road of attachment to our civilizational projects and have also objectified and commodified nature beyond recognition. This is why, writes Richard Dillon, Jesus employs a "combination of sapiential insight and apocalyptic vision . . . aimed at shocking the old world's citizens out of their instinctive adherence to its illusions of self-mastery and self-sufficiency. . . . God's gift requires swearing off the 'managerial complex' most people have toward the future."[16]

Jesus's first positive object lesson is the raven (12:24a), which alludes to two Hebrew Bible texts that marvel at God's gracious provision to all living things, particularly in times of hunger:[17]

> Job 38:41: "Who provides for the raven its prey when its young ones cry to God and wander about for lack of food?"
>
> Psalm 147:9: "God gives to the animals their food, and to the young ravens when they cry."

Also in the background here is Elijah, who is fed by a raven during a drought he has inflicted, Exodus-style, on Baal-serving King Ahab (1 Kg 17:1–7). The prophet then calls down divine provision for the widow of Zarephath (1 Kg 17:8–16), a story already alluded to by Luke in Jesus's Nazareth *drash* (4:25–26).

Jesus now takes aim at the rich landowner whose portrait he's just painted (12:18): ravens "neither sow nor reap, have neither storeroom nor barn," yet find provision in the Great Economy. Indeed, corvids are impressive foragers, whose "success as a species is due to their omnivorous diet; they are extremely versatile and opportunistic in finding sources of nutrition, feeding on carrion, insects, cereal grains, berries, fruit, small animals, nesting birds, and food waste. Some notable feats of problem-solving provide evidence that the common raven is unusually intelligent."[18] Artist and theologian Ted Lyddon Hatten's work gracing the cover of this book pays homage to this very point: a raven takes over Zacchaeus's perch in a sycamore tree, staring down a tower—or barn—in the distance (see if you can find Elijah's cave). Ted weaves both biblical and ecological threads into an amazing and deeply thoughtful and sophisticated body of "ornitheological" writing and art; I recommend taking a moment to reflect on his explanatory note about the cover piece.[19]

The NRSV renders 12:24c: "Of how much more value are you than birds!" The verb (*diapherō*), however, means "different."[20] We would do better to read this in relation to the parallel teaching about sparrows a few verses before this (12:7), which exhorts humans to *learn* from birds. While the special worth of human life is an essential strand of the biblical worldview, there is also a recurrent emphasis on our creatureliness, putting us on par with other animals.[21] One could plausibly infer from Jesus's teaching here that special divine care for humans is necessary precisely because it is *we* who have abandoned the Great Economy, making us more vulnerable (and infinitely more dangerous!) than other creatures.

This would explain the assurance that God knows our needs—and our apparent inability to meet them without worrying ourselves to death. Jesus could assume that ancient people accepted they could not add length to their stature or lifespan (12:25; *prosthêinai*, whence "prosthetics"). We moderns, however, continue to labor under the fantasy that we *can*, pursuing technological prosthetics, from robotics and AI to geo- and genetic-engineering, which only serve to feed our cultural plague of anxiety. Jesus is alluding to Psalm 39: "Let me know my end, and what is the measure of my days. . . . You have made my days a few handbreadths" (39:4–5). The Psalmist further underscores the moral of the rich farmer parable regarding mortality and possessions: "Surely for nothing we are in turmoil; we heap up, and do not know who will gather" (39:6).

Jesus's second positive object lesson turns our attention to wild lilies, probably *Anemone coronaria*, which bloomed around the Jordan Valley in early spring (12:27).[22] Images of lilies adorned Israel's shrines (Exod 25:31–34) and Solomon's Temple (1 Kg 7:19, 22, 26)—with which the flower is here ironically contrasted! Jesus is moving from critique of rich landowners to Israel's most powerful king—who was a regional imperialist. Lilies do not engage in the hard labor of spinning cloth, "but I tell you" (says Jesus with rhetorical insistence), "Solomon in all his glory never 'wrapped himself around' like one of these." This is likely a euphemism for the Second Temple, the zenith of Israel's civilizational aspirations. Jesus's polemic is a pointed addition that breaks the rhythmic parallelism to verse 24 and should not be dismissed as mere hyperbole. It asserts that the greatest technological and political achievement known to his Judean contemporaries has *less intrinsic worth than one wildflower* in the Great Economy. Yikes, what if he *means* it?

As extreme as Jesus's assertion would have seemed to his disciples, this valuation is the very opposite of our capitalist cosmology. Our technological hegemony authorizes a continuing holocaust of extinction and endangerment, routinely sacrificing species and habitats—and now, under climate crisis, whole ecosystems—to the idol of expansionism and profiteering.[23] Pay attention to the spotted owl or the Saint Helena olive, says Jesus. *Blather*, respond our severe modern economic orthodoxies dismissively. But it is not blather: it is the cosmology of Great Economy, articulated in Exodus 16 and echoed by Indigenous and traditional peoples the world over and throughout history. For millennia this translated into economic lifeways characterized by symbiosis with nature, sustainable local production and consumption, and cooperative and equitable work patterns.[24] Jesus is doing nothing more and nothing less than re-centering us in the oldest wisdom on the planet.

If he is right, our capitalist economic cosmology falls down like a house of cards. The history of progress has been predicated on the ideas that nature is an object to exploit for our industrial purposes, and that value is only what *we* impute through our relentless attempts to reengineer the biosphere for profit. Yet our project has placed both ecological and social systems on the brink of collapse. So who is the fool here—an economic cosmology that sustained human life for a hundred thousand years or more, or one that may not last another hundred?

In keeping with the parallelism of the two object lessons, another rhetorical question follows: "How much more" (as in 12:24) will the Creator who "clothes" the hay in the field clothe humans (12:28a–b)? "You of little faith" (*oligopistoi*, only here in Luke), a shaming epithet, prefaces Jesus's final exhortation of the sequence (12:28c–29). "Do not seek food and drink" is a repudiation of the rich landowner's decadent feasting in the shadow of his barns of greed. This negative imperative is repeated: "Do not keep being anxious" (*meteorizomai*, only here in the New Testament). This time Jesus targets Roman culture: "All the nations of the world hustle after such things" (12:30a; *epizēteō* is an intensification of the previous verb *zēteō*). Imperial cultures historically have spawned widespread anxiety, alienation, and addiction due to both artificial scarcity among the poor majority and the artificial abundance of the affluent minority, who compete to accrue private wealth in order to satisfy engineered appetites.

The Divine Parent, on the other hand, is "well-pleased" to gift us with enough (12:30b).[25] Jesus does not try to transcend human material life by invoking a heroic or ascetic imperative; rather, he emphasizes that God is mindful of our legitimate needs.[26] As this sequence has stressed repeatedly, these will be "added to us" as we embrace the Great Economy—unlike our own efforts to add a single day to our lives through anxiety, engineering, or accumulation, as the rich landowner discovered. The Creator is portrayed here as a *father who is acting like a mother* (looking after everyone's needs and calming fears as befits the ancient Mediterranean maternal householder), or like a caring shepherd tending this "little flock" (12:32).[27]

"Seek instead" is in the imperative not because the Great Economy is hidden but because its ethos of sharing equitably the divine gift is so counterintuitive to our economic formation. In other words, we are to act in the *opposite* manner of the rich landowner (12:33). The double command to "sell . . . and give" will be repeated in Jesus's later challenge to the rich ruler, but with important resonances and differences that give insight into Luke's economic theology:

> 12:33: Sell your possessions (*pōlēsate ta huparchonta humōn*) and give (*dote*) alms and provide yourselves . . . with a treasure in the heavens that does not fail (*thēsauron en tois ouranois*).
>
> 18:22: Sell all you have (*panta hosa echeis pōlēson*), distribute to the poor (*kai diados ptōchois*), and you'll have treasure in heaven (*exeis thēsauron en tois ouranois*).

Disciples and the rich man are both called to divest in order to enter the Great Economy. But in the former case, the proceeds are given (*didōmi*) as solidarity in the tradition of almsgiving (*eleēmosunēn*, from the verb *eleēō*, "to show mercy").[28] In the latter case, it is a matter of reparative justice for the poor (*diadidōmi* is "to redistribute"). And unlike the rich man's expectation to inherit the Great Economy (12B), in Jesus's teaching it is only *given*.

"Treasure in heaven" is an apocalyptic image of reversal, a glimpse of God's parallel universe. In this alternate reality, "purses don't wear out" (though true disciples have already given these up; 10:4; 22:35).[29] The rationale for this is simple: thieves can't steal what isn't held privately, and moths can't eat what isn't stored up.[30] To underscore the point, Jesus follows this sequence with a real world scenario: a rich landowner's household, in which servants must stay awake in order to be at the beck and call of the master, while he worries about when thieves might come to take his property (12:35–39). The insomniac apocalyptic verb *grēgoreō* is used in 12:37, echoing the other "thief in the night" warning tropes in the New Testament.[31] Jesus uses the irony of apocalyptic reversal in 12:40: The Human One comes *in the guise of the rich man's greatest fear*: a midnight burglar!

Jesus's teaching here is taken to heart by Wendell Berry, who pleads for our economic behavior to *serve* social and ecological relationships, not *pillage* them. One of the most compelling contemporary articulations of this traditional economic cosmology is the model proposed by feminist economist Hazel Henderson, who passed in 2022. Henderson pointed out that most economic calculations of worth, such as a nation's GDP, give monetary value only to private and public sector goods and services. This ignores, however, what she called "the love economy," which consists of all the *non-monetized* expressions of household, neighborhood, and community production and consumption, including mutual aid and "sweat equity." This social cooperative economy, in turn, is itself predicated upon nature's resources and processes, by which ultimately we all

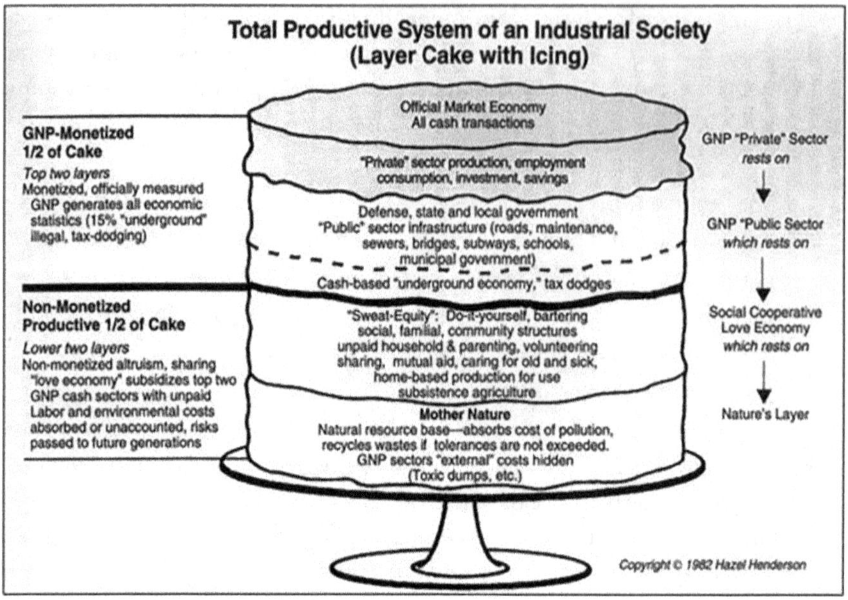

Figure 5. "Total Productive System of an Industrial Economy," layer cake model (Originally developed by Hazel Henderson, 1982).

live or die. Henderson beautifully portrayed these sectors in terms of a cake (see Figure 5).[32] Yet capitalism imputes no intrinsic market value to these two foundational layers of the cake, content instead to skim off the icing for private profit.

The catechism of 12:21–34 instructs us how *not* to live and die like a rich fool. It resonates with Henderson's call to revalue the foundational layers of this cake; it even resonates with her model's maternal tones of baking, loving, and Mother Nature! Jesus advocates apprenticeship to the Great Economy, beginning by being attentive to Creation—a discipline being rediscovered through the keystone modern permaculture design principle of observation.[33] If our world is to survive the extractive cannibalism of the two top layers of our economy, we must do battle with our anxiety, alienation, and addiction, even as we learn to work for transformation from the bottom up through regenerative practices of communion, community, and constraint.

Luke's remarkable sequence, so long shrugged off by the church as Jesus's cute little Saint Francis moment, concludes with a proverb: "Where your treasure is, there also will your heart be (12:34). It is an apt summary—and doubles as a challenge to us to discern just *where* that is!

CHAPTER NINE

Lessons from Bodies and Banquets

Second Rich Man Sequence

> If a man eats and drinks a great deal, but is never filled, he sees a physician, inquires what ails him, what is wrong with his system, and how to rid himself of the disorder. But if the owner of five couches goes looking for ten, and the owner of ten tables buys up as many again, and though he has lands and money in plenty is not satisfied but is bent on more, losing sleep and never sated by any amount, does he imagine that he does not need someone who will prescribe for him and point out the cause of his distress?
>
> —Aristippus[1]

THE THREAD I will follow in this chapter is a little different than in the other rich man sequences in Luke's special section. I first look at two healings that present archetypal portraits of a poor (13:10–17) and a rich (14:1–6) person respectively. They are twinned by their common association as healings on the Sabbath, Jesus's practice that continues to provoke conflict. These stories demonstrate Luke's embodied symbolism, narrating somatic conditions that mirror the disease of the body politic. The latter healing leads directly into Jesus's most extended Sabbath Economics teaching, in three parts, which illustrates how to transform table fellowship from a reflection of systemic disparity to a model for just community (14:7–24).

A. The Bent Over and the Bloated

Luke's Somatic Symbolism (13:10–17, 14:1–6)

Before tackling the healing that begins at 13:10, let's overview the series of Q and L sayings that precede it (12:35–13:9). In this sequence, Jesus continues to point out brutalities endured by lower classes who work and live in the world of the *kurios* ("lord"):[2]

- household servants enduring sleeplessness (12:37) and beatings (12:47)
- debtor's prison (12:58–59)

- Galileans suffering violence at the hands of Roman authorities (13:1–3)
- Pedestrians killed by dangerous urban construction (13:4–5)[3]
- unreasonable demands on peasants for agricultural production by absentee landlords (13:6–9)

Jesus's warning to "settle out of court" in the second example above refers to a judicial system that routinely imprisoned the poor for indebtedness. His scenario "reflects a situation in Roman Palestine where . . . it is better to have a patron in the creditor . . . than to face the courts controlled by the landlord class."[4]

Jesus, invoking the fire and baptism of the wilderness prophet John (12:49–50), repudiates the "peace" of an imperial system that generates such violations (12:51). Instead, he foments "division in the house": not just in the Pax Romana that protects the strong man's palace (11:17–21), but also the domestic household (12:52–53).[5] Families then (as today) were pressured to conform (and to so teach their children) to the dominant political-economic system. But these social structures will inevitably be disrupted by the gospel of the Great Economy. Then once again, Jesus directs our attention to nature's cycles for help in discerning the *kairos* of our historical moment (12:54–56).[6]

This brings us to the first of two twinned Sabbath healings. To help make sense of their political character, I turn to an important conceptual lens used throughout my reading of Luke. Modern interpreters must take into account the "problem of cross-cultural communication" in our attempts to try to "explain the healing narratives from antiquity."[7] Our modern Western worldview assumes that gospel healing stories relate "supernatural" cures of medical and/or psychological disorders (whether or not we ourselves accept that possibility). The ancient Mediterranean world, however, like other non-modern cultures, was not biomedical in its approach to illness, but bio-symbolic. While traditional medicine (herbal, somatic, and spiritual) in antiquity was widely used to address physiological and psychological symptoms, chronic or congenital illnesses or "abnormalities" required other methods, since these were understood primarily as "socially disvalued states" that threatened communal integrity.[8]

All human societies (then and now) seek to order themselves by regulating and socializing human bodies within the body politic. The majority culture or regime in power defines what is pure or impure, safe or threatening, legal or illegal. For example, according to ancient Hebrew patriarchy, menstruating women were considered unclean and dangerous, and were required to quarantine from men. Closer to home, from the beginning of a colonial project in the Americas predicated on white supremacy, racial purity codes considered dark-skinned bodies to be "inferior" (and according to the US Constitution, only 60 percent human), resulting in repeated patterns of brutal enslavement, exploitation, criminalization, and racialized law enforcement. Black bodies today continue to be the most reliable mirror of social health in the US.[9] And in modernity up until very recently, disabled bodies were quarantined, segregated, and pathologized.

Frantz Fanon's essay "Colonial War and Mental Disorder" gave clinical credence to the notion that people reproduce dysfunctional politics in their own personalities or bodies.[10] He noted cases during the Algerian independence struggle of the late 1950s, in which patterns of colonial violence were replicated in pathological conditions among those living under that political system—both among colonizers and colonized. Sometimes this manifested through somatic illness, sometimes through mental disorders (including demon possession).

Cultural anthropologist Mary Douglas also reflected on this phenomenon in a seminal essay entitled "Two Bodies":

> The physical body can have universal meaning only as a system which responds to the social system, expressing it as a system. What it symbolized naturally is the relations of parts of an organism to the whole. Natural symbols can express the relation of an individual to his society at that general systemic level. The two bodies are the self and society.[11]

Douglas alludes to a mirroring between the two:

> The social body constrains the way the physical body is perceived. The physical experience of the body, always modified by the social categories through which it is known, sustains a particular view of society. There is a continual exchange of meanings between the two kinds of bodily experience so that each reinforces the categories of the other.[12]

This is especially evident in traditional cultures, which do not make radical distinctions between self and society as moderns do; it was certainly characteristic of first-century Palestine.[13] In light of such studies, Botha asserts that for ancient healers, "attention is focused on the social and symbolic conditions of the sickness" more than individual physical ailments.[14]

I have adopted and adapted these sociological frameworks in my study of Luke. I speak of how the *body politic*—the imperatives, hierarchies, symbols, and structures of a dominant sociopolitical order—is reproduced (or resisted!) by how, where, and when individuals and groups present their *political bodies*. This helps us understand gospel accounts of Jesus's healing and exorcism as *expressions of political engagement*, and not just as individual interactions devoid of social meaning, as Western Christians typically assume. As a practitioner, Jesus takes a *radical* approach to physically or spiritually impaired bodies, addressing the *root* causes of a presenting pathology or disorder—the person's social "dis-memberment" as enforced through dominant cultural codes of debt and purity. The political character of Jesus's healings was certainly intelligible in its original cultural context, since all our gospel narratives attest that they inevitably incited conflict with authorities. When we use literalizing, theologizing, or spiritualizing lenses to read gospel healing and exorcism stories, we miss these sociopolitical dimensions.

Part of the problem for those in power was how the status of a subject was disrupted through healing, especially if Jesus's intervention violated accepted protocols. For example, he is perceived as an "unlicensed" practitioner in his first two healing stories in Luke: declaring a leper clean despite not being a priest, then absolving a paralytic of sin despite not being a scribe (5:12–26).[15] But another part of the problem was how Jesus placed his *own* body within public space, often transgressing accepted or expected social boundaries of power and prestige (e.g., 4:31–37; 7:1–17). In Luke, this often occurs at banquets hosted by powerful men, as we've already seen (5B)—which is precisely the setting of the second healing I will look at in this chapter (14:1).

Luke "the physician" often represents diseased bodies as archetypes, maps, mirrors, or microcosms of the unjust social systems that generate and perpetuate their condition. This is especially the case with the two Sabbath healings under consideration here. Both are uniquely Lukan, occur in close narrative proximity, and have parallel structure. Though in neither case is the subject labeled rich or poor, the symbolics of their respective somatic conditions tell an economic story. Several factors suggest that each person functions as a social type; they:

- have no names;
- have no backstory (both suddenly appear on and leave the scene);
- are not described as sick or disabled; and
- never speak.

They show what Luke has been telling us concerning pathologies of indebtedness and affluenza in the body politic: the "bent-over" woman (13:10–17) is literally crippled by debt, while the bloated man (14:1–6) embodies the social disease of "too muchness."

Duncan Derrett was the first to demonstrate how these two episodes are narrated "in mutual relation, arranged as a diptych," even though they do not appear consecutively.[16] They are twinned as Sabbath conflicts between Jesus and the authorities, but also by Luke's narrative placement of them in relation to lengthy teachings concerning economic equity, which are punctuated by shorter proclamations about the criticality of the historical moment, as shown in this plotting of the entire sequence:

- Sabbath Economics teaching: greed (12:13–34);
  - series of sayings/parables: coming justice (12:35–48), "signs of the times" (12:57–13:9);
    - Sabbath Object Lesson: "bent-over" woman (13:10–17);
  - series of sayings/parables: the Great Economy as surprise and mystery (13:18–21), the "narrow Way" (13:22–30), the cost of discipleship (13:31–35) ;
    - Sabbath Object Lesson: "too big" man (14:1–6);
- Sabbath Economics teaching: table fellowship justice (14:7–24).

This kind of compositional interweaving is another way in which Luke expresses disparity between wealthy and poor as the heart of the social crisis of his time.

The bent-over woman is a curious episode in Luke—a blend of call and controversy as well as of healing and exorcism. Natalie Houghtby-Haddon's study of this text and its social implications then and now contends it is a key interpretive text for seeing Luke's social vision for his community.[17] It opens in a synagogue on the Sabbath (13:10), again symbolizing the intersection of sacred time and space (as in 6:6–11). Luke began Jesus's ministry narrative at such a venue (4:15–44), but starting at 6:7, the synagogue becomes an increasingly contested place, then a zone of outright hostility (12:11).

The phrase "just then," or "and behold" (*kai idou*), underlines the awkward appearance of a woman who is clearly beat down (13:11). She is described as having labored under a "spirit of weakness" (*astheneia*, literally "lack of strength"), a condition Luke depicts as common among those to whom Jesus ministers (5:15; 8:2; see Acts 28:9). Oakman notes that "many of the people 'healed' by Jesus were perhaps suffering the effects of malnutrition . . . due simply to vitamin deficiencies."[18] This has caused her to become "bent over" or "completely overcome" (*sugkuptō*, only here in the New Testament). Given Luke's literacy in the Septuagint, the detail about the duration of her misery may likely be an allusion to the deep history of subjugation suffered by her people: "Eglon the Moabite king and the Philistines . . . oppressed the Israelites *for eighteen years*" (Judg 3:12–14; 10:7–8). This would suffice to reframe the condition of her political body relative to the body politic of Roman occupation.

Jesus summons her over, conspicuously *before* engaging the synagogue leader (13:12), again defying gender conventions. He declares her "set free" (*apoluo*, 13:13), suggesting that the issue is not disease but *bondage*.[19] Only then does he lay hands on her, "making her erect again" (13:14).[20] The synagogue leader objects to doing work on the Sabbath and tries to make an object lesson out of him to the audience (13:14). Jesus rebuffs such theatrics, calling him a hypocrite—a term borrowed from Greco-Roman theater, which connotes "playing a role." He then cites Deuteronomy 5:12–15, which enjoins Sabbath rest for the whole household, including beasts of burden. If animals are to be "untied" (*luō*), Jesus reasons, how much more deserving of release is a "daughter of Abraham" (Luke 13:16, a phrase unique in the New Testament, but which anticipates its counterpart in 19:9). Her "bonds" here allude to prison chains (as in all but one of twenty appearances of *desmos* in the New Testament). As noted, indebtedness led either to bonds of servitude or of prison. This also alludes to Torah's obligation to redeem "daughters" sold into slavery during the Sabbath year (Exod 21:7–11).

Richard Lowery summarizes how, "by the very nature of her debilitating ailment, the woman is a living embodiment of the standard metaphor for indebtedness and oppression":

> The image of untying and releasing the ox and the donkey also connects the story of the woman's healing with Sabbath-year release. . . . [As in] "shaking off the yoke" of debt in Nehemiah 5:13, indebtedness, servitude, and oppression are often described as bearing a yoke. The root meaning of *shemittah* in the Sabbath-year passage refers to loosening a yoke and letting it drop from the shoulders. With shoulders now unbound, the one released can stand completely erect.[21]

Her political body was doubled over—and today we still routinely talk about "crippling debt," or how individuals, social groups, and whole nations "groan under debt burdens." Debt remains the most widespread symptom (and mechanism) of economic injustice.

Jesus "puts his opponents to shame" (*kataischunō*, only here in the Gospels, but often in Paul), but the crowd "rejoices at the glorious things Jesus was doing" (13:17). Still, this is the last time Jesus visits a synagogue in Luke's narrative, perhaps because this woman's liberation fulfills the promise he made in his inaugural synagogue *drash* to realize Isaiah's vision of "loosing bonds" (4:18 = Isa 58:6). Yet it also anticipates Jesus's later promise: "When these things begin to take place, stand erect . . . your redemption is drawing near" (21:28).[22]

* * *

Placing this story side by side with that of the "bloated man" a chapter later helps us see the obvious twinning:

Woman Bent Over (13:10–17)	Man Too Bloated (14:1–6)
[10]Now he was teaching in one of the synagogues on the Sabbath.	[1]On one occasion when Jesus was going to the house of a leader of the Pharisees to eat a meal on the Sabbath, they were watching him closely.

<table>
<tr><td rowspan="2">11 And just then (kai idou) there appeared a woman with a spirit that had crippled her for eighteen years...</td><td>2 Just then (kai idou), in front of him, there was a man who had dropsy.</td></tr>
<tr><td>3 And Jesus asked the lawyers and Pharisees, “Is it lawful to cure people on the Sabbath, or not?”</td></tr>
<tr><td>12 When Jesus saw her, he called her over and said, “Woman, you are released (apolelusai) from your ailment...”</td><td>4 But they were silent. So Jesus took him and healed him, and released him (apelusen).</td></tr>
<tr><td>14 But the leader of the synagogue, indignant because Jesus had cured on the Sabbath...</td><td rowspan="2">5 Then he said to them, “If one of you has a child or an ox that has fallen into a well, will you not immediately pull it out on a Sabbath day?”</td></tr>
<tr><td>15 But the Lord answered him and said, “You hypocrites! Does not each of you on the Sabbath untie (luei) his ox or his donkey from the manger, and lead it away to give it water?”</td></tr>
<tr><td>16 And ought not this woman ... be set free from this bondage on the Sabbath day?”</td><td rowspan="2">6 And they could not reply to this.</td></tr>
<tr><td>17 All his opponents were put to shame.</td></tr>
</table>

The latter story is more concise because of the earlier “template.” Yet the subject of healing could not be a more different social type.[23]

The scene setup is similar to the earlier banquet at the house (*oikos*) of Simon the Pharisee (7:36). But as Stuart Love points out, Jesus's immediately preceding lament over Jerusalem sets a foreboding tone: “Behold, your *house* is left empty” (13:35).[24] Though that alluded to the Temple, Jesus is now inside another *oikos* of the elite *on the Sabbath* (14:1a). Since 6:7, scribes and Pharisees have been “watching him, to see whether he would heal on the Sabbath, so that they might find an accusation against him”—and they continue to do so here (14:1b). Yet as the ensuing episode reveals, Jesus is observing *their* habits closely too, and will soon turn from suspect to prosecutor.

The man with dropsy suddenly appears (14:2), just as the bent-over woman did. In the same way that her political body problematized the integrity of the synagogue community, so this man's pathology haunts this banquet room. “Dropsy” was an ancient medical term (*hudrōpikos*, only here in New Testament) that described the swelling of soft tissues due to the accumulation of excess water (*hudor*). Today we would call this condition edema, possibly due to congestive heart failure. A late medieval medical text describes "the Dropsy as an unnatural Tumour, in which all the Body, or some one of its parts, is swelled to an immeasurable Bulk."[25] But given that Luke's was not a biomedical culture, what was the *symbolic* meaning of this disease?

Michael Gilleland has researched how dropsy was understood in classical antiquity: "The view was prevalent in ancient medicine that dropsy sufferers were insatiably thirsty. . . . This led to a comparison between *avarice* (a disease of the soul) and *dropsy* (a disease of the body). In both cases, what the sufferer wanted (more water or more possessions) only aggravated the problem."[26] He cites numerous classical Greek and Roman writers who made this connection:

- Stobaeus: "Diogenes used to liken greedy men to those suffering from dropsy. For the latter, although filled with liquid, still desired to drink."
- Polybius: "He was unaware that as in the case of a dropsy the thirst of the sufferer never ceases and is never allayed by the administration of liquids from without, unless we cure the morbid condition of the body itself, so it is impossible to satiate the greed for gain, unless we correct by reasoning the vice inherent in the soul."
- Horace: "Indulgence bids the dropsy grow / Who fain would quench the palate's flame / Must rescue from the watery foe / The pale weak frame."
- Ovid: "Riches have grown and with them the frantic lust for wealth, and they who have the most possessions still crave for more. They strive to gain that they may waste, and then to repair their wasted fortunes, and thus they feed their vices by ringing the changes on them. So he whose belly swells with dropsy, the more he drinks, the thirstier he grows."
- Seneca: "Even if all these things are heaped up, they will never fill a soul incapable of being filled, no more than any amount of liquid will be enough to satisfy him whose desire arises not from any lack but from the heat of his blazing innards. For that is not thirst but rather a disease."[27]

Given this literary evidence, there is little doubt that Luke portrays this man's dropsy as the spirit of affluenza lurking in this banquet. Jesus heals (exorcizes?) it as the prolegomenon to his serial challenges to those at the gathering that immediately follow.

Jesus preempts his opponents by posing their objection as a question: "Is it lawful to heal people (*therapeuō)* on the Sabbath, or not?" (14:3). In so doing, he is returning to the scene of his first "crime," in which his synagogue healing on the Sabbath launched a conspiracy against him (6:11). There Luke followed Mark in shaping Jesus's query as a Deuteronomic ultimatum: "Is it lawful on the Sabbath to do good or to do harm, to save life or to destroy it?" (6:9 // Mark 3:4). That carefully choreographed political theatre invokes the memory of Moses on the mountain, overlooking the Promised Land, urging his people to "choose life" (Deut 30:15–19). Here in 14:3, Jesus again presses the question that lies at the heart of the matter: *What exactly are we about as a people?* In the US we might think of Dr. King's 1963 speech in front of the Lincoln memorial on the centenary of the Emancipation Proclamation, challenging white America "to keep the promises you made on paper."

As he did in 13:14–16, Jesus interrogates the purpose of Sabbath: prohibition or liberation? His opponents "keep silent" (14:4a; *ēsuchazō*)—a classic "no comment." Such studied avoidance is the refuge of political figures who imagine they are too powerful to be held accountable. Or, as the most recent federal bailout of the banking and mortgage industry again revealed, of plutocrats who deem their institutions too big to fail. Or of the studied silence of most churches around issues of economic disparity. Jesus answers his own question by taking action.

In three dramatic gestures, he takes *ahold* of the man, *cures* him, and *releases* him (14:4b). Again, this last is a Jubilee verb (*apoluō*), used by Luke for releasing someone from sin (6:37), forgiving debt (as in 13:12), or setting a prisoner free (23:16–25). Jesus then turns back to the silent spectators with another cutting rhetorical question, linking this episode firmly to the bent-over woman: "If any of you has a child or an ox that has fallen into a well, will you not immediately pull it out on a Sabbath day?" (14:5).[28] His adversaries would be well aware that Torah enjoins aid to a neighbor's ox or ass if it strays, concluding: "So you shall do with any lost thing of your brother's" (Deut 22:3). The man with dropsy, "too big because of too much," is clearly lost, but Jesus came to seek and save such (as intoned at the conclusion of the later Zacchaeus story, 19:10; 13A). Those who object to Jesus here are similarly diseased, unable to welcome this healing lesson about Sabbath Economics.

Jesus challenges conventional interpretations of prevailing law with actions meant to animate moral imagination, which is what Dr. King attempted to do through civil disobedience action. For both Jesus and King, the issue was not the particular legal prohibition itself, but how laws often ignore or exclude those in need—often putting property ahead of people. Luke's episode concludes with his adversaries' inability to "answer back" (14:6; *antapokrinomai*, only here and in Rom 9:20). But Jesus is only getting started.

The next episode moves us from the parlor into the dining room, where the Nazarene will go on the offensive with a parable aimed at deconstructing the architecture of elite meal fellowship. Braun recognizes that the healing of dropsy opens up "the thematic center of the remainder of the dinner episode," which is about "the cure or transformation of character from greed to generosity, defined as both the disposition of wealth and the renunciation of an ethos of exclusive social interaction."[29] This table, like the bodies around it, represents a map of wider social and economic disparities.

B. Justice Seeks the Lowest Places

Table as Social Map (14:7–24)

The healing of an archetypal figure suffering from affluenza sets the tone for Luke's most extended banquet narrative. Jesus now tells in painful detail what recovery from this disease will entail for patrons of this privileged gathering. The full sequence can be outlined as follows:[30]

Frame: 13:31–35: Jesus anticipates *his* cost of discipleship
- i. 14:1–6: Healing the somatic archetype of affluenza:
- ii. 7–11: Critiquing a "seating chart"
- iii. 12–14: Critiquing the "guest list"
- iv. 15–24: Transforming the "guest list" for the Great Banquet

Frame: 14:25–33: Jesus clarifies to his followers *their* cost of discipleship

In 14:7, Jesus turns "to those who were invited" (*tous keklēmenous*) and launches into his longest parable, repeating that verb no fewer than eight times, and ending with a warning that uses the same perfect participial phrase (*tōn keklēmenon*, 14:24).

Luke gave us a foretaste of this section in 13:29, which imaged the Great Economy as a space where people come from the four directions to sit at table together. This is not proposed as a heavenly banquet, nor as a eucharistic metaphor, but a scenario from the heart of first-century Eastern Mediterranean village culture: the commensality that stood at the center of social intercourse. That earlier vignette warned, however, that the guest list would be turned upside down: "Some are last who will be first, and some are first who will be last" (13:30), which is exactly what this teaching will advocate. This underlines Jesus's conviction that there are issues of justice that must be worked out before God's table can be realized among us.

The imaginary of a cosmic communal meal is primal and profound, since eating is the most essential human practice, both habitual and symbolic. Food sustains and enriches our lives and cultures, yet when there is too little or too much of it, desperation or greed follow. Food brings people together but also divides them. In ancient Mediterranean culture (and still in our societies today), table fellowship mirrored the inclusions and exclusions of the wider society. Jerome Neyrey shows how a map of social relations is reflected in "the roles and statuses of participants at a meal: who sits and who waits on table, what specific actions one performs during the meal, who sits close or far from the host, what and how much food one eats, and when one eats, either first or last."[31]

Thus Jesus uses banquets as opportunities to teach about justice and inclusion. This partly echoes the Hellenistic philosophical tradition, in which critical public conversation took place at meals (as well as alliance-building, power brokering, and political influencing among elite male participants). Plato always sets the discourses of Socrates at *symposia*, dinner parties-cum-schools of learning. It is not surprising, therefore, that Jesus turns partaking into pedagogy; where he differs from the philosophers is what he talks about, and how!

An earlier meal at a Pharisees's house was "interrupted" by an uninvited woman, after which Jesus took the host to task—*and* implicated all the guests (5B). Here we must prepare for another very long evening (I like to call this "the party from hell")! With the atmosphere already tense from his adversaries' silence in 14:6, the trouble deepens as Jesus reads the room (*epechōn* means to "focus on" or "zero in on," 14:7b). He notices how guests are "choosing places of honor" (14:8); *prōtoklisias* is "first couch," similar to the "first seats" in synagogue (*protokathedria*) coveted by Pharisees (11:43) and scribes (20:46). In response Jesus spins a thinly veiled commentary on the present banquet in the guise of a story about "some wedding feast" (14:7a); Luke calls it a parable because it speaks prophetic truth and asks for radical change.

The first two sections of the banquet teaching begin in parallel fashion, a negative example followed by a positive one:

> 14:8: "When you are invited by anyone. . ." *don't do this*;
> 14:13: When you give a feast, invite. . . *do this.*

Jesus takes aim first at guests who are maneuvering around the "seating chart" (14:8–12). As in State dinners today, politics and power determined where and with whom one sat at an ancient *symposium*. "From the Greek and Latin literature one gathers that the dominant etiquette of issuing and accepting dinner invitations adhered to a strict sense of social gradation and segregation . . . where 'snobbery,' sycophancy, and humiliation . . . lurk menacingly in the background."[32]

Jesus counsels fellow invitees to abandon *voluntarily* positions of privilege in order to foreclose on the possibility of demotion by the host (14:8–9). As a strategy of self-interest (avoiding public shaming), this echoes the advice of

Proverbs 25:6–7. Jesus makes this alternative strategy explicit: occupy *at the outset* the "last/least" position (14:10; *eschaton*, as in 13:30). It will cost the host prestige to have to invite someone to "move up." Such subversive behavior undermines a hierarchical social system of positional management predicated on competing upward.

Jesus's conclusion is just a refrain from his mama's song-of-reversal:

> 14:11: For all who exalt (*hupsōn*) themselves will be humbled, and those who humble themselves (or "have been humiliated," *tapeinōthēsetai*) will be exalted (reiterated in 18:14).
>
> 1:52: God has brought down the powerful from their thrones and lifted up (*hupsōsen*) the lowly (*tapeinous*).

To a room full of male "executives" intent on ladder-climbing, the subversive idea that social transformation comes from below would have been unintelligible![33] Yet Jesus's strategy of downward mobility only echoes Amos's famous exhortation to Israel's leaders: "Let justice roll *down* like water" (Amos 5:24). Like water, "level" relentlessly seeks the lowest places.

Luke doesn't bother to record the audience's reaction, which we can easily imagine (and possibly share). Instead, Jesus moves on to critique the guest list, this time directed toward his host, as the parable seems to dissolve into unsettling instruction (14:12–14). In the honor culture of the elite, formal meal invitations were made with expectation of reciprocation; for the patron class, gifting was the primary mechanism for building influence.[34] Prestige was expanded by hosting both social *equals* (in order to do deals) and social *inferiors* (in order to secure them as indebted dependents). But a conventional guest list of those who will "repay" (*antapodoma*, only here and in Rom 9:11) is roundly rejected by Jesus point by point: "Do *not* invite your friends or your brothers or your kinsmen or rich neighbors" (14:12). The last example is marked out as particularly odious by its lack of a personal pronoun; inviting economic superiors to gain their patronage (so-called "negative reciprocity") functions only to strengthen the social hierarchy.

Instead, exhorts Jesus, invite only those who *cannot* reciprocate. His alternative guest list privileges "the poor, the 'crippled' (NRSV), the disabled, the blind" (14:13), and will be repeated in 14:21.[35] Such persons have been already named multiple times in Luke: in Jesus's inaugural sermon (4:18, poor and blind), the Beatitudes (6:20, poor), and his report to John (7:23, poor, blind, disabled). It becomes problematic, however, when human beings categorized into such groups are stereotyped and objectified, or worse, instrumentalized (by writer or reader) as mere props for healing stories.[36] Fortunately, there is a growing body of literature challenging ableist hermeneutics.[37] Luke portrays how such political bodies were categorically marginalized in the ancient body politic, especially when their physical conditions were correlated to poverty (thus his lists always mention *both*). Jesus pushes back hard on elite perceptions—fueled by purity concerns, economics, or prejudice—that such persons have nothing to bring to the table.

Jesus now utters the last of his *makarios* blessings in Luke's narrative, this time to those who are not looking for recompense (*antapodidomi*) or social advancement but who only long for God's justice (14:14).[38] After Jesus has publicly critiqued both guests and host—while also appealing for change—the tensions at this deteriorating dinner party are surely at a breaking point. In a desperate effort to make nice, one of the guests blurts out his own *makarios*: "Blessed is the one who will eat bread in the kingdom of God!"—one of very few times someone other than Jesus uses that phrase in the Gospels (14:15). This epitomizes a perennial, if disingenuous, religious response to conflict: we ignore what is in front of us and focus on the hereafter!

In Jesus's time, it was common to invoke the eschatological banquet as a symbol of salvation, inspired by traditions such as Isaiah 25:6. Such a devout entreaty would, according to Kenneth Bailey, have elicited the equally pious response: "May we be counted among the righteous in that day."[39] But the assumption was that this gathering would be limited to Israel's chosen; Qumran, for example, had a long list of those who would be excluded, including the disabled!

This man's effort to bring a pious ceasefire to the conflict rising in the room postpones the Great Economy to the hereafter, whereas Jesus is trying to realize it *here and now*. So, in the last section of this discourse (14:15–24), Jesus tells a story, which may be the actual parable signaled in 14:7. It is a tale about a great banquet gone bad—being told at precisely such a banquet!

The scenario would have been perfectly recognizable to those at table. In ancient Palestinian custom, first one invited guests to the village feast; then based on acceptances, slaughtered the appropriate meat and cooked it (a necessary strategy without refrigeration); then summoned the guests (14:17).[40] But what follows here is a systematic repudiation of the host's summons, narrated in triple, formulaic refrain:

- A first man sends regrets because he "bought a field that he must go inspect" (14:18). In fact, no one in this cultural context, even an absentee owner from the city, would purchase a field without knowing it and its history thoroughly.[41] Not only is the scenario a clear fabulation; it puts the economic transaction before the banquet relationship, intensifying the insult to the host.

- A second man similarly bought oxen, which he had to inspect (4:19). This is a similarly bogus excuse; no one would buy draft animals without testing them. Five oxen implies this man had a huge estate to plow, and as in 14:5, his care for animals excludes social relations!
- The parallelism of the third man's response seems to imply that his wife was an economic transaction (as was often the case). The curt report that he has gotten married (a feast to which this host was not invited) "implies that he already has enough reciprocal social obligations."[42] Moreover, the second stanza of the formula is missing, meaning he does not even signal regret!

To be rejected thrice, and in such backhanded manners, represents a thorough shaming by those who deem the host unworthy of their company. He has lost the game he was trying to play; a glass ceiling has shattered him to pieces.

The punch line to this nightmarish scenario is how the householder channels his anger at this rejection into a repudiation of his own colleagues (14:21). He embraces the very advice Jesus just suggested at the real-life banquet: throws out both seating chart and guest list, and starts again from below. Messengers are dispatched to search the "highways and alleys," which is to say, the cracks of urban society where the destitute dwell (14:21–22).[43] The story escalates, as he then turns to country "roads and hedges" (14:23). This signals a seeking out of those "afforded neither the protection of city walls nor attachment to a village," who were "isolated from city elite, city non-elite, and villagers alike. . . . They are from the lowest ranks one could possibly find."[44] In some cases, the messengers have to *compel* these folk to come—a realistic touch, since in an honor culture, those of low estate would assume they must decline such an invitation as improper or embarrassing to all concerned.[45]

The story ends abruptly with the host's avowal that "none of those he had invited will taste his food" (14:24). This is a double entendre. On one hand, the host is severing ties with his former associates. On the other hand, he also realizes that, having broken bread with outcasts, other power brokers will never again come to his door! He has committed class suicide—yet in Jesus's upside-down universe, he has just been born again by fully embracing Jubilee redistribution.[46]

"The banquet parable is a story about the 'conversion' of a wealthy urban householder-host," writes Braun, summarizing:

> The householder exemplifies the argument for a transformation of character which the elaboration has taken up as the theme of *chreia* at all its crucial points. An ostensibly wealthy householder sets out to seek honor

> (exalt himself in a "dropsical" manner) by hosting an ostentatious banquet to which he invites many of his wealthy colleagues noted for their ("dropsical") interest in accumulating assets; the result of this quest is not honor, but shame; consequently, the text implies that he undergoes a change of heart ("cure" for his previous "dropsical" ambitions) and abandons the quest for a reputable place among the social elite, "lowers" himself, does what is necessary . . . to become a benefactor and member of a group of people from the very lowest social rank; he finds this to his taste . . . and declares he no longer desires the company of his former wealthy colleagues and the "well-being" that he once thought they would provide.[47]

Does this story-within-a-story represent a happy ending to the dinner party Jesus is attending? Whether Jesus's *actual* host converts, as in the parable, is left like an unresolved chord—which surely also hangs over wealthy North American churchgoers!

Jesus wants to take *ahold*, *heal*, and *release* us, as he did with the dropsical man at the outset of this sequence. The powerful medicine of building community with those who have too little can restore the humanity of those of us who have too much. The two healing stories and extended banquet narrative examined in this chapter make an argument through showing and telling. It is that healing bent-over poverty on one hand, and bloated affluenza on the other, can be achieved only when the former fully regains membership in the body politic and the latter abandons privilege and entitlement in order to explore a life of downward solidarity. In the Sabbath Economics imagination of Luke, the liberation of political bodies is crucial to the work of deconstructing a body politic beholden to social disparity.

Can a simple meal story animate such robust social imaginary? I drafted this paragraph on February 1st, 2024: my sixty-ninth birthday, and the sixty-fourth anniversary of the famous Woolworth's lunch counter sit-in. Four African American university students sat down in segregated space at a cafeteria in Greensboro, North Carolina in a determined bit of political theater. It launched sit-in protests by Black political bodies and their allies across the South, which in turn breathed new life into a flagging civil rights movement and ended up changing the US body politic forever.[48] We should never underestimate the power of a strategic meal for justice.

CHAPTER TEN

Lessons from Improvisation and Defection

Third Rich Man Sequence

> *Gemeinschaft* lies in the household and the concept of kinship, in the ties of blood, friendship and neighborhood. . . . *Gesellschaft* lies in commerce and the conception of contract, its ties are the ties created by the transaction between (abstract) persons, its measure for all things is money.
>
> —Eugene Kamenka[1]

Eugene Kamenka concisely summarizes sociologist Ferdinand Tönnies's illuminating 1887 framing of two economic cosmologies. By the end of the nineteenth century, US capitalism had achieved continental hegemony through industrialization and urbanization, resulting in unprecedented social displacement, environmental destruction, and economic disparity. Tönnies was one of many European intellectuals (such as Karl Marx, Max Weber, and Marcel Mauss) who were trying to understand this brave new world as it was reshaping North Atlantic societies.

Tönnies argued that the market economy, and the state apparatuses developed to facilitate it, were steadily unraveling the fabric of older relational modes of economic exchange.[2] He articulated this in terms of a broad but fundamental distinction between what he called the integrating forces of traditional *Gemeinschaft* (community)—such as kinship, ethnicity, religion, and local literacy—and the disintegrating, instrumentalist forces of *Gesellschaft* (capitalist society). He defined *Gemeinschaft* as everything that holds human relationships together despite all that would pull them apart. *Gesellschaft*, in contrast, represented everything that would pull human relationships apart despite all that holds them together.

A similar distinction was elaborated two generations later by Hungarian political economist Karl Polanyi in his 1944 *The Great Transformation: The Political and Economic Origins of Our Times*.[3] Modernity, Polanyi contended, is defined by the struggle between the forces of the self-regulated market and what he called the "countermovement of social protectionism." Another two generations later, this antagonism was again summarized by Wendell Berry in terms of "Two Economies" and by Hazel Henderson in terms of the invisibilizing and exploitation of the bottom two layers of the "economic cake" by the top two layers.[4]

These analogous attempts to understand the roots of inequality and unsustainability remain the most succinct statements I have encountered regarding our modern economic crisis, from the last Gilded Age to the present one. They resonate strongly with biblical language about the struggle between the Great Economy (symbolized by *manna* in Exodus 16) and the forces of *pleonexia* (symbolized by "mammon" in Luke 16). In a world on the edge of a nervous breakdown from global social disparity and ecological overshoot, Luke's Jesus calls us to a discipleship of recovering, rebuilding, and advocating for community amidst the ever more insatiable, predatory, and destructive power of capital.

The next two chapters explore the two deeply related rich man stories narrated in Luke 16: a parable illustrating the difficulty of defecting from the cosmology of mammon (16:1–13) and a warning tale about the consequences of failing to deconstruct the chasm between rich and poor (16:19–31). These stories are, respectively, Luke's most nuanced and most unequivocal, representations of the two economies.

A. Capital or Community? Caught between Two Economies (16:1–8a)

We pick up Luke's narrative at the conclusion of the banquet parable, where Jesus engages a growing crowd with further reality checks about the demanding journey of discipleship. This sequence is shaped as a unit by three sharp refrains ending with an identical ultimatum: "unless . . . one cannot be my disciple" (14:26c, 27c; 33c, *ou dunatai einai mou mathētēs*). The discourse is illustrated with analogies drawn from the imperial world:

- *14:26: First ultimatum—family*: This call to transcend conventional kinship networks includes the troubling phrase "unless one hates" their family (*miseō*). This verb is mostly used by Luke to describe how adversaries feel about disciples.[5] Only here and in 16:13 (the impossibility of serving two masters) does Jesus require it of followers, in order to emphasize the need to resist two powerful socializing forces that can undermine and constrain discipleship commitment: the personal (the family system) and the political (the economic system).
- *14:27: Second ultimatum—the cross*: This is the second time Luke's Jesus clarifies the fate of those whom the empire deems dangerously

dissident (see 9:23). Here he follows Mark's blunt reckoning statement (Mark 8:34). This is followed by two examples of counting the cost, using uniquely Lukan images which, like crosses, were familiar presences on the Judean landscape under empire:

  - *14:28–30: building a tower*: Jesus alludes back to his examples in 13:1–4 of the violent ruler and the dangerous tower (*purgos*) as indicators of their disastrous historical *kairos*. The example of an unfinished tower project illustrates the overreach of the rich, revealing their presumption.
  - *14:31–32: king going to war*: Suing for ceasefire likely is another parody of the Herodians (Rome never conceded militarily). Why invoke such examples when this class of elites are not in Jesus's audience? It may be to show that in the real world, powerful people "count the cost" before embarking on *their* major commitments, while poking fun at them when they fail.
- *14:33: Third ultimatum—renouncing possessions*: The above two scenarios are contrastive, not comparative, to disciples whose vocation is the opposite of amassing wealth and power. Followers must take up the cross (not the king's sword), and here, must "take leave of" (*apotassō)* their belongings (*huparchousin*), not capitalize edifices.[6]

This string culminates in one more analogy: salt (14:34). This likely alludes to salt's healing or covenantal properties—after all, these are painful choices to be made.[7] The sequence concludes with the appeal to "ears that hear," repeated from 8:8.

The narrative now resets, with Jesus's audience increasingly polarized between "tax collectors and sinners coming near to listen" and "Pharisees and scribes grumbling" (15:1–2). Jo Bailey Wells sketches the next sequence (15:3–16:8) as four parables told in continuous sequence:

> We hear a story of a lost sheep, a lost coin, a lost son and then . . . a dishonest manager. The connections between the first three seem pretty natural: they are all cases of "lost and found." Are we to view the fourth under the same heading?[8]

Probably all four parables are about economics. The first two are about village life, in which the community rejoices when lost precious assets are found; these scenarios illustrate heavenly joy over persons who repent (15:7, 10). The lost sheep story may also, however, allude to Nathan's searing parable to King David, about how powerful people exploit the poor (2 Sam 12). In Luke's single most popular parable, the Prodigal Son (15:11–32), the two homebound characters embody the contrasting ethos of balanced (the jealous firstborn) and generalized reciprocity (the generous father). The fourth story illustrates a different meaning of repentance: improvising ways of turning around in systems we don't control. It is about someone stuck in the vexing and painfully real context of being caught between two economic cosmologies, who nevertheless takes what action he can. To this story we now turn.

Luke 16 is structured around two stories with identical opening lines, and bracket Jesus's teaching concerning mammon and the love of money:

16:1–8: "There was a rich man who. . ." (16:1)
    16:9–13: Teaching on God and mammon
    16:14–18: Criticism of Pharisees as "lovers of money"
16:19–31: "There was a rich man who. . ." (16:19)[9]

This literary unit is firmly linked to Luke's previous and subsequent sections. The Manager story hooks back to the Prodigal Son: both envision rescue by the household love economy and both deploy the verb *diaskorpizō* ("scatter," 15:13). The Lazarus tale hooks forward to Jesus's teaching about causing "little ones" to stumble (17:1–4).

Luke 16:1–8 is usually referred to as the Parable of the Unjust/Dishonest Steward, subtitled as such in many versions of the New Testament. This already biases our reading, encoding a hermeneutic of moralistic capitalism that takes the side of the boss and vilifies his manager in the story—despite the fact that both master and Jesus *commend* the steward's action. I therefore refer to this as the tale of a "Defect-ive Manager," interpreting him as someone caught between the two economies.

For modern managerial class folk, this story scenario might be analogized to that of a mid-level supervisor in a large corporation. Just as he is about to be downsized because of below-expected sales numbers, he ventures an act of resistance that he hopes will ingratiate him to clients who in turn will offer him hospitality. This is an attempt to defect to the relational economy (*Gemeinschaft*) that survives just below the surface of the Master's system (*Gesellschaft*) that is about to disenfranchise him. I propose this manager as the protagonist of this parable, and as an archetype for those of us who are ensnared in the toxic and oppressive imperatives of plantation capitalism. His efforts to use the resources at his command to rebuild social relations represent an improvisational embrace of Sabbath Economics meant to animate the imaginations of all of us similarly squeezed.

The rhetorical structure of the parable proper is chiastic:

A: 16:1–2: rich man's charges against and dismissal of the manager
B: 3: manager's internal dialogue about his fate
C: 4: manager's decision and rationale (focal point)
B′: 5–7: manager's action: writing off debt
A′: 8a: rich man's response to manager's action

This focuses attention on 16:4, which encodes the moral of the story: to act "so that people might welcome us into their homes" (reiterated in 16:9b).

The system of patron–client relationships—the cornerstone of social stratification in Roman Palestine—is foregrounded in this parable. Witherington points out that as the hierarchical structures of the Roman Empire imposed themselves on traditional participatory institutions around the Mediterranean world, patronage increasingly defined all social, economic, and political relations, from family to craft guilds to tribal structures.[10] Moreover, the social safety net of the older relational ethos was increasingly eroded by the pressure of economic structural adjustments throughout the Pax Romana, which was steadily displacing local subsistence peasant farming and fishing with managed production for export. Resulting latifundialization and landlessness, which caused the atrophy of village mutual aid, made the patronage of the great households a practical necessity (discussed at length by Hanson and Oakman).[11] The elite thus cast a long and chilling shadow across the landscape, which is reflected in this parable.

"There was a certain *plousios*. . ." (16:1a = 16:19a). Jesus's world was ruled by an absentee landlord class, toward which he already made his attitude clear in his first rich man parable (12:16–21; 8A). Like that landowner and his ever-bigger barns, the estate implied here is vast, indicated by the significant amounts of wheat and oil owed by the master's debtors (16:6–7).[12] Kenneth Bailey assumes that these debtors are sharecroppers working the estate, while Malina and Rohrbaugh think the huge amounts depicted suggest that these are whole villages owing percentages of their harvest, or perhaps merchant commodity traders competing to distribute produce to foreign markets.[13]

"Who had a steward. . ." (16:1b, *oikonomos*, "house manager," whence comes our word "economics"). This man would have belonged to what Gerhard Lenski called a dependent retainer class, which he described as "officials, professional soldiers, household servants and personal retainers, all of whom served in a variety of more or less specialized capacities."[14] Estate managers "had the authority to rent property, to make loans, to liquidate debts in the name of the master . . . usually paid in the form of a commission or fee on each transaction they arranged. . . . Traditional Israelite law provided that an agent was expected to pay for any loss incurred by his employer for which he was responsible. He could also be put in prison."[15]

This literate bureaucratic class had a tenuous existence: they had to ensure exorbitant profits for the master through merciless resource extraction and labor exploitation while at the same time maintaining working relations with peasant producers and competitive merchants. As Herzog puts it, such a manager was forever "caught in the crossfire between the master's greed and excessive demands . . . and the tenants' or debtors' endless complaints."[16] This is where the broad analogy with we who are middle-class, educated folks applies: like this *oikonomos*, we are privileged people who are nevertheless subservient to an economic system that both benefits and dehumanizes them. While most of Jesus's parables feature subjects who are either peasants (as protagonists) or elites (as antagonists), this story uniquely addresses *people like us*.

"And charges were brought to him that this man was wasting his goods" (16:1c). The two verbs here tell an interesting story. The first (*diaballō*, only here in New Testament) connotes accusations made "with hostile intent, either falsely or slanderously."[17] Herzog sees an implication that the manager is being undermined by fellow stewards, who are ever competing for increased prestige and influence within the master's system. The second verb (*diaskorpizō*) normally refers to a physical or geographic scattering: of a flock (Mark 14:27), seed (Matt 25:24), or people (John 11:52; Acts 5:37). Only here and in the immediately preceding Parable of the Prodigal Son (Luke 15:13) is it translated "squandering," thanks to capitalist hermeneutics. There is good reason in the context of this parable to argue that the verb here implies that this manager is *already* skimming and redistributing some of the resources under his control, a practice he will shortly intensify. After all, earlier in Luke, *diaskorpizō* appears in a key phrase in the Magnificat: God has "scattered the proud," which is synonymous with "pulling down the mighty from their thrones" (1:51f), referring to just the sort of rich and powerful people portrayed in this parable.

Though the charges against this manager are portrayed as hearsay, his dismissal is summary, confirming the absolute authority of the master (16:2, perhaps a faint echo of Isaiah 22:19). The accused does not try to argue or defend himself, knowing there is no recourse or due process in this system. Instead, in a poignant internal dialogue (16:3), he focuses on the stark alternatives facing him, knowing he "won't ever be able to work in this town again"! The soft-handed bureaucrat realizes he is not physically able to endure the brutal exploitation that was the lot of day laborers; on the other hand, seeking alms would obliterate what remained of his class honor. Herzog calls these options "death by digging or death by begging."[18]

As suggested by its structure, the story turns on the fired manager's conclusion in 16:4. Though his action plan is not revealed, the hoped for result is: he is going to do whatever it takes to cross over from the economy of *Gesellschaft* to that of *Gemeinschaft*. He has decided to defect from his patron's world, in which all social relations are cannibalized in service of accumulating wealth for the elite. His strategy is to intensify what he has already begun, hoping that by scattering assets he will be welcomed back into the older village-based ethos of generalized reciprocity, mutual aid, and hospitality. In exchange for his facilitation of debt-relief, "they will receive me into their *oikous*." Having been kicked out of the great household, he now must bet on the older tradition of Henderson's "love economy" for survival.

The rest of the story unfolds quickly (16:5–7), revealing the manager's subversive initiative. Presumably having a narrow window of time between his firing and its public announcement to the village, he hurries to his place of business. Still acting as official agent, he summons "his master's debtors one by one," perhaps so they can't compare notes (16:5a).[19] The phrase "tell me how much you owe" indicates either that he had lost access to the books or that he is already crossing over into the older honor code (16:5b). The manager does, however, ask for their handwriting on the revised bill that would make it an official transaction (16:6–7). The amounts of oil (approximately nine hundred gallons) and wheat (150 bushels) were substantial amounts—possibly representing contracts made with whole villages. Herzog contends that the amount written off is roughly equivalent to the 25–50 percent hidden interest charged in produce contracts that represents the master's profit margin.[20] It is a fire sale on debt, a sort of partial Jubilee moment. But only two examples are narrated here, as opposed to the more traditional parabolic rule of three (see, e.g., 14:18–20; 19:16–21). That is because *this* scene isn't the punch line of the story; that comes in the next verse, where the master, unaccountably, *commends* his feral ex-manager (16:8).

The landowner concedes that his system is corrupt (as in the later Parable of the Pounds, 19:22, 13B), acknowledging that the one he fired is a "manager of injustice."[21] However, the plutocrat gives him credit for acting "shrewdly."[22] Herzog makes sense of this surprising reaction by showing how the manager's action put the master in a bind.[23] The clients would have immediately praised their patron publicly for authorizing this debt reduction. Now the master is a local hero, and to save face he must follow through on the write-off, so as not to place the whole system in crisis.[24] He is, in other words, begrudgingly admitting that the manager has outmaneuvered him. Nevertheless, there is no hint here that he will welcomed the defector back into his system. The ex-manager's fate now lies in the hands of the villagers who benefited from his unilateral debt restructuring.

B. Defect-ive Discipleship in a World Ruled by Mammon (16:8b–14)

Jesus now begins decoding the parable: "For the children of this age are shrewder than the children of light in dealing with their own generation" (16:8b).[25] The phrases "this age" and "their generation" are apocalyptic in tone, the traditional rhetoric of resistance in Jewish antiquity. They convey an indictment of the entire system of exploitation, characteristic of the world that must "pass away." Yet Jesus nevertheless acknowledges that as long as "this age" persists, being "shrewd" (repeating the master's approbation) will be required to survive it. In this case, the manager has defected from the master's house to the debtor class, helping them in order to help himself. His gesture has rebuilt social relations instead of capital: hard-pressed peasants get a measure of relief, and he'll have a place to stay now that he's out on his ear. Jesus is not holding up this protagonist as a model disciple; he is, however, saying that disciples can learn from his improvisation.

This brings us to the moral of the story. Jesus has spun a tale about the predatory world of ancient commodity managing presided over by the "children of this age." He chooses this moment to introduce a unique term, in order to underline a crucial lesson for the "children of light": "Make friends for yourselves by means of the mammon of injustice" (16:9a). Mammon seems to be Jesus's dark metaphor for the dominant economic system.[26] The unqualified opposition between mammon and God articulated in the conclusion to Jesus's teaching (16:13) intensifies apocalyptic dualism. As so often in Luke, such rhetorical heat is Jesus's way of politicizing the issue.

We hear clear resonance between Jesus's exhortation in 16:9b and the manager's strategy at the center of the parable:

> v 4: In order that when (*hina hotan*) I am put out of the economy they may receive me into (*dexōntai me eis*) their homes.
> v 9b: In order that (*hina hotan*) when it fails they may receive you into (*dexōntai humas eis*) the eternal tents.

For Jesus, the question is not *whether* the unsustainable mammon system will fail; only *when*. Interestingly, he refers to the eschatological resting place for those displaced by the mammon system (like Lazarus in the next tale) in terms of the hospitality of "eternal tents" (*aiōnious skēnas*). This hints that redemption lies in a return to Israel's primal wilderness traditions—which is to say, the origins of Torah's vision of Sabbath Economics (2A).[27]

I interpret Jesus's extraordinary pronouncement here as an endorsement of improvisational monkeywrenching. Like the bureaucrat in the parable, disciples caught and complicit in the mammon system must figure out ways to defect from it while working to rehabilitate the traditional ways of the Great Economy. "Defect" is a double entendre, both a noun and a verb: to defect is to be dismissed by the dominant culture as defective. But this is the *only way people of privilege can become trustworthy*—which is precisely the focus of the next three verses (16:10–12), in which the Greek *pisteuō/pistos* (belief/trust) appear no fewer than five times!

Two assertions frame this little triplet on trust.

- 16:10: The first is a reminder that small experiments in trusting Sabbath Economics *matter*—but so do small acts of injustice.
- 16:11: Sandwiched between the two assertions is a rhetorical question about the mammon of injustice that clarifies both assertions. If Kittel is right that *mamōnās* is a transliteration of an Aramaic word meaning "that in which one trusts," it would make this a pun: "If then you have not been trustworthy (*pistoi*) in the unjust 'thing in which you place your trust' (*mamonâ*), who will entrust (*pisteusei*) you with true things (*to alēthinon*)?"[28] This underlines the lesson of the parable: attempts of the managerial class to redeploy capital to rebuild community are necessarily ambiguous and partial but nevertheless meaningful.
- 16:12: The second assertion is easily lost in translation. It is best rendered "that which belongs to the other" (*allotrios*), alluding to how those caught in oppressive systems often must handle what is not their own. How we go about this—exemplified by the manager's scattering—is how we earn trust.

Jesus's parable debrief concludes with a *pronuncamiento* that represents the pivotal midpoint of Luke's series of six rich men stories.

So as to not to be misunderstood as endorsing equivocation about the two economies, Jesus reiterates their fundamental *incompatibility* with a figure about serving conflicting masters, then thunders: "You cannot serve God and mammon!" (16:13). As the radical Southern Baptist farmer Clarence Jordan liked to point out: "It doesn't say ya *shouldn't*, it says ya *can't*!!"[29] Or as Wendell Berry paraphrases: "If we do not serve what coheres and endures, we serve what disintegrates and destroys."[30] This prepares us for equally unsettling polarities in the story of Lazarus to follow.

In a pointed bridge to the next rich man story, Luke narrates that "the lovers of money heard all this and ridiculed him" (*exemuktērizon*; 16:14). The adjective *philarguros* ("lover of money") appears only elsewhere in 2 Timothy 3:2, while the noun *philarguria* is roundly condemned as the proverbial "root of all evil" in 1 Timothy 6:10. The verb derives from *muktēr* ("nose"), conveying exactly our English phrase "they turned up their noses," or "sneered," at him! It occurs only once more in the New Testament: when local rulers "look down their noses" at Jesus as he hangs on a Roman cross (Luke 23:35). The profound disdain of the moneyed class for Jesus's Sabbath Economics teaching continues today. Now, as then, no heed is paid to Torah, the prophets, or to the possibility of a Great Economy (16:16).

* * *

The story of the manager trying to defect from the mammon system—in tension with the dialectic of its debrief—articulates what we might call a "trialectical" challenge to persons of privilege today under capitalism:[31]

i) The managerial class must realize that the system that *appears* to benefit us is a social and ecological endgame. We must figure out how to act creatively and concretely to use whatever economic means are in our hands to rebuild social relations with those oppressed by this system.
ii) Our best efforts will only ever bring *partial* relief or justice to a world ruled by capital. Nevertheless, we must persist, knowing that the system is ultimately unsustainable, and in the conviction that every experiment in re-centering the community in all economic decision-making helps build alternatives.
iii) The ambiguity of our position (complicit), and of our efforts to resist (fractional), should never delude us, as it has mainstream economic theologians, that the two economies are compatible. They are not, and the struggle to defect from one to the other matters, politically and personally.

This tale is an extraordinary call to discipleship in the real world: it refuses to exonerate us from a responsibility to act, however improvisationally, while making it clear that such efforts do not constitute an acceptance of what Dorothy Day famously called the "filthy rotten system."[32]

This is one of many biblical stories that encode in their characters our *own* resistances to the Great Economy, thus challenging us profoundly.[33] We have been thoroughly socialized into the world of mammon, where capital routinely destroys community. Financing can move freely across borders, but desperate workers can't; neighborhoods are redeveloped for the rich, while driving out the poor; and government policy bails out bankers who made predatory loans, but not working-class people who lose homes to foreclosure because of those same loans.[34] We cannibalize social relations to accumulate money in a thousand ways, large and small, working so compulsively we can't nurture our families, leaving beloved home places to follow promotions, too busy to sustain true community, and far more anxious about our net worth than the fate of the disenfranchised.

Even if we do recognize the fundamental corruption of capitalism, we are half-hearted at best in our efforts to resist or change the mammon system.

This tale can help deconstruct and reconstruct our consciousness around money. We are deeply entwined in capitalist culture, and for the foreseeable future are stuck in and with the money economy. Dissociative rhetoric or oppositional activism cannot exonerate us from our practical responsibility to handle the resources we do have subversively. We must be clear that money is neither a rational exchange mechanism nor a morally neutral tool; it can, however, be a means of either negating or affirming social relationships.

Unlike poor folk, middle-class Christians have far more choice about how we deploy our financial resources than we are socialized to imagine, as demonstrated by growing movements such as fair trade, community-supported agriculture, and social investing (appendix II, i–ii). A defect-ive discipleship will seek to use capital consciously, critically, and creatively to rebuild some measure of community and justice, even as we organize for systemic transformation. Nothing less can change the economic cosmology that is killing us and animate our political imaginations to embody ever more radical alternatives. The alternative is to do nothing differently, which ensures the endgame of disaster. That is the lesson of the story that now follows, which drives home why it is imperative to resist the structural, endemic socioeconomic disparity of the mammon system.

CHAPTER ELEVEN

Catechism of the *Chasma Mega*

Fourth Rich Man Sequence

Art is the lie that enables us to realize the truth.

—Pablo Picasso[1]

THE FIRST PART of Luke 16 narrates ambiguity; the second, stark clarity. Neither are explicitly named as parables, as are twelve other stories throughout Luke's Gospel. The Defect-ive Manager *can* be read as a parable because of its internal structure (story and explanation) and because it is the fourth in a series of consecutive scenarios about being lost. It is harder to make a case for the Lazarus episode, since it is not continuous with that series; on the other hand, the fact that most of its plot takes place in the afterlife tempts us to see it as parabolic, with Abraham giving the moral.[2] Still, with my teacher William Herzog, I read it rather as a real-world warning tale about—indeed, a catechism on—the cruel world of inequality. The end (in both senses of that word) of plutocracy is purgatory: for the poor in life, for the souls of the rich here and hereafter, for prospects of peaceable equilibrium in society, and (if we allegorize the flames of Hades) for our warming planet under climate crisis.

Building on Jesus's pivotal ultimatum about God and mammon (16:13), this next story of "a rich man who..." shows the fatal consequences of failing to deconstruct systems of vast social and economic disparity that hold our world hostage. It is Jesus's harshest teaching, yet represents the fulcrum of Luke's entire Sabbath Economics argument.[3] The *chasma mega* that segregates the desperately poor outcast and the wealthy mansion owner is uncrossable *because it has been designed that way by its architects.* These architects, and all of us who abide by their social constructions, will understand the truth of this gulf *only* by seeing it from the other side.

To compel us to see the historical crisis of disparity clearly, Luke's narrative moves from the all-too-real (the conflicted scenario of the *oikonomos*) to the surreal (taking us through a dark mirror to the afterworld). It confronts us with the brutality of social divides of our own engineering by representing that world turned upside down. If the Beatitudes and Disciples' Prayer proclaim good news to the poor, and the Defect-ive Manager addresses those caught between two economies, this story "speaks plainly" to plutocrats—and also "speaks to our condition" as people infected with the affluenza virus (to borrow two venerable Quaker phrases). Luke's succinct articulation of how mammon ultimately ravages both haves and have-nots, if in different ways, and provides refreshing clarity about disparity, centering it as the defining problem of both ethics and history. After all, as indicated next, the divide between rich and poor is the context for *both* ancient gospel *and* contemporary North American readers of it—except in our case, more so.

A. The End of Plutocracy

Disparity as Purgatory (16:19–22)

In 2009, historians Walter Scheidel and Steven Friesen published a paper analyzing economic disparity in the Roman Empire at its population peak in around 150 CE. They estimated that the elite orders and other wealthy groups made up only about 1.5 percent of the seventy million inhabitants, but controlled around 20 percent of the wealth, while middling households (perhaps 10 percent of the population) consumed another fifth.[4]

In contrast, a study by the Federal Reserve reported that the top 1 percent in the US owned 38.5 percent of the country's wealth in 2016; a 2021 analysis reported that the top 10 percent control almost 70 percent of national wealth.[5] Which is to say, the richest sector in the US economy controls *twice* as much wealth as did that of the ancient Roman Empire. The *chasma mega* portrayed in Luke's ghostly tale *should* haunt us because it persists today, constructed and maintained by segregationist policies (such as redlining and law enforcement "bluelining") and social architecture (such as freeway construction and urban redevelopment), but also by our own internalized class prejudices.[6]

Luke's story opens as a political cartoon employing archetypal symbols of wealth and poverty.[7] The first character is introduced through a concise sketch of decadent wealth (16:19); since the fourteenth century, tradition has called him "Dives."[8] In fact, Luke leaves this main character nameless, likely in order to portray him as a generic cipher for his class. He "always clothed himself" (imperfect tense) with "purple and fine linen" (*porphuran kai busson),* both luxury imports equivalent to today's high-end Italian power suits. These fabrics are named together again by John the Revelator as part of doomed cargo mourned by the profiteering merchants of a burning Babylon (Rev 18:12).

This man, moreover, was "feasting sumptuously every day." This would have been a slap in the face to the original peasant hearers of this tale, for whom feasting only took place occasionally and always in shared community festivals. It is meant to tutor us in the solipsism of affluenza, portrayed earlier in Jesus's parable about the wealthy landowner whose singular concern was with how to store and consume *privately* his surplus (8A). That cautionary tale similarly cut short such presumptive feasting (12:19, the only other use of *euphraino* in Luke) with sudden death-as-judgment!

Finally, this story is set at Dives's gate (*pulōn)*, indicating the fortress nature of his mansion. Herzog wonders if this might allude to the scenario denounced by the prophet Amos:

> They hate him who convicts in the gate (LXX *pulē*), and they abhor him who speaks the truth. Therefore because you trample upon the poor . . . you have built houses of hewn stone, but you shall not dwell in them . . . you who afflict the righteous, who take a bribe, and turn aside the needy in the gate. . . . Hate evil, and love good, and establish justice in the gate (Amos 5:10–12, 15).[9]

I think Amos is more than just in the background here; Luke's story is a full-throated *midrash* on this oracle's judgments on the rich.

The contrasting character has nothing *except* a name (Lazarus is a colloquial derivation of the Hebrew Eleazar, "God is my help"). His positioning outside the gate reflects spatial as well as economic disparity (16:20), and his description is equally archetypal of those at the bottom of the social pyramid. Lazarus is someone *made* poor: by debt (displaced from his land and kinship network); by disease (he has "sores"); and/or by discrimination from purity codes. So Herzog: "The verb here (the passive of *ballō*) . . . connotes one who has been 'thrown down'," so beaten that he does not even have the status of beggar."[10] Lazarus "longed for" (*epithumeō*) cast-off pieces of bread that had been used as napkins by the rich at table, for which apparently he could not even compete with street dogs (16:21). There was a charitable patronage practice by wealthy households in which clients, especially poor ones, would stand outside the door during a feast and hope for a "*sportula*, which is either a basket of food or some money to buy food for the day."[11] But Lazarus isn't one of these supplicants; he is roadkill in a death-dealing system.[12]

Having established a scenario of extreme social disparity in bold strokes, Luke's plot commences simply: both characters die—mortality being the only thing they have in common (16:22). The contrasts continue: Dives "was buried," implying all the pomp of a funeral for his class, while Lazarus receives no interment, his body probably disposed of in a refuse heap. At this point, the deconstruction of this cruel world commences. Lazarus's corpse is carried by angels to the "bosom of Abraham."[13] The noun *kolpos* signals intimacy at a banquet (see John 13:23), and for Luke the image confirms the Baptist's promise that "God is able from these stones to raise up children to Abraham" (3:8). In contrast, Dives is cast into Hades (16:23a), in classical antiquity the underworld, "a waiting place where righteous and sinners alike are gathered after death but separated from each other."[14] This realizes Jesus's warning vision in 13:28 about an Abrahamic banquet at which those relying on their entitlement are "cast out."[15]

These respective "destinations" of the two characters are stated matter-of-factly and reiterated in 16:23. The opening spatial opposition is now intensified cosmically: the "gate" that separated them in life has become a gulf in death. Lazarus's longing for crumbs from the table has become Dives's plea for "the end of his finger dipped in water to cool my tongue" (16:24). Lazarus never speaks in this story, as the second part now focuses on the painful yet tragi-comical exchange between Dives (who never truly awakens to the truth of his new space) and Abraham (who never relents in telling it to him). Is what now transpires merely a kind of *Trading Places* plot? If so, this would connote a crude form of divine retribution-in-kind. I think it is more helpful to read this "split screen" vision of Dives and Lazarus/Abraham through the lens of apocalyptic discourse.

The Greek word *apocalypsis* means unmasking, in which visions see through the dominant stories of empire: its self-aggrandizing fictions of sovereignty, its militaristic triumphalism, its seductive delusions of entitlement, and its severe orthodoxies of law and order. Apocalyptic decodes what the sage Morpheus, in the film *The Matrix*, calls "the world that has been pulled over our eyes."[16] It endeavors to see reality from the standpoint of redemption in two ways:

- by stripping away layers of denial and propaganda that keep us distracted, to expose realities of suffering and injustice—thus seeing the world *as it really is* from the perspective of the poor and victims of violence;
- by transfusing our dulled and dumbed-down imaginations with visions of the world *as it can and should be* from the perspective of divine love and justice.

Such double vision is able to recognize the world enslaved, and to envisage it liberated. This political cartoon is trying to jolt us into having "eyes that see."

B. Abraham's Warning

Fulcrum of Luke's Gospel (16:23–31)

The rich man now begins his "loud calls" (*phōneō;* see 8:54; 23:46) across the gulf. Astonishingly, he is trying to *negotiate* with Father Abraham. This crucial figure is invoked eight other times in Luke, more than in any other gospel. The story thus far:

- has problematized who *really* belongs to the Abrahamic family (3:8)
- a poor woman crippled by debt was welcomed back into that family against objections from the synagogue authorities (13:16)
- elites were warned that many of those who presume "chosen" status will *not* sit at table with Abraham at the eschatological banquet (13:28)
- in Luke's final rich man story, a rich man will be embraced as a "son of Abraham"—*after* he redistributes his wealth (19:9)

Here the patriarch receives Luke's most elaborate treatment, portrayed as a cosmic pedagogue.

The caricature of Dives now hits high notes of sarcasm about the entitlement of the ruling class. Despite his demotion, he calls upon his ethnic status (after the requisite preface "have mercy on me"), while persisting in class presumption. Dives tries to enlist Abraham to dispatch Lazarus on servant errands not once but *twice*; that he calls Lazarus by name damningly reveals that he actually knew him in life (16:24, 27)! The Ancestor, in turn, addresses Dives as a (petulant!) "child" (16:25). To Dives's first attempt to *order Abraham to order Lazarus* to serve him, the Patriarch responds curtly, directing his attention back to the unjust world over which the rich man once presided. In this rejoinder, "good" and "evil" are defined in clearly material terms: the shoe now on the other foot, Dives experiences the pain of deprivation, while Lazarus is "comforted" (*parakaleō*, which can also mean "consoled" or "encouraged"). Herzog points out that the story neither portrays Dives as impious nor Lazarus as pious; it is strictly about class distinction, or what liberation theology calls "God's preferential option for the poor."[17]

Abraham affirms that there is a "great gulf" (*chasma mega*, only here in the New Testament) between haves and have-nots, holding up a cosmic mirror to the insolent rich man (16:26). Insofar as Dives abided by the social architecture of extreme disparity in his world, he must also live by it in the next, in order to learn the truth of its impassability *from its other side*. There is restorative justice logic here: if inequality is criminal, then "convicted" perpetrators (and accomplices) must try to comprehend their complicity in violation by witnessing to victims' perspectives and experiences, for the purpose of making repair through concrete repentance and restitution.[18]

Still, sometimes the implicated refuse to change, and Dives is depicted as such a "hard case." Undeterred and unrepentant, he now doubles down on his request, exuding patriarchal entitlement (16:27–28). He presumes that just as his privilege will be passed on through the patrilineal line, so do his brothers deserve "fair warning." (Note that Dives has dropped the address "Father Abraham," now appealing on behalf of his own "father's household" in 16:27.) He proposes another errand for Lazarus: to "bear solemn witness" (*diamarturomai*) to the violent nature of the gulf (16:28).

Dives is not wrong that testimony "from the other side" of social gulfs is essential to change hearts and minds. But this plutocrat, having ignored Lazarus at his doorstep for years, has the gall to imagine he can bid the poor man to leave his "consolation" and traverse the *chasma mega* in order to enlighten Dives's rich relatives! "Just as the rich man fails to see Lazarus as a brother and kin, he fails to hear Abraham. The pedagogy of the oppressor has failed."[19] Dives has still not reckoned with Lazarus's experience of marginalization, desiring only the poor man's attestation to spare his own kin *who still live in luxury*. This is, needless to say, the opposite of "restorative justice"; today it is referred to as *revictimization*. Indeed, privileged people are practiced at displacing responsibility, ever expecting oppressed people to bear the emotional labor of speaking truth.[20]

The third and final exchange is the punch line to this cautionary tale. Abraham waves off Dives's attempts to make the victim responsible for change and points instead to the testimony of scripture (16:29). Specifically, he counsels a rereading of Moses and the prophets and their Sabbath Economics catechism of the dire implications of structural inequality (chapter 2). Dives's last gambit is to move from special pleading to full-blown quarrel: "No! But if only. . ." (16:30a). His people will only repent (16:30b; that is, change behavior) "if someone is sent to them *from the dead*." More irony: it is Dives who is in the place of the dead, not Lazarus.

What a dramatic illustration of the resistance of the rich toward the biblical witness, even when they profess Scripture's authority. Surely this moment is reproduced every week in churches of privilege and piety; a minister who preaches this text in such spaces can count on similar resistance, even if only expressed through disapproving silence. Instead, we ape Dives's desire for a miracle, a special circumstance, a divine intervention to resolve *our* problem. There is so much in these exchanges between the rich man (self-referential and defiant to the bitter end) and the Ancestor (equally stubborn in defending Lazarus and insisting on biblical literacy)! It should be enough to undermine every theology of entitlement and immunity by which we exonerate ourselves from responsibility to deconstruct social disparity in the world.

The clincher is Abraham's stunning closing argument: "If they do not listen to Moses and the prophets, neither will they be convinced even if someone rises from the dead" (16:31). In this phrase, "rising" (*anistēmi*) contrasts with Dives's notion of Lazarus "proceeding (*poreuomai)* from the dead." The former clearly refers not to Hades but to Jesus's resurrection.[21] This, of course, is how Luke's narrative ends (or rather, continues). Yet at this midpoint of his overall story arc, Luke insists that it is only the *scriptural vision of justice*, not the *novum* of resurrection, that can "convince or persuade" us to repent.[22]

This astonishing assertion—especially for those who regard the resurrection mostly as a dogmatic requirement, or worse, as a "get out of jail free" card—anticipates how Luke will conclude his Gospel. This is why my project began with a reflection on the Road to Emmaus narrative, where an unrecognized Risen Christ exhorts disillusioned disciples to study "Moses and the prophets." Luke's resurrection Christology does not rescue us from history. Rather, Luke points us back to the discipline of biblical literacy in prophetic faith. Disciples are empowered for, but not exonerated from, the work of deconstructing disparity by the Risen Jesus.

Herzog summarizes the "codification" function of this story for first-century Judaism: "By selecting a figure whose value for legitimating the social order was great, Jesus increased the shock value of the representation while enlisting Abraham as advocate of the desperately poor."[23] I believe this story, coming midway through the series of rich man object lessons, represents the hermeneutic key to Luke's Gospel, functioning in two ways as a fulcrum:

1. It holds up an eschatological mirror to our economic realities, challenging us to either live against or die with the inhumane gulfs that divide our social landscape.
2. It points us back to the Sabbath Economics vision of Moses and the prophets, as the Risen Christ will do again in the Emmaus epilogue.

This tale shakes up those who would rather daydream about the hereafter with the rude awakening that the *here* persists in that *after*. It exhorts us to reread the Bible, our history, and our own social geography in order to commit to a discipleship of deconstructing injustice and inequity. For Luke, this is the only way to be rescued from the *chasma mega*, as will be dramatized in the story of Zacchaeus (19:9; 13A).

Directly on the heels of this unsettling lesson, Jesus warns his disciples against complicity in practices and systems that "entrap" the vulnerable (the original meaning of *skandalizō*; 17:1), upon which Jesus utters a Woe (17:2). It may be "impossible" (*anendektos*; only here in the New Testament) to prevent *all* injustice, but this does not lessen God's fierce solidarity with every "one of these little ones entrapped," as illustrated by the Lazarus story. Jesus invokes another apocalyptic image of judgement: a dark metaphor about drowning-by-millstone (Mark 9:42). The same image appears in John the Revelator's vision of the collapse of Rome's oppressive economy: "Then a mighty angel took up a stone like a great millstone and threw it into the sea, saying, 'So shall Babylon the great city be thrown down'" (Rev 18:21). Jesus reiterates this grim trope again a few verses later, insisting that true faith can send formidable structures to that same watery fate (Luke 17:6b).

The deeply archetypal tale of Lazarus and Dives haunts Christian history and has continually reappeared in the art of Christendom for more than fifteen hundred years.[24] Given that our society is more than twice as disparate as was the one to which Luke originally addressed his Gospel, the obvious questions include:

- Where, who, and how are Dives and Lazarus today?
- Why and how do we aspire to the affluenza of the former, while scapegoating, invisiblizing, or ignoring the misery of the latter?
- How long will we live peaceably with the *chasma mega* in our world?

This story truly afflicts the comfortable and comforts the afflicted—and it bubbles up in the lectionary every Year C on the Sixteenth Sunday after Pentecost (see appendix I). We would do well not to miss the opportunity to direct the attention of congregations to inconvenient truths about the *chasma mega* in our world—letting the Gospel do the heavy lifting.

CHAPTER TWELVE

Lessons from Power and Presumption

Fifth Rich Man Sequence

> I suspect that Jesus spoke many of his parables as a kind of sad and holy joke. . . . I don't mean the kind of godly jest the preacher starts his sermon with to warm people up and show them that . . . he can laugh with the rest of them and is as human as everybody else. I mean the kind of joke Jesus told when he said it is harder for a rich person to enter Paradise than for a Mercedes to get through a revolving door. . . [or] for Nelson Rockefeller to get through the night deposit slot of the First National City Bank.
>
> —Frederick Buechner, *Telling the Truth*[1]

THIS CHAPTER PICKS up Luke's narrative at 18:1 and works through the sequence leading up to and through the penultimate rich man story (18:24–30). I begin with a parable that pits a widow's tenacity against a judge's obstinacy (18:1–8), then look at a second that contrasts a Pharisee and a toll collector (18:9–14). In each case, the marginalized character illustrates aspects of true prayer: persistence on one hand, honest self-assessment on the other. The powerful characters, on the other hand, are caricatures of presumption and entitlement. This sets the stage for Jesus's encounter with the fifth of Luke's rich men—the only place in the whole gospel tradition where Jesus's call to discipleship is *explicitly* rejected. We close by considering Jesus's debrief of that episode, which features the dreaded (but as Buechner contends, also hilarious) text of terror about the eye of a needle.

A. Contesting Delusions of Affluenza (18:1–17)

I will not exposit Luke 17 but offer this brief summary of that sequence:

- 17:1–4: This teaching concisely articulates the dialectic of justice and grace. On one hand, Jesus warns against causing "little ones to stumble" (1–2; discussed at the close of chapter 11). On the other, he enjoins the hard work of community members holding themselves accountable while also practicing restorative processes—as many times as is necessary (3–4).[2]

- 17:5–6: The famous "mustard seed faith" saying promises that small kernels of trust in the Great Economy can uproot tall sycamore trees of injustice—as will be demonstrated in the Zacchaeus story (13A).[3]
- 17:7–10: Another real-life scenario from the world of the servant class, though on the smallholder's end, since just one slave does both fieldwork and cooking.[4] Often moralized as a parable about servility, it is better understood as a kind of koan, as it undermines hierarchy by addressing the listener first as a "master," then as a "servant," blurring what was usually considered an absolute distinction.
- 17:11–19: The ten lepers represent another object lesson, showing how otherness is centered by Jesus (the protagonist's Samaritan identity is as marginalizing as his leper status). This again conjures the Nazareth Jubilee sermon's example of Naaman's healing (4:27; as in 5:12–14). As is appropriate in honor culture, the Samaritan gives thanks to God, the True Patron (17:16–17); Malina and Rohrbaugh suggest that Jesus accepts his gratitude as "payment."[5]
- 17:20–21: Jesus's response to yet another interrogation by Pharisees about the visibility of "the Kingdom of God" is L material. The translation "it is within you" (21b) is favored by Western religious interiority but is better rendered by the NRSV "among you." Zerwick and Grosvenor suggest that the adverb *entos* could even be translated "yours if you choose it," appropriate given that these local authorities have agency in many social matters.[6]
- 17:22–37: To reflect further on the matter of "signs," Jesus turns instead to his disciples. In a mix of Q sayings and synoptic apocalyptic traditions, he counsels them to ignore those who chase spectacle (22–23); the Human One's advent will be evident (24). He then quickly redirects attention back to the Way of the Cross (25) and offers analogies from the Genesis tales of Noah and Lot (26–33): life-as-usual continued until it was too late for them to avoid disaster. (Surely a warning to those of us living under climate catastrophe!) The sequence ends with his reiteration of the cost of discipleship (33 = 9:24), and how crisis will divide people (34–35). The final verse is clear about the origins of apocalyptic violence: the predatory Roman "eagle" that hovers over Jewish bodies and body politic (37).[7]

This brings us to 18:1, and two more unique Lukan stories about prayer and struggle.

These two parables are twinned (18:1–14). The first also has significant resonance with the "friend at midnight" tale examined earlier (11:5–13; 7B):

- Both feature two main characters (in 11:1 they are social equals, in 18:2–3 social opposites). Twinning male and female protagonists is typically Lukan.
- The first story is set in the relational ethos of a village, where it is expected that the protagonist's request would be met; the second is set in a city (*polis*), where the widow's petition to a powerful judge would seem futile (18:2).
- Both stories use the identical phrase: "keeps bothering me" (*parechein moi kopon*, 11:7 = 18:5), literally "makes trouble," or "makes my work difficult."
- Each concludes with Jesus's moral: God's compassion is imperfectly mirrored by a human parent (11:11) and God's justice starkly contrasts with an "unjust judge" (*kritēs tēs adikias,* 18:6).

These stories exhort listeners to persist in pressing for what is needed and just, because God stands with and for them.

Unlike the friend at midnight, however, the widow and judge story is introduced as a parable, which illustrates the necessity of persistence so as not to "lose heart" in a cruel world (18:1; *egkakein* is found four times in Paul's letters). An intransigent "judge in some city" (*en tini polei,* perhaps alluding to a notorious political figure) fears "neither God nor public opinion" (18:2). Herzog thinks this might imply that he only grants cases in which he has been bribed.[8] In that same city, a widow seeks vindication against an "opponent" or accuser (18:3).[9] Herzog assumes she is likely trying "either to claim her maintenance from [her deceased husband's] estate or to reclaim her *ketubah,* that is, the amount of money her husband pledged to her as an inheritance in the event of his death. . . . If there was no written agreement, the case could require litigation" that other family members could contest.

That she has to advocate for herself indicates she is alone (or alienated from her husband's family), with no male to represent her. "The Hebrew word for widow connotes one who is silent, unable to speak. In a society in which males played the public role and in which women did not speak on their own behalf, the position of a widow . . . was one of extreme vulnerability . . . the stereotypical symbol of the exploited and oppressed."[10] Imperatives to protect widows were as ubiquitous in the Hebrew Bible as they were rare elsewhere in the ancient world. For example:

- You shall not abuse any widow or orphan. If you do abuse them, when they cry out to me, I will surely heed their cry; my wrath will burn, and . . . *your* wives shall become widows and your children orphans (Exod 22:22–24).
- Yahweh is not partial and takes no bribe. . . . Cursed be anyone who deprives the alien, the orphan, and the widow of justice (Deut 10:17; 27:19).
- The Lord watches over the strangers; upholds the orphan and the widow (Ps 146:9).
- Seek justice, rescue the oppressed, defend the orphan, plead for the widow (Isa 1:17).

Such Torah and prophetic traditions hang heavily over Luke's scenario.

The widow's petition to "grant me justice" (18:3) echoes through the next two scenes (18:5, 7).[11] But unlike the story of the friend at midnight, this judge could *not* be shamed into doing the right thing (18:2, 4; *entrepō* is to be shamed), since the power differential between him and the widow precludes reciprocity. Herzog sketches the political context of this story:

> In Palestine, the use of an oral torah to interpret the Torah provided an institutionalized procedure and framework for continually recodifying the Torah to protect special interests while presenting the process as merely applying the principles of justice. . . . The judges whose decision applied those codes and set precedents for their implementation were in the service of the elites. The problem they faced was how to appear as representatives of justice while consistently rendering decisions in favor of the richer and more powerful. The only surprising element in the parable is that the judge seems to have abandoned all pretense of impartiality and has become openly what he has been covertly, a judge of injustice.[12]

Because the widow refuses to settle for anything short of justice, her only option is to make his life impossible—a kind of irresistible-force-meets-immovable-object scenario.

Germane is another, final illustration of widow exploitation, this time in a Temple setting, in Luke 20:45–21:6 (Mark 12:38–13:2). Jesus publicly warns people against the predation of scribal retainers "who devour widow's estates" as trustees, covering their crimes with public piety (20:45–47). He then points to the radically different relationships that rich (*plousios*) elites and a poor (*penichros*) widow have to the Temple treasury (21:1–4).[13] This is the final time in

Luke's narrative that Jesus will denounce the disparity between haves and have-nots. Like Mark, Luke portrays the episode as a final straw, after which Jesus abandons the Temple precinct and calls for its demise (21:5–7). Luke's last widow story thus contrasts starkly with his first: the prophetess Anna who spoke in the Temple about the coming Messiah and the "liberation of Jerusalem" in 2:36–38. Indeed, Luke's five widow vignettes alone (the three just mentioned, plus 4:25–26 and 7:12) are a mini-catechism in the imperative of Sabbath Economics justice.

With the scene set in 18:1–3, the plot proceeds but takes place entirely in the judge's head! At two previous points in Luke's special section he deploys internal dialogue to penetrate the armor of an elite character, revealing:

- the self-focused greed of an estate owner (12:17–19);
- the scheming of a bureaucrat (16:3–4);
- and now the frustration of this judge.

Perhaps Luke is trying to persuade his audience: "Rich people and their official agents are actually *afraid* of you exercising your power"—a word we ourselves should also heed! Sure enough, the judge relents *only* because the widow "wears him out" (the verb *upōpiazō* means literally "to strike under the eye" or "browbeat"; otherwise only used by Paul in 1 Cor 9:27).

Her determined strategy was twofold: she approached the judge directly and publicly. Though it may have been a breach of patriarchal etiquette, it created a spectacle that could raise questions about his system and confound his stalling tactics, as well as his likely intention to cut a backroom deal with her possibly bribe-paying opponents. She prevailed "not by denouncing the judge but by demanding he do his duty."[14] Herzog concludes that she tested "the limits of his expediency," in order that he

> may eventually decide that it is simply too costly to continue the stalemate . . . forcing the judge to reevaluate the cost-benefit ratio of her case . . . cut his losses and move on. . . . She was able to analyze her limit situation and design a limit action that broke the spell of inevitability cast by the ruling elites.[15]

In modern terms, we might see this as an efficacious campaign of nonviolent direct action.

To paraphrase Jesus in 18:6: "Pay attention to the unarticulated anxieties and fears of the powerful—you can outlast them!" His commendation of the widow puts her in the exemplary, if admittedly risky, company of the Defect-ive Manager (16:1–8; 10A). Even more dramatically than in his commentary on the friend at midnight story (11:9–13), Jesus emphasizes the distinction between the antagonist and God (18:7). He poses two rhetorical questions (each implying a negative answer), contrasting with the two most unsavory characteristics of the judge:

- Will God refuse to vindicate the elect?[16]
- Will God delay?[17]

Because God's universe "bends toward justice," neither public advocacy nor praying for justice are exercises in futility; in fact, they are the very substance of faith. Yet Jesus closes with a haunting question—not so rhetorical—concerning whether the Human One will find such faith among us (18:8b). It still hangs over our history.

This parable clearly correlates persistent organizing and prayer. Action and contemplation are *not* opposed to each other but are two sides of the same commitment. The story shows the way the world is but also the way it *could be* if enough people, no matter how marginalized, refused to remain silent in the face of injustice. It is not a fairy tale about a superwoman who topples patriarchal plutocrats with amazing magical powers. But it *is* about strength. If the weeping woman in 7:41 represents one expression of power, this widow demonstrates the other meaning of "crying out." A painting entitled *Saint Lucy before the Judge* by Renaissance painter Lorenzo Lotto (1532) captures this parable's scenario beautifully: a woman gestures fiercely at a judge high above her on his bench while two court officials try to hold her back; a crowd of men around flail their arms; and in the foreground, a baby runs toward her in joy.[18] These are the kind of women Jesus knew—not least his mother—as well as knew of through his tradition, from Sarah to Myriam and Rahab to Esther. Such advocates have always been the backbone of poor and oppressed communities: inconvenient, indefatigable, indomitable.

* * *

A second parable follows that also indicts elites like the judge (18:9–14). This time it targets those who justify their privilege with religious presumption and disguise their predatory power with public piety—perhaps striking closer to home for those of us in churchly circles. The setting, like that of the impoverished widow in 21:1–4, is the Temple Court, possibly during the offering (18:10). Both characters separate themselves from the afternoon crowd: the Pharisee "stands by himself" in order not to be contaminated by contact with anyone impure; the toll collector "stands far off" because of his despised status in the community (18:11, 13a).

Again, Herzog provides a good summary of how the two main "redemptive media," Torah and Temple, functioned in first-century Jewish Palestine to

> define the nature of the obligation or indebtedness incumbent on every member of the society. Only when this debt was identified and its ideological justifications were articulated in a persuasive manner would the second function, extraction of a surplus, be feasible.[19]

In addition to the three major annual tithes and offerings required by the Temple, workers and producers labored under direct taxes extracted by Roman officials and

> a vast array of indirect taxes in the form of tolls, imposts, duties, tariffs. . . . The Temple system was no less oppressive than the Roman occupation, but the combination of the two systems of tribute produced a crisis among the peasant population base.[20]

This parable contrasts two differing representatives of this extraction system: one honored, the other shunned. The Pharisees' interpretations of Torah helped legitimate the Temple-based purity and debt system. The toll collector was a street-level representative of Roman tax apparatus, "who staffed the booths and cheated the public on behalf of the chief . . . toll farmers whom they served."[21]

Luke again twins characters to make a point of their social dissimilarity. The Pharisee's prayer is longer and self-congratulatory, particularly regarding his tithing (18:12b); he endorses the Temple obligation because he benefits from it. His public denunciation of "extortioners, swindlers *(adikoi),* and adulterers . . . can also be read as three ways of describing the toll collector," thus accentuating his own piety while humiliating the other.[22] Belittled, the toll collector's prayer is short—"God, be merciful to me, a sinner"—accompanied by gestures of extreme remorse (18:13).[23] Herzog calls it "a bold and audacious prayer," in which he dares to consider himself worthy of redemption despite his implication in an unjust system *and* his public humiliation by the Pharisee.[24]

At a narrative level, the toll collector's petition echoes Peter's lament in 5:8, the first occurrence of *hamartōlos* in Luke. Ironically, an indebted fisherman and a collector of debts (*telōnēs*) are the *only* characters in the story to confess their own sinfulness. According to Jesus, when accompanied by change, this is the gateway to healing (5:32). He thus decodes the story by pronouncing the toll collector "acquitted" (18:14a; the meaning of *dikaiō* in the passive voice). This resonates with the judicial context of the previous parable and with Jesus's earlier censure of Pharisees who "justify themselves before people" (*dikaiountes heautous*, 16:15; also used of the lawyer in 10:29).

These back-to-back parables draw implicating portraits of powerful figures operating from a deep sense of entitlement and contrast them with two marginalized individuals battling for their dignity. Jesus now concludes this teaching by reiterating, almost word for word, his pronouncement from 14:11: "the exalted (*hupsoō*) will be brought down, and the humbled lifted up" (18:14b). Jesus's mama taught him to hope for this (1:52), and it will soon be realized in the story of Zacchaeus and a blind beggar (13A).

The next episode deepens Jesus's subversion of power and prestige: over his disciples' protest, he holds "even infants," again seeking proximity to the most vulnerable (18:15).[25] In antiquity, "infant mortality rates sometimes reached 30 percent, another 30 percent of live births were dead by age six, and 60 percent were gone by age sixteen."[26] Jesus "exalts" these young ones to a status they did not enjoy in their culture and sternly warns against impeding them (using the imperative of *aphiēmi* in 18:16–17). The Great Economy can only be "welcomed" like children (8:17; *dechomai*, the hospitality verb examined in 6A). All three of the unsettling encounters in 18:1–17, with their social dissidence and reversals, prepare us for Luke's penultimate rich man story.

B. Reckoning with the Needle's Eye (18:18–30)

Lukan scholars agree that his special section begins at 9:51, the point at which Jesus "sets his face toward Jerusalem." There is some disagreement, however, over where it should end. When judged strictly on the density of L material it concludes at 18:14, since from there forward Luke follows Mark's narrative relatively closely until his unique Emmaus epilogue.[27] When judged by the geographical subplot of the overall narrative, however, this middle section of the Third Gospel ends at 19:28: the point at which Jesus prepares to enter Jerusalem, where he remains until Emmaus (we've been reminded of his "march to the Holy City" at 13:22, 17:11; 18:31; and 19:11). I follow the latter approach, which accommodates the inclusion of the final two sequences in Luke's series of rich man stories. The first sequence I turn to now; the second (a key L text which culminates this thematic thread) I examine in chapter 13.

Luke follows Mark's rich man story closely (Mark 10:17–31), often reproducing it word for word, though with a few notable edits.[28] He omits Mark's transitional setting of this scene "on the way" (Mark 10:17a), such that the man's question comes abruptly on the heels of Jesus's teaching about "entering the Great Economy like a child" (18:17)—with which he could not be more out of step! He is a "ruler" (*archōn*). This term has described a variety of high positions heretofore in Luke's narrative: Jairus, a ruler of a synagogue (8:41); Beelzebul, a ruler of demons (11:15); a court magistrate (12:58); and a Pharisaic official (14:1). In the Passion narrative, *archōn* will denote political officers in Jerusalem (23:13, 35; 24:20). But *this* ruler's question—"What shall I do to inherit eternal life?"—appears to be a straightforward theological inquiry about salvation (18:18).

So how does such a promising opening end up in a disappointed departure? And why does Jesus seem to shrug off this discipleship *rejection* with a crude class explanation? The story is all too familiar to Christendom yet has never seemed to be overly troubling; after all, our theologians and preachers have spent great intellectual energy undermining its plain meaning. This infamous encounter has occasioned countless homilies (often on Stewardship Sunday!) exhorting those who are "blessed with wealth" to take care not to let their affluence "get in the way of their love for God and the church"—despite the fact that such an interpretation is *precisely* what this text clearly rules out. So has this tale—like so much of Luke's critique—been domesticated.

From his direct, even aggressive, approach, we can tell this man is socially powerful. He wants something from Jesus, so begins by offering him an accolade, fully expecting it to be reciprocated as befits honor culture (18:18b). Not only does Jesus refuse to return the compliment; even more impolitely, he rebuffs the man with a theological objection (18:19). Jesus thus immediately subverts all the protocols of "civil" conversation between male leaders. Yet Luke's overall narrative, not least the two preceding parables, have prepared us for his no-nonsense approach toward the entitled. The problem here is that the ruler's question assumes he can inherit (*klēronomeō*) eternal life. This is the second time Jesus has been approached with exactly this request; the first time it was a lawyer (10:25), which similarly propelled Jesus into theological sparring (6B).

In both cases, these gentlemen are exhibiting the false consciousness of class entitlement: they assume that eternal life is heritable, just like their wealth. Beneficiaries of a socioeconomic system typically envision religion as a reproduction of their own privilege—hence Marx's famous contention that "the mode of production in material life determines the general character of the social, political, and spiritual processes of life."[29] This ruler will shortly be revealed as *very* wealthy, and indeed his tiny class took great care to protect entitlements across generations. But we readers are supposed to recall that it was a dispute over inheritance that animated Jesus's inaugural rich man story (12:13; 8A). Moreover, Jesus will soon spin a parable about the struggle over land, in which insurgent tenant farmers try to kill the heir (*klēronomos*) in order to wrest the *klēronomia* from the absentee landlord—reminding us that the politics of inheritance was often bloody business (20:9–19).

In response to Jesus's interrogation concerning Torah's ethical commands (18:20), the ruler makes a grandiose claim: "All these I have observed from my youth" (18:21). This flies in the face of Jesus's insistence that "no one is good but God alone" (18:19b). Jesus doesn't contest the ruler's delusion but simply responds with a facade-puncturing caveat: "One thing you still *lack*."[30] He proceeds to make three invitations to change (18:22):

- "Sell *everything* you have . . ." *Panta hosa* is emphatic, used also in 18:12, where the Pharisee boasted that he gave a 10 percent tithe on *all* of his income. Here, by way of contrast, Jesus is asking for 100 percent!
- ". . . distribute it to the poor, and you will have treasure in heaven . . ." We hear two important echoes here. The first is to the story of a strongman disarmed by the Stronger One, who "distributes his plunder" (11:22, the only other appearance of *diadidōmi* in Luke; 7B). The second is to the conclusion of his catechism on the Great Economy, where the phrases "sell and give" and "treasure in heaven" (*thēsauron*) also appear together (12:33; 8B). This reversal radically revalues the currency!
- ". . . and come follow me" (*akoloutheō*, a discipleship term in the Gospels).

From Jesus's perspective, in order to truly observe the commandment not to steal (18:20), this man must quickly restore to the poor what had been taken from them by the wealthy. Jesus is not inviting him to change his attitude toward his wealth, nor to treat his servants better, nor to reform his personal life. Rather, he is plainly asserting that restitution is the precondition for the ruler's discipleship. "Deeply disquieted," the ruler turns on his heel and walks away from the Way.[31] Luke gives us a singular, telling reason: he was "exceedingly wealthy" (18:23; *plousios sphodra* is only here in the New Testament).

This stark scenario requires debriefing, then and now. The second part of the passage complies, if only to compound the shock. In Mark's text, Jesus turns to address the disciples, but in Luke he looks at the ruler as he begins speaking (18:24a). It is not clear whether Jesus is addressing him directly or musing aloud to his disciples as he watches the man depart. The plot now changes focus from the ruler's concern about eternal life back to the previous episode's concern about "entering the Great Economy" (18:17). And it elicits Jesus's most notorious, and widely ignored, teaching (18:24b–25):

> How hard (*duskolōs*) it is
> for those having wealth (*chrēma*) to enter the Great Economy.[32]
> For it is easier for a camel to go through the eye of a needle
> than for a rich man to enter the Great Economy![33]

So the audience will not forget—repetition being the key to pedagogy—the essential point is reiterated using the razor's edge of absurdist humor. It is like trying to get Palestine's largest animal through its smallest aperture: not *difficult*, but *impossible*.

The clarity of this saying has escaped the church through the ages, and it instead has concocted countless disingenuous reasons why the passage cannot mean what it says.[34] Christians have been so anxious that Jesus might be categorically excluding the rich that they have missed the fact that this doublet is not a statement about them at all, but about the *nature of the Great Economy*. Jesus's has already asserted—in the very first line of the Sermon on the Plain (6:20)—that it is a space that has no entry requirements for the poor. Conversely, here he stipulates that the Great Economy, defined as that social condition in which there is "enough for everyone," is a space where the rich cannot enter—insofar as their wealth is predicated upon structural disparity. Their entry requirement is redistributive justice.

This text remains as dissonant to our ears today as it was to "those who heard it," who can only muster an anguished, incredulous protest: "*Who* then can be saved," if not the rich? (18:26). Jesus is attacking the sacred ideologies that rule over us, which associate wealth and power with divine blessing or election (antiquity), or with the entitlement earned by "hard work" and/or entrepreneurial genius (modernity). The Jubilee imagination circulates at a low rate of exchange within contemporary Christianity because in our capitalist cosmology, redistributive justice is high heresy; we believe in "salvation by works." Practices of generalized reciprocity only make sense within the divine cosmology of "salvation by grace." By the time this rich man is invited to relinquish control over his surplus, however, Luke's narrative has firmly established the vision and practice of Sabbath Economics. In the Great Economy, the last are first, or in this case, the impossible is possible (18:27).[35] Jesus will now show how.

Peter is quick to remind Jesus that he and his fellow disciples *have* "left their own and followed" (18:28 = 5:11). Jesus neither confirms or denies Peter's claim, but does promise this:

> Amen I say to you, there is no one who has left house or spouse or brothers or parents or children, for the sake of the Great Economy, who will not *receive* multiplication in this time (*kairos*), and in the age to come eternal life (18:29–30).

This is the fourth of Jesus's six "solemn sayings" in Luke, and echoes the one immediately preceding this episode (18:17). Peter's claim to have sacrificed "our own (*ta idia*)" likely refers to family and homes, which Malina and Rohrbaugh point out would have been the only real assets a peasant possessed.[36] But Jesus assures them (in the conditional subjunctive mood) that *whosoever* "releases" (*aphiēmi*, the Jubilee verb) these will *receive* them back (*not* inherit!) multiplied through community sharing in the Great Economy.[37]

"...and in the age to come, eternal life." *This* is the answer to the rich ruler's question. But he has not stuck around to hear it, possessed by his possessions, unpersuaded by Jesus's alternative cosmology, and thus unwilling to change his economic practice. Luke's penultimate rich man story is, like the preceding one (chapter 11), is a warning tale that when undomesticated has not lost its bite in our time. Privately controlled wealth is the backbone of capitalism and is predicated upon the exploitation of natural resources and human labor. Profit maximization renders socioeconomic stratification, objectification, and alienation inevitable. According to this story, those who are privileged within *this* system cannot enter the Great Economy nor be rescued by entitled fantasies of eternal life (just ask Dives). Such stories are *not* good news for those of us who are inheritors of, and in, the rich man's legacy. The only antidote to personal and political "damnation" is the lifelong journey of Sabbath Economics.

The disciples' incredulity at Jesus's teaching here anticipates our own. Does Jesus *really* demand that we who are caught in affluenza and beholden to plutocracy must participate in wealth redistribution as a condition for discipleship? Can we even imagine a world in which there are no presumptive rich and desperate poor? To our skepticism, Jesus replies: "What seems impossible to you is possible for God" (18:27). Which is why economics is ultimately a theological matter.

CHAPTER THIRTEEN

Healing Affluenza, Resisting Plutocracy

Sixth Rich Man Sequence

> The story ends so brutally, both for the slave, who loses everything, and for those who opposed the rule of this king and are slaughtered. The ending is harsh because this isn't about God's kingdom. This story is told in Zacchaeus's house for Zacchaeus's sake. Sometime in the near future, Zacchaeus is going to have some appointments with the bureaucrats above him. He is supposed to have collected the tax amount and some extra to line their pockets. He was probably chosen for his job because he was the best at squeezing money out of the people. As a result of meeting Jesus, he won't have extra for kickbacks. He is going to be like that third slave—unable to deliver the economic goods to the harsh ruler.
>
> —Keesmaat and Walsh, "Outside of a Small Circle of Friends"[1]

JESUS'S ANNOUNCEMENT OF the final leg of his journey to Jerusalem (18:31a) signals the closing sequence of Luke's middle narrative, which began back at 9:51. For a third and final time he briefs his disciples concerning the fate that awaits him in the Holy City, about which they remain in denial (18:31b–34).[2] The triptych that follows begins with an encounter with a poor man (18:35–43), and then the richest character yet (19:1–10). It is Luke's final literary twinning of somatic symbolism to show the crisis of economic disparity. The third episode is a parable about an even wealthier baron and another defector (19:11–17). This is the capstone to Luke's six rich man sequences, after which Jesus presses on "up to Jerusalem" (19:28).

A. Mary's Song Realized, Abraham's Family Reunified (18:35–19:10)

The triptych begins with the inconvenient interruption of a blind beggar, as Luke follows Mark's story of Bartimaeus (10:46–52).[3] He is begging because he is both disabled and poor—social conditions that reinforced each other in ancient societies, and too often still do today. He positions himself at the gates of Jericho because pilgrims on their way up to Jerusalem would have been in a mood to give alms (18:35). This is how he survived—just as Zacchaeus thrived by managing the predatory tax extraction system centered in that administrative urban center. As in so many gospel healing stories, the poor man takes initiative to reach out to the healer, despite opposition from those around him. But for the first time, so does a rich man. The commotion of a crowd (*ochlos*) gets each of their attentions, and each has to make a pointed effort to encounter Jesus—connecting their otherwise vastly disparate prospects (18:36, 19:3).

Upon inquiring, the blind man is informed that "Jesus of Nazareth is passing him by" (18:37).[4] The healer's reputation clearly preceded him, and desperate not to miss the opportunity to receive liberation, the blind man becomes insistent (18:38–39). He addresses Jesus as "Son of David," perhaps invoking royalty to get his attention.[5] Verbal repetition underlines the ensuing war of wills:

- 18:38: The blind man "shouts out" (*boaō*), a verb that heretofore described John the Baptist (3:4), a desperate father (9:38), and tenacious prayer (18:7).
- 18:39a: Those at the front of the crowd "rebuke (*epitimaō*) and silence (*sigaō*)" him, suggesting they are trying to clear him out of the way, attesting to his low social status as one of the invisible and expendable poor.[6]
- 18:39b: He responds by "screaming" (*krazō*), used elsewhere by Luke to describe a father's tortured son (9:39) and the stones that break human silence (19:40).

The man stubbornly repeats his petition for mercy (see 17:13). When the marginalized advocate for themselves too loudly and insistently, it creates a scene, as we saw previously with the wailing woman (7:35–40) and the persistent widow (18:1–6).

Jesus stops in his tracks, a fourth resonance with the Zacchaeus story (18:40; see 19:8a). In another strong verb, he commands (*keleuō,* only here in Luke) his "handlers" to bring the blind man forward. Jesus *inquires* after, rather than ignoring, the fracas (18:41a), yet again embracing the divine vocation of listening for the cry of the poor (Exod 3:7). This man desires "to see again" (Luke 18:41b, *anablepō*), the same verb Jesus used in reciting his mission back in 7:22. He's asking for "a hand up, not a handout" (to use the infamous presidential cliche). To prioritize symbolism over physiology, we might translate this compound verb as "to re-vision." Jesus again affirms, as in 7:9, 50; 8:48; and 17:19, that it is the man's trust exhibited through initiative that liberates him (18:42). He leaves what little he has (his mendicant franchise) in order to follow Jesus—discipleship as the embodiment of true vision.

* * *

Entering Jericho, we are immediately told Jesus sought to "pass through" it, as if in a hurry to leave (19:1). He had his reasons; possibly the oldest city in the world, it would be no more hospitable to a wilderness prophet than Jerusalem to come. But let us consider this episode in geopolitical context. The main route for Galilean pilgrims to Jerusalem would have taken them through Samaria, but given his earlier expulsion from this region, Jesus had likely taken the longer eastern route (see Figure 6), entering Jericho from the east and then heading west.[7]

While east of the Jordan he would have likely revisited the place where he was baptized by John, where Jesus went deep into Jordan's waters to remember the stories held by that sacred river (3:21–22). Primary among them was the old Israelite saga preserved in Joshua 1–6, its serial episodes laced with magical symbolism:

- Rahab's subterfuge that outwits Jericho's urban police (Josh 2);
- Israel's Red-Sea-like crossing of the swollen Jordan from the east (Josh 3)—a crossing which Jesus would just have made;
- taking twelve river stones to erect a sacred cairn announcing Israel's insurrection against Canaanite overlords in Jericho (Josh 4);
- a camp celebrating circumcision, Passover, the end of *manna* and holy ground (Josh 5);
- and the defeat of Jericho—a heavily fortified city-state—by a peasant militia armed with nothing more than Jubilee trumpets and a Sabbath circle dance (Josh 6)!

Jesus would have carried a consciousness of this legacy of resistance and renewal into Jericho. Now, something equally improbable is afoot, as Luke introduces his final archetypal rich character (*plousios*, 19:2).

The Zacchaeus story is the single clearest New Testament text about a practice of economic reparation. This is a fraught but crucial issue that white churches in North America today must face in the wake of a half-millennium of Christian-sponsored colonization and enslavement. It is a conversation in which scripture can again do the heavy lifting, but unfortunately, we are handicapped by how middle-class churches trivialize this story, an effective strategy for avoiding it. The main character is portrayed as a "wee little man" with no particular social identity or context, whose most important action is to climb a tree to see Jesus, as canonized in the cloyingly cute Sunday School ditty.[8] Such sentimentalizing obscures the real economic and political terrain of the story—and thus its edge.

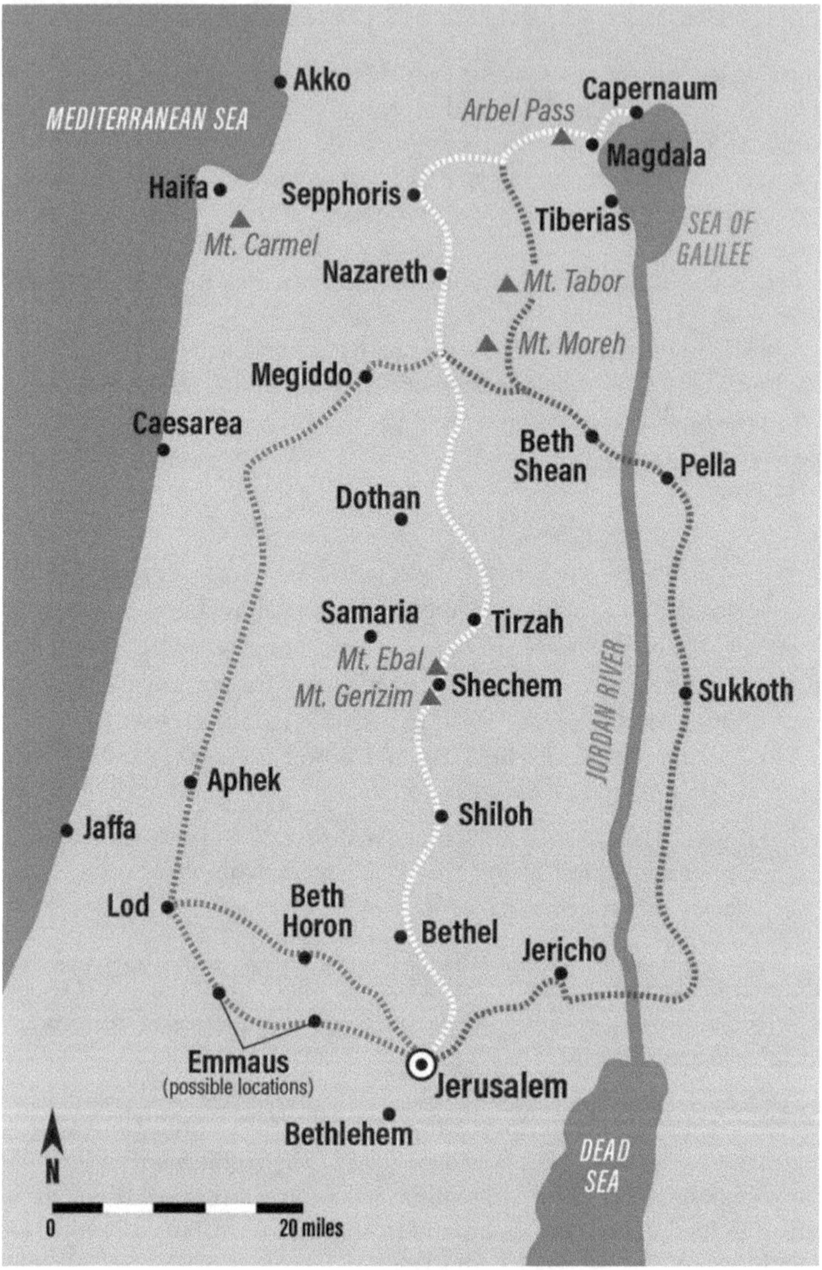

Figure 6. Map of ancient pilgrimage routes (courtesy of the Biblical Archaeology Society).

This is our sixth and final encounter with tax collectors in Luke. As we've seen, these local Jews were street level representatives of an oppressive tax-farming system. While major tax and tribute burdens were taken directly by agents of Rome with official policing power, native collectors held low-level contracts to collect duties, levies, tolls, and customs on lands, products, and persons, living from whatever commissions they could get. Taxpayers had no idea what sort of financial arrangement had been negotiated by the collector, and thus were inevitably victims of extortion. Because they were viewed as agents of a hated Roman occupation, publicans were socially rejected, religiously impure, and disdained as political traitors.

They were not, however, necessarily as well-off as Levi (5:27–30; 4B), since they were at the bottom of a professional hierarchy in which profits flowed upward. This is why they keep showing up in the crowds of marginalized people in Luke. Luke takes a special interest in low-level tax collectors because he understands how key they were to the political captivity and economic oppression of the Roman occupation. Their trade symbolized everything that had gone wrong for and with the nation. In Luke's story they are attracted to John the Baptist (3:12) and his proclamations about the justice of God (7:29, 34); they keep coming to the table with Jesus (5:27; 15:1); and they are capable of expressing deep regret about their entrapment in a rotten system (18:10–13; 12A).

The *chief* tax collector (*architelōnēs*), on the other hand, was at the top of this extractive pyramid, exploiting those under him who exploited the people, and thus would have been the most rapacious, wealthiest, and most despised among them (19:2). His office was strategically headquartered in Jericho, a regional center for trade, and the port of entry for all traffic crossing into Palestine from east of the Jordan. This rich man has a name—*for the first time* in Luke! Was Zacchaeus "short" of stature, or "young in age" (as *hēlikia* is translated in every other usage in New Testament; 19:3)?[9] The latter would imply that he inherited his lofty franchise as the result of family patronage, probably to the royal house of Herod, who kept a winter palace in Jericho. Zacchaeus's privilege since birth contrasts sharply with the unnamed blind man's years of poverty and neglect. Luke's culminating pair of archetypes thus represents the very top and bottom of the social hierarchy.

This story is full of surprises, however, the first of which is that this universally scorned exploiter was actually "trying to see Jesus." Like the beggar, Zacchaeus mobilizes so that Jesus does not "pass him by." The fact that both characters want to see—and that both are "blind," though in radically different ways—is how Luke binds their fate together. The narrative until this point has suggested that it is impossible for the rich to cross the *chasma mega*. But when Zacchaeus climbs a *sukomorea* tree, we are meant to recall what Jesus had promised earlier: "If you had faith the size of a mustard seed, you could say to this *sukaminō* tree, 'Be uprooted and planted in the sea,' and it would obey you" (17:6).[10] In the Zacchaeus story, Luke yet again shows what Jesus told: a rich and powerful man, perched high up in a sycamore tree, is about to be uprooted and replanted into the soil of Sabbath Economics.

Passing that tree, Jesus "looks up" (*anablepō,* another verbal hook with the blind man in 18:41), re-visioning the possibility of healing for this plutocrat. He issues a double command:

- First, Zacchaeus must "hurry down" (the verb *speudō* appears in 19:5a and 6a, connoting a sense of urgency) from his position *above* the crowd. Repentance requires social repositioning. This is Luke's symbolic fulfillment of the Magnificat (1:52), showing what Jesus's mama sang: in the crowd below, the blind man disciple was lifted up from his trampled position as a beggar; this rich man is now brought down from his privileged perch of superiority. Mary's revolutionary vision of leveling was *not* a delusion: the Great Economy will be animated from the bottom up, and the mammon system will collapse from the top down.
- Second, Jesus demands hospitality—an aggressive and perhaps risky strategy. "It is necessary (*deî*) that I stay at your house today" (19:5c). While this verb often connotes the inevitability of prophetic suffering in Luke, it can also refer to an equally costly sense of responsibility concerning "what needs to be done" to animate radical change.[11] From his experience with Levi at the start of his ministry (5:27–29), Jesus realizes that only a full intervention will suffice here.

Despite having no kind words about the wealthy in his teaching thus far, and having just had his call to discipleship summarily rejected by a rich ruler two episodes earlier (12B), Jesus nevertheless continues to take initiative.

This surprise is immediately followed by another: Zacchaeus hurries down and "receives him joyfully" (19:6).[12] This is an unexpected and courageous pivot for someone of his social station and living in his insular bubble. Surely it is evident to him that by welcoming the homeless man Jesus, he is also welcoming his entourage—which now specifically includes the poor blind man, who would still be considered unclean.

Imagine this raggedy group of folk trooping into the elegant home of the head of the regional tax farming industry. If *we're* not unsettled by this awkward class-mixing, the other characters in the story certainly are. There is immediate resistance from Jesus's people, who object to sharing table fellowship with an oppressor (19:7). They "grumble aloud" (the wonderfully onomatopoetic *diagogguzō*), just as the local authorities did at the prospect of eating with "tax collectors and sinners" (5:30; 15:1–2)—and as the Israelites did in the Exodus wilderness just before their Sabbath Economics catechism (Exod 16:2, 7–8, LXX).[13] No doubt Zacchaeus's people protest too, likely worried about the proverbial fine china and silverware! But as Jesus will point out, this violation of social boundaries is literally liberation walking into the house of the rich.

Apparently, Zacchaeus can sense the tension. Luke tells us "he stood still" (*statheis*)—the exact phrase that described Jesus's halt when he heard the poor man screaming, taking the time to feel and hear the man's distress (18:40). Now it's the tax farming executive who stops dead in his tracks, a rhetorical repetition Luke uses to suggest that he is encountering not only Jesus, but also disenfranchised neighbors he has never truly seen, but in whose impoverishment he likely had a hand. In that Zen moment of pause, he realizes Jesus is interested in more than hospitality.

Uncharacteristically for those of his class, his response is not to turn heel as did the previous rich man; or to indulge in a photo opportunity for a public lament about inequality, make a ritual apology in front of the crowd, call for a high-level committee to study the problem, or rant about government policy. Rather, unbidden, in his greeting of Jesus he blows the door of his class-standing off its hinges by committing to two substantial practices of redistributive justice:

1. "Half of my assets (*huparchonton*) I give (*didōmi*) to the poor. . ." (19:8a). This is not charity, benefaction, a 10 percent tithe, guilt-money (in modern parlance) with strings attached, or a donation to the nonprofit industrial complex. *It is restitution according to Torah*, in which someone who has stolen from another must restore equity plus four- or fivefold in order to make up for breach of trust, aggravation, and injustice (Exod 2:2).
2. "And if I have defrauded (*sykophanteō*) anyone of anything, I restore (*apodidōmi*) it fourfold" (19:8b). One can imagine Jesus raising an eyebrow and muttering "*If*?"[14] This is another echo of Torah:

> If any one sins and commits a breach of faith against the Lord by deceiving his neighbor in a matter of deposit or security, or through robbery, or if he has oppressed his neighbor, or has found what was lost and lied about it,

> swearing falsely . . . he shall restore what he took by robbery, or what he got by oppression, or the deposit which was committed to him, or the lost thing which he found, or anything about which he has sworn falsely; he shall restore it in full, and *shall add a fifth to it*, and give it to him to whom it belongs" (Lev 6:2–5).[15]
>
> The verb in 19:8b intensifies the one in 19:8a: we have now moved from *restitution* to *reparations*. Zacchaeus goes beyond Torah's 20%, suggesting the massive extortion that built his franchise.[16]

Zacchaeus is doing nothing more or less than rediscovering and embracing the teachings of his ancestors. It is a first step toward transforming his whole estate back into Commonwealth and is accepted as such by Jesus. This story contrasts dramatically with every other rich man vignette in Luke, not least the immediately preceding one. What the rich ruler refused to do is confirmed here as the only avenue into the Great Economy—and *not* an impossible task (18:27–28).

There is a second hermeneutical problem surrounding how this episode is read, this time arising from the academic side of the street. As Sylvia Keesmaat notes, "the disagreement over how to tell this story in Luke 19.1–10 reveals some ideological fault lines in the world of biblical scholarship."[17] Many interpreters (including Malina and Rohrbaugh!) have argued that in 19:8, Zacchaeus was reporting on what he was *already regularly giving*, and that his reputation for generosity and justice were widely known, which is why Jesus solicits his hospitality and seems to commend him. This is an astonishingly eisegetical, even fraudulent, solution to the challenge that redistributive justice poses to middle-class hermeneutics under capitalism, one more example of our modern attempts to squeeze Luke's rich men through the eye of the needle.

There are multiple reasons why such a reading does not cohere:

- Zacchaeus's alleged reputation for kindness and community would not square with the clear antipathy of the crowd toward him in 19:7.[18]
- There is not a shred of evidence that this man had ever made such gestures. Zerwick and Grosvenor translate the present indicative *didōmi* in 19:8a as intention ("I am determined to give";[19] similarly, *apodidōmi* signals a conditional commitment ("if I have . . . I give back").
- Jesus invokes the temporal marker "today" (*sēmeron*) twice in this episode (19:5, 9). In Luke this often connotes a watershed moment

of liberation (2:11; 4:21; 5:26), and Jesus's pronouncement that "today salvation has come to this house" is no exception (19:9). This is the *beginning* of Zacchaeus's momentous turn toward repentance and repair.

- Above all, the notion that a head of the tax-farming operation would *regularly* give away half his assets (which would include the profits of his Herodian patrons), *and* redress any hint of extortion (despite its normalcy and the absence of any mechanisms for prosecution), is absurd. It would have meant financial and political suicide, meaning that Zacchaeus would not still be in his position!

This is not a story about a patron's self-congratulation but his *conversion*. And it is the culmination of the Jubilee argument Luke has been building since Mary's Magnificat.

Perhaps Zacchaeus had heard reports of Jesus's parables, such as the sobering tale of Lazarus and Dives (chapter 11). But Luke's longer story arc offers the best explanation for Zacchaeus's immediate material penance at the door to his home. He had certainly received intelligence from his underling Levi in Capernaum; after all, these two episodes virtually frame the entire narrative of Jesus's pre-Jerusalem ministry. Levi would have stressed to his overlord that this prophet from Nazareth was serious about repairing the socioeconomic divide through redistribution of wealth. And Levi didn't just *tell* Zacchaeus about Jesus's call to Jubilee; he *showed* it by abandoning his toll office and inviting Jesus to his home for a feast (4B).

There were, as we've seen, objections raised about Levi's defection, but Jesus's rationale may have gotten certain elites to thinking about repentance as *medicine*. You can't heal people, he'd said, who don't know they're sick; only those who acknowledge the personal disease of affluenza and the political disaster of plutocracy and decide to change direction (5:31). Perhaps Levi was among the disciples now trooping into his former boss's house to testify to the Way. We can only speculate about the mix of reasons that motivated Zacchaeus to embrace Jesus's movement for healing and repair: disillusionment or determination, contradiction or conviction, insubordination or imagination. But we surely ought to reflect on how he managed to get so clear that following Jesus requires reparations when over the long history of the church, so few Christians have come to terms with it!

Jesus, for his part, takes a moment to celebrate, making an extraordinary, three-part response to Zacchaeus's commitment. First, he declares that "today salvation has come to this house" (19:9a). He means this quite literally: when he and all his funky friends crossed the *chasma mega* into the palace of a robber baron, they brought with them the ingredients for his healing and liberation. Encounter animates transformation.

Second, by calling him a son of Abraham, Jesus restores Zacchaeus's membership in his ancestral community, a kinship that wealth and oppression had shattered (19:9b). He is now family with poor folk such as the bent-over woman, whom Jesus similarly acknowledged as a "daughter of Abraham" (13:16). Luke's rhetorical resonance means to argue that the poorest debtor and the richest creditor must both be healed for the Abrahamic body politic to be made whole.

Third, he emphasizes that the Human One seeks and saves the *lost* (19:10). The bent-over woman and the blind beggar were dehumanized by isolating economic disparity, and Jesus's embrace restored them to the fullness of community. Zacchaeus and his economic and political class, on the other hand, are *lost*, hopelessly addicted to privilege and power unless and until they repent, which means practicing concrete redistributive justice. As Wendell Berry put it succinctly for us modern progeny of Zacchaeus under racial capitalism: "The great obstacle is simply this: the conviction that we cannot change because we are dependent upon what is wrong. But that is the addict's excuse, and we know that it will not do."

At the climax of Luke's sprawling series of sequences about rich people, Jesus challenges and accompanies the richest among them to take step one, the portal to recovery. But true sobriety must lead to a searching moral inventory, amends, and reparations. In our historical moment, the addict's excuse will not do: not for climate crisis; not for racialized disparity; not for legacies of genocide. If *we* who are so diseased by the virus of affluenza want to follow Jesus, we must start by following Zacchaeus. But that requires defecting from mammon—both its narrative and its systems—and that carries a cost.

B. The Cost of Defection (19:11–28)

Luke's transition to the third part of this triptych is an overlapping technique, which functions to bind it tightly to the preceding episode (19:11a). The phrase "as they were listening to these things" (meaning the exchange between Zacchaeus and Jesus) refers not only to the crowd in the story; it is also a gesture to us as listeners/readers. They and we both need to be warned against interpreting the breakthrough story of Zacchaeus though a triumphalist or happily-ever-after lens.

As narrator, Luke offers two glimpses into the consciousness of the characters (19:11b,c):

- "because he was near to Jerusalem" indicates that Jesus understands that nothing transpired in Jericho that will change his fate in Jerusalem.

- "and because they supposed that the kingdom of God was to appear immediately" indicates that from the perspective of the non-elite, Zacchaeus's announcement of reparations was perceived as the dawn of the Great Economy they had been hearing about. The *architelōnēs* was that prominent, and his actions that unexpected and potentially that revolutionary.

But Jesus recognized, as must we, that one conversion—no matter how dramatic, unprecedented, or infectious—does not system-change make. So Jesus "proceeds" (or "provides," *prostithēmi*) to spin a parable about one more rich and powerful ruler ("*Therefore* he said," 19:12a). It will illustrate that just as the Defect-ive Manager's redistributive initiative didn't change the architecture of his rich boss's system (chapter 10), neither can Zacchaeus's Jubilee gesture alone bring down a plutocratic regime. Alas, there will be no Hollywood ending.

The Parable of the Minas (18:12–28) is another notorious text, not because it has been ignored as with so many of Luke's other rich man stories, but because it is interpreted so credulously. Matthew's "Talents" version (Matt 25:14–30) receives far more ecclesial attention for three reasons:

- it comes up in the lectionary, whereas Luke's parable does not;
- it contains only economic violence instead of the brutal political violence of Luke's version, the former apparently being more palatable; and
- the popular (mis)reading of "talents" in terms of a disciples' capacity fuels pious homilies about the need to put one's "money, time, and talents" at the service of the church—typically on Stewardship Sunday.[20]

Both versions of the parable, which differ substantially but exhibit the same structure, have long been sentimentalized in North American churches as a capitalist morality tale about making money on money, thinly disguised by paeans to the virtues of hard work, responsible investing, and obedience to the boss. In contrast, I and a growing minority of interpreters read it as a warning tale about the cost of discipleship for those who would resist the plutocratic system, focusing on the third servant as a defector.[21] His fate portends that of Zacchaeus, about whom we do not hear again in the New Testament.

Whether this parable is based on Q tradition or another folk story is debated.[22] What is clear is that Luke's narrative framing puts it in a plainly political context—both Jesus's own as he heads for the center of Judean power, and that of the story-world:

A: . . . he went on to tell a parable, because he was near Jerusalem . . . (19:11).

B: "A nobleman went to a distant country to get royal power for himself and then return. . . . But the citizens of his country hated him and sent a delegation after him, saying, 'We do not want this man to rule over us.' When he returned, having received the kingly power. . ." (19:12,14–15a).

C: Parable of the Minas (19:13, 15b–26)

B′: "But as for these enemies of mine who did not want me to be king over them—bring them here and slaughter them in my presence" (19:27).

A′: After Jesus had said this, he went on ahead, going up to Jerusalem (19:28).

This frame, distinctive to Luke, has been recognized by an increasing number of commentators over the last half century as a parody of Herod Archelaus.[23] As such, it provides both a deeply empire-critical conclusion to the triptych, and a sobering finale to the series of rich man stories.

A synopsis of the convoluted political history of Archelaus is necessary to provide context. He was one of seven sons of Herod the Great, three of whom struggled for succession in Palestine, as recounted by Jewish historian Josephus. The father passed in 4 BCE in Jericho, his will dividing his geopolitical domain into three tetrarchies. One of Archelaus's first acts was to slaughter three thousand Jewish protesters in the Temple who had been mourning those killed by his father after the "Golden Eagle" incident shortly before his death.[24]

Not long after, both Archelaus and Antipas traveled to Rome to ask Caesar Augustus to adjudicate their rival claims to kingship.[25] During the months the emperor was deliberating, a delegation of fifty Judean leaders traveled to Rome for an audience with him, opposing Archelaus because of his cruelty to his own people. The emperor eventually decided in favor of Archelaus, confirming his rule over half the Herodian territory, now called the "ethnarchy" of Judea; Philip and Antipas each received a quarter of the remaining half. Archelaus, in turn, retaliated by killing those who had tried to oust him. Less than a decade later, after the census of Quirinius (a watershed event that Luke acknowledges in 2:1–2), Archelaus was removed by the emperor and exiled for excessive incompetence and violence; the province of Judaea was then placed under direct Roman rule.

It is not difficult to see Luke's allusions to such events in his introduction and conclusion to the parable. It coheres with Frank Dicken's argument that Luke-Acts plays with the ancient literary technique of "composite characterization"; this narrative strategy, which emphasizes "ideological (or theological) concerns," is borne out by the thinly veiled caricature of the nobleman in 19:12–27. For Luke, all Herodian rulers (and their imperial sponsors) were cut from the same cloth—as suggested by the Second Temptation (4:5; 3B).

Again, scene-setting matters. In 19:12, Jesus is departing Jericho, a base of Herodian power. It would be up to one of the city's noblemen to retaliate against the elite retainer Zacchaeus for ruining his provincial tax-farming franchise. Ed Visser imagines that on the road west, "Jesus and his disciples (and others making their way to Jerusalem for Passover) would have walked right past the palace" of Herod the Great, Antipas, and Archelaus. "It is very likely that he used the occasion . . . to tell a story right out of the pages of their recent history!"[26]

This parable pulls back the veil shrouding the plutocratic system Luke has been *telling* us about all along, and for the first time *shows* how the rich get richer and the poor get poorer: it is by making money on money. The Archelaus figure commands his retainers to grow the capital he entrusts to them, and commends the results, warning: "I tell you, that to everyone who has will more be given; but from him who has not, even what he has will be taken away" (19:26). This caricature as political and economic critique is lost, however, on conventional readings of the parable, which insist on seeing it as a theological allegory that *reproduces* this cutthroat system: the ruler must be a figure for God (or Jesus), and we must aspire to be profitable servants—and never dare to not cooperate!

Medieval and Reformation readings of the story approved of the hard working servants who multiplied their master's money, while castigating the third servant who refused to play the game.[27] This interpretation has gone virtually unchallenged in modernity because it coheres so perfectly with the capitalist ethos we live and breathe. It is championed as a self-congratulatory story about investment banking. And we consume it unquestioningly, having been socialized into the culture of economic hierarchy and meritocracy, which we internalize through our habits of aspiring *upward* and scapegoating *downward* on the social ladder (however unconsciously). For example, conservative evangelical R.J. Moeller writes:

> Look at the parable of the talents in Luke 19, where wealth is unevenly distributed and where the poorest of the three men is condemned for lazily squandering his opportunity. . . . If we have to "choose between unequal prosperity and shared poverty," I'll choose the former.[28]

But such readings of the parable are in fact laced with contradictions, not to mention deeply problematic. Allegorizing the ruler as God requires us to accept a social Darwinist deity who is ruthless, unforgiving, and brutal, exploiting for profit (19:22), commending usury (19:23), and publicly executing adversaries (19:27). Needless to say, such a take cuts directly against the grain of *everything*

Luke has heretofore told and shown about Jesus and Sabbath Economics. Nevertheless, Christians continue to cite the parable in isolation, imposing presumptions about the glories of a system that rewards venture capital—and thus read it exactly backwards!

Luke's original audience would not have had to allegorize the scenario to make sense of it. Its portrait of a great household was all too recognizable. When a powerful patriarch went away on economic or political business, his affairs would be handled by retainers or slaves (as in 19:13, *doûlos*), who had risen to prominent positions in the household hierarchy.[29] Luke's version of the tale diverges from Matthew's in the number of such agents (ten versus three) and the amount capitalized, but the three-part plot structure is the same.

The *mina* was an ancient Near Eastern unit of weight for silver or gold, and became a unit of currency equivalent to sixty shekels. In the first century CE, it was equivalent to about a hundred *denarii* (one *denarius*, according to Matt 20:2, paid a typical day's wage to an agricultural worker). One calculator estimates that a *mina* would be worth about $8,700 in modern US dollars: not the fabulous sum envisioned by Matthew's *talanta*, but not chump change either.[30] The slaves are told to "do business" with them on behalf of the king. The verb *pragmateuomai* (the first of three consecutive verbs that appear only here in the New Testament) can connote the work of a moneychanger, trader, or even a tax farmer. In short, their purpose is to generate handsome profits for the ruler.

Once the nobleman returns with his sovereignty secured, he summons his agents to see what they have "gained by trading their silver" (19:15; *diapragmateuomai*, an intensification of the verb above). The first two agents report that they "multiplied" (*prosergazomai*) their master's investment, tenfold and fivefold respectively. This was well beyond the 100–200 percent return expected (and doesn't count what the agents would have kept for themselves). It was likely achieved through luxury commodity trading, loansharking, extortion, and/or land seizures. The two agents are granted a corresponding number of cities over which they will "assume authority" (19:16–19). This is, after all, the patronage of a *king*, who promotes them from the economic to the political sphere to continue to do his bidding.[31] Their reward is a deeper immersion into the ruler's world of mammon and domination.

Though lauded by modern readers, such profits would have elicited disgust from a first-century audience. In traditional Mediterranean society, stability was the ideal, not self-advancement; strategies of wealth accumulation imperiled the equilibrium of society. "In the 'limited good' world of the peasant . . . honorable people did not try to get more, and those who did were automatically considered thieves."[32] Luke's portrait of the king and his co-exploiters here echoes his earlier sketches of the rich landowner's many barns, or Dives feasting every day. It is impossible that Luke would suddenly intend this scenario to be seen as *exemplary*—which is why efforts to undermine Luke's plain meaning have required extreme theological gymnastics!

Conversely, modern interpreters love to reprimand the third slave who, cautious and unproductive, is turned into an object lesson of entrepreneurial failure. But if the profiteering portrayed was understood by Jesus's audience as rapacious, then this uncooperative third slave should be seen as the *hero* of this parable. The punch line of this three-part folktale is his explanation of his (in)action (19:20–21). It is part of Luke's parody that he hid his *mina* away in a "rag": a *soudarion* was used to wipe sweat or to clean corpses (as in Acts 19:12; John 11:44; 20:7). It would have been considered highly unclean—thus symbolizing the dirty work or death-dealing associated with the *minas* of his two colleagues.

Worse, the defective slave now dares to speak his mind about the king's system, offering a triple indictment:

> I was afraid of you. . .
> . . .because you are a harsh man. . . [*austēros,* only here in the New Testament];
> you take up what you did not place, and reap what you did not sow (19:21).

The king's franchise is unmasked as harsh and exploitive, profiteering off the labor and land of others. As Herzog puts it, the ruler returned to a "reckoning with two sets of servants, loyal subjects (*douloi*) and disgruntled citizens (*politai*). The third servant is revealed as a spokesman for the citizens who opposed the ruler, and in his speech he articulates their discontent (19:14) and shares their fate (19:27)."[33]

The king makes no effort to refute the monkey-wrencher's analysis (19:22), driving Luke's point home. "You knew, did you?" he rages, repeating the indictment. It is not unlike the cliched Hollywood scene in which the villain congratulates the hero for finding him out—just before he kills him! Appreciating only appreciation, the king then excoriates the third servant for not at least seeking a "banker's return" (19:23). The noun *trapeza* is wrongly translated as "bank," however; there were no such institutions in antiquity. Rather, it is a "table"—such as those of Temple moneychangers that Jesus overturns in his Temple protest (Matt 21:12 // Mark11:15)!

The real problem here is the king's entitlement to interest (*tokos*), which means literally "offspring"—money breeding money. While usury may be the fundamental building block of modern finance capitalism, it was prohibited by Torah.[34] Often translated "oppression," it is one of the central complaints leveled by the prophets. Jeremiah accused the ruling class of Israel of "oppression upon oppression, deceit upon deceit" (Jer 9:6)! Ezekiel sees it as the cardinal sin of an unjust economic system:

> If you do not oppress anyone, but restore to the debtor his pledge, commit no robbery, give your bread to the hungry and cover the naked with a garment, do not take advance or accrued interest (*tokō*), withhold your hand from iniquity, execute true justice . . . you shall surely live" (Ezek 18:7–9).

Nor was the Bible alone in antiquity in denouncing the sin of making money on money. Aristotle explicitly condemned it, counting "usurers who lend money in small sums at a high rate of interest" among "degrading trades" whose "common characteristic . . . seems to be sordid greed."[35]

The king's response is immediate and punishing as he turns to make an example of this whistleblower in a matching triple indictment:

- First, he confiscates the *mina* (19:24a), which the third slave, from a peasant perspective, had honorably preserved. As Keesmaat notes, this is an allusion to Zacchaeus's assured fate: "When it becomes clear that Zacchaeus no longer has enough wealth to line the pockets of the official who gave him his position, he will have his city taken away and given to a tax collector who is willing to squeeze as much land and money out of people as possible."[36]
- Second, the king redeploys the "unused" *mina* to his obedient top earner (19:24b). Luke provides a "Greek chorus" to express the horror we are supposed to feel here (19:25)—again, something ignored by traditional interpreters! The ruler then defiantly points to this example of "redistribution upward" as a confirmation of the goal of his economic strategy: to facilitate the urban landowning rich getting richer while pushing poor smallholders off their land (19:26).[37]
- As if this chilling pronouncement isn't enough, his third response returns to the political conflict that opened the parable: the king vows to execute publicly those who rejected his sovereignty (19:27). In the Herodian security state, spectacles of capital punishment were engineered to terrorize any who might consider dissent or defiance of the regime in the future—a policy that mimicked the Roman Empire's use of the cross.

The Parable of the Minas is truly a horror tale, which has been defanged and domesticated as pedantic and platitudinous to keep aright the world that Jesus's storytelling meant to turn upside down. We must bring Jesus's parables back down to earth in order to come to terms with their interrogation of entrenched arrangements of power and privilege, such as this story's commendation of resistance to usurious business as usual.

"And when he had said this, Jesus went on ahead, going up to Jerusalem" (19:28). These are perhaps the most poignant and foreboding words in Luke's whole story. Jesus has just narrated truth-speaking and its consequences, not only as exhibited by Zacchaeus and the third servant, but in anticipation of his own confrontation with what Keesmaat calls the world of "crucifixion economics."[38] From here, Luke picks up Mark's narrative one last time, following it through Jesus's Jerusalem conflicts and his *inevitable* arrest, trial, and *Via Crucis*.[39]

* * *

Because there is very little L material from 19:28–24:12, I conclude my investigation here. But in many respects, the closing triptych we have just examined stands as a microcosm of Luke's story as a whole. It portrays:

- Jesus's attention to, and solidarity with, the most marginalized (the blind beggar);
- a fierce challenge to the rich, who have been consistent targets of critique, yet who he *also* wishes to liberate (Zacchaeus); and
- his unequivocal indictment of a system that is the antithesis of Sabbath Economics, from which disciples are called to defect (parable of the Minas).

There is more to Luke's narrative, of course. In the epilogue, I trace one more thread: how the theme of liberating table fellowship extends through Jesus's death, resurrection, and the rebirth of his Sabbath Economics movement at Pentecost—and how a sacred meal teaches us how to re-member and recover the Way.

Luke wrote his Gospel with a clear sense that the mammon system, though flourishing under the Roman Empire, was in crisis. He curated stories of Jesus, and of the first generation of his movement, in the conviction that those following Jesus's Way could embody anew the old ways of the Great Economy, which alone represents good news for the poor.

At the heart of his sprawling narrative sits primal ancestor Abraham, with a poor man at his breast, directing the attention of a rich man to the cruelties of the *chasma mega* and to the visionary power of Torah and Nevi'im. This is exactly the goal of the Third Gospel: to press readers/listeners to see and reckon with the persistent disparities of their world and to insist on personal and political alternatives by apprenticing ourselves to the cosmology and practices of Sabbath Economics. The true vocation of the Jesus movement is this: to carry on the work of healing affluenza, resisting plutocracy, and realizing the Great Banquet, where poor and rich are no more.

Epilogue

Re-membering Three Meals

> We remember Christ's death
> We proclaim Christ's resurrection
> We await Christ's coming in glory.
>
> —Memorial Acclamation[1]

I CLOSE THIS book by tracing one more Lukan thread: the daily practice of eating as an embodiment of Sabbath Economics, which is re-membered and empowered through communal liturgical practices of sharing Eucharist. This reflection carries Luke's narrative forward into his second volume and serves to summarize key findings of this study.

Throughout the Third Gospel, as we have seen, meals represent key moments of revelation and instruction. It is fitting, then, to conclude this project by recognizing and exploring the three sacred meals that form a bridge between Luke's story of Jesus and that of the church in Acts. In the Last Supper, Jesus looks back to the story of Exodus liberation commemorated in the Passover feast but also ahead to his own death as a new sign of redemption. The second meal occurs in the middle of Luke's Emmaus Road epilogue: a Strange Teacher of Moses and the prophets is mystically revealed as the Risen Christ in the breaking of bread. The third is the common meal at the center of the Pentecost church, which animates a communitizing of possessions.

Two millennia after Jesus, Communion rightly remains constitutive of the ritual life of the Christian church across confessions and geographies. The Anglican Memorial Acclamation cited above corresponds nicely to Luke's three bridging meals, which commemorate respectively Jesus's death, resurrection, and continuing presence among us through the Spirit. Each meal also expresses and exhorts Sabbath Economics as the heart of the Gospel.

i. The Last Supper as Sabbath Economics Ritual (22:15–30)

Jesus's final meal with his companions prior to his crucifixion is at the Pesach (Passover) table, the ritual meal of memory for Jews. It takes place in the attic of a safe house in Jerusalem as security forces are closing in upon the hunted community. During the course of the meal, Jesus tries to help his friends reckon with his coming execution and its meaning for a continuing movement. This moment has been adopted by the church as its ritual meal of memory.[2]

Given our lamentable historic alienation from one another, both Jews and Christians today would do well to recognize the kindred nature of our respective sacred meals, which are perhaps the oldest still continually observed on our planet. Pesach and the Lord's Supper each birthed a people. Passover commemorates the liberation of Hebrews from the imperial straitjacket of Pharaoh's Egypt (Exod 12). Eucharist gathers Christians around the life of Jesus of Nazareth, a Jewish prophet whom Caesar's execution stake could not vanquish. Each time these meals are celebrated, our two peoples—cousins estranged for too long—are born again. They help (and push) us to carry on the stories that save us from illness and death in order to combat the agnosia, confusion, and oppression sowed by imperial plutocracy.

Pesach and Paschal Banquets, though distinct, have much in common. Both:

- commemorate a journey of faith which, in the old saying of the Black Church, "makes a way out of no way": Exodus march and discipleship road.
- are rituals of remembering. "Why is this night different from all other nights?" ask Jews (Exod 12:14, 42). "Do this in memory of him," say Christians (1 Cor 11:23–26).
- were celebrated by communities on the run. Passover was eaten in haste by Hebrew slaves with their bags packed, fixing to go feral (Exod 12:11). Eucharist was convened by a prophet marked for death, shared with a handful of betrayal-bound disciples in hiding from the authorities (Luke 22:1–13).[3]
- culminated a campaign of nonviolent resistance to empire. Both acknowledge symbolically that blood *given* is the power of life over death: of lambs on doorposts to spare inhabitants (Exod 12:7, 13) and of a Lamb who was slain in order to ransom every captive (Rev 5:9).
- are living traditions that have animated countless slave revolts and liberation movements and have inspired believers famous and forgotten to embrace struggles for freedom.[4]

Above all, both meals proclaim the unique characteristics of a biblical God who stands with the marginalized: YHWH who hears the cry of the oppressed (Exod 3:7–8) and who mystically resides as Christ in and with the poor, the prisoner, and the persecuted (Matt 25:31–46). This undomesticatiable and inconvenient God can neither be named or tamed by imperial civilization, then or now; is patron of no royal family, wealthy class, or religious hierarchy, then or now; and promises through these meals to deliver humanity and all of creation from bondage to slavery, sin and death.

When abstracted from their real-world origins, however, these sacred meals become sentimentalized, merely performative, or deteriorate into fairy-tale rites of magical redemption. Today, our two kindred communities too often fail to preserve and observe the revolutionary character of our respective sacred meals, domesticating them into religious "entertainment."[5] Case in point: I write this during the seasons of Easter and Passover 2024, under the shadow of a genocidal war on Gaza's civilian population, through which Jewish and Christian leaders of militarized regimes have betrayed the best of their traditions.

Specifically, most Christian churches have become blind to the economic dimensions of Eucharist as a Sabbath Economics ritual. As we saw earlier (6B), the chain of verbs used in the Last Supper ("Took... blessed... broke... gave...") repeats a formula introduced in Jesus's shared wilderness meal with the poor (9:16). At the intertextual level, this meal is remembering not only Passover and Cross but also the stories of Exodus *manna* and Elijah's conjuring of bread, which emphasize "enough for everyone" as the central principle of the Great Economy.

Three changes made by Luke to Mark's narrative of the Last Supper further strengthen this correlation:

- *Jesus's preface to the words of Institution (22:16).* He confesses a poignant, reiterative "desiring desire" to eat Pesach with his disciples before suffering (16a), alluding to the desperate hunger of both the Prodigal Son and Lazarus.[6] And he vows to fast until this meal is "fulfilled (*plēroō*) in the Great Economy" (16b), alluding to the eschatological banquet in which all are satisfied (13:29). In the next episode, his final words to his disciples include an intention to appoint them to "eat and drink at my table" there (22:30), at which the poor are welcomed (6:20) but the rich are not (at least not with their wealth intact; 18:25).
- *The shared cup (22:17).* Jesus instructs his disciples to "take this, and divide (*diamerizō*) it among yourselves"; Luke alone uses this verb, which will also describe the distribution of languages at Pentecost (Acts 2:3) and the subsequent redistribution of property (Acts 2:45; see iii).
- *Jesus's exhortation to servanthood (22:24–30).* Luke has moved this teaching (which appears much earlier in Mark's narrative, Mark 10:42–45) into this fraught context, placed right *after* Jesus's laments about his body broken and his friend's betrayal (22:19–23), giving it greater pathos.[7] It also renders tragicomic the disciples'

"dispute" (*philoneikia*) over "which of them was to be regarded as the greatest" (22:24).[8] In one concise sentence, Luke captures the ideology of empire: "The *kings* of the nations lord over them, and those with power over them are called *benefactors*" (22:25).[9] We have met these kings and patrons (here both are Lukan additions to Mark) over the course of this long story, and their dysfunctional ethos is internalized whenever disciples aspire upward. Jesus then turns that cosmology upside down one final time, calling his disciples to *servant* leadership (22:26). As he did at the "banquet from hell" (9B), he again invokes downward mobility at table (22:27). At the Third Gospel's final meal, Jesus takes the lowest position—showing his disciples the Way into the Great Economy (22:28–30).[10]

Even as he turns this Pesach meal into a meditation on his own death at the hands of empire, then, Luke's Jesus presses his followers to embrace Sabbath Economics.

ii. Loaves and Fish

Realizing the Risen Jesus (24:27–45)

The strongest indication of how important "getting Communion right" was to Luke is the fact that he, alone among the Gospels, reiterates this ritual meal in two subsequent sequences. The first occurs in the middle of the Emmaus Road story. My reading in chapter 1 of this epilogue-as-prologue only mentioned this bread-breaking briefly, so I return to it here.

The Emmaus episode involves disciples who are still on the lam. Fleeing on a back road in the wake of their leader's execution, two of them encounter a Stranger, who inquires about their distress. After listening to their recitation of the traumatic events, he commences tutoring them in Moses and the prophets to help them make sense of this traumatic event. As it grows dark, the two prevail upon the Stranger to stay with them at another safe house (24:28–29). A meal follows, about which Luke's brief two-verse account freights a great deal of meaning.

The Stranger "reclines" with them (24:30a). The verb *kataklinō* (only in Luke's Gospel in the New Testament) prompts us to review three strategic meals narrated earlier:

- 7:36–50: During Jesus's visit to Simon's house, as he *reclines* (7:36) he receives the intimate grief of a marginalized woman, who embodies an object lesson directed to the host about seeing the poor and enacting Jubilee release to liberate them from indebtedness (5B).

- 9:10–17: A crowd follows Jesus to a "deserted place," and as in the Emmaus story, it grows late. This prompts his disciples to propose sending people away to provision themselves (9:12). Instead, after determining what resources his community has on hand, Jesus organizes a wilderness meal (9:13). Twice he invites thousands of people to *recline* (9:14–15)—for Luke, this is banquet language. It is here that Jesus inaugurates the aforementioned gesture of taking/blessing/breaking/giving (9:16), the ritual that invokes the Great Economy in which "and all eat and are satisfied" (9:17; 6B).
- 14:7–14: Amidst another banquet at a Pharisee's house, Jesus again addresses both guests and host (as in 7:34–47). He examines the "politics of *reclining*" (14:8), commending voluntary downward mobility as a strategy to deconstruct hierarchy (9B).

The Emmaus meal, like the ones above, also narrates Sabbath Economics, as the Stranger repeats for the *third* time in Luke's narrative the loaves and fishes formula: "took . . . blessed . . . broke . . . gave . . ." (24:30b).[11]

The chiastic literary structure of this mystical second eucharistic moment, and its placement in the middle of the Emmaus narrative, reveals the formula as a fulcrum:

A: "And beginning with Moses and all the prophets, he interpreted to them in all the scriptures the things concerning himself" (24:27).
    B: The disciples invite the Stranger to stay with them (24:28–29).
        C: "When he was at table with them, he took the bread, blessed, broke it, and gave it to them" (24:30).
    B′: The disciples recognize the Stranger as Jesus Risen (24:31).
A′: "They said to each other, 'Did not our hearts burn within us while he talked to us on the road, while he opened to us the scriptures?'" (24:32)

Its tight framing by the Stranger's catechism in prophetic literacy, which immediately precedes it and continues after (24:44–48), binds the ritual to the Sabbath Economics traditions of the ancestors. Moreover, the two disciples offer a double testimony:

- "our hearts burned within us . . . while he opened the scriptures to us" (24:32);
- Jesus was "known to them in the breaking of the bread" (24:35).

These narrative signals introduce the Easter church as a community nurtured and sustained *equally* by Word and Sacrament—a dialectical balance that neither Protestants nor Catholics have yet sufficiently achieved.

One more intertextual allusion is worth noting. Jesus's breaking and *giving of bread* (24:30) is reciprocated in the final Emmaus scene: his disciples *give him fish* to eat (24:42; *epididōmi* in both verses). This is one last allusion to the wilderness loaves and fishes demonstration project. Luke's first two sacred meals have both nodded to that archetypal connection. The third will fully embody Sabbath Economics.

iii. Meals and Property in Common

Realizing Sabbath Economics at Pentecost (Acts 2)

Luke begins his second volume with a review of the Risen Jesus's last days, which overlaps with the close of his Gospel. The Acts account repeats, but in greater detail, three crucial plot points. Jesus:

- commissions the disciples as "witnesses" (*martus*; Luke 24:48 // Acts 1:8b);
- counsels them to wait in Jerusalem for divine power (Luke 24:49 // Acts 1:4, 8a);
- ascends (Luke 24:50–51 // Acts 1:9).

A cloud (*nephelē*) surrounds him, echoing the Transfiguration (Luke 9:34–35). Immediately, the disciples are accosted by two angelic figures (Acts 1:10–11). We've seen such "men" before: at the beginning of Luke's story (Luke 1:34) and again at its end at the empty tomb, where the disciples similarly receive a pointed rebuke (Luke 24:4–6). They are exhorted to "cease gazing into heaven"—may our churches pay heed!

Accordingly, the disciples return to Jerusalem—the scene of their leader's lynching only weeks earlier (Acts 1:12). We should not miss the fact that here, for the *third* time in the Lukan bridging sequence we're tracing, they gather in an "upper room" (Acts 1:13).[12] This suggests they are still underground; indeed, they have reason to fear in the wake of the brutal suppression of their movement. After prayerfully debriefing with Jesus's family (1:14), they begin deliberating about replacing Judas (1:15–26). It seems important to "the 120 gathered" that the apostolic group should again be numbered *twelve*. I contend these numbers symbolize their ancestral Israelite tribal confederacy, a decentralized governing structure that represented the *political* shape of Sabbath Economics.

The next scene commences with the unusual phrase "When the day of Pentecost was being *fulfilled*..." (Acts 2:1).[13] The Feast of Weeks, or Shavuot, occurring between Passover and the Feast of Tabernacles was originally a celebration of the first fruits of harvest (Exod 23:14–17; Lev 23:9–22; Deut 16:9–12).[14] I earlier noted the rhetorical resonances between Shavuot and the Levitical Jubilee (2A), reminding Israel that Sabbath Economics applies at *each* harvest. Luke's narrative of Pentecost now fulfills these Jubilee implications for the first fruits of a new messianic movement—which is about to come out of hiding, pushed onto the streets by an empowering Spirit to contest Jesus's murder and proclaim his resurrection.[15]

What sort of practices the Spirit animated at Pentecost, and continues to enable, has been a tragically divisive issue in the life of the modern church. The debate about what it means to be Spirit-filled has, over the last century and a half, typically focused on the expression of individual charismatic gifts. The historical context of Luke's narrative, however, as well as the agricultural roots of the feast being celebrated, means that we should rather look at the *political* and *economic* character of Acts 2. The narrative consists of three parts, culminating in the third of Luke's sacramental meals:

- the "tongues" (1–12)
- Peter's speech (13–41)
- the breaking of bread and community of goods (42–47)

This sequence is framed by two "distributions" (the only appearances of *diamerizō* in Acts): tongues at the outset (2:3), possessions at the end (2:45). In between, Peter proclaims the "gift" of the Spirit and the unilateral cancellation of debts in Christ (2:38), echoing Jesus's inaugural Jubilee pronouncement at Nazareth (4A). In other words, Pentecost has far more to do with redistributive Sabbath Economics than with the religious spectacle of glossolalia.

Before focusing on the meal, let us briefly consider the first two parts of the sequence:

Tongues of fire. The "storm" of wind and fire (2:2) correlates to the baptism "with the Holy Spirit and with fire" promised by the wilderness prophet John (Luke 3:16, reiterated in Acts 1:5).[16] The "tongues" have caused much consternation, despite the fact that their purpose is immediately revealed: cross-cultural communication (2:3–4)! "Jews from every nation" now hear about the "powerful works of God" *in their own language* (2:5–11). Unaccountably, the cosmopolitan crowd is being instructed by rural and uneducated (yet suddenly polyglot!) Galilean peasants (see also 4:13). Moreover, women are clearly identified as part of the core discipleship group (1:14), which Peter will shortly justify from the prophet Joel (2:17–18). This scene thus portrays the disciples as following Jesus in transgressing boundaries of ethnicity, class, and gender—the very structures that hold empire together. The Spirit has animated a community insurrection to challenge the personal and political status quo.

The crowd debates what the reader is wondering: "What does this mean?" (2:12). This "sign of tongues" is not primarily foreshadowing the international missionary reach of the Gospel in Acts, as traditionally argued. Luke is alluding to something much more profound: the ancient Hebrew argument with the imperial Tower of Babel (Gen 11:1–9). That primal tale—a nomad's polemic against the powerful city-states of Mesopotamia—fiercely condemned the Tower (a cipher for the ziggurat), the architectural representation of centralized, hierarchical domination and idolatry (Gen 11:2).[17] The *centripetal* power of empire draws resources and people into itself, inevitably imposing cultural and linguistic conformity on its subjects (Gen 11:1, 6). The divine counterstrategy calls for *centrifugal* dispersion and diversification (Gen 11:7–8). Heterogeneity is a restraint upon monoculture—an ecological *and* political insight that several millennia have only confirmed! Luke recontextualizes Babel's lesson, portraying Jerusalemites as "confused" by hearing the Gospel in their *own* language rather than Greek, the lingua franca of the eastern empire (Acts 2:6).[18] This multicultural insurgency is the *cultural* shape of Sabbath Economics.

Peter's speech. The scene's skeptics dismiss the disciples' "babble" as drunken behavior (2:13)—a typical dismissal of upstart poor people by the well-heeled. To be sure, as Bill Wylie-Kellermann points out, "After what's been done to Jesus, you'd have to be either crazy or drunk to be shouting his name in the streets and pointing accusing fingers at the executioners."[19] Their disdain seems to kick Peter into gear (2:14–15), and the camera now zooms in on his impromptu sermon from Joel (2:17–21 = Joel 3:28–32a). The Shavuot context resonates with the prophet's rich harvest imagery and promise of abundance after pestilence (Joel 2:19, 21–25a). For Joel, renewal comes first to the land, *then* the spirit "pours out" on the people (Joel 2:28a).[20] This judgment motif informs the rest of Peter's speech (Acts 2:22–35).

The remarkably transformed Peter, who just weeks earlier had pled ignorance about the arrested Jesus in order to save his own skin (Luke 22:54–62), now thunders a politically volatile public indictment: "This Jesus who you crucified, now be assured that God has made him both Lord and Messiah" (2:36).[21] He challenges the crowd—firmly under the boot of Caesar's *kyriarchy*, which pitilessly suppressed all messianic movements—to transfer its allegiance from executioner to victim (2:38). It is a treasonous proclamation that will shortly land him in jail (3:17–4:4), as it did his predecessors John and Jesus. Luke's portrait of Peter here, bravely defying the very authorities before whom he had cowered, is meant to demonstrate how the Spirit can embolden even the most beat-down and disheartened of us.

This brings us to the third part of the Acts 2 sequence, and Luke's final sacred meal scenario. Those who welcome Peter's message are baptized (2:41).[22] In turn they are welcomed into a community that has resuscitated the practice of Sabbath Economics in the daily practice of breaking (*klasis*) bread. In Luke's description, this eating frames the "signs and wonders":[23]

> They devoted themselves to the apostles' teaching and community, and to the breaking of bread and prayers.
>
> Awe came upon everyone; because many wonders and signs were being done by the apostles. All who believed were together and had all things in common; they would sell their properties and possessions and distribute them to all, as any had need.
>
> Day by day, as they spent much time in the temple together, they broke bread in their homes, and ate their food with glad and generous hearts (Acts 2:42–46).

The principal *sign* is that the community "holds all things in common" (*hapanta koina*, 2:44). The principal *wonder* (or portent, *teras*) is how the household table has eclipsed the Temple as primary symbolic center of the movement.[24] This third sacred meal does not replicate the loaves and fishes formula of the first two because it is being *embraced as a way of life*.[25] The commonwealth is being restored, as "properties and possessions" (*ta ktēmata kai tas huparxeis*) are sold and the proceeds "distributed among all in need" (2:45; *diamerizō,* as in 2:3). At the birth of the church, Luke's vision of Sabbath Economics is being fully realized.

This snapshot—a programmatic passage for Acts—is so important that, of all the signs and wonders Luke relates in his second volume, only the miracle of economic sharing is described twice. The more detailed narrative of 4:32–37 has strong verbal resonances with the first, including the identical phrases "all things in common" (*hapanta koina*, 4:42) and "to each as had need" (*kathoti an tis chreian eichen* 4:35). The fulfillment of Sabbath Economics is captured in the result: "there was not a poor person (*endeēs*) among them" (4:34). That noun, only here in the New Testament, appears often in the LXX, first in the Deuteronomic communal discipline of seven-year debt amnesty ("so that there will be no poor among you," Deut 15:4, 7, 11). Proverbs 3:27 states the principle sharply: "Do not withhold good from the poor (LXX *endeē*) when it is in your power to do it." By "distributing" (*diadidōmi*, Acts 4:35) their surplus, the disciples follow the way of Zacchaeus (13A).

In a well-established Lukan narrative pattern (such as the contrasting stories of the rich young ruler and Zacchaeus), this longer account of community sharing includes positive and negative object lessons about those who sell property. Joseph/Barnabas contributes his proceeds to the community treasury (4:36–37), while Ananias and Sapphira hold some back, lie about it, and keel over (5:1–10). The latters' sudden death is another example of somatic symbolism by Luke (9A): when the political bodies of disciples are infected by the lies of mammon, the spirit of Sabbath Economics can die in the church's body politic. This lesson resonates throughout our history.

As a portrait of communitized economics, this third sacred meal story is another Lukan text of terror for North American Christians, most of whom long ago yielded to the enchantments of mammon. Thus, this aspect of the Pentecost uprising has been discounted, devalued, or disappeared in our seminaries and sanctuaries. I'll name just three classic strategies of dismissal, each of which offers a case study in capitalist hermeneutics:

1. *The claim that Paul organized his apostolic collection to bail out the Jerusalem church, which was bankrupted by its "communistic" economic practices.* There isn't a shred of evidence that suggests Paul's collection was in response to bankruptcy—or to any other crisis for that matter (e.g., famine or persecution). Rather, he invites the churches of Asia Minor to "share their resources with the poor among the saints at Jerusalem" (Rom 15:25f; see also 1 Cor 16:1–3; 2 Cor 9:12) as a principled expression of trans-ethnic solidarity. Even clearer is 2 Cor 8–9, the apostle's most elaborate rationale for this economic sharing project: the principle of social equality. His argument centers on an appeal to Exodus 16:18—that foundational catechism of Sabbath Economics (2 Cor 8:15).[26] So the opposite is the case: inspired by the practice of mutual aid, Paul's collection sought to *nurture* this ethos among the churches, not *rescue* those who embraced it!
2. *The assertion that the first Christians thought the world was going to end soon, and therefore didn't need to worry about property management or economic planning.* This remarkably pejorative caricature fails to note that there is no hint of apocalyptic rationale in Acts 2 (other than the judgment of God alluded to in Peter's sermon, 2:16–20, 40). Indeed, most scholars believe that Luke-Acts is the *least* apocalyptic literature in the New Testament. The economic sharing of Acts (and of Paul just noted) appeals to Torah principles of Sabbath Economics and flow seamlessly from the teaching and object lessons of Luke's Gospel outlined in this book—none of which invoke an "eschatological interim ethic."

3. *The declaration that the portrait of economic sharing in Acts 2 and 4 is an idealization of the early community and cannot be used to guide "normative Christian behavior.* In this argument, the Acts scenario is considered either fictional (liberal scholars) or strictly unique to the apostolic Pentecost community (conservative scholars); in either case, it is not instructive for later generations.[27] This fails to acknowledge all the ways in which Acts 2 follows seamlessly from Luke's pervasive gospel pedagogy of Sabbath Economics. It also ignores the dark warning tale about Ananias and Sapphira just noted (Acts5:1–11), which hardly qualifies as an idealization! On the other hand, to take that story seriously is to have to reckon with all the ways we ourselves equivocate on the vision of Sabbath Economics: rationalizing our possessiveness, giving with half a heart, and refusing to circulate the gift. Not to mention disregarding challenging texts![28]

Above all, each of these popular "workarounds" of Acts 2:43–47 and 4:32–37 misses entirely what I've just demonstrated: namely, that the Pentecost community's embrace of generalized reciprocity and mutual aid was *rooted* in sacred table fellowship. Luke's three eucharistic meals fuse the sacrament of memory and the practice of Sabbath Economics, in the power of the Spirit.

According to the Acts narrative (and other traditions), the apostle Paul and Luke both promoted this fusion.[29] This is why Paul was so furious that wealthier Corinthian Christians were "profaning" the Lord's Supper, celebrating it according to the conventions of economically stratified and segregated Greco-Roman table fellowship, in which the rich eat first and best (1 Cor 11:17–34). Paul had little patience with those who fetishized the mystical body of Christ in liturgy while ignoring the social body of Christ in reality, especially those in need. Yet most affluent Christians today do just that. Few churchgoers imagine that whenever we take Communion we should also "re-member" Sabbath Economics. Yet if we could fully recover the Eucharist as a ritual that both envisions and empowers the Great Economy, how different our personal and political Christian witness in a world of disparity would be!

iv. Remembering the Prophets
A Closing Thought

This concludes my overview of Sabbath Economics in Luke. May it be of use to preachers and teachers who proclaim and practice the Third Gospel in season and out (for lectionary resources, see appendix I). For persons of faith and conscience struggling to deconstruct socioeconomic disparity in our body politic, appendix II provides a short list of US organizations. These colleagues provide analysis, organizing, and practical experiments to inspire and accompany personal and political change. My prayer is that this study of Luke—the fruit of a quarter century of pedagogy and practice around Sabbath Economics—might contribute to building vision and capacity in our churches for the work of justice in this new Gilded Age.

A poignant question posed by Jesus to his disciples near the end of Luke's story hangs heavily over churches in our critical historical moment: "Will the Human One find faith on earth?" (Luke 18:8). This depends, according to Luke, on whether or not we "listen to the prophets" (16:29, 31). God raises up such prophets in every place, time, and culture—not least among our Indigenous kin. As I was completing the copyediting review of this manuscript, Elaine and I were reading a trusted theologian for our morning devotions: Choctaw elder and Episcopal Bishop Steven Charleston's wise and pertinent new book, *We Survived the End of the World: Lessons from Native America on Apocalypse and Hope.*[30] He profiles four native prophets whose apocalyptic visions helped their people endure the apocalypse of settler colonialism. One of them is Shawnee seer Tenskwatawa (younger brother of the famous leader Tecumseh).

In 1805—the beginning stage of the double apocalypse of the industrial revolution and the American settler march "from sea to shining sea," both of which culminated in the First Gilded Age—Tenskwatawa proclaimed his manifesto of how believers should respond to this threat. As Charleston summarizes them, Tenskwatawa's teachings include broad precepts that we ourselves would do well to heed: "No more war or killing between Native nations. Truth telling in all negotiations. Respect for all women. Reverence for the earth and all her creatures." But poignantly, Tenskwatawa's *conclusion* echoes the old ways of Sabbath Economics as embraced by the Pentecost community of Acts 4: "Private ownership of land was to be repudiated. No more land was to be ceded or sold. Native people should hold all things in common and share whatever they had with one another. Generosity was to be a cornerstone of the new faith as it restored ancient values and traditions."[31]

In a similar prophetic vein, McCarraher's closing words to *The Enchantments of Mammon* urge us to resist the dominant capitalist economic system today: "We can do this in the midst of imperial decay and in the face of seemingly impossible odds. We can practice, in the twilight of a senescent empire, love's radiant, unarmed, and penniless dominion."[32] So I close by reiterating the conviction, so beautifully articulated by the sage Pueblo poet Leslie Silko with which I began. Our scriptural narratives of the Great Economy, contextually read and practiced, are the ancient wisdom we need to save us from the illness of affluenza and the social death of plutocracy. In our age of ecclesial forgetfulness, may our liturgical meals empower us to re-member and reanimate this vocation. And in our culture of confusion, may the imaginary of our biblical traditions be unleashed anew through engaged study, advocacy, and above all, embodiment. Because the enchantments of mammon cannot stand up to our sacred stories.

APPENDIX I

Strategies for Preaching and Studying Luke in Year C

> Do we know our Bible and our tradition well enough to preach series that are both profoundly biblical and profoundly relevant? . . . Do we know our congregation in its social context well enough to preach a series that speaks to the depths and heights of their personal and social experience? . . . Our people deserve no less.
>
> —Alyce M. McKenzie, "Lectionary or Series?"[1]

THIS APPENDIX OFFERS suggestions for how the content of this book might inform a rhythm of preaching or study. There is plenty of online discussion about pros and cons of following the logic of a lectionary versus topical preaching.[2] In my opinion, a curated, ecumenical lectionary—an ancient "scheduling" practice that may go as far back as Jesus's *drash* on Isaiah 61 in Luke 4 (4A)—has three primary strengths:

1. It is constructed around the church's (or synagogue's) liturgical year, which functions to re-narrate secular time through "seasons" of sacred story.
2. The Revised Common Lectionary (hereafter RCL) centers the Gospel, around which the other readings orbit. Its three-year cycle rotates among each of the three synoptics, giving ample opportunity for congregations to build literacy in the Jesus story as the core of the Christian faith.
3. It serves as a mechanism by which a wide spectrum of churches wrestle with the same texts on any given Sunday. This collective rhythm *could* be a powerful engine for consolidating and strengthening our ecclesial witness—even if it rarely functions that way.

In my own occasional preaching, I almost always use one or more of the week's RCL texts, whether or not that is the practice of the congregation I am addressing.[3] And in my (more frequent) teaching of scripture, whenever possible I reference lectionary opportunities to proclaim passages we are studying.

The lectionary's steepest downside is that it is a poor guide for extended thematic proclamation, and tends to discourage close study of whole narratives. Its diverse cross section of texts provides a measure of biblical breadth, but neither depth nor coherence for purposes of sustained exposition. While its pericope orientation may suit homiletics, its atomized selections mitigate *against* scripture's narrative or rhetorical integrity. To be sure, interrelating lectionary texts of the day can be a creative challenge for preachers or teachers—especially when the choice of those texts might seem idiosyncratic or even inscrutable! But focusing narrowly on these excerpts can easily miss broader thematic and compositional patterns, not to mention long narrative arcs. And all but one of the "four stories" necessary to critical interpretation are typically ignored or decontextualized (introduction, i). The "Narrative Lectionary" project initiated by Luther Seminary in 2010 is a thoughtful attempt to mitigate these problematic aspects, and some readers may embrace it as a compromise alternative to the RCL.[4]

In short, it is a considerable challenge to correlate a sustained interpretation of a whole biblical book or theme with a rarely sequential, seasonally fragmented reading schedule. Nevertheless, I make three suggestions here, focusing solely on the texts explored in my study of Luke and Sabbath Economics. First, recognizing that the ecumenical lectionary is an important shaping force in our churches, I overview both challenges and opportunities for preaching the Lukan texts highlighted in this book. Then I offer a non-lectionary approach that covers all the texts exposited above, but still follows the year's liturgical seasons. Finally, I make a few suggestions for what a year-long, non-preaching-oriented group study might look like.

i. Correlating This Book with the Year C Lectionary

The table below shows only the RCL Gospel readings for Year C (excluding certain non-Sunday Feast Days), as that is the focus of my comments; find the other readings for each of the six seasons at https://lectionary.library.vanderbilt.edu/lections.php?year=C&season=Advent. (Remember that each cycle changes slightly, depending on which Sundays are excluded or included in that calendar year.) Lukan texts are in bold, as are the sections where I discuss them in the book (my references to all or part of a text can also be found by consulting the Scripture index). Given the uneven representation of Luke's Sabbath Economics texts throughout the Year C lectionary, I have highlighted in gray the best Sundays to explore this theme and have put in italics my occasional suggestions for possible substitutions.

Lectionary Schedule		
Advent Year C	**Gospel**	**My Comments**
1st Sunday	**Luke 21:25–36**	An "apocalyptic season of turning" bridges Pentecost and Advent. The First Sunday offers an excerpt from Luke's version of the synoptic Little Apocalypse.
2nd Sunday	**Luke 3:1–6**	The introduction of John the Baptist (**see second part of 3A**) gives an opportunity to discuss the importance of the wilderness prophetic tradition in Luke's narrative. The Malachi reading lends further focus.
3rd Sunday	**Luke 3:7–18**	The "edge" exhibited in John's mission statement is discussed in **the second part of 3A**.
4th Sunday	**Luke 1:46–55**	Mary's Magnificat is the focus of **the first part of 3A**. Because it is a programmatic passage, this is a key opportunity to introduce Luke's Sabbath Economics vision of leveling social disparities, which resonates throughout his narrative.
Christmas Year C	**Gospel**	**My Comments**
Christmas Eve or Day	**Luke 2:1–20**	Luke's Christmas story emphasizes God's "preferential option for the poor," referred to in the **first part of 3A**, and is a chance to open up that side of the Jubilee vision.
1st Sunday	**Luke 2:41–52**	The story of Jesus as a child in the Temple is briefly noted in the **first part of 3A**.
2nd Sunday	John 1:1–18	*To keep a Third Gospel focus, substitute here another part of Luke's Christmas story or even Luke's genealogy (3:23–38).*
Epiphany Year C	**Gospel**	**My Comments**
1st Sunday	**Luke 3:15–22**	The Feast of Jesus's Baptism, discussed **variously on pp 56, 59, 61, 83, 107, 136, 207**, is an opportunity to talk about why Jesus chose to apprentice to the politically dissident wilderness prophet John. This primal moment is referred back to often in Luke's story (e.g., 7:29–30; 12:49–50; Acts 2:2).
2nd Sunday	John 2:1–11	*See note on 5th Sunday in Epiphany.*
3rd Sunday	**Luke 4:14–21**	This and the following Sunday features Jesus's inaugural sermon in Nazareth *in its entirety*. Don't miss this chance to open up Luke's full Jubilee theme in this, another "programmatic passage," drawing **on 4A**.

4th Sunday	**Luke 4:21–30**	As discussed in the second part of **4A**, Jesus's spin on the Isaiah 61 text challenges insider entitlement. This theme is reiterated through demonstration in 7:2–23 (see **second part of 5A**). This important correlation is best discussed here, since the Luke 7 text is scheduled for Propers 4 and 5 of Ordinary Time, which do not come up every cycle. See also my notes on 7:11–16 at the **beginning of 5B**.
5th Sunday	**Luke 5:1–11**	The momentum of Sabbath Economics continues for three more Sundays, offering one of the best opportunities during the year to center this theme. This magical call text, fully explored **in 4B**, allows a preacher to show both how this fishing tradition is narrated differently in all four Gospels as well as to bring out more socio-economic background to Luke's story. *Luke 5:12–39, because it follows Mark, does not appear in Year C. One could take license to substitute this important sequence for Second Epiphany's Johannine reading; my comments are in the* ***second part of 4B****.*
6th Sunday	**Luke 6:17–26**	This blessings and woes section of the Sermon on the Plain dramatically opens up Luke's critique of disparity, covered in **5A**. A good opportunity to explore differences with Matthew's Sermon on the Mount.
7th Sunday	**Luke 6:27–38**	The nonviolence focus of this next part of the Sermon keys on the economic violence of indebtedness; see **second part of 5A**.
Transfiguration Sunday	**Luke 9:28–43a**	While I do not explore Luke's Transfiguration story (aside from brief comments on pp. **97, 108, 206**), see my comments on Mark's version (Myers, *Strong Man*, 249–251). Jesus's mystical communion here with "Moses and the prophets" is an opportunity to reflect on how they represent the hermeneutic key to Luke's whole narrative (e.g., 24:27, 44, as discussed **in 1B and 11B**).
8th Sunday	**Luke 6:39–49**	In years this passage does come up, take the opportunity to focus on the village setting and agricultural metaphors at the heart of Jesus's teaching. This text also appears in Proper 3 after Pentecost because neither date makes the lectionary calendar very often.
9th Sunday	**Luke 7:1–10**	This text also appears in Proper 4 after Pentecost. The scenario twins with Jesus's earlier allusion to Elisha and Naaman and should *not* be seen as a Lukan apologia for Roman occupation (see **chap 3, n. 30, chap 5, n. 12**).

Lent Year C	Gospel	My Comments
1st Sunday	**Luke 4:1–13**	Jesus's testing in the wilderness is rightly the traditional text for the first Sunday in Lent; I reflect on the first temptation in **3B**. I correlate it with the deep story of Israel, focusing on the first temptation. This allows a preacher to summarize the "Sabbath Economics catechism" of Exodus 16 (see **2A**). This foundational text is not well represented in the RCL, reflecting the church's failure to understand its importance. Exodus 16:1–15 (omitting the instructions!) is read on the 17th Sunday after Pentecost in Year A, awkwardly correlated with Matthew's Parable of Laborers in the Vineyard. It also appears (though broken up) in the 11th Sunday after Pentecost in Year A, correlated with John's Bread of Life discourse—and thus is typically interpreted in a de-economized spiritual fashion. *This is the Sunday to repair this oversight.*
2nd Sunday	**Luke 13:31–35**	This text underlines Jesus as a prophet, first in his sharp retort to Herod, then in his embrace of the prophet's fate. I discuss his critique of the ruler at the **end of 5A (see esp. fn. 13)**.
3rd Sunday	**Luke 13:1–9**	This text similarly reflects Jesus's commentary on the perils of everyday life under empire; see **pp. 135–136, esp. fn. 3**, and the connections to 14:28–30 (see **p. 153**).
4th Sunday	**Luke 15:1–3, 11b–32**	The Prodigal Son is Luke's most popular parable. See context at the **beginning of 10A**; it is connected to the Defect-ive Manager Parable through the verbs *diaskorpizō* and *epithumeō* (a desperate hunger that will settle for scraps) experienced by both the Prodigal (15:16) and Lazarus (16:21)!
5th Sunday	John 12:1–8	*To remain in Luke, you might substitute his story of the raising of the son of the widow of Nain (Luke 7:11-17; see my comments in **5A-B**), which usually is omitted in the RCL's Year C calendar. This would replace the scheduled Johannine story of the raising of Lazarus; similar theme, though quite different treatments.*
Palm Sunday	**Luke 19:28–40**	Though this book doesn't tackle Luke's story of Jesus's entry into Jerusalem, based on Mark's narrative of carefully choreographed street the-ater, hear my comments from a 2013 webinar: "Jesus's March on Jerusalem in Political and Economic Context: Luke 19" https://bcmonline.org/2013/03/19/node-276/.

Easter Year C	Gospel	My Comments
Resurrection Sunday	**Luke 24:1–12**	Luke's empty tomb narrative roughly follows Mark's, with a few interesting differences: omitting the lament before the stone (Mark 16:3), adding another angel (Luke 24:4) and the famous phrase "Why do you seek the living among the dead?" (24:5c). Most importantly, Luke adds a gender polemic that notes three women (24:10, see 8:2–3) whose testimony the male apostles did not believe (24:11)! Plenty there for an Easter sermon! *Note: The reading for both the Easter Vigil and Easter Evening is the Emmaus Road story (24:13–49), an important text for this book (see **chapter 1**). In order to keep Eastertide focused on Luke, the following sequence of passages from the Emmaus narrative could be spread out over the next five Sundays in lieu of the Johannine readings, as suggested below.*
2nd Sunday	John 20:19–31	*Per the previous note, a first segment of the Emmaus Road story could be **Luke 24:13–18**, re-placing the scenario in the real world of occupied Jerusalem in the aftermath of Jesus's execution (**1A**).*
3rd Sunday	John 21:1–19	***Luke 24:19–24:** The disciples' passionate lament to the Stranger about their frustration speaks volumes about the trauma experienced by the movement after Jesus's lynching (**1A**).*
4th Sunday	John 10:22–30	***Luke 24:25–27, 32, 44–47:** A great opportunity to drill down on the importance of prophetic literacy for Luke (**1B**).*
5th Sunday	John 13:31–35	***Luke 24:28–35, 41–42:** Jesus revealed in the breaking of bread is highlighted in my study as the second of three sacred meals that bridge the Gospel and Acts, reiterating the "loaves and fishes" Sabbath Economics motif (see **epilogue, ii**).*
6th Sunday	John 14:23–29	***Luke 24:36–40:** In this "traumatic somatic" moment, the Risen Christ is revealed as the Crucified One (**1B**), centering the disciples' epistemology in a reckoning with mangled flesh and bone.*
7th Sunday	**Luke 24:44–53**	Ascension Day, usually celebrated on the last Sunday of Eastertide, could neatly culminate a series on Luke 24. The first RCL reading is **Acts 1:1–11**, Luke's "second" account of the Ascension (see beginning of **epilogue, iii**).

Pentecost Sunday	**Acts 2:1–21**	The narrative of Pentecost is deeply rooted in Shavuot's Sabbath Economics redistributive justice—especially if the narrative is extended to include **Acts 2:42–47** and if the first reading (**Gen 11:1–9**) is correlated with the multicultural insurrection of "tongues" (see **epilogue, iii**).
Ordinary Time Year C	**Gospel**	**My Comments**
Trinity Sunday	John 16:12–15	
Proper 3 (8)	**Luke 6:39–49**	Not observed some years (see 8th Sunday of Epiphany).
Proper 4 (9)	**Luke 7:1–10**	Not observed some years (see 9th Sunday of Epiphany).
Proper 5 (10)	**Luke 7:11–17**	Luke's widow of Nain resuscitation story is paired with that of Elijah's healing of the widow of Zarephath, explored at the **beginning of 5B**, anticipating a sequence of women witnesses.
Proper 6 (11)	**Luke 7:36–8:3**	A fun text to preach—and dramatize! **6B** explores it as a key Sabbath Economics object lesson, a meal story that addresses social disparity, the economics of indebtedness and gender dynamics (deepened in the epilogue of 8:1–3). Unfortunately this text rarely makes the cut in the Ordinary Time calendar; *if not, I recommend switching it up with Proper 7.*
Proper 7 (12)	**Luke 8:26–39**	Luke's version of Mark's exorcism of the "Legion"; see index and my comments on Mark 5:1–21 in Myers, *Strong Man*, 190–194.
Proper 8 (13)	**Luke 9:51–62**	A watershed moment in Luke's plot: Jesus "sets his face to go to Jerusalem." This opens the Special Section (9:51–18:14), which is the terrain of most of Year C's Ordinary Time lectionary. This is thus a good time to start a series on Luke and Sabbath Economics. The rejection by Samaritans (see **pp. 97, 105**) sets up next week's text.
Proper 9 (14)	**Luke 10:1–11, 16–20**	Luke's second iteration of Jesus's teaching regarding missionary ethics and the importance of respecting hospitality (see also 9:1–6) is explored in **6A.**
Proper 10 (15)	**Luke 10:25–37**	The Good Samaritan parable is a demonstration of Sabbath Economics mutual aid towards outsiders; see **second half of 6B.**
Proper 11 (16)	**Luke 10:38–42**	Preachers often miss how Luke's Mary and Martha story flips the script on gender roles for women regarding table versus Torah. The oddly paired Amos 8:1–12 reading is a keystone text of social justice.

Proper 12 (17)	**Luke 11:1–13**	The Disciples' Prayer offers a shorter catechism on Sabbath Economics, as explored in **7A**. It's a key opportunity to help the church get right the prayer we allegedly know by heart. Prayer as tenacity in a cosmology of grace is the focus of the second part of the text, investigated in **7B**.
Proper 13 (18)	**Luke 12:13–21**	The good news: the lectionary includes the first rich man story of the special section, which foreshadows much of what is to come (see **8A**). Let this text do some heavy lifting around issues of intergenerational affluenza! The bad news: it skips over most of Jesus's Great Economy catechism (12:22–34; see next).
Proper 14 (19)	**Luke 12:32–40**	This is one of Year C's most frustrating, inscrutable redactions of Luke's narrative—and testimony to how alienated modern Christians are from the wisdom of nature! The example of lilies and ravens is ignored in favor of the "thief in the night" parable. Thus the demanding conclusion of the former teaching (about selling possessions and discerning what we treasure, 12:32–34) is implicitly linked instead to a master-slave image, which is typically interpreted in a way that Jesus's "return in glory" resolves the discipleship mandate (12:39–40; on this see **8B, fn. 31**). The apocalyptic exhortation to "stay awake" is always needed, but the Sabbath Economics heart of Jesus's teaching is lost. *I strongly recommend reinstating 12:21–34 (explored in* ***8B****), either with or without 12:35–40, in order to hear Jesus's (and Hazel Henderson's) challenge to our unsustainable industrial economic cosmology.*
Proper 15 (20)	**Luke 12:49–56**	Jesus invokes the "fire" and "baptism" of John while repudiating the "peace" of a violent imperial system (see **pp. 58, 136**). His movement will "divide the house": both the Pax Romana that protects the palaces of the strong (11:17–21) and the domestic household that socializes conformity (12:52–53). We may ignore nature, but seem to "interpret" it better than we do the *kairos* (12:56).
Proper 16 (21)	**Luke 13:10–17**	This is an important opportunity to introduce Luke's "somatic symbolism" and to talk about indebtedness and poverty (**first part of 9A**). *Since this text's "twin" (14:2–6) is skipped over by next week's lection, I recommend including it in today's reading to capture the contrasting political bodies of rich and poor, both healed on the Sabbath* ***(second part of 9A)****.*

Proper 17 (22)	**Luke 14:1, 7–14**	A key scenario at a table of elites, but again truncated, with two-thirds of Jesus's unitary Sabbath Economics teaching stripped away (**see 9B**). The interlocking lessons about social positioning, entitlement and radical hospitality are so painfully relevant to our own context that *I recommend reinstating at least vv. 15–24*!
Proper 18 (23)	**Luke 14:25–33**	This teaching about "counting the cost" of discipleship—which begins by reckoning with the cross and ends with renunciation of possessions, also alludes to the violence of imperial life in first-century occupied Palestine, noted at the **beginning of 10A**.
Proper 19 (24)	**Luke 15:1–10**	The first two of a string of "lost and found" parables (the third is the Prodigal Son, 4th Sunday in Lent); see context at the **beginning of 10A**. Why Psalm 14 was deployed here and not in Proper 13 is beyond me…
Proper 20 (25)	**Luke 16:1–13**	The next two Sundays allow a fulsome engagement with two "texts of terror" in Luke 16 (not to mention with powerful readings from Amos 8 and 6). The "defect-ive manager" here (explored in detail in **chapter 10**) is for us a deeply germane, but inveterately misinterpreted, story about acting improvisationally to use capital to restore community (rather than the other way around typical of our society).
Proper 21 (26)	**Luke 16:19–31**	**Chapter 11** focuses on today's text, which is a fulcrum not only for Luke's entire argument about disparity but also for his insistence that we must recover Sabbath Economics cosmology through literacy in Moses and the prophets. *Do not miss* this opportunity to let the Gospel do extremely heavy lifting around issues your congregation will resist—but for which preaching Luke through Ordinary Time will have prepared them!
Proper 22 (27)	**Luke 17:5–10**	I engage the proleptic image of "uprooting a sycamore tree" in the middle of my comments about the Zacchaeus story (**13A, especially fn. 10**), and one could have fun posing it as a riddle that will be solved five weeks later (Proper 26)! At the **start of 12A**, I consider the text's other real-life scenario, from the servant class. Often moralized as a parable about servility, it is better understood as a kind of *koan* that undermines hierarchy by addressing the listener first as a "master," then as a "servant," blurring what was usually considered an absolute distinction.

Proper 23 (28)	**Luke 17:11–19**	Another object lesson showing how "otherness" is centered by Jesus (the protagonist's Samaritan identity is as marginalizing as his leper status). This again conjures the Nazareth sermon's example of Naaman's healing (**4:27** ; as in **5:12–14**). See **beginning of 12A**.
Proper 24 (29)	**Luke 18:1–8**	The amazing story of the tenacious widow (and its parallel with the scenario in 11:5–8) is explored in **12A**. This is a perfect text to discuss how prayer and persistence are both needed in the work of personal and political change.
Proper 25 (30)	**Luke 18:9–14**	Also covered in **12A**, this is yet another contrastive scenario featuring two "servants" of the dominant economy. Its portrait of elite entitlement sets the stage for the rich man's rejection of Jesus's call to discipleship, which doesn't come up Year C (**12B**).
Proper 26 (31)	**Luke 19:1–10**	The culminating story in Luke's rich man series, this is a truly frightening text for affluent North Americans (no wonder it comes up around Halloween!). Explored in **13A**, this passage can again do the heavy lifting for the fraught conversation around redistributive justice, and specifically reparations to those who have been dispossessed by a rapacious economic system. It can be a perfect, challenging conclusion to an Ordinary Time preaching series on Sabbath Economics and a great way to ring in the All Saints Triduum (and talk about ancestral wealth).
Proper 27 (32)	**Luke 20:27–38**	Luke's version of Mark's story about Jesus's debate with Sadducees about resurrection (see Myers, *Strong Man*, 314–317).
Proper 28 (33)	**Luke 21:5–19**	This begins Luke's Little Apocalypse and the season of turning (see 1st Advent). Jesus's judgment on the Temple system is provoked by the preceding story of an exploited widow *(20:45–21:4)—which is a good reason to include it in this Sunday's Gospel reading. This Markan tradition functions as the seventh and last of Luke's rich man stories. If the Zacchaeus tale is comic (a happy outcome), this is tragic, portraying how a poor woman is made destitute by exploitive lawyers and the tithing demands of the Temple system (I touch upon this in the first part of **12A**).* Jesus then exits the Temple and pronounces doom on its economic structures—his final repudiation of the "end of the world as we know it." The wars, lies, and social upheaval of empire (21:8–11) will challenge disciples to bear costly witness (21:12–19).

Proper 29 (34)	**Luke 23:33–43**	The text for Reign of Christ Sunday is Luke's portrait of Jesus on the cross. It generally follows Mark (though with elements in different order) but adds the exchange with one being crucified alongside him. Only Luke calls these men "criminals" (23:32–33, 39), implying they are poor; this makes sense of Jesus's promise of immediate deliverance into paradise (24:43), which echoes the fate of Lazarus back in 16:23.

ii. An Alternative Schedule for Preaching Luke and Sabbath Economics Across the Liturgical Year

Should one be unable or unwilling to abide by the RCL's considerable strictures in trying to preach or teach through Luke and Sabbath Economics, the next best strategy is to plot a "revised RCL" journey that covers all the texts centered in this book. Below is a suggestion of how this can be done in accordance with the liturgical seasons, so as not to abandon ecclesial rhythms altogether. I have shaped this suggested schedule to correspond with RCL readings wherever possible, especially around feast days (highlighted below in gray); in those cases, refer to the preceding RCL table for more of my comments.

Here is just one way to experiment with an alternative lectionary:

A Non-RCL Schedule		
Advent Year C	**Text**	**Topic/Reference**
1st Sunday	**Exod 16:1–18**	Israel's first catechism and first instruction (**2A**).
2nd Sunday	**Exod 16: 20–36**	Second and third instructions, and the *manna* as a Sabbath Economics sign for all generations (**2A**).
3rd Sunday	**Luke 3:1–14**	Introduction of wilderness prophet John the Baptist (**second part of 3A**). Note: Include here RCL's Malachi reading for 2 Advent, which coheres with the Baptist's coming in the wilderness.
4th Sunday	**Luke 1:46–55**	The Magnificat (**first part of 3A**).
Christmas Year C	**Gospel**	**Topic/Reference**
Christmas Eve or Day	**Luke 2:1–20**	Luke's Christmas story (**first part of 3A**).
1st Sunday	**Lev 25**	The Jubilee tradition (**2B**).
2nd Sunday	**Deut 15:1–11**	Seventh year debt-release tradition (**2B**).
Epiphany Year C	**Gospel**	**Topic/Reference**
1st Sunday	**Luke 3:15–22**	Feast of Jesus's Baptism (see comments in RCL section).
2nd Sunday	**Luke 4:14–21**	Jesus's inaugural sermon in Nazareth (**first part of 4A**).

3rd Sunday	**Luke 4:21–30**	Jesus's controversial *drash* (**second part of 4A**).
4th Sunday	**Luke 4:31–44**	First two healings (see Myers, *Strong Man*, 141–151).
5th Sunday	**Luke 5:1–11**	Call of fishermen (**first part of 4B**).
6th Sunday	**Luke 5:27–6:5**	Three food stories: Levi, fasting, gleaning (**second part 4B**).
7th Sunday	**Luke 6:17–26**	"Blessings and woes" from Sermon on the Plain (**5A**).
Transfiguration Sunday	**Luke 9:28–43a**	Jesus's mystical communion with Moses and the prophets and the hermeneutic key to Luke's story as a whole (see **1B**).
Lent Year C	**Gospel**	**Topic/Reference**
1st Sunday	**Luke 4:1–13**	Jesus's testing in the wilderness (**3B**).
2nd Sunday	**Luke 7:1–10**	Healing of a centurion, demonstrating Elisha's healing of foreign officer Naaman in Jesus's *drash* (**beginning of 5B**).
3rd Sunday	**Luke 7:11–17**	Widow of Nain resuscitation story, demonstrating Elijah's healing of the widow of Zarephath (**beginning of 5B**).
4th Sunday	**Luke 7:35–8:3**	A key Sabbath Economics meal story as object lesson that addresses social disparity, the economics of indebtedness, and women's agency (**6B**).
5th Sunday	**Luke 9:1–6**	Luke's first iteration of his missionary instructions (**first half of 6A**) and why this is still important for Christian missions.
Palm Sunday	**Luke 19:28–40**	Luke's story of Jesus's entry into Jerusalem, based on Mark's carefully choreographed street theater (hear my comments at https://bcmonline.org/?s=political+street+theater&id=6797).
Easter Year C	**Gospel**	**Topic/Reference**
Resurrection Sunday	**Luke 24:1–12**	Luke's empty tomb narrative. Use as introduction to following series on the Emmaus Road story.
2nd Sunday	**Luke 24:13–18**	Replace the Emmaus Road scenario in the real world of occupied Jerusalem in the aftermath of Jesus's execution (**1A**).
3rd Sunday	**Luke 24:19–24**	The disciples' lament to the Stranger speaks volumes about the movement's trauma after his lynching (**1A**).
4th Sunday	**Luke 24:25–27, 32, 44–47**	Drill down on the importance of prophetic literacy for Luke's Sabbath Economics vision (**1B**).

5th Sunday	**Luke 24:28–35, 41–42**	The Stranger is revealed in the breaking of bread, the second of three sacred meals that bridge the Gospel and Acts, reiterating the "loaves and fishes" motif (see **epilogue, ii**).
6th Sunday	**Luke 24:36–40**	The "traumatic somatic" moment in which the Risen Christ is confirmed as the Crucified One (**1B**).
7th Sunday	**Luke 24:44–53 Acts 1:1–11**	Ascension Day can culminate a series on Luke 24, including Luke's second Ascension account (see **epilogue, iii**).
Pentecost Sunday	**Acts 2:1–21, 42–47, Gen 11:1–9**	Pentecost/Shavuot Sabbath Economics redistributive justice, correlated with the multicultural insurrection of "tongues" (**epilogue, iii**).
Ordinary Time Year C	**Gospel**	**Topic/Reference**
Trinity Sunday	**Luke 8:40–56**	Not covered in the book, but this story of two contrasting political bodies is an important demonstration of Jesus's radical prioritizing of the marginalized in order to heal the diseased, disparate body politic of Israel (see my comments on the Markan diptych in Myers, *Strong Man*, 197–205).
Proper 7	**Luke 9:10–17**	Luke's wilderness feeding, as a keystone text of Sabbath Economics, is an excellent way to kick off Ordinary Time.
Proper 8	**Luke 9:51–56**	A watershed turn in Luke's journey plot opens his Special Section. Jesus's rejection by Samaritans sets up the next two weeks.
Proper 9	**Luke 10:1–11, 16–20**	Luke's expanded iteration of Jesus's teaching about missionaries respecting hospitality (**6A**).
Proper 10	**Luke 10:25–37**	The Good Samaritan parable demonstrates Sabbath Economics mutual aid towards outsiders (**second half of 6B**).
Proper 11	**Luke 10:38–42 Amos 8:1–12**	Though not discussed in the book, the Mary and Martha story argues that women's place is studying Torah, not just serving at table (see p. 269, n. 35). Include Amos's keystone text of social justice.
Proper 12	**Luke 11:1–13**	The Disciples' Prayer as a "shorter catechism" on Sabbath Economics (**7A, first part of 7B**).
Proper 13	**Luke 12:13–21**	Luke's first rich man story in his Special Section series—and critique of intergenerational affluenza (**8A**).
Proper 14	**Luke 12:22–28**	Jesus's Great Economy catechism calls us to pay attention to the testimony of lilies and ravens, so elegantly depicted on the cover of this book (**first part of 8B**). Since this text is ignored in the RCL, it deserves focus for two Sundays!

Proper 15	**Luke 12:29–34**	Jesus (and Hazel Henderson!) challenge us to "seek first" the Great Economy and wean ourselves off of our unsustainable industrial economic cosmology (**second part of 8B**).
Proper 16	**Luke 13:10–17**	Introduce Luke's "somatic symbolism" and talk about indebtedness and poverty (**first part of 9A**).
Proper 17	**Luke 14:1–6**	Another Sabbath healing twinned to previous week's text, showing contrasting "political bodies" of rich and poor and setting up the long banquet teaching (**second part of 9A**).
Proper 18	**Luke 14:7–14**	Jesus's Sabbath Economics teaching at a meal of elites (**see 9B**). Because its interlocking lessons about "table as social map" and the delusion of upward mobility are so painfully relevant to our own context, it also deserves two Sundays.
Proper 19	**Luke 14:15–24**	The concluding parable shows a host's conversion to radical hospitality and the Great Economy (**second part of 9B**).
Proper 20	**Luke 16:1–13** **Amos 8:4–7**	The "defect-ive manager" story is deeply germane for middle-class churches but needs to be disentangled from long-standing misinterpretations (**chapter 10**). Use Amos too.
Proper 21	**Luke 16:19–31** **Amos 6:1–7**	The fulcrum for Luke's entire argument about disparity and for recovering Sabbath Economics cosmology through literacy in Moses and the prophets (**chapter 11**).
Proper 22	**Luke 18:1–8**	The amazing story of the tenacious widow (**first part of 12A**) begins a series on the ravages of entitlement; this and next week's choice illustrate how prayer and persistence are both needed for personal and political change.
Proper 23	**Luke 18:9–14**	Another illustrative scenario about social opposites (**second part of 12A**).
Proper 24	**Luke 18:18–30**	A ruler's rejection of Jesus's call to discipleship, another key rich man story. The epilogue conversation is particularly crucial to a discipleship of Sabbath Economics (**12B**).
Proper 25	**Luke 18:35–43**	The front end of Luke's final contrastive dyad in this series is a blind man who *does* follow (**first part of 13A**).
Proper 26	**Luke 19:1–10**	The culminating story in Luke's rich man series, perfect for fraught conversations around redistributive justice and reparations to those who have been dispossessed by a rapacious economic system (**13A**).

Proper 27	**Luke 19:11–27**	Luke's Parable of the Pounds as a lesson about the cost of discipleship (**13B**).
Proper 28	**Luke 20:45–21:4**	Jesus's judgment on the Temple system is provoked by two stories of widows made destitute by an exploitive legal and tithing system; they function as the seventh and last of Luke's rich man scenarios (see **first part of 12A**). Jesus exits the Temple and denounces on its economic structures.
Proper 29	**Luke 22:15–30** **Acts 2:42–47**	These two eucharistic meals realize Sabbath Economics and provide a fitting conclusion to the year's teaching (**epilogue, i, iii**).

iii. A Longer Study Series

The pulpit is not the only (nor the best) way to articulate Luke's vision of Sabbath Economics. This book is primarily geared for close study and discussion, preferably done in groups, which can include Sunday or midweek adult education for the congregation. The Third Gospel—our most extensive story of Jesus—really deserves a year-long engagement, through which participants can explore and metabolize Jesus's call for economic discipleship.

The architecture of this book was designed for 34 sessions: two for the introduction, each chapter, the epilogue, and each appendix. If a group meets twice a month, that is a year-and-a-half commitment. Obviously, the task of sustaining such a long period of concentration is a daunting prospect in our culture of short attention spans, and may need to be divided up over a longer period. It does not, of course, need to be restricted to the Year C calendar! However structured, the profundity of Luke's vision and narrative deserves a deep dive into critical literacy, reflection, and most importantly, embodiment—for which the next appendix offers resources.

APPENDIX II

Resources for Personal and Political Sabbath Economics Practices

> How does God's love abide in anyone who has the world's goods, sees a sibling in need, yet refuses help?
>
> —1 John 3:17

> The logic of capitalism is not simply incorrect; it is also a "technology of desire" that trains people to desire, act, and shape institutions in ways that are consistent with the problematic underlying anthropology and ontology. The practices and organization of the Church rest on a different set of assumptions, offer a different account of the social world, and form people in ways that are consistent with a true anthropology that is dependent on God.
>
> —Steven McMullen, "Radical Orthodox Economics"[1]

IN LIGHT OF Luke's Gospel, and of the unsustainability and cruelty of continuing economic disparity in our world, people of faith have a responsibility to promote and practice significant change in personal and political realms. This appendix recommends a short list of resources and organizations that can empower a discipleship of healing affluenza and resisting plutocracy here in North America. It is organized into three primary spheres of engagement: with household economies, with faith institutions, and with systems that perpetuate disparity. Of the many groups currently doing economic justice work in the US, the recommendations below give priority to faith-rooted groups whose efforts we at Bartimaeus Cooperative Ministries (BCM) know and trust, and with whom we have collaborated.

Affluenza and plutocracy are terminal diseases that can only be healed through collective, intergenerational recovery and deep political transformation. This book has endeavored to provoke, animate, and strengthen our *will* to change; the groups noted below show ways to do so.

i. Working a Sabbath Economics Household Covenant

Over twenty-five years of Sabbath Economics education and organizing, our small shop at BCM has developed resources to help ourselves and others focus practically on repentance as "turning our economic lives around." As discussed at the outset of this book, most North Americans see economic systems and behaviors as too abstract, complicated, or mystifying to engage critically. Yet the more we feel powerless to make meaningful changes, the more likely we are to conform to dominant economic perceptions and habits that perpetuate the crisis.

Experience has taught us that for ordinary middle-class folk, the best place to discover agency and activism is where the economic system "out there" intersects most concretely and intimately with our lived experience: our household economy. This is the space from which *every day* we work and consume, save and spend. Our household practices express most accurately our real (as opposed to professed) social values. Are our habits mindful and critical, or compulsive and credulous, regarding the enchantments of mammon?

For most of us, enduring and substantive personal changes only unfold incrementally, and require significant discernment and deliberation. Thus at the heart of our pedagogy is a method for tracking and evaluating our experiments with economic discipleship we call the "Sevenfold Sabbath Economics Household Covenant."[2]

This model (see Figure 7) represents the basic components of our household economies. Though there are many other instructive ways to diagram this terrain, we have stipulated seven aspects in the spirit of Sabbath symbolism. Because each aspect is deeply related to the others, one can start at any point in the circle, but all of it must be considered.

The first three aspects reflect our strong emphasis on money habits, since in our capitalist culture everyone is socialized into the primacy and power of capital—regardless of how much or little we own, owe, or share.

- *Surplus Capital*: Most folks in (over)developed societies have at least some resources deposited in a bank. A good first Sabbath Economics step is to move one's savings from corporate banks (whose business is concentrating capital on Wall Street) to locally owned banks or credit unions (whose focus is to provide financial services to their community; see https://www.betterbankingoptions.com/). Not everyone has surplus beyond modest savings (indeed, only a minority of Americans hold investments). But for those who do, the next best thing to divestment and redistribution is to move assets out of mainstream corporate investment firms whose mission is to make money on money (the concise definition of usury), and to reinvest them in Community Development Financial Institutions (CDFIs) whose mission is to make capital available to low-income people, businesses, and organizations (learn more at https://www.cdfifund.gov/). Minimally, investments should be screened for social and ecological responsibility (SRI),

Figure 7. Sabbath Economics Household Practices Covenant, Bartimaeus Cooperative Ministries.

based on the principle that the capital one entrusts to a financial institution represents a measure of power.[3] The SRI movement is mainstream now, though one should beware of greenwashing. We also encourage people to calculate a "social mortgage" or wealth tax on their surplus capital, and to tithe that amount to low-wealth entities and/or those deserving of restitution or reparations. This modest discipline helps us remain ever mindful of our inevitable entanglement in an exploitive usury system and structures of inequity.

- *Negative capital*: By this we mean one's aggregate household debt (including mortgage, car notes, credit cards, student loans, etc.). We encourage participants to calculate and assess their debt-to-savings ratio with the goal of reducing it, since debt should never be considered an asset, given usurious interest rates. Restricting the number and limits of credit cards is a good step (a popular strategy has been to place reminder notes right on one's cards).[4] So is using savings to pay off a percentage of debt to reduce the amount of interest serviced. More recently, groups have experimented with cooperative loan and debt pools as a practice of mutual aid.[5]

- *Giving*: This book has repeatedly pointed out that the gift economy is constitutive of the Great Economy and helps build social relations. Covenant participants explore the history and values of their giving and assess their relationship with organizations to whom they give (relational giving helps move us beyond anonymous charity to solidarity). We encourage formulating a strategic giving plan and examining the balance between our giving of money, time, and talent. Some have experimented with communitizing their decision-making process to focalize collective priorities, move from charity to justice, and strengthen accountability.

The other four aspects of our covenant model address a cross section of "lifeway" patterns. It is important to continually monitor and reduce the ecological footprint of our household habits, such as housing, transportation, and energy.[6] The same goes for our consumption: becoming more literate in assessing commodities in terms of their geographic origins and shipping carbon footprint; resource extraction; production and labor practices; packaging and durability; and impacts on the waste stream. Our model also includes examining our relationships with marginalized communities and exploring ways to overcome our insulation from, and solidarity with, them. The final (and too often overlooked) aspect is critically looking at our labor *and rest* habits, a key area of compulsive behavior in our society that has been intensified through the increasing dominance of online communications.

Working the covenant empowers us to begin or continue transforming our practices. This approach draws on the addiction-recovery tradition of conversion, already highlighted at several points in this book (see pp. 20, 77, 144, 192). In Twelve-step language, repentance-as-recovery means recognizing how deeply captive we are to an economic system that has infinite tolerance for both poverty and extreme wealth. The model challenges us to take regular inventory of what must change in our daily habits and to make amends to those harmed directly and indirectly by our economic practices (including poor communities and the environment).

This journey covenants to lifelong change, and to "working a program" that continually assesses, audits, and adjusts our economic behaviors:

- *Assessing*: The model challenges us to think through *each* of seven areas of the lived economy of our individual or family household, and to do so in light of gospel values such as those expressed in this study of Luke's story of Jesus. To paraphrase the apostle Paul (Rom 12:2): Where are we *conforming* to the mammon system, and what habits will we begin *transforming* toward the good? Because individual or private intentions are rarely fruitful, covenant work best takes place in a small group of persons committed to the recovery process and to mutual accountability. A group builds courage to break social taboos that keep us silent about money, class, and lifestyle, as we listen carefully to each other to nurture greater transparency and transformation.
- *Auditing*: The model challenges us to identify *at least one* specific commitment our household can make in *each of the seven* areas over the course of a year (or some other time frame). Honesty and humility are particularly crucial to a group process. Virtue signaling about how much one has accomplished in a given area, or comparing oneself favorably to someone else, is counterproductive. Our task is to figure out and work with our *own* growing edges. Similarly unhelpful are ideological statements about what we should all be doing. We can encourage and push each other only if we recognize that every household can only begin where it is, which can be quite different, for different reasons. The most important principle is: *No step is too small, and no step is too large*! And the most relevant ongoing question is: What are *next* steps that will take our household deeper into Sabbath Economics in the context in which we live and work, here and now?
- *Adjusting*: Periodic re-covenanting is essential, wherein we review commitments in order to renew, amend, or fine-tune them, and support each other to go deeper in each covenant area. Each step is an experiment from which we learn and grow—as do our companions on the journey.

Over time, households (or even whole congregations!) can collaborate to make a deeper collective impact. For example, some years ago BCM partnered with a local presbytery on a pilot project to change banking and investment habits. Over the course of a year, forty-five households moved almost three million dollars of their respective surplus capital into socially responsible and community investments! Other groups have experimented with collective tithing or debt-relief, reducing their carbon footprint, and journeying together outside their comfort zone toward marginalized communities.

Through convening, facilitating, and resourcing groups around the country, we have discovered that honest conversations among participants has two empowering effects:

1. *It de-privatizes our anxieties.* We are all socialized and constrained under our capitalist system to be very private about our economic lives, which effectively undermines critical conversation and collective action. We end up struggling "alone together" with similar frustrations and disempowerment. Breaking powerful taboos and silences helps free us from such isolation and alienation and changes patterns of denial or defensiveness on one hand, or blaming and shaming on the other.
2. *It communitizes our imagination.* The cosmology of capitalism is severe and absolute in its efforts to persuade us that there are no real alternatives to itself. But when we start to experiment with "defect-ive" behaviors (chapter 10), we realize other life patterns are possible, and begin mustering common courage to change. Because we each bring different backgrounds and perspectives, we help one another see things differently and overcome deeply socialized fear, paralysis, and ambivalence in order to think and act outside our boxes.

Most participants in covenant work have experienced palpable relief in a space where they can tackle difficult but necessary issues. One ongoing accountability group in Minneapolis has lasted more than fifteen years!

While this covenant process is effective in challenging and accompanying persons to reimagine their household economic practices, its focus on personal habits is not a *substitute* for engaging wider political aspects of economic justice but rather a *complement* to organizing and advocacy. Household covenant work is not by itself *sufficient* for creating a world that conforms more deeply to the Great Economy. It is, however, *necessary* as a spiritual discipline for the long haul of faith development and social transformation. The lifelong journey of learning to resist the culture of mammon and embrace the culture of *manna* consists of small, concrete steps. What are *your* next steps?

ii. Support for Household Covenant Work

There are several organizations that have specifically evolved to support this kind of work. Chief among them is **Faith and Money Network** (https://faithandmoneynetwork.org/), based in Washington, DC. These friends, formed through the Washington DC-based Church of the Savior (a radical ecclesial experiment over three generations), are committed to curating spaces for people of faith and conscience to reckon with and repair their economic discipleship. FMN offers online and in-person introductory sessions, money autobiography and genealogy workshops, household covenant groups, and "trips of perspective." They have long been part of a North America-wide Sabbath Economics collaborative, which continues to convene strategic gatherings and develop resources for this work. If you wish to join us, contact https://bcmonline.org/.

Other groups doing similar work of education, advocacy, and training around Sabbath Economics discipleship include:

- California- and Mexico-based **One Earth Jubilee** (https://oneearthjubilee.com/)
- **Simple Living Works!**, a long-standing online, resource-rich site (https://simplelivingworks.wordpress.com/)
- **Gospel Living**, a Catholic site (https://www.gospelliving.org/money.html)
- **Manna Gum: Enough for All**, a group doing contextual Sabbath Economics work in Australia (www.mannagum.org.au)

Most relevant to this book's focus are those working around issues of surplus capital, reparations, and structural justice. Key colleagues in this growing field of socioeconomic change-making include:

- **Just Money Advisors** in Louisville, KY (https://www.justmoneyadvisors.com/) are faith-rooted financial counselors who have helped lead the socially responsible and social investment movement in the US and who look for creative ways to leverage capital to build community, especially on behalf of low-wealth groups. We commend them highly. (Parallel work is being done in the U.K. by the unrelated ecumenical Just Money Movement; see https://justmoney.org.uk/.)
- **Ancestors and Money** animator Morgan Curtis facilitates cohorts in money genealogy work (https://www.morganhcurtis.com/ancestors-money).
- **Chordata Capital** is an anti-capitalist wealth management firm that supports clients to redistribute rather than continue accumulating capital in the spirit of solidarity economics (https://chordatacapital.com/impactreport/).

- The **Francesco Collaborative** helps faith-based investors reimagine practices anchored in Catholic Social Teaching (https://francescocollaborative.org).
- The **Criterion Institute** is a nonprofit think tank expanding possibilities for how finance can be used for social change (https://www.criterioninstitute.org/).
- **The Land Clinic**, a project of Sustainable Law Group, recomposes property, contract, estate planning and real estate law practices to focus on the systems, tools, and processes that support reparations and connecting people to the ecologies and histories of place (https://www.landclinic.org/annual-report).
- **Foundation 99** focuses on "building economic security for the 99%," especially working people and racial minorities (https://foundation99.org/).
- **The Cooperative Fund of the Northeast** offers community-based investments, loans and support for democratic enterprises (www.cooperativefund.org).

iii. Faith Communities

Christian denominations have made important statements about the disparity crisis. Here are two notable examples, from Protestant and Catholic officials respectively:

> The root causes of massive threats to life are above all the product of an unjust economic system defended and protected by political and military might. . . . This crisis is directly related to the development of neoliberal economic globalization . . . an ideology that claims to be without alternative, demanding an endless flow of sacrifices from the poor and creation. It makes false promises . . . claiming sovereignty over life and demanding total allegiance, which amounts to idolatry . . .
>
> We believe that human beings are called to choose God over mammon. . . . Therefore we reject any ideology or economic regime that puts profits before people, does not care for all creation, and privatizes those gifts of God meant for all. We reject any teaching which justifies those who support, or fail to resist, such an ideology in the name of the gospel.
>
> —*Confessional declaration, World Alliance of Reformed Churches, 2004*[7]

> I think of the words spoken to [Francis of Assisi] from the Crucifix in the little church of San Damiano: "Go, Francis, repair my house, which, as you see, is falling into ruin." The repair of that house concerns all of us. It concerns the Church, society and the heart of each individual. Increasingly, it concerns the environment, which urgently demands a sound economy and a sustainable development that can heal its wounds and assure us of a worthy future. . . . [E]ach one of us is called to rethink his or her mental and moral priorities, to bring them into greater conformity with God's commandments and the demands of the common good . . . [of] a different kind of economy: one that brings life not death, one that is inclusive and not exclusive, humane and not dehumanizing, one that cares for the environment and does not despoil it.
>
> —*Letter from Pope Francis to "Economy of Francesco" gathering, 2020*[8]

No matter how on point, however, statements alone are insufficient unless accompanied by collective action.

In North America over the last half century, most mainline denominational institutions have issued public statements about social inequality and economic disparity. Unfortunately, their constituencies in the pews have mostly ignored them, settling instead for middle-of-the-road counsels to generosity and good stewardship. Many denominations no longer have national education, advocacy, or organizing programs focused on economic justice.[9] On the other hand, conservative Christian groups and preachers concentrate their hortative energy on qualifying or dulling what the New Testament teaches about wealth disparity. Most are eager to assure their people that capitalism has no fatal moral flaws (apart from human hearts), as a cursory web search of "Christians and wealth" reveals.

It thus falls upon a small number of national and regional entities across the ecumenical spectrum to keep a focus on faith and economic justice. These include the following twenty organizations, with whom we collaborate most often (listed alphabetically):

1. **Beloved Community Center** (https://belovedcommunitycenter.org/)
2. **Catholic Committee of Appalachia** (https://www.ccappal.org/)
3. **Catholic Worker Movement** (https://catholicworker.org/)
4. **Center and Library for the Bible and Social Justice** (https://clbsj.org/)
5. **Christian Community Development Association** (https://ccda.org/)
6. **Christians for Social Action** (https://christiansforsocialaction.org/)

7. **Church of the Saviour** (https://inwardoutward.org/ministries/)
8. **Clergy and Laity United for Economic Justice** (https://www.cluejustice.org/)
9. **Green Sabbath Project** (https://www.greensabbathproject.net/)
10. **Institute for Christian Socialism** (https://www.christiansocialism.com/)
11. **Interfaith Center on Corporate Responsibility** (https://www.iccr.org/)
12. **Network Advocates for Justice**, inspired by Catholic Sisters (https://networklobby.org)
13. **Jubilee USA Network** (https://www.jubileeusa.org/)
14. **Kairos Canada** (https://www.kairoscanada.org/)
15. **Kairos Center** (https://kairoscenter.org/)
16. **Poor Peoples Campaign** (https://www.poorpeoplescampaign.org/)
17. **Repairers of the Breach** (https://www.breachrepairers.org/)
18. **Shalom Center** (https://theshalomcenter.org/)
19. **Sojourners** (https://sojo.net/)
20. **Wendland-Cook Program in Religion & Justice** (https://www.religionandjustice.org/)

Some of these groups focus on analysis and education, others on organizing and advocacy, others on sustenance and reflection; all of them we commend. I again single out (as in the introduction) the **Poor Peoples' Campaign** as a crucial grassroots mobilization and resourcing national collaborative around issues of disparity that deserves support.

iv. Organizing for Systems Change

Systemic change is neither simple nor one-dimensional. My fifty years of social movement involvement has taught me to think of the task as a complicated jigsaw puzzle with many parts. While keeping the big picture and broad strategic goals in mind, we cannot meaningfully engage the whole; rather, we must discern which piece or pieces we can best directly tackle and which ones we can support indirectly. Because the work of eradicating dehumanizing disparity is such a vast field, my recommended list here is shorter, so as not to overwhelm. Each of the sites below can lead you to further aspects of educating and organizing around economic justice.

United for a Fair Economy, cofounded by Chuck Collins, who wrote the foreword to this book, is the best place to start learning about and responding to the forces that create and sustain structural inequality (https://www.faireconomy.org/). UFE sponsors many specific programs, including Inequality.org, which provides its own curated list of think tanks, academic centers, public interest groups, and organizing projects directly addressing disparity (https://inequality.org/resources/organizations/). To these I would add:

- **Center for the Advancement of Steady State Economics** (https://steadystate.org/) calls for a sustainable, now-growth economy with stabilized population and consumption, beginning in the wealthiest nations.
- **Excessive Wealth Disorder Institute** takes a diagnostic approach, defining "*EWD* as a societal sickness resulting in the insatiable need to acquire more . . . [which] affects not only the excessively wealthy, but everyone in our society" (https://www.excessivewealth.org/).
- **Opportunity Agenda** engages inequality through cultural strategies, messaging and training (https://opportunityagenda.org/).
- **Oxfam** is a global organization that has been fighting inequality and to end poverty and injustice since 1942 (https://www.oxfamamerica.org/).
- **Peterson Institute for International Economics.** For those still wondering whether "inequality is an urgent problem," PIIE offers a downloadable, forty-page PDF that gives a compelling, global overview of trends, causes, and broad suggested responses (see it at https://www.piie.com/microsites/how-fix-economic-inequality).
- The American College of Trust and Estate Counsel's "**Planning for a Diverse and Equitable Future**" site offers several snapshots of current disparity (especially around race) in the US and some strategies for addressing it (https://www.actec.org/planning-for-a-diverse-and-equitable-future/understanding-economic-disparities/).
- The "**solidarity economy**" paradigm is being used globally to inform practice and organizing. To explore it see:
    - A definition of "solidarity economy": https://solidarityeconomyprinciples.org/what-do-we-mean-by-solidarity-economy/
    - The Solidarity Economics Project: https://solidarityeconomics.org/

- The United Nations links solidarity economics with its sustainable development goals: https://www.un.org/sites/un2.un.org/files/social_and_solidarity_economy_29_march_2023.pdf

There are obviously many other places to look for information, analysis, and action. What is important is that we choose a piece of the vast puzzle of economic justice and work it faithfully as an expression of our discipleship!

NOTES

ACKNOWLEDGMENTS

1. See Murphy Davis, *Surely Goodness and Mercy: A Journey into Illness and Solidarity*, Atlanta: Open Door Community Press, 2020 (https://opendoorcommunity.org/resources/publications/).
2. Daniel Erlander, *Manna and Mercy: A Brief History of God's Unfolding Promise to Mend the Entire Universe*, Minneapolis: Augsburg Fortress, 2011. See also http://mannaandmercy.org/.
3. See the forthcoming tribute volume to Gottwald's work: Matthew Coomber and Ludwig Noya, ed., *Class and Intersectionality in the Hebrew Bible: Engaged Biblical Studies in the Academy and on the Streets* (Eugene, OR: Cascade Books, 2025), which includes my essay on Norman and his work with Word and World and the CLBSJ experiments in alternative theological training for activists.
4. Learn about the amazing ongoing work of CCA (https://www.ccappal.org) and see an aching obituary at https://www.newsandsentinel.com/obituaries/2021/05/michael-john-iafrate/.
5. See https://www.lacatholicworker.org/. Hear Catherine talk about her life at https://catholicworker.org/catherine-morris-of-hennessy-house-of-hospitality-on-coffee-with-catholic-workers/. Learn about Dietrich's books at https://www.ncronline.org/news/la-catholic-worker-reflects-50-years-journalism-and-resistance.
6. See her *Sabbath Economics: A Spiritual Guide Linking Love with Money* (https://judithfavor.com/sabbath-economics-2020/).
7. Cain Hope Felder and Charles Herbert Smith. *The Jubilee Legacy Bible*, Nashville, TN: Townsend Press, 1999; see David Crumm, "For Blacks, a Unity Bible: Edition Designed to Appeal to Young and Old, Provide Link to African Heritage," The Washington Post, December 17, 1999. For more on Wood see https://www.belovedeconomies.org/research-collaborators-31-60/blog-post-title-one-zdapl.
8. See Michelle Boorstein, "Rebel pastor Gordon Cosby left lasting mark on mainstream Christianity," The Washington Post, April 5, 2013; and https://inward-outward.org/. My Biblical Vision of Sabbath Economics booklet (see below, Introduction, fn. 25) was originally produced and distributed by CoS's Tell the Word Press.

ARTIST'S STATEMENT

1. Elaine Scarry, *On Beauty and Being Just*, Princeton, NJ: Princeton University Press, 2001, 95, 97.

2. To read and view two of Ted's expressions of "ornitheology," see http://www.tedlyddonhatten.com/#/seeing-ahead/ and https://www.theporchcommunity.net/essays/2019/8/21/bird-chess-ted-lyddon?rq=ted%20lyddon%20hatten.

INTRODUCTION

1. Leslie Marmon Silko, *Ceremony* (New York: Viking Press, 1977), 2.
2. "Survivance" is a term coined by native activist and writer Gerald Vizenor that combines disciplines of resilience and survival (see https://en.wikipedia.org/wiki/Survivance). For a deep engagement with personal and political histories and legacies of settler colonialism in North America, and the prospects of healing these hauntings through a discipleship of decolonization, see Elaine Enns and Ched Myers, *Healing Haunted Histories: A Settler Discipleship of Decolonization* (Eugene, OR: Cascade Books, 2024).
3. Numbers 11 represents a "minority report" of the more famous manna story in Exodus 16 (see 2A). Yet it was remembered and cited twice by the Psalmist (Ps 78:27–31; 106:13–15). As we'll see, in both testaments biblical instructions to live within limits are articulated in a variety of ways: Exodus storytelling, Levitical legislation, Deuteronomic exhortation, prophetic pronouncement, gospel parable, and apostolic pleading. Other old cultures also knew the danger of unrestrained appetites, as we find for example in classical cautionary tales, such as the demise of old King Midas or young Icarus, or in Indigenous stories about greed (see www.native-languages.org/legends-greed.htm).
4. Paul Ricoeur, "The Model of the Text: Meaningful Action Considered as a Text" in *Understanding and Social Inquiry*, ed. F. Dallmayr and T. McCarthy (Notre Dame, IN: University of Notre Dame Press, 1977) 320.
5. For an orientation to the complex world of hermeneutics—which pertains to any text, from literature to social media—see https://en.wikipedia.org/wiki/Hermeneutics. See also my comments in Ched Myers, *Binding the Strong Man: A Political Reading of Mark's Story of Jesus* (Maryknoll, NY: Orbis Books, 1988), 4–8.
6. Brian Biery, "A Tribute to Dorothea Bradley, Who Represented the 'Power of One,'" *Pasadena Now*, May 13, 2020, www.pasadenanow.com/main/dorothea-bradley-representing-the-power-of-one.
7. See interviews of poor people globally chronicled by Deepa Narayan, "Poverty Is Powerlessness and Voicelessness," *Finance & Development* (International Monetary Fund quarterly), December 2000, 37:4, https://www.imf.org/external/pubs/ft/fandd/2000/12/narayan.htm; Herbert Gans, *The War Against the Poor: The Underclass and Antipoverty Policy* (New York: Basic Books, 1995); and testimonies gathered at www.poorpeoplescampaign.org/resource/.
8. The rider of the black horse holds a monetary scale and boasts of an imperial economy that inflates the cost of basic foodstuffs through scarcity while protecting luxury items enjoyed by the rich (Rev 6:6). John's other horsemen are imperial conquest (Rev 6:2), military violence (6:4), and Death (6:8). See more in Wes Howard-Brook and Anthony Gwyther, *Unveiling Empire: Reading Revelation Then and Now* (Maryknoll, NY: Orbis Books, 1999), 141–142.

9. King's 1967 "Breaking the Silence" speech named the other two triplets as militarism and racism. This, his most courageous and consequential public address—delivered *exactly* one year before he was assassinated by his own government—can be read at www.americanrhetoric.com/speeches/mlkatimetobreaksilence.htm. For my analysis of this speech and its legacy, see https://bcmonline.org/2017/04/06/040517recordedwebinarapr2017/.
10. I highly recommend the Public Broadcasting System's documentary *The Gilded Age* for an introduction: www.pbs.org/wgbh/americanexperience/films/gilded-age/. David Huyssen argues that the Second Gilded Age is more disparate than the first in "We Won't Get Out of the Second Gilded Age the Way We Got Out of the First," *Vox*, April 1, 2019, https://www.vox.com/first-person/2019/4/1/18286084/gilded-age-income-inequality-robber-baron. In 2021, the World Inequality Lab found that "the globe's 2,750 billionaires [are] now . . . wealthier than half the planet" (www.cbsnews.com/news/wealth-inequality-billionaires-piketty-report/). On racial capitalism, see https://en.wikipedia.org/wiki/Racial_capitalism. The chart of wealth stratification in the US found at https://paulkivel.com/resource/social-service-or-social-change/.
11. Karl Evers-Hillstrom, "Majority of Lawmakers in 116th Congress Are Millionaires," at www.opensecrets.org/news/2020/04/majority-of-lawmakers-millionaires/, April 23, 2020.
12. Sam Mace, "Book Review: Limitarianism: The Case against Extreme Wealth," *Theory Matters* (Substack), March 17, 2024, https://theorymatters.substack.com/p/book-review-limitarianism-the-case. See Nolan Higdon, "Elon Musk and the Oligarchs of the 'Second Gilded Age' Can Not Only Sway the Public—They Can Exploit Their Data, Too," *The Conversation*, April 27, 2022, https://theconversation.com/elon-musk-and-the-oligarchs-of-the-second-gilded-age-can-not-only-sway-the-public-they-can-exploit-their-data-too-181936. On plutocracy and the media, a recent series of articles outline the various key characteristics of "American Oligarchy" at www.motherjones.com/politics/2024/01/american-oligarchy/.
13. Monbiot George, "For the sake of life on Earth, we must put a limit on wealth," *The Guardian,* Sep 19, 2019, https://www.theguardian.com/commentisfree/2019/sep/19/life-earth-wealth-megarich-spending-power-environmental-damage.
14. This term has been popularized by civil rights legend James Lawson (see Jim Conn, "Plantation Capitalism," *Capital & Main: Investigating Power, Money and Society*, June 25, 2013, https://capitalandmain.com/plantation-capitalism.) See a longer historical discussion by Matthew Desmond, "In Order to Understand the Brutality of American Capitalism, You Have to Start on the Plantation," *The New York Times—The 1619 Project*, August, 14, 2019, https://www.nytimes.com/interactive/2019/08/14/magazine/slavery-capitalism.html; and especially Desmond's recent *Poverty, by America* (New York: Crown Publishing, 2023).
15. A portmanteau of "affluence" and "influenza," it was first deployed to describe psychological problems of the wealthy. "Fred Whitman, a wealthy San Franciscan, takes credit for coining the term in the 1950s as a somewhat humorous description of the children of inherited wealth . . . but [it] became a household word in 2013

when the concept of affluenza was used in a court case" (https://grammarist.com/new-words/affluenza/).

16. Wendell Berry, *What Are People For? Essays* (Berkeley, CA: Northpoint Press, 1990), 201.
17. On plutocracy, see Ronald Formisano, *Plutocracy in America: How Increasing Inequality Destroys the Middle Class and Exploits the Poor* (Baltimore, MD: Johns Hopkins University Press, 2015); Chrystia Freeland, *Plutocrats: The Rise of the New Global Super-Rich and the Fall of Everyone Else* (New York: Penguin Press, 2012); Tavis Smiley and Cornel West, *The Rich and the Rest of Us: A Poverty Manifesto* (New York: Smiley Books, 2012); and the new Excessive Wealth Disorder Institute (www.excessivewealth.org). I acknowledge my debt to the tireless work of two friends and mentoring over many years. One is John Cobb, whose work broke new ground (John Cobb and Herman Daly, *For the Common Good: Redirecting the Economy toward Community, the Environment, and a Sustainable Future*, second updated ed. [Boston: Beacon Press, 1994]) and who continues to sustain it (see his Institute for Ecological Civilization at https://ecociv.org/). The other is Ulrich Duchrow, whose studies of global capitalism have been prophetic and resourceful: *Global Economy: A Confessional Issue for the Churches?*, trans. David Lewis (Geneva, Switzerland: WCC Publications, 1987); *Alternatives to Global Capitalism: Drawn from Biblical History, Designed for Political Action* (Heidelberg: International Books/Kairos Europa, 1995); and Duchrow Ulrich and Franz Hinkelammert, *Property for People, Not for Profit: Alternatives to the Global Tyranny of Capital* (London, UK: Zed Press, 2004) . On affluenza, see: John De Graaf, David Wann, and Thomas Naylor, *Affluenza: How Overconsumption Is Killing Us—and How to Fight Back*, 3rd ed. (Oakland, CA: Berrett-Koehler Publishers, 2014); Oliver James, *The Selfish Capitalist: Origins of Affluenza* (London: Vermilion, 2008); and Paul Wachtel's classic *The Poverty of Affluence: A Psychological Portrait of the American Way of Life* (Santa Cruz, CA: New Society Publishers, 1989).
18. Eugene McCarraher, *The Enchantments of Mammon: How Capitalism Became the Religion of Modernity* (Cambridge, MA: Harvard University Press, 2019), 1. For two other important recent deep dives into the culture and history of capitalism, see: Stan Goff, *Mammon's Ecology: Metaphysic of the Empty Sign* (Eugene, OR: Cascade Books, 2018); and Justin Pack, *Money and Thoughtlessness: A Genealogy and Defense of the Traditional Suspicions of Money and Merchants* (New York: Palgrave Macmillan, 2023). I also strongly recommend my friend Cynthia Moe-Lobeda's *Building a Moral Economy: Pathways for People of Courage* (Minneapolis, MN: Fortress Press, 2024).
19. See https://en.wikipedia.org/wiki/Poor_People%27s_Campaign. Rev. Barber—in my opinion the foremost exemplar of Dr. King's spirit and vocation today—also leads Repairers of the Breach (www.breachrepairers.org) and Yale's Center for Public Theology and Public Policy (www.theologyandpolicy.yale.edu).
20. See Chuck Collins, Felice Yeskel and United for a Fair Economy, *Economic Apartheid in America: A Primer on Economic Inequality & Insecurity* (New York: The New Press, 2005). Collins cofounded UFE as part of his own recovery from affluenza; he now directs the Program on Inequality and the Common Good

(https://ips-dc.org/inequality-and-the-common-good/), coedits www.inequality.org, and writes prolifically (see https://ips-dc.org/ips-authors/chuck-collins/).

21. John C. Haughey, *Virtue and Affluence: The Challenge of Wealth* (Kansas City, MI: Sheed & Ward, 1997), 7.
22. Those events are narrated and analyzed in detail in Myers, *Who Will Roll Away the Stone? Discipleship Queries for First World Christians* (Maryknoll, NY: Orbis Books, 1994). Other issues I immersed in during that period included: rural water rights, Hawaiian sovereignty, labor solidarity, antiracism and affirmative action organizing, affordable housing, LGBTQ advocacy, Palestinian human rights, environmental protection, and especially borderlands justice and immigrant rights (on this last issue, see Ched Myers and Matthew Colwell, *Our God Is Undocumented: Biblical Faith and Immigrant Rights*, Maryknoll, NY: Orbis Books, 2012).
23. See Ched Myers, "Reconnecting Seminary, Sanctuary, Streets and Soil: Curating Alternative Spaces for Theological Education," in *Let Your Light Shine: Mobilizing for Justice with Children and Youth*, ed. Reginald Blount and Virginia Lee (New York: Friendship Press, 2019), 59–74. These included a national collaborative called Word and World Peoples' School from 2001–2015 (www.wordandworld.org/schools.html) and our Bartimaeus Kinsler Institute from 2007 to the present (https://bcmonline.org/bcm-online/programs/bartimaeus-institute/).
24. See the Canadian Ecumenical Jubilee Initiative, *A New Beginning, A Call for Jubilee: The Vision of the Canadian Ecumenical Jubilee Initiative* (Toronto: Canadian Ecumenical Jubilee Initiative, 1998). The Jubilee USA Network continues this work (see www.jubileeusa.org/). See also Ann Pettifor, "The Jubilee 2000 Campaign: A Brief Overview," in Chris Jochnick and Fraser Preston, eds., *Sovereign Debt at the Crossroads: Challenges and Proposals for Resolving the Third World Debt Crisis* (Oxford: Oxford Academic, 2006), 297–318.
25. Ched Myers, *The Biblical Vision of Sabbath Economics* (Washington, DC: Tell the Word Press, 2001). The booklet was originally produced and distributed by Church of the Savior in Washington, D.C., the oldest continuing alternative church experiment in the U.S., co-founded by Gordon Cosby, to whom this book is co-dedicated (see Boorstein, 2013). With over ten thousand copies sold or given away, it is now available online at https://bcmonline.org/2022/06/01/the-biblical-vision-of-sabbath-economics-v1-5/, and has been republished in the U.K. and translated into German. It has been widely used in faith and justice movements, and has inspired a parallel Australian collaborative (https://mannagum.org.au/).
26. Matthew Colwell, *Sabbath Economics: Household Practices* (Washington, DC: Tell the Word Press, 2007). See more in appendix II, i.
27. Ched Myers, ed., *Watershed Discipleship: Reinhabiting Bioregional Faith and Practice* (Eugene, OR: Cascade Books, 2016).
28. Enns and Myers, *Haunted Histories*.
29. The https://en.wikipedia.org/wiki/Two-source_hypothesis page provides a helpful overview of this theory, which "proposes that Matthew and Luke used Mark for narrative material as well as for the basic structural outline . . . and use a second source, Q (from German *Quelle*, "source"), not extant, for the sayings found in both of them but not in Mark." Luke's use of Markan material is easily

identified by using a Gospel parallels tool (see an overview at www.gospelparallels.com/).

30. In this book, I intentionally use the dictionary form (first-person singular) of Greek verbs, not the conjugated forms that appear in Luke's text. This unorthodox approach means to make it easier for a non-Greek reader to find the verb in a Greek dictionary, lexicon, or thesaurus. I have not done this for most nouns, adjectives, et cetera, because they rarely change except for endings, so can be easily found. The LXX was almost certainly the version of the Hebrew Scriptures that Luke used and in which he was impressively literate; see overview at https://www.britannica.com/topic/Septuagint.
31. Myers, *Strong Man*, 12–80, 92–106.
32. See William Herzog, *Parables As Subversive Speech: Jesus As Pedagogue of the Oppressed* (Louisville, KY: Westminster John Knox Press, 1994) and Douglas Oakman, *Jesus and the Peasants* (Eugene, OR: Cascade Books, 2008).
33. Robert Tannehill, *The Narrative Unity of Luke-Acts: A Literary Interpretation*, vol. I. (Minneapolis, MN: Fortress Press, 1986); Charles Talbert, *Reading Luke: A Literary and Theological Commentary on the Third Gospel* (New York: Crossroad, 1992); Frank Dicken, *Reading Luke* (Eugene, OR: Cascade Books, 2023).
34. Jerome Neyrey, ed., *The Social World of Luke-Acts: Models for Interpretation* (Peabody, MA: Hendrickson Publishers, 1991); Oakman, *Peasants;* Robert Brawley, *Luke: A Social Identity Commentary* (London: T&T Clark, 2020).
35. Walter Pilgrim, *Good News to the Poor: Wealth and Poverty in Luke-Acts* (Minneapolis, MN: Augsburg, 1981); Halvor Moxnes, *The Economy of the Kingdom: Social Conflict and Economic Relations in Luke's Gospel* (Eugene, OR: Wipf & Stock, 2004); David D. M. King, *Reclaiming the Radical Economic Message of Luke* (Eugene, OR: Pickwick Press, 2022).
36. Richard Cassidy, *Jesus, Politics and Society: A Study of Luke's Gospel* (Maryknoll, NY: Orbis Books, 1978); Luise Schottroff and Wolfgang Stegemann, *Jesus and the Hope of the Poor*, trans. M. O'Connell (Maryknoll, NY: Orbis, 1986).
37. José Miranda, *Communism in the Bible*, trans. by Robert R. Barr (Maryknoll, NY: Orbis Books, 1982); Elsa Támez, *Bible of the Oppressed*, trans. by Matthew O'Connell (Eugene, OR: Wipf & Stock, 2006). Támez, whose work I highly recommend, was a colleague of Ross and Gloria Kinsler in Costa Rica; all three mentored me in Latin American readings of Scripture. See the Kinsler's *The Biblical Jubilee and the Struggle for Life: An Invitation to Personal Ecclesial and Social Transformation* (Maryknoll, NY: Orbis Books, 2000) and *God's Economy: Biblical Studies from Latin America* (Maryknoll, NY: Orbis Books, 2005); The Kinslers are memorialized in the name of our annual study program, the Bartimaeus Kinsler Institute (https://bcmonline.org/bcm-online/programs/bartimaeus-institute/).
38. King, *Reclaiming.*
39. King, *Reclaiming*, 1–3.
40. King, *Reclaiming*, 8–24.
41. This detailed treatment of Luke and Sabbath Economics thus falls between my commentary on Mark (Myers, *Strong Man*) and my follow-up articulations of what

that study meant for us (Myers, *Stone,* 1994 and Ched Myers, Stuart Taylor, Cindy Moe-Lobeda, Joseph Nangle and Marie Dennis, "*Say to This Mountain": Mark's Story of Discipleship*, Maryknoll, NY: Orbis Books, 1996).

42. Matthew Coomber, ed., *Economics and Empire in the Ancient Near East: Guide to the Bible and Economics*, Vol. 1 (Eugene, OR: Cascade, 2023), 2. See also Anthony Keddie, *Class and Power in Roman Palestine: The Socioeconomic Setting of Judaism and Christian Origins* (Cambridge: Cambridge University Press, 2019); and a more popular treatment in Richard Horsley, *Covenant Economics: A Biblical Vision of Justice for All* (Philadelphia: Westminster, 2009).
43. See a more detailed summary in Oakman, *Peasants*, 33–39. For an excellent and accessible overview of political economy in the New Testament period, see Richard Horsley, *You Shall Not Bow Down and Serve Them: The Political Economic Projects of Jesus and Paul* (Eugene, OR: Cascade Books, 2021). See also David A. Fiensy, *Christian Origins and the Ancient Economy* (Eugene, OR: Cascade Books, 2014).
44. In addition to those just named, I would highlight Kenneth Bailey's work on the cultural and social background of parables helped stimulate a boom in social-scientific work in the New Testament: *Poet and Peasant and Through Peasant Eyes: A Literary-Cultural Approach to the Parables in Luke,* combined edition (Grand Rapids, MI: Eerdmans, 1983). My mentor Norman Gottwald's re-visioning of the history of Israel did the same for Hebrew Bible studies: *The Tribes of Yahweh: A Sociology of the Religion of Liberated Israel, 1250–1050 BCE* (Maryknoll, NY: Orbis Books, 1979). I recommend two good overviews of how the social sciences have impacted New Testament scholarship. The late John Elliott (a cofounder of the Center and Library for the Bible and Social Justice) helped pioneer sociological approaches; see "From Social Description to Social-Science Criticism," *Biblical Theology Bulletin,* 38 no. 1 (Spring 2008): 26–36. Halvor Moxnes is another leader; see "Social-scientific readings of the Bible" in *The New Cambridge History of the Bible,* ed. by John Riches (Cambridge: Cambridge University Press, 2015) 160–171. David Fiensy, "The Galilean Economy in the Time of Jesus: Can You Dig It?" *The Bible and Interpretation* (2013) https://bibleinterp.arizona.edu/articles/2013/07/fie378015, summarizes some of the tensions between sociological and archeological methodologies; for a deeper dive see his *The Realia Jesus: An Archaeological Commentary on the Gospel of Luke* (Eugene, OR: Cascade Books, 2024).
45. Bruce Malina and Richard Rohrbaugh, *Social Science Commentary on the Synoptic Gospels* (Minneapolis, MN: Fortress Press, 1992); K. C. Hanson and Douglas Oakman, *Palestine in the Time of Jesus: Social Structures and Social Conflicts* (Minneapolis, MN: Fortress Press, 1998). Alan Culpepper's new *The People of the Parables: Galilee in the Time of Jesus* (Louisville, KY: Westminster John Knox Press, 2024) offers a thorough, readable overview of social context as refracted through Jesus's parables—thus often focusing on peasants and other non-elites—and presents recent data and analysis across a broad range of disciplines.
46. See Oakman's overview of its relevance to the New Testament, *Peasants*, 53–69.
47. From an excellent online introduction to these models at https://socialsci.libretexts.org/Courses/HACC_Central_Pennsylvania's_Community_College/

ANTH_205%3A_Cultures_of_the_World_Perspectives_on_Culture_(Scheib)/07%3A_Economics/7.04%3A_Modes_of_Exchange_and_Reciprocity. See also definitions at www.masterclass.com/articles/generalized-reciprocity#gaazqNIiN63MU9ialUu9g.

48. See more detail at Hanson and Oakman, *Palestine*, 99–129.
49. Neyrey, *Social World*, 368.
50. See summaries in Bruce Malina, *The Social World of Jesus and the Gospels* (London: Routledge, 1996).
51. Oakman, *Peasants,* 162–163.
52. Nickolas Fox, *The Hermeneutics of Social Identity in Luke-Acts* (Eugene, OR: Pickwick Publications, 2021), 171.
53. See 11A.
54. Ricoeur, *Model*, 320.
55. The term "Anthropocene," now common shorthand for our interlocking social and ecological crises, obscures the fact that it is not humanity in general that has brought us to this crossroads. Indigenous peoples, Mexican farmworkers, African American factory workers, Syrian refugees, and Filipino contract laborers have not brought this upon us. Rather, it is a half-millennium legacy of settler colonialism and extractive capitalism that has wrought displacement, destruction, and disparity in every corner of our world. A small part of humanity (including at least half of us in the US) has both driven and derived social and economics privileges from industrialization and globalized markets, which is why some analysts more accurately refer to this epoch as the "Capitalocene." See a summary at https://en.wikipedia.org/wiki/Capitalocene; an overview of the conversation in Jason Moore, ed., *Anthropocene or Capitalocene? Nature, History, and the Crisis of Capitalism* (Oakland, CA: PM Press, 2016); and a constructive engagement in Donna Haraway, *Staying with the Trouble: Making Kin in the Chthulucene* (Durham, NC: Duke University Press, 2016).
56. Stephen Fowl and Gregory Jones, *Reading in Communion: Scripture and Ethics in Christian Life* (Grand Rapids, MI: Eerdmans, 1991), 29.
57. Paul Ricoeur, *Freud and Philosophy* (New Haven, CT: Yale University Press, 1970), 27.
58. My partner Elaine was privileged to work with the late Cheyenne Peace Chief and Mennonite pastor Lawrence Hart, who helped build a movement for repatriation of remains, and the establishment of the Native American Grave Protection Act in the US (see www.clintondailynews.com/obituaries/lawrence-homer-hart). See Elaine's profile of this amazing man in Elaine Enns and Ched Myers, *Ambassadors of Reconciliation II: Diverse Christian Practices of Restorative Justice and Peacemaking* (Maryknoll, NY: Orbis Books, 2009), 121–132.
59. Moxnes, *Social-Scientific*.
60. Wendell Berry, "Two Economies." *Review and Expositor*, 81 no. 2 (May 1984): 189–90. The lovely conversation with Jackson and articulation of the "indispensable" notion of the Great Economy is online at www.worldwisdom.com/public/viewpdf/default.aspx?article-title=Two_Economies_by_Wendell_Berry.pdf. I first adopted this lovely framing in Myers (1994:168–170).

61. Berry, "Two Economies," 188.
62. Berry, "Two Economies,"193–194.
63. See 6B, n. 29.
64. Berry, "Two Economies," 199.
65. See summary at www.addictioncenter.com/treatment/12-step-programs/, and Gerald May's beautiful *Addiction and Grace: Love and Spirituality in the Healing of Addictions*, annotated edition (San Francisco: HarperOne, 2007). For a detailed discussion of this analogy, see Myers Ched, "Beyond the 'Addict's Excuse': Public Addiction and Ecclesial Recovery" in *The Other Side of Sin: Woundedness from the Perspective of the Sinned-Against*, ed. Susan Nelson and Andrew Sung Park (New York: SUNY Press, 2001), 77–108.
66. For reflections on approaching scripture with neither authoritarianism nor diffidence, see Ched Myers, "Neither Authoritarian Nor Diffident: Conversing about Biblical Differences," *Uniting Church Studies* (Melbourne, Australia), 4, no. 2, August 1998; also at https://bcmonline.org/1998/08/01/articles-biblical-interpretation-neither-authoritarian-nor-diffident-conversing-about-biblical-diffe/. On "Interrogatory Theology" see Myers, *Stone*, 13–44.

CHAPTER ONE

1. See a definition at https://en.wikipedia.org/wiki/Docetism.
2. For a classical European example, see Noël Coypel, "Resurrection of Christ," ca. 1700 (Musée des Beaux-Arts de Rennes), https://useum.org/artwork/La-Resurrection-du-Christ-Noel-Coypel. For a contemporary American lowbrow version, see Simon Dewey, "He Lives," 2023 (Altus Fine Art), https://altusfineart.com/products/simon-dewey-he-lives-resurrected-christ. For more examples, see Anna Swartwood House, "The Long History of How Jesus Came to Resemble a White European," (*The Conversation*, July 17, 2020), https://theconversation.com/the-long-history-of-how-jesus-came-to-resemble-a-white-european-142130.
3. Robert Zünd, "Gang nach Emmaus," 1877 (Kunstmuseum Luzern), https://www.kunstmuseumluzern.ch/wp-content/uploads/2018/06/2004-zuend-emmaus.jpg.
4. See "The Roman Inscriptions of Britain, High Rochester (Bremenium) RIB-1284" (*Athena Review* 1, no.2, 1996), http://www.athenapub.com/aria1/_Brit/rib1284.htm.
5. The verb *poreuō* connotes potentially fatal journeys in 22:22 and Acts 20:1, 22, and 25:12.
6. Flavius Josephus, *War of the Jews* (Book VII, Chapter 6, para. 6), https://penelope.uchicago.edu/josephus/war-7.html. Also see David Bivin, "Farewell to Emmaus Road," *Jerusalem Perspective* (Jan 13, 2017), https://www.jerusalemperspective.com/16208/.
7. Thomas Moran, "Slave Hunt, Dismal Swamp, Virginia," 1862 (Philbrook Museum of Art) https://philbrook.emuseum.com/objects/1830/slave-hunt-dismal-swamp-virginia?ctx=f292490dbeb5d0e9695cc32d48bd0cc4fce172e5&idx=498. For commentary, see "The Great Dismal Swamp," podcast #271, producer Sharif Youssef (*99% Invisible*, Aug 15, 2017), https://99percentinvisible.org/episode/great-dismal-swamp/.

8. See “Songs of the Underground Railroad,” Harriet Tubman Historical Society (accessed April 2024), http://www.harriet-tubman.org/songs-of-the-underground-railroad. Also see Arthur C. Jones, *Wade In The Water: The Wisdom of the Spirituals* (Maryknoll, New York: Orbis Books, 1993).
9. Ched Myers, “Jesus's risen, mutilated body,” *The Christian Century*, Vol 136, Issue 19 (September 11, 2019), https://www.christiancentury.org/article/critical-essay/jesus-risen-mutilated-body. See images at Lisa Whittington, “#MuseumsSoWhite: Black Pain and Why Painting Emmett Till Matters—Interview with Dr. Lisa Whittington,” (*NBC News*, March 26, 2017), at https://www.nbcnews.com/think/news/museumssowhite-representation-black-pain-why-emmett-till-painting-matters-ncna737931. See also Katie Nodjimbadem, “Emmett Till's Open Casket Funeral Reignited the Civil Rights Movement,” *Smithsonian Magazine* (September 2, 2015), at https://www.smithsonianmag.com/smithsonian-institution/emmett-tills-open-casket-funeral-reignited-the-civil-rights-movement-180956483.
10. See photo essay by Bill Preston, “1968 Civil Rights Movement in Memphis,” *The Tennessean* (Feb 24, 2014), www.tennessean.com/picture-gallery/news/2014/02/24/1968-civil-rights-movement-in-memphis/5775743.
11. Hanna Rioseco, “MLK's Assassination: The Story Behind the Photo” (Thirteen, *PBS*, Jan 14, 2024), https://www.thirteen.org/blog-post/mlk-assassination-the-story-behind-the-photo.
12. A jury in a 1999 civil trial, brought by the King family to the 30th Judicial District court in Memphis, took only ninety minutes to find that the federal government, City of Memphis and state of Tennessee conspired to kill Dr. King, a stunning verdict that was virtually ignored in the US press. Sue Anne Pressley, “Memphis Jury Finds Conspiracy Led to King Assassination,” (*The Washington Post*, Dec 8, 1999), at https://www.washingtonpost.com/archive/politics/1999/12/09/memphis-jury-finds-conspiracy-led-to-king-assassination/318b25c1-e5cd-44f4-8522-231c7a54f880. See William Pepper, *The Plot to Kill King: The Truth Behind the Assassination of Martin Luther King Jr* (Skyhorse, 2018).
13. Tony Henry's obituary confirmed that he “coordinated transportation and food for the Martin Luther King ‘tent city’ until King's death.” “Anthony Ray Henry,” obituary (*Houston Chronicle*, Jan 11, 2008), www.legacy.com/us/obituaries/houstonchronicle/name/anthony-henry-obituary?id=25762860.
14. See Ruby Sales, “Where Does It Hurt?” interview at On Being with Krista Tippett (The On Being Project, September 15, 2016), https://onbeing.org/programs/ruby-sales-where-does-it-hurt.
15. See more on walking and talking among Greek philosophers at Sean O'Connor, “Aristotle's Thinking Hack,” (*Medium*, Nov 13, 2016), https://medium.com/stoicsunday/stoic-sunday-aristotles-thinking-hack-50114e529f44. This pedagogic tradition influenced many Hellenistic rabbis but was also influenced *by* Jewish storytelling. The peripatetic Jesus appears throughout Luke's story (e.g., Luke 12:22–34).
16. Again the analogy of Till's body helps us understand the subversive power of this story. Mamie Till Mobley's retrospective assessment of the impact of the traumatic somatic was couched in resurrection language: “When people saw what happened to my son, men stood up who had never stood up before.” Jesus's mother

might well have expressed similar sentiments two millennia earlier! See Stanley Nelson, director, "The Murder of Emmett Till," (clip); "Emmett Till's Mother Speaks" (American Experience, *PBS*, 2003), at https://www.pbs.org/wgbh/americanexperience/features/emmett-till-sacrificial-lamb.

17. See a sixth-century fresco in Davit Gareja monastery in eastern Georgia, www.pinterest.com/pin/my-lord-savior--373728469061425709.

CHAPTER TWO

1. M. Douglas Meeks, *God the Economist: The Doctrine of God and Political Economy* (Philadelphia: Augsburg Fortress Press, 1989), 78. I strongly recommend Meeks's book to those wishing to explore more deeply the theological basis for my framework of Sabbath Economics.
2. On the Jewish roots of catechesis see Kaufmann Kohler and E. Schreiber "Catechisms" *Jewish Encyclopedia* (New York: Funk & Wagnalls, 1901–1906), https://www.jewishencyclopedia.com/articles/4149-catechisms.
3. This section builds out the first chapters of Myers, *Biblical Vision*. There are innumerable debates and conundrums regarding the historical dating, authorship, and redaction of both Torah and prophetic texts; see Norman Gottwald's *The Hebrew Bible: A Brief Socio-Literary Introduction* (Minneapolis, MN: Fortress Press, 2009) for an overview. For complexities of reconstructing late Bronze Age economic systems and practices in the Ancient Near East, see Coomber's recent *Economics and Empire*; Roger Nam, "Israelite and Judean Society and Economy," in Brad Kelle and Brent Strawn, ed. *The Oxford Handbook of the Historical Books of the Hebrew Bible* (online publication, 2020), https://digitalcommons.georgefox.edu/cgi/viewcontent.cgi?article=1163&context=gfes.
4. A concise way to portray the ecological exhaustion of modern capitalism is to track "the date when humanity has exhausted nature's annual budget"; see www.footprintnetwork.org/our-work/earth-overshoot-day/.
5. See https://en.wikipedia.org/wiki/Mount_Horeb for the debate about whether this was the same peak as Mount Sinai.
6. On this "theonym" see https://en.wikipedia.org/wiki/Tetragrammaton. There are volumes of commentary about its meanings. Rabbi Arthur Waskow teaches that it is unpronounceable because its "aspirate consonants" invite us to "simply breathe" (see www.haggadot.com/clip/excerpt-why-yahyhwh-rabbi-arthur-waskow. See also Arthur Waskow, *Dancing in God's Earthquake: The Coming Transformation of Religion* (Maryknoll, NY: Orbis Books, 2020). For a comparison of YHWH's otherness to "undocumented status," see Myers and Colwell, *Our God is Undocumented*, 56–57.
7. Evan Eisenberg, *The Ecology of Eden: An Inquiry into the Dream of Paradise and a New Vision of Our Role in Nature* (New York: Vintage Books, 1998), 75.
8. Eisenberg, *Ecology of Eden*, 82–83.
9. See Ched Myers, "Nature against Empire: Exodus Plagues, Climate Crisis and Hard Heartedness," *Direction* (49:1), Spring 2020, 5–17.
10. See more in Meeks, *God the Economist*.

11. Richard Lowery, *Sabbath and Jubilee* (St. Louis, MI: Chalice Press, 2000), 86–87.
12. Lowery, *Sabbath and Jubilee*, 93.
13. Ellen Davis, *Opening Israel's Scriptures* (Oxford: Oxford University Press, 2019), 50.
14. Indigenous peoples historically the world over have typically preferred hunting and gathering over cultivation and had to be forced (or enslaved) into agriculture by imperial expansion (see James Scott, *Against the Grain: A Deep History of the Earliest States*, New Haven, CT: Yale University Press, 2017). In California, autumn acorns dropping copiously from native oak trees provide a good lesson in making bread from that which "falls from heaven" (see Kat Anderson, *Tending the Wild: Native American Knowledge and the Management of California's Natural Resources*, Berkeley: University of California Press, 2005). Tellingly, this staple resource is ignored by settlers here, since its abundance defies commodification, monopolizing, and scarcity economics. Paul Shepard, in *The Only World We've Got* (San Francisco: Sierra Club Books, 1996) and *Coming Home to the Pleistocene* (Washington, DC: Island Press, 1998), argues that human beings are far more biologically adapted to these ancient lifeways than to modern economic behavior: "The prototype to which the genome is accustomed is Pleistocene society." The best study of the viability of hunter-gatherer societies is Marshall Sahlins's now-classic *Stone Age Economics* (New York: Aldine de Gruyter, 1972); see also John Gowdy, *Limited Wants, Unlimited Means: A Reader on Hunter-Gatherer Economics and the Environment* (Washington, DC: Island Press, 1998) and Colin Tudge, *The Time Before History: 5 Million Years of Human Impact* (New York: Simon & Schuster, 1996). These lifeways still survive among more remote Indigenous peoples—and in certain traditional practices that have been preserved in almost every culture.
15. Lowery, *Sabbath and Jubilee*, 95.
16. Karl Marx, *Capital: A Critique of Political Economy*, Volume One, Chapter 24, Section 3, trans. Samuel Moore and Edward Aveling, Marx/Engels Internet Archive, https://www.marxists.org/archive/marx/works/1867-c1/ch24.htm#S3.
17. Lowery, *Sabbath and Jubilee*, 93–94.
18. See https://www.law.cornell.edu/wex/blue_law.
19. See Oliver Balch, "The Relevance of Gandhi in the Capitalism Debate," the *Guardian*, Jan 28, 2013, www.theguardian.com/sustainable-business/blog/relevance-gandhi-capitalism-debate-rajni-bakshi.
20. To understand more see www.masterclass.com/articles/generalized-reciprocity. Marshall Sahlins described these lifeways as "the original affluent society," *Stone Age Economics*, 5; see fn. 14.
21. Waskow writes: "*B'Har* [Lev 25] begins with and *B'Chukkotai* [Lev 26] ends with asserting 'this comes from Sinai,' like the Ten Utterances." He further wonders why "though B'Har is the most radically justice-pursuing in all of Torah, *tzedek* and *mishpat*—two different aspects of 'Justice—do not appear. The crucial concepts are religious & spiritual: *dror*, 'release' and *Shabbat*, 'pause to rest'" (private correspondence, May 23, 2024).
22. I encourage readers who want reliable treatments of the long-running biblical debate about Jubilee legislation to consult Lowery, *Sabbath and Jubilee*; Meeks,

God the Economist; and Michael Hudson (see next footnote). Robert North, *Biblical Jubilee after Fifty Years* (Rome, Italy: Gregorian & Biblical Press, 2000) offers a summary of Catholic thought, though reflecting mainstream scholarly skepticism.

23. Michael Hudson, "Proclaim Liberty throughout the Land: The Economic Roots of the Jubilee," *Bible Review* 15, no. 1 (February 1999), https://library.biblicalarchaeology.org/article/proclaim-liberty-throughout-the-land. This article is a précis of his booklet *The Lost Tradition of Biblical Debt Cancellations* (New York: Social Science Forum of the Henry George School, 1993), at https://michael-hudson.com/wp-content/uploads/2010/03/HudsonLostTradition.pdf. He has since expanded his research into the monumental . . . *And Forgive Them Their Debts: Lending, Foreclosure, and Redemption from Bronze Age Finance to the Jubilee Year* (Dresden, Germany: ISLET-Verlag, 2018). According to the late dean of ancient debt studies David Graeber, this established Hudson as "the most important economic historian of the last half century." Graeber's own opus, *Debt: The First 5,000 Years* (New York: Melville House Publishing, 2011) devoted only a few pages to the biblical material (80–84) but closed with the startling declaration: "We are long overdue for some kind of Biblical-style Jubilee" (390)!
24. Hudson, *Lost Tradition*, 6–7; he summarizes how these practices were deployed in various dynasties in 17–43.
25. Hudson, "Proclaim Liberty."
26. Summarized in Hudson, *Lost Tradition*," 43–54.
27. James W. Watts, "Leviticus 25's History of Inspiring Freedom as a Moral Challenge to Literary-Historical Interpretation," *Biblical Interpretation* (online 2022, print 2023), 21, doi:10.1163/15685152-20221703.
28. Watts, "Leviticus," 2.
29. Watts, "Leviticus," 1, 2, 22.
30. Michael Walzer, *Exodus and Revolution*, rev. ed. (New York: Basic Books, 1986).
31. See the whole song, and others by Spence, at www.marxists.org/history/england/britdem/societies/spenceans/songs1.htm. Peter Linebaugh has published many good pieces on these movements, as well as on the early origins of African American Jubilee songs; see https://libcom.org/article/jubilating-peter-linebaugh). See also the fascinating story of eighteenth-century Caribbean Black "Jubilationist" Robert Wedderburn, in Peter Linebaugh and Marcus Rediker, *The Many-Headed Hydra: Sailors, Slaves, Commoners and the Hidden History of the Revolutionary Atlantic* (Boston: Beacon Press, 2013); see it online at https://freeuniverseity.files.wordpress.com/2012/12/mhh-9.pdf. In contrast, during the same period, Charles Wesley's "Blow Ye the Trumpet Blow" (1750) shows the spiritualizing tendency among white Christians, interiorizing the Jubilee as an atonement trope (www.hymntime.com/tch/htm/b/l/o/w/blowblow.htm).
32. See the full original 1845 text at https://aadl.org/signalofliberty/SL_18450317-p1-02. Learn about Garrison at https://www.britannica.com/biography/William-Lloyd-Garrison.
33. Bennett Parten, "Blow Ye Trumpet, Blow: The Idea of Slavery and Freedom," *Journal of the Civil War Era* 10:3 (University of North Carolina Press, Sept 2020), 298.

34. Pamela Brown, "Reimagining Jubilee: A Political Horizon for Our Times," *Tikkun* 30:1 (2015), 26.
35. See Mat Callahan, *Songs of Slavery and Emancipation* (Jackson, MS: University Press of Mississippi, 2022); online at https://academic.oup.com/mississippi-scholarship-online/book/45036.
36. See Dave Paulson, "The Trials and Triumph of the Fisk Jubilee Singers, One of America's Great Musical Institutions," *Nashville Tennessean*, Feb 1, 2021; at https://www.tennessean.com/in-depth/entertainment/music/2021/02/01/how-fisk-jubilee-singers-became-american-musical-institution/3730118001. The Public Broadcasting Service produced a lovely (if long overdue) documentary in 2019 on the Jubilee Singers; see www.pbs.org/wgbh/americanexperience/films/singers/. An 1886 testimony verifies Harriet Tubman's use of "Go Down Moses" as underground railroad code (https://docsouth.unc.edu/neh/harriet/harriet.html, 37). Learn the history of "Wade in the Water" at www.cpr.org/2021/04/19/spirituals-radio-project-how-a-grand-vision-of-jesus-on-a-white-horse-signaled-triumph-over-slavery/. For a theo-political reading of the spirituals, see James Cone, *The Spirituals and the Blues* (Maryknoll, NY: Orbis Books, 1991).
37. An example is a lengthy 1850 correspondence between pro-slavery theologians laying out their biblical justification (indeed imperative) for slavery, at https://docsouth.unc.edu/church/stringfellow/stringfellow.html.
38. See Ann Pettifor, "The Jubilee 2000 Campaign: A Brief Overview," in *Sovereign Debt at the Crossroads: Challenges and Proposals for Resolving the Third World Debt Crisis,* Chris Jochnick and Fraser Preston, ed. (Oxford: Oxford Academic, 2006), 297–318, and the briefer assessment at https://thoughtfulcampaigner.org/2020/04/19/jubilee-2000-five-enduring-lessons-for-campaigners/. In the US, it continues in the work of Jubilee USA Network (www.jubileeusa.org/) as well as experiments such as the Debt Collective's Rolling Jubilee campaign (https://debtcollective.org/what-we-do/debt-abolition/).
39. Ellen Davis, *Scripture, Culture and Agriculture: An Agrarian Reading of the Bible* (Cambridge: Cambridge University Press, 2008), 111.
40. See Enns and Myers, *Haunted Histories*, 141–151 for a reading of the Naboth story in conversation with the history of the US annexation of Hawai'i.
41. See Mark 12:1–10 (commentary at Myers, *Strong Man,* 308–310). Luke follows Mark closely in his account of the parable (Luke 20:9–19).
42. See Lowery, *Sabbath and Jubilee*, 45, where he also discusses the historicity and moral lesson of this text.
43. A majority of scholars accept (give or take a myriad of details!) that our canonical Torah consists of at least three major redactional strands. The earliest is attributed to a Deuteronomist source (late seventh century BCE); the Yahwist source is dated to the mid-sixth century, during the Exile; and a Priestly source is the latest (fifth century BCE); see https://en.wikipedia.org/wiki/Dating_the_Bible. See an overview of this complex and changing academic debate at https://en.wikipedia.org/wiki/Composition_of_the_Torah.
44. Ingrid Robeyns, "What, if Anything, Is Wrong with Extreme Wealth?" *Journal of Human Development and Capabilities*, Volume 20, Issue 3 (2019), 251 266,

https://doi.org/10.1080/19452829.2019.1633734. See an interview with Robeyns about her *Limitarianism: The Case Against Extreme Wealth* (Westminster, MD: Astra House, 2024) at www.theguardian.com/books/2024/jan/21/limitarianism-the-case-against-extreme-wealth-ingrid-robeyns-extract.

45. George Monbiot, "For the Sake of Life on Earth, We Must Put a Limit on Wealth," *The Guardian,* Sep 19, 2019, at https://www.theguardian.com/commentisfree/2019/sep/19/life-earth-wealth-megarich-spending-power-environmental-damage.
46. Brian Czech, *Supply Shock: Economic Growth at the Crossroads and the Steady State Solution* (Washington, DC: Steady State Press), 2021. See https://steadystate.org/.

CHAPTER THREE

1. The efforts of the Jubilee Singers, particularly Work, "ensured that these songs, once confined to the memories of those who suffered and hoped under slavery, found a permanent place in the annals of American music" (www.hymncharts.com/2023/11/21/the-story-behind-go-tell-it-on-the-mountain/).
2. These liturgical titles are derived from the opening words of each song in Latin. Prelude and Prologue function equivalently in music and literature respectively.
3. C.S. Song, *Third-Eye Theology: Theology in Formation in Asian Settings* (Maryknoll, NY: Orbis Books, 1979), 137–140.
4. See Elizabeth Johnson, "Mary, Mary, quite contrary: How can the image of Mary be construed as a source of blessing rather than a blight for women's lives in both religion and politics?" *U.S. Catholic* 68:12 (Dec 2003), 12.
5. R. Alan Streett, *Songs of Resistance: Challenging Caesar and Empire,* (Eugene, OR: Cascade, 2022), 63–68.
6. See an exhaustive list at https://en.wikipedia.org/wiki/List_of_Magnificat_composers.
7. Frank Dicken, *Reading Luke,* (Eugene, OR: Cascade Books, 2023), 45.
8. See Cristina Buffa, "The Magnificat and the Song of Hannah: Comparing Social Conditions," *Revue des Sciences Religieuses* 92:3 (July 2018), 377–392.
9. The woman of Revelation 12 is an extraordinary conflation of the Mary story and Exodus 1. She takes refuge in the wilderness, surviving (as in Exodus) only because of nature's alliance (Rev 12:6, 14–16). Her evocative celestial appearance—clothed with the sun, standing on the moon and crowned with stars—has been appropriated beautifully in Catholic iconography portraying Our Lady of Guadalupe, patroness of Indigenous peasants displaced by Spanish colonization of Mexico and the US Southwest. Myers and Colwell, *God Is Undocumented,* 170–178, correlate Luke's nativity story to the powerful Hispanic public liturgy of Posadas.
10. Streett, *Songs*, 68.
11. Streett, *Songs*, 68–69.
12. Streett, *Songs*, 70.
13. Luke here uses a participle of the verb *plouteō* (as in 12:21, Luke's inaugural object lesson about the rich; 8A); everywhere else in Luke the adjective *plousios* is used.
14. Dicken, *Reading Luke*, 45. Dicken provides a good introductory overview of Luke, and shows in details how the Magnificat exemplifies a programmatic passage

(39–53). See also Kelly Nikondeha (*The First Advent in Palestine: Reversals, Resistance, and the Ongoing Complexity of Hope*. Minneapolis: Broadleaf), 2022.

15. Keesmaat, Sylvia, *A Fountain of Tears: Ecological Grief in the Biblical Story*, Center and Library for the Bible and Social Justice Series (Eugene, OR: Cascade Books, 2025). For an overview of some of the historical issues associated with this census, see https://en.wikipedia.org/wiki/Census_of_Quirinius.
16. Such displacement continues for Palestinians in Bethlehem today, a town divided and locked down by an Israeli security wall. The irony is backlit by artist Banksy's famous image of Mary and Joseph stopped in front of the wall (see it at https://thesource.com/2015/12/22/banksys-joseph-and-mary-christmas-card-resurfaces-on-social-media/). For more of the story, see the testimonies of Presbyterian minister Don Wagner (*Glory to God in the Lowest: Journeys to an Unholy Land*, Olive Branch Press, 2022) and of Palestinian naturalist and activist Mazin Qumsiyeh (http://qumsiyeh.org/).
17. This is the only childhood story of Jesus in the entire New Testament, though later apocryphal works reveled in speculative tales (see examples and sources at www.wisdomwordsppf.org/2018/08/10/the-wild-child-jesus-tales-from-the-apocryphal-literature/). Significantly, from 3:12 onward, Jesus is addressed as a teacher (*didaskalos*) fifteen times, more than in any other Gospel.
18. The Greek adjective *syngenēs*, by which Elizabeth is described to Mary in 1:36, defines the familial relationship only as "kin," which in traditional cultures can be understood quite broadly. Luke does seem to be more interested in kinship networks generally (using the term five times in his two volumes, versus the other Gospels using it only twice). However, he is more interested in both John and Jesus's *prophetic* lineage (1:17).
19. Though most of Luke's references to Herod are to Antipas, his mention of "Herod, king of Judea" (1:5) may allude to the ill-fated Archelaus Herod, who is later parodied by Luke in the Parable of the Minas (13B). Dicken reviews the historical problems around Luke's "Herod" nomenclature, and proposes a "composite Herod," a conflation of Herod the Great, Archelaus, and Antipas "into a gospel-rejecting, prophet-executing, Messiah-mocking, apostle-decapitating composite 'Herod.' Positing a composite character, not only in Luke-Acts but also other ancient texts, gives us a new way of understanding various historical anomalies with regard to events and characters" (Frank Dicken, "Composite 'Herod' in Luke-Acts," *The Bible and Interpretation* June 2015, at https://bibleinterp.arizona.edu/articles/2015/06/dic398023). For debate over Lysanias see https://en.wikipedia.org/wiki/Lysanias#%20.
20. For an overview of the nationalist rebellion, Roman siege, and destruction of the Second Temple, see David Rhoads, "Children of Abraham, Children of God: Metaphorical Kinship in Paul's Letter to the Galatians," *Currents in Theology and Mission* 31, no. 4 (Aug 2004): 282-95. For longer studies, see Doron Mendels, *The Rise and Fall of Jewish Nationalism: Jewish and Christian Ethnicity in Ancient Palestine* (New York: Doubleday, 1992) and Susan Sorek, *Jews Against Rome: War in Palestine AD 66–73* (New York: Continuum, 2008).
21. This is a key thread for Luke. The noun *metanoia* occurs twenty-two times in the New Testament, with half of those in Luke-Acts; the verb *metanoeō* is used thirty-four times, fourteen in Luke-Acts.

22. See 4A. Tannehill (*Narrative Unity*: 65–66) is correct in noting that the noun *aphesis* appears elsewhere in Luke-Acts only in the phrase *aphesis tōn hamartiōn* ("release of sins," but usually translated "forgiveness of sins"). Luke's narrative uniquely establishes equivalences between release and forgiveness, and sin and debt (see 7A).
23. It is likely a Q tradition, and Matthew puts it in the mouth of Jesus *twice* in the context of heated adversarial exchanges with Pharisees: when they accuse him of casting out demons by the power of Beelzebul (Matt 12:25–34) and again when they try to dissociate themselves from ancestors who killed Israel's prophets (Matt 23:29–35)!
24. Malina and Rohrbaugh, *Social Science*, 203.
25. The Greek is *hriza* (whence comes our word "rhizome"; see Luke 8:13); the Latin word is *radix*, whence comes our term "radical."
26. See Enns and Myers, *Haunted Histories*, 213–238.
27. The verb *metadidōmi* is here in the imperative mood. Ephesians 4:28, which also uses this rare verb, offers us a commentary germane to our capitalist system that routinely distributes wealth upward rather than downward: "Do not steal from people, but rather do good, honest work in order to share with them."
28. Stegemann and Stegemann, *Jesus Movement*, 92–93.
29. For background on tax farming see Malina and Rohrbaugh, *Social Science*, 387–388; Hansen and Oakman, *Palestine*, 113–116; and especially Oakman's discussion of "tax resistance" in *Peasants*, 280–298.
30. John is likely addressing Jewish police surveilling his movement (Paul makes a wry comment on soldier's pay in 1 Cor 9:7a). It is also possible that these were Roman soldiers, given the political tensions of the era (see interaction with centurions by both Jesus in Luke 7:2–9 and Peter in Acts 10). *Daseiō* means to take something by violent shaking (only here in the New Testament), while *sukophanteō* can also mean to harass, oppress, blackmail, or *extort* (as in the case of Zacchaeus in 19:8, its only other appearance in the New Testament).
31 Acts 7:30 also recalls the revelation of YHWH to Moses in a fiery bush and, perhaps in a sardonic nod to John's preaching, notes that the apostle Paul uses *fire* to destroy a *viper* (28:5)!
32. Heretofore in Luke the verb *euangelizō* has only described angelic messaging (1:19, 2:10). For a discussion of the term as an appropriation and subversion of Roman propaganda, see Myers, *Strong Man*, 122–23.
33. See that account at www.livius.org/sources/content/josephus/jewish-antiquities/josephus-on-john-the-baptist/. Luke expands on Mark's brief proleptic report of the arrest (Mark 1:14) but omits Mark's flashback account of John's execution (Mark 6:16–29).
34. John Meier, *A Marginal Jew: Rethinking the Historical Jesus, Volume II: Mentor, Message, and Miracles* (New Haven, CT: Yale University Press, 1994). Meier is one of the few scholars to discuss extensively the notion of John's mentorship of Jesus.
35. See basic definitions at www.wordreference.com/definition/mimesis. For this concept in Rene Girard (following Eric Auerbach), see https://mimetictheory.com/mimetic-theory-resources/faq/what-is-art-a-mimesis/. This section draws from my reading of the Temptations through the lens of a decolonial response to the Columbus Quincentenary (Ched Myers, "The Wilderness Temptations and the American Journey: Resistance and Contemplation in a Quincentennial

Perspective" in *Richard Rohr: Illuminations of His Life and Work*, ed. Andreas Ebert and Patricia Brockman (New York: Crossroads, 1993), 143–157. I expanded this reflection after participating in a deeply impactful 2002 Uniting Church of Australia retreat moving around Victoria, curated by Aboriginal leaders.

36. See https://en.wikipedia.org/wiki/Genealogy_of_Jesus for a detailed analysis of Luke's genealogy, including comparison to Matthew's. An interesting note there is Augustine's claim that "the count of generations in the Book of Luke is 77, a number symbolizing the forgiveness of all sins." I would add that seven is *the* key number in Sabbath Economics calculations.
37. See https://aktalakota.stjo.org/seven-sacred-rites/hanblecheyapi-crying-for-a-vision/. Choctaw Episcopal bishop Steven Charleston has written a beautiful account of a contemporary vision quest spirituality entitled *The Four Vision Quests of Jesus* (Harrisburg, PA: Morehouse, 2015), which I highly recommend.
38. Christopher Vecsey, *Imagine Ourselves Richly: Mythic Narratives of North American Indians* (San Francisco: Harper & Row, 1991), 20–21.
39. See 7A for how Luke's ordering of the temptations corresponds, in reverse order, to the first three petitions of his Lord's Prayer (11:2–3). Jesus will also reenact these three themes in the course of his ministry as object lessons for his disciples: his wilderness feeding (9:10–17), his refusal of hierarchy (22:24–26), and his embrace of the way of the cross (9:22–25).
40. Eisenberg, *Ecology of Eden*, 106.
41. Eugene McCarraher, *Enchantments*.
42. I briefly discuss the other two temptations in the context of the Lord's Prayer (7A).
43. Silko, *Ceremony*, 2.

CHAPTER FOUR

1. From a sermon given at Binkley Baptist Church, Durham, North Carolina, on June 30, 2013, just four days after the US Supreme Court struck down a key provision of the Voting Rights Act of 1965. View a seven-minute excerpt at www.youtube.com/watch?v=1PASlMPsqwI. As noted in the introduction, Dr. Barber is cochair of the Poor Peoples' Campaign (www.poorpeoplescampaign.org/).
2. Dicken analyzes it as such; *Reading Luke*, 40–42.
3. Richard Horsley and Neil Asher Silberman, *The Message and the Kingdom: How Jesus and Paul Ignited a Revolution and Transformed the Ancient World* (London: Penguin Publishing Group, 1997), 24.
4. See Michael Brenes, "How the Philippines Were Crucial to the Making of American Empire, review of *Bound by War: How the United States and the Philippines Built America's First Pacific Century* by Christopher Capozzola (Basic Books, 2020)," *Jacobin* (August 13, 2021), at https://jacobin.com/2021/08/philippines-filipinos-us-empire-military-bases-colonialism-christopher-capozzola-bound-by-war-review.
5. Modern scholars call this "Third Isaiah," part of a collection compiled by post-Exilic disciples of the great eighth-century prophet (see a concise summary of this theory at https://stephencook.com.au/2020/11/14/

third-isaiah-theres-only-one-isaiah-in-my-bible-so-why-do-some-scholars-think-there-was-more/). The historical moment of Third Isaiah would have been parallel in many ways to occupied Galilee in the first century.

6. Michael Prior, *Jesus the Liberator: Nazareth Liberation Theology, Luke 4:16–30* (Sheffield, UK: Sheffield Academic Press, 1995), 152–153. This book is highly recommended for a close study of this text.
7. André Trocmé, *Jesus and the Nonviolent Revolution* (Ossining, NY: Orbis Books, 2003) originally published in 1962; John Howard Yoder, *The Politics of Jesus* (Grand Rapids, MI: Eerdmans, 1994), originally published in 1972; Robert B. Sloan, *The Favorable Year of the Lord: A Study of Jubilary Theology in the Gospel of Luke* (Austin, TX: Schola Press, 1977); and Prior, *Jesus the Liberator*. Sharon Ringe, *Jesus, Liberation, and the Biblical Jubilee: Images for Ethics and Christology* (Minneapolis, MN: Fortress Books, 1985) offers a sympathetic but more nuanced view, while Christopher James Luthy and Keith Dyer, in *Rethinking the Acceptable Year: The Jubilee and the Basileia in Luke 4 and Beyond* (Eugene, OR: Wipf & Stock, 2019), adopt the majority's diffidence. More recently, a few evangelicals have rediscovered and affirmed Jesus as a Jubilee practitioner. See Paul Hertig, "The Jubilee Mission of Jesus in the Gospel of Luke: Reversals of Fortunes," *Missiology* 26, no. 2 (1998), 167–179; Michael Schluter, John Ashcroft, and James Jones, ed., *Jubilee Manifesto: A Framework, Agenda & Strategy for Christian Social Reform* (Downers Grove, IL: InterVarsity Press, 2005); and Christian T. Collins Winn, *Jesus, Jubilee, and the Politics of God's Reign* (Grand Rapids, MI: Eerdmans, 2023).
8. Though the verb is mostly used for "forgiveness of sins" (*aphesin hamartiōn*) throughout Luke's work (1:77; 3:3; 5:20–23; 11:4; 17:3f; 23:24; 24:47; Acts 2:38; 5:31; 10:43; 13:38 and 26:18), *aphiēmi* also carries Jubilee connotations of "leaving possessions" (Luke 5:11; 18:28f) and "releasing from debt" (11:4).
9. See Ched Myers. "Nature against Empire: Exodus Plagues, Climate Crisis and Hard Heartedness," *Direction* 49, no. 1 (Spring 2020): 5–17.
10. Martin Luther King Jr, "A Time to Break Silence (Declaration against the Vietnam War)" 1967. https://www.americanrhetoric.com/speeches/mlkatimetobreaksilence.htm. Read my commentary at https://bcmonline.org/2007/03/01/articles-peacemaking-time-break-silence-again-reflection-40th-anniversary-kings-riverside-speech/.
11. King, " A Time to Break Silence."
12. For Mark's crowd as character, see Myers, *Strong Man*, 156–157; on Mark's version of these events see *Strong Man*, 141–143.
13. Just as Luke alludes to events in Capernaum prior to bringing Jesus there, as noted, he introduces Simon (4:38) *before* the fisherman is called to discipleship. This is probably prolepsis, "anticipations" of coming scenes.
14. K. C. Hanson, in "The Galilean Fishing Economy and the Jesus Tradition," *Biblical Theology Bulletin* 27, no. 3 (August 1997): 99–111, was the first to outline the context I summarize here. See also Hanson and Oakman, *Palestine*, 106–110; Crossan, *God and Empire*, 108–123; and a popular overview by John Petty at www.progressiveinvolvement.com/progressive_involvement/2008/01/lectionary-bl-2.html.
15. John Dominic Crossan, *God and Empire: Jesus against Rome, Then and Now* (San Francisco: HarperOne, 2007), 122–123.

16. Between Tiberias and Capernaum on the west shore was Magdala (or Migdal, "lighthouse"), a major harbor also known as Tarichaea, which means "processed fishville" (see https://en.wikipedia.org/wiki/Tarichaea). Luke later tells us this is where Mary hailed from (8:2), possibly a refugee from the fish factories.
17. Map at www.ritmeyer.com/2014/12/04/harbours-of-the-sea-of-galilee/. On the "Jesus boat," see https://en.wikipedia.org/wiki/Sea_of_Galilee_Boat; Crossan, *God and Empire*, 121–123. Though Luke does not associate Jesus with his father's construction work, both Mark 6:3 and Matthew 13:55 do.
18. Douglas Oakman, "The Shape of Power and Political Economy in Herodian Galilee," ed. Laurel Dykstra and Ched Myers, in *Liberating Biblical Study* (Eugene, OR: Cascade Books, 2011), 157.
19. The verb *zōgrōn* means to capture alive. Its only other appearance in the New Testament is perhaps germane; Christians are exhorted to "correct their opponents with gentleness, that God might grant that they will repent and come to know the truth, so they may escape from the snare of the devil, having been *captured* by him to do his will" (2 Tim 2:26).
20. For commentary on Mark's version of these vignettes see Myers, *Strong Man*, 143–55.
21. On how uses of an oral Torah tried to "recodify the redemptive media" in this period, see Herzog, *Subversive Speech*, 182–183).
22. Herzog insists upon the latter, *Subversive Speech*, 180–181.
23. Pyung Soo Seo, *Luke's Jesus in the Roman Empire and the Emperor in the Gospel of Luke* (Eugene, OR: Pickwick Publications, 2015), 71.
24. Seo, *Luke's Jesus*, 82–83 notes that the phrase *dochēn megalēn* is not found elsewhere in the New Testament but does appear in three telling passages of the LXX (Gen 21:8, I Esdras 3:1, and Dan 5:1), each indicating feasts given by nobles or kings. A home that would accommodate so many dinner guests would have needed to be large. The only other use of *dochē* in the New Testament is Luke 14:13, a scenario this story prefigures. Elsewhere Luke uses the term *deîpnon* for a main meal or banquet.
25. Seo, *Luke's Jesus*, 83.
26. I prefer the synonym "Human One" over the doubly patriarchal "Son of Man," a term that Luke, following Mark, introduces in 5:24. See my commentary of Mark's version of these food stories in Myers, *Strong Man*, 157–163.

CHAPTER FIVE

1. David King, *Reclaiming*, 73.
2. For historical background on the crisis of indebtedness, see Oakman, *Peasants*, 33–39.
3. I recommend three (very different) studies of Matthew's Sermon: Warren Carter, *Matthew and the Margins: A Sociopolitical and Religious Reading* (Maryknoll, NY: Orbis Books, 2000), 128–195; Gene Davenport, *Into the Darkness: Discipleship in the Sermon on the Mount* (Eugene, OR: Wipf & Stock, 1988); and Pinchas Lapide, *The Sermon on the Mount: Utopia or Program for Action?* (Maryknoll, NY: Orbis

Books, 1986). Luke abbreviates or omits many parts of Matthew's sermon, placing many parallel sayings elsewhere in his narrative (e.g., 11:2–4, 9–13, 33–36; 12:22–34, 57–59; 13:23–27; 14:34–35; and 16:13, 18).

4. For a technical discussion of the Q text of the Sermon tradition, its social function in early Palestinian Jewish Christianity, and its later appropriations, see Simon Joseph, "A Social Identity Approach to the Rhetoric of Apocalyptic Violence in the Sayings Gospel Q," *History of Religions*, 57, no.1 (University of Chicago Press Journals, 2017), at https://www.journals.uchicago.edu/doi/full/10.1086/692316#.
5. See Johnson Thomaskutty, "A Sociolinguistic Reading of *ptōchos* in Luke's Gospel, Part I," *New Testament Scholarship Worldwide* (blog), October 15, 2013, https://ntscholarship.wordpress.com/2013/10/15/a-sociolinguistic-reading-of-ptochos-in-lukes-gospel-part-i-2/.
6. The verb "to laugh" (*gelaō)* appears only here and 6:25b in the New Testament (see an echo of Luke's vocabulary in James 4:9). In contrast, Matthew mostly uses a different verb (*klauthmos*) for the phrase "wailing and gnashing of teeth" (six times, versus once in Luke 13:28).
7. See Matt 7:15. The "false prophet" moniker seems to have had a technical meaning in the New Testament (Acts 13:6; 2 Pt 2:1; 1 John 4:1), especially in apocalyptic traditions (Matt 24:11, 24; Mark 13:22; Rev 16:13; 19:20; 20:10).
8. For a study of the rhetoric of reversal in Luke, see John York, *The Last Shall Be First: The Rhetoric of Reversal in Luke*, Journal for the Study of the New Testament, Supplement Series 46 (Sheffield, UK: JSOT Press, 1991). For an overview of the history and social function of apocalyptic literature, see Michael Zank, "Apocalyptic Literature," *Michael Zank blog*, October 25, 2019, https://blogs.bu.edu/mzank/2019/10/25/apocalyptic-literature/.
9. Matthew 5:38–45, which Luke here condenses, has been interpreted by Walter Wink through the lens of Gandhian nonviolent resistance; see Wink, *Engaging the Powers: Discernment and Resistance in a World of Domination* (Minneapolis, MN: Augsburg Fortress, 1992) 175–193. Wink's exegesis is contested. See the 2021 debate between Kevin Carnahan ("Jesus Did Not Teach Nonviolent Resistance in the Sermon on the Mount," *Political Theology Network*, October 14, 2021, https://politicaltheology.com/jesus-did-not-teach-nonviolent-resistance-in-the-sermon-on-the-mount/) and Scott Paeth ("Walter Wink, the Powers, and the Sermon on the Mount," *Political Theology Network*, October 28, 2021, https://politicaltheology.com/walter-wink-the-powers-and-the-sermon-on-the-mount/). But I recommend Wink's moral-political reading, which has rightly been influential.
10. "Credit" appears in the RSV in both Phil 4:17 and 1 Pt 2:20, but the Greek verbs are different.
11. The adjective "merciful" (*oiktirmōn*) oddly appears in the New Testament only here and in James 5:11 but describes YHWH throughout the LXX.
12. Luke calls him a "centurion" (*hekatontarchēs*, used only by Matt and Luke in the New Testament; Mark 15:39, 44–45 uses *kenturiōn*, a Latin loan word). But Alan Culpepper reasons that because "the Hellenization of Galilee did not make great advances until . . . the settlement of Roman garrisons in Galilee around 120 CE"; and "the story of Jesus and the centurion (Matt 8:5–13, Luke 7:1–10) is the only

record of an encounter between Jesus and a gentile in Galilee; the centurion was probably a Herodian officer rather than a Roman soldier." See Culpepper, *The People of the Parables: Galilee in the Time of Jesus* (Louisville, KY: Westminster John Knox Press, 2024), 27.

13. Suggested by the Oxford Reference, which continues: "Reeds were the vegetation motif on the first coins issued by Herod Antipas, who founded his capital city on the border of the Sea of Galilee, where reeds were prolific" (see www.oxfordreference.com/display/10.1093/oi/authority.20110803100409829). Luke's earlier vignette about Herod (9:7–9) suggests that while the king may be cunning about power, he is easily confused about protest movements, unable to distinguish Jesus from John. Or the wavering image could be an allusion to 1 Kg 14:15 ("The Lord will smite Israel, as a reed is shaken in the water"), part of the aging prophet Ahijah's oracle of judgment on the house of Jeroboam, which by implication also hangs over Herod. Either way, the phrase is decidedly uncomplimentary of the king. Jesus will again deride Antipas in 13:31, where Pharisees (surprisingly) warn him the king is hunting him. There he calls Herod "that fox," an allusion to *vulpes vulpes palaestina*, an opportunistic predator who is nonetheless vulnerable to larger hunters (i.e., Rome). Pyung Soo Seo points out that Jesus is mocking the king, not the *alōpēx*, which he invokes respectfully in 9:58, *Luke's Jesus*, 44–45. Jesus assures (warns?) the Pharisees that he will carry on with his work despite being stalked (13:32). But he also acknowledges that soon enough his work will indeed be "brought to an end" (*teleioō,* 13:32c)—in large part because of Herod's collusion (see 23:7–11). On Luke's damning portrait of Herod's complicity in the railroading of Jesus, see Seo, *Luke's Jesus*, 41–47.
14. The noun *mikroteros* refers here to those who are marginalized; the rhetorical contrast with "greatest" (*meizon*) is used again in Jesus's later teaching about servanthood (22:26–27).
15. See K. E. Corley, "The Anointing of Jesus in the Synoptic Tradition: An Argument for Authenticity," Journal for the Study of the Historical Jesus 1, no.1 (2003).
16. A. Pesonen, "The Weeping Sinner: A Short Story by Luke?" *Neotestamentica* 34, no.1 (2000).
17. A classic expression, or perhaps protest, of this gendered burden is found in the Mexican folklore of "La Llorona," the ghost woman who lost her children and is forced to wander the Earth searching, forever caught between the world of the living and the dead (see https://en.wikipedia.org/wiki/La_Llorona). It aptly describes the trauma of grieving the disappeared, especially in the absence of justice. Wailing in many non-Western traditions is loud and unbounded, often because it is an expression of frustration and rage. This is not welcome in polite Western society—especially northern Euro-American Protestant culture, which mostly represses grief, turning it inward. The southern European Pablo Picasso painted a series of "Weeping Woman" protest portraits that are both poignant and gruesome (see https://en.wikipedia.org/wiki/The_Weeping_Woman). The excoriated face of the woman was part of Picasso's response to newspaper photographs of Luftwaffe bombing of Guernica on behalf of Franco in the Spanish Civil War on April 26, 1937 (see further www.pablopicasso.org/guernica.jsp). The very fact that Luke's wailing woman is unnamed represents a lacuna through which we might hear her

cries today: women having their children taken away at the US-Mexico border, or standing in the ruins of bombed out buildings in Gaza, or holding vigil in public plazas in Latin America demanding justice for the disappeared. Yet Luke's archetypal Llorona somehow knew that her tears, and all they held, would be received by the weeping prophet Jesus. Which is why it is important to pause and *feel* the mournful details of this Gospel story!

18. Four of only six appearances of this verb in the New Testament are in Luke-Acts. While the most famous "kiss" in the Gospels is one of betrayal (Matt 26:49), it is normally an act between men of welcome (Luke 15:20) or farewell (Acts 20:37). Only here in the New Testament is it across genders!
19. Jesus has just lamented popular ignorance of what makes a prophet (7:33–34). The verb *haptetai* is often used in New Testament healing stories (e.g., 7:14, 22:51) but in at least one instance connotes sexual touching (1 Cor 7:1).
20. *Para* + *bole* means to put side by side; think of it as a similitude wrapped inside a story with a twist. The word appears eighteen times in Luke, though some stories that function parabolically are not so labeled, as we'll see. The first full-blown parable will be the story of the sower immediately following this sequence (8:4–15).
21. The particularity of Luke's vocabulary here is likely significant. The noun *daneistēs* ("creditor") appears only here in the New Testament, but four times in the LXX. One of those is 2 Kings 4:1, the story of Elisha's multiplication of oil jars to rescue a widow dying from debt, to which Luke may be alluding as a hermeneutic lens for Jesus's parable. *Chreopheiletēs* is a compound noun, which seems to mean "loan-debtor," and appears only here and in Luke 16:5, a rhetorical link we'll explore there (10A).
22. Malina and Rohrbaugh write: "In Roman law that prevailed in Palestine in the first century, a court could grant a creditor one of two options in order to recover a defaulted loan: 1) the debtor could be forced to work for the creditor until the debt was paid off, or 2) the debtor could be put in prison. If imprisoned, the expectation was that relatives would pay a 'ransom'. . . [and] could sell the debtor's property to pay the debt" (*Social Scientific Commentary*, 333). See also the overview of indebtedness in ancient Palestine in Oakman, *Peasants*, 39.
23. The verb here is not "release" (*aphiemi*) but "freely grant" (*charizomai*). The latter verb is also part of Jesus's Jubilee program, as its other appearance in Luke is the previous episode where Jesus similarly "grants" a blind person sight (7:21). It connotes an act of grace so powerful that Paul places it at the center of his theology (Rom 8:32; 1 Cor 2:12; Gal 3:18).
24. "He refers to the [collection] project ten times in 2 Cor 8–9 as the work of 'grace' (*charis*). . . . Paul opens and closes his appeal to the Corinthians by reminding them that this financial partnership only mirrors the grace of God (2 Cor 8:1; 9:14)" (Myers, *Biblical Vision*, 57). See epilogue iii.
25. See Robert Tannehill's discussion of this text, which points out that forgiveness isn't actually pronounced until the next verse (*Narrative Unity of Luke-Acts*, 116–118).
26. The double healing in 8:40–56 is similarly a highly choreographed tale illustrating the priority of the outcast. I read it as one of Luke's several "political cartoons" (see

6A, n. 3; 8A; and 11A). It contrasts the two female political bodies, insider and outsider, in order to argue that the health of the body politic (symbolized by their respective association with the number 12, 8:42–43) is contingent upon the restoration of the radically excluded woman to the "family" (8:48). Since Luke generally follows Mark's account, I don't examine this story here; see my comments in *Strong Man*, 197–203.

27. J. L. Resseguie calls the story's "strange behavior, indecorous actions, and 'startling' language. . . an artful way to force the reader to reexamine staid conventions" ("Automatization and Defamiliarization in Luke 7:36–50," *Journal of Literature and Theology* 5, no. 2, 1991). B.E. Reid sees the tale as a "paradigm for feminist hermeneutics" ("'Do You See This Woman?' Luke 7:36–50 as a Paradigm for Feminist Hermeneutics" *Biblical Research* 40, 1995). J. A. Sanders agrees it should be read through the lens of "Jubilee legislation in Deut 15" ("Extravagant Love," *New Blackfriars* 68, no. 806, 1987).
28. On Magdala see 4B, n. 12; and Hanson and Oakman, *Palestine*, 110. Mary's "seven demons" may allude to Jesus's strange parable in 11:24–26 (see 7B and Enns and Myers, *Haunted Histories*, 40–41.
29. Her husband Chuza is called a "steward" (*epitropos*, only here in Luke), meaning that he managed Herod's property. It would have been extraordinary for someone of Joanna's stature to travel with Jesus, who Herod saw as a political threat, and in a company of unrelated men, most of whom were peasants. Bauckham contends she should be identified with the Junia of Romans 16:7, thus having become a prominent apostle herself. See Richard Bauckham, *Gospel Women: Studies of the Named Women in the Gospels* (Grand Rapids, MI: Eerdmans, 2002). The third woman mentioned by Luke here, Susanna, does not appears again in the New Testament.
30. Malina and Rohrbaugh, *Social Science*, 334.
31. For my note and resources on the important concept of fictive kinship in the Bible see chapter 6, fn 2.

CHAPTER SIX

1. See my comments on Mark's parable, including its socioeconomic background, in Myers, *Strong Man*, 174–180.
2. K. C. Hanson, "BTB Readers Guide: Kinship," *Biblical Theology Bulletin* 24 (1994), 183–194 provides a sociological overview. Scott Bartchy, "The Sibling Secret (Revealed)" *Leaven* 9, no. 1, Article 5 (2001) https://digitalcommons.pepperdine.edu/leaven/vol9/iss1/5 and "Who Should Be Called Father? Paul of Tarsus between the Jesus Tradition and Patria Potestas," *Biblical Theology Bulletin* 33, no. 4 (Nov 2003): 135–147 helped bring to both scholarly and popular attention the importance of fictive kinship in the New Testament, especially in the apostle Paul's writings. David Rhoads, "Children of Abraham, Children of God: Metaphorical Kinship in Paul's Letter to the Galatians," *Currents in Theology and Mission* 31, no. 4 (Aug 2004): 282–297, prefers the term "metaphorical kinship." A. Destro and M. Pesce, in "Fathers and Householders in the Jesus Movement: The Perspective of the Gospel of Luke," *Biblical Interpretation*, 11, no. 2 (2003): 211–238, conclude

that the model of discipleship transformed the model of the household. Donald Ker, "Family Finances: 'Kinship' and the Collection," *Irish Biblical Studies* 25, no. 1 (2003): 2–30, argues that Paul's international mutual aid effort, known as the collection, was driven by this kinship ethos. I show how 2 Corinthians 8–9 is a key Sabbath Economics text in Myers, *Biblical Vision*, 52–59. Sandra Richter, in *The Epic of Eden: A Christian Entry into the Old Testament* (Downers Grove, IL: InterVarsity Press, 2008), discusses fictive kinship in the covenant models of the Hebrew Bible. Norman Gottwald's *Tribes* used the concept in his epic work on the "tribes of YHWH," positing that the patriarchal narratives helped construct a fictive family identity for Israel. See also Gunnar Lehmann, "Ancient Israel's Social Structure(s)," in *The Ancient Israelite World*, ed. Kyle Keimer and George Pierce (London: Routledge, 2022), 212.

3. Luke follows Mark's version closely; see my comments on Mark in Myers, *Strong Man*, 190–194.
4. See comments on Mark's story, whose key components are preserved by Luke, in Myers, *Strong Man*, 197–203.
5. This is reflected, for example, in the *Didache*, an early manual that devotes considerable attention to the ethics of hospitality for itinerant disciples (see overview at https://en.wikipedia.org/wiki/Didache). But its instructions were directed to *receiving* communities, whereas Jesus's addressed the *traveler*. For academic discussion of the *Didache* and itineracy in the early church, see Stephen Patterson, "Didache 11–13: The Legacy of Radical Itinerancy in Early Christianity," in *The Didache in Context: Essays on Its Text, History, and Transmission*, ed. Clayton Jefford (Novum Testamentum Supplements, Vol. 77, 1994), 313–339.
6. In late medieval Europe, Christendom's mission of hegemonic expansion began fusing with powerful mythologies of ethnic superiority, codified in papal pronouncements that became the doctrine of discovery, which heralded enlightenment for "pagan" inhabitants and entitlement for Christian subjugators. White supremacist ideologies continued to drive a long history of missions-as-conquest, with which modern churches have not fully come to terms.
7. Roger Epp, *We Are All Treaty People: Prairie Essays* (Edmonton: University of Alberta Press, 2008), 133.
8. Most settler Christians today prefer either to ignore (conservatives) or disassociate (liberals) from the painful, half-millennium-long history of missionary entanglements with European imperialism. But Western society was fundamentally shaped by the intimate collusion between church and empire, and the privileges enjoyed by white settlers on Indigenous lands throughout the world are rooted in this legacy. See more on this, and the struggle to decolonize the church's missions past, present and future, in Enns and Myers, *Haunted Histories*, 132–141.
9. Mark 8:27–9:41 functions as a fulcrum for his discipleship narrative (see Myers, *Strong Man*, 235–256).
10. The verb *poreuomai* appears five times in 9:51–57! It is often used in Luke when speaking of travel that will require hospitality (1:39; 2:3, 41; 4:42; 7:11; 9:13; 24:28) or encountering hostility (4:30; 9:51–53; 13:31–33; 14:31; 15:4, 8; 19:28; 21:8; 22:22; see also Acts 20:1).

11. "The Human One has nowhere to lay his head" makes this clear (9:58). His seemingly harsh challenge to those who wished to complete their family obligations prior to following reflects two problems. In traditional culture, such duties could take months or years (9:59, 61). More importantly, such requests reflect an assumption that the recruit could continue their symbiotic relationship with their family household. The discipleship community entails radically different duties of fictive kinship and mutual aid, as discussed.
12. Mathew's omnibus version of the instructions also draws on Q (Matt 10:9–16), as does Luke here. Purse (*ballantion*) appears again as part of Jesus's exhortation to disciples to sell their *huparchonta*, because "commonwealth purses" don't wear out (Luke 12:33). Jesus's strange exhortation just prior to Gethsemane, which reverses his admonitions and tells disciples now to take purse, bag, and sell their coat to buy a sword (!), appears only in Luke (22:35–36). But he immediately explains that it is only for the purpose of fulfilling Isaiah 53:12, and when they respond with a call to arms, he abruptly shuts down the conversation (Luke 22:37–38).
13. Malina and Rohrbaugh, *Social Science*, 346.
14. Patrick Wolfe, "Settler Colonialism and the Elimination of the Native," *Journal of Genocide Research* 8, no. 4 (Dec 2006), 388.
15. Lewis Hyde, *The Gift: Imagination and the Erotic Life of Property* (New York: Vintage Books, 1983), 4.
16. Christopher B. Hays, "Commentary on Isaiah 55:1–13," WorkingPreacher.org (Dec 17, 2017), https://www.workingpreacher.org/commentaries/narrative-lectionary/word-accomplishes-gods-purpose/commentary-on-isaiah-551-13.
17. Mark 6:31–32. Similar to English, the Greek adjective *erēmos* means "desolate place"; as a noun, "desert" or "wilderness." In Luke this is a space where John the Baptist lived and ministered (1:80; 3:2; 7:24) and where Jesus was tested (4:1) and withdrew to pray (4:42; 5:16). The adjective is used in 9:10b but is obscured by NRSV: "he withdrew privately to a city called Bethsaida." The KJV is a better translation: "he went aside into a desert place belonging to the city called Bethsaida" (since most Palestinian villages were surrounded by desert).
18. The verb to follow (*akoloutheō*) is introduced in Luke's narrative as a discipleship term (5:11, 27–28), which connotation remains in all but a few appearances after.
19. Provisions (*episitismos*) appears only here in the New Testament. The fact that fields (*agros*) are included here implies that gleaning might be an option, as in 6:1–5.
20. The verb *agorazō* has only a negative connotation in Luke's story (see 14:18–19; 17:28; 19:45; 22:36).
21. Oakman surmises that if Luke's number "has historical value. . . . Jesus could fall under the same suspicion that his predecessor John the Baptist did . . . likely to incur the wrath of the political authorities" (*Peasants*, 52). Extrapolating from demographic modeling, he sketches population density and dispersal in this period. Magen Broshi's review of the literary and archaeological evidence concludes "the population of Palestine in antiquity did not exceed a million persons" ("The Population of Western Palestine in the Roman-Byzantine Period," *Bulletin of the*

American Schools of Oriental Research 236, Autumn 1979, 7), though Oakman argues for a quarter of that.

22. Mark calls these "companies" *symposia* (Mark 6:39), Luke uses *klisias*; both words are unique in the New Testament.
23. The only difference is the thanksgiving: here Luke uses *eulogeō*; at 22:19, *eucharisteō*.
24. For example, according to Genesis 47:13–21, the Israelites ended up in Egypt because of Joseph's "management" of famine conditions to benefit Pharaoh's interests. Still today, natural cycles of flooding and fire turn into social disasters because of political and economic conditions of exploitation, especially in poor countries.
25. The verb *anaginōskō* ("to read/interpret") appears only twice more in Luke: Jesus reading from Isaiah (4:16) and in his response to Pharisees challenging his gleaning by questioning their biblical literacy (6:3). It is used in the Acts episode of the Ethiopian eunuch's reading of Isaiah (Acts 8:32–36) and twice refers to how "Moses and the prophets" are read in synagogue each week (Acts 13:27; 15:21). For my reflections on hermeneutic disciplines, see Myers, "Neither Authoritarian Nor Diffident," also at https://bcmonline.org/1998/08/01/articles-biblical-interpretation-neither-authoritarian-nor-diffident-conversing-about-biblical-diffe/.
26. Fowl and Jones, *Reading in Communion*, 17.
27. The "text" the lawyer cites is already a reinterpreted one, a *midrashic* conflation of Deut 6:5 and Lev 19:18. It may even have derived from Jesus himself (see Mark 12:29–31)—in which case the lawyer is giving the answer he thinks Jesus wants to hear.
28. For a full exploration of this, see Brandon Scott, *Hear Then the Parable* (Minneapolis, MN: Fortress Press, 1989).
29. As noted previously, my late teacher Herzog's *Subversive Speech* is a groundbreaking treatment of Jesus's storytelling I often lean on.
30. Oakman, *Peasants*, 171–172.
31. Oakman, *Peasants*, 173–177.
32. Oakman, *Peasants*, 178.
33. Oakman, *Peasants*, 44–45. In Luke 7:41, Jesus posits two debtors owing five hundred and fifty *denarii* respectively. In Mark 6:38 the disciples complain that they would need to find "two hundred denarii worth of bread" to feed the five hundred in the wilderness (see John 6:7). The woman's ointment in Mark 14:5 "could have been sold for three hundred denarii" (see John 12:5). These are all huge amounts of money. Yet in 20:24, Jesus can't muster a single *denarius* (though presumably he doesn't carry the Roman coin because of its idolatrous image of Caesar).
34. In his prelude, between the songs of Mary and Zechariah (1:50–78), Luke uses *eleos* five times, then only here.
35. The Samaritan episode rightly challenges the Protestant dogma of "salvation by faith, not works," and the theological idealism it has spawned. Yet Luke's dialectical approach is delightfully demonstrated in his very next story—about Mary, Martha, and Jesus's critique of the "idolatry of doing" (10:38–42)!

CHAPTER SEVEN

1. Obery M. Hendricks Jr., "Guerilla Exegesis: 'Struggle' as a Scholarly Vocation," in *Liberating Biblical Study*, Dykstra and Myers, 127.
2. For an overview of the complex tradition history of the Prayer, see Oakman, *Peasants*, 199–242, and his interesting correlations with early Passover Haggadot (*Peasants*, 104). Wilton gives etymological background on the evolution of the English Prayer: www.wordorigins.org/big-list-entries/trespass-sin-debt.
3. Oakman, *Peasants*, 119.
4. Oakman, *Peasants*, 228.
5. See Seo, *Luke's Jesus*, 131–133. This connotation of *oikoumenēs* is clear in 2:21 (the imperial census; see also Acts 19:27; 24:5) and implied in the apocalyptic saying of Luke 21:26 (see also Acts 11:28; 17:6, 31).
6. Jacques Ellul, *Anarchy and Christianity*, trans. Geoffrey Bromiley (Grand Rapids, MI: Eerdmans, 1991), 46–55, at https://theanarchistlibrary.org/library/jacques-ellul-anarchy-christianity-en.
7. As explained in the introduction, most everywhere else in this book I have chosen to paraphrase this traditional metaphor as the "Great Economy," in keeping with the main theme of this project.
8. See my reflections on early Israel's "earth spirituality" at https://bcmonline.org/2006/04/01/articles-ecology-faith-surely-gate-heaven-bible-and-earth-spirituality/
9. As suggested in Herzog, *Subversive Speech*, 209–210. See 6A.
10. Herzog, *Subversive Speech*, 194–202.
11. Malina and Rohrbaugh, *Social Science*, 351.
12. Herzog, *Subversive Speech*, 205–206.
13. The noun *anaideia* appears only here in the New Testament; the KJV's awkward "importunity" prevailed until the NRSV substituted "persistence." Herzog overviews a long history of interpretive struggle over this verb, and concludes it connotes "shameless," see Herzog, *Subversive Speech*, 202–203, 212–213).
14. The adjective *kōphos* can mean inability to speak, or hear, or both (as in 7:22). In Mark's longest healing narrative, a possessed boy has a silencing spirit that seeks to destroy him through the archetypal forces of fire and water (Mark 9:14–28). The disciples are impotent to exorcize it, and in an epilogue, Jesus challenges them to pray and discern whether they are possessed by the very demons they seek to cast out. For my commentary on this important passage for inner and outer journeys, see Myers, *Stone*, 76–110.
15. Mark's version of this indictment (Mark 3:25) inspired Abraham Lincoln's famous lines: "A house divided against itself cannot stand. I believe this government cannot endure, permanently half slave and half free." It is from a speech on June 16, 1858, after Lincoln accepted the Illinois Republican State Convention's nomination as candidate for US senator. He lost to Democrat Stephen Douglas, as even Lincoln's political allies regarded that speech as too radical (see www.abrahamlincolnonline.org/lincoln/speeches/house.htm).
16. This phrase is in the first of two Q additions that Luke and Matthew insert into the Markan pericope (Luke 11:18b–20 // Matt 12:27–28; the other is Luke 11:23 //

Matt 12:30). Luke's *daktulos theou* (versus Matthew's "Spirit of God") is taken from the LXX of Exodus 8:15. The divine digit appears only elsewhere in the Hebrew Bible as the writer of the stone tablets of the Decalogue (Exod 31:18; Deut 9:10)!

17. The only other parallel usage of the adjective *ischuros* in the New Testament is in a list of imperial oppressors that includes "the rich and the strong" (Rev 6:15, *hoi plousioi kai hoi ischuroi*; see also Rev 19:18). For comments on Mark's passage as master metaphor for Jesus's resistance to empire, see Myers, *Strong Man*, 164–167.
18. Luke might have taken this military term from the Maccabean tale of Apollonius, governor of Syria, who went up "fully armed" to seize the Temple treasury, only to be turned away by angelic forces (4 Macc 7:11), a somewhat similar scenario. However, the dating of 4 Maccabees, written in Koine Greek, is uncertain; it may have been contemporary to or after Luke.
19. In 12:51, Jesus pronounces: "Do you think that I have come to give peace on earth? No, I tell you, but rather division" (the noun *diamerismos* echoes the verb *diamerizō* in 11:17–18, and in Acts 2:3 and 45 specifically means "distribute"). For a persuasive argument that Luke's Jesus is portrayed throughout the Gospel as "Lord" in specific contrast to the myth of Caesar Augustus, see Seo, *Luke's Jesus*, 116–175.
20. The compound verb *eperchomai* (to "appear") appears in Luke-Acts eight times, almost always in an apocalyptic sense of revelation or disruption; it is used only twice in the rest of the New Testament.
21. In its active transitive form here it means "to conquer"; as intransitive "to overcome." *Nikaō* appears only here and in John 16:33 in the gospels, but five times in 1 John and 15 times in Revelation. Seo, *Luke's Jesus*, 134–135, points out that this "victory" echoes the vanquishing of Rome's Legions in the Gerasene demoniac (8:26–39).
22. The term *panoplia* ("full armor") is known to many from Ephesians 6:11 and 13, the only other time it appears in the New Testament. The pluperfect *epepoithein* means to "trust in" or "depend on" (see, e.g., 18:9).
23. This phenomenon is also graphically described in a later pastoral epistle's warning about "backsliding." 2 Peter 2:20 uses the identical phrase as Luke 11:26b, "the last state being worse than the first" (*ta eschata cheirona ton proton*), as well as the same rare adjective, "waterless" (Luke 11:24).
24. Avery Gordon, *Ghostly Matters: Haunting and the Sociological Imagination* (Minneapolis: University of Minnesota Press, 1997), 7. See our discussion in Enns and Myers, *Haunted Histories*, 36–41, and the literature cited there. We cannot repair deep historical legacies of oppression and violence without reckoning with the ghosts that inhabit our psyches, communities, social structures, and lands (we recommend Luke's story there too).
25. Eve Tuck and C. Ree, "A Glossary of Haunting," in *Handbook of Autoethnography*, ed. S. Jones, T. Adams and C. Ellis (London: Routledge, 2018), 642.
26. Martin Luther King, *Why We Can't Wait* (New York: Harper & Row, 1963), 109–110.
27. The story invokes the archetypal number seven, so foundational to the Sabbath consciousness of Judaism, and resonant in other mystical traditions. One might

think immediately of Thomas Merton's *The Seven Storey Mountain* (San Diego, CA: Harcourt Brace, 1948)—except that *this* ghost story speaks of traversing a seven storey *valley*.

CHAPTER EIGHT

1. An excerpt from a prophecy that was, along with one from Hopi spiritual leader Thomas Banyacya, delivered to the United Nations on December 10, 1992, the waning days of the Columbus Quincentenary. See context in a 2005 piece from *Indian Country Today*: http://www.senaa.org/HopiProphecy/hopiwarningstothe-world.htm. See the full text of both at https://crab.rutgers.edu/users/omaha/NAI/Hopi_Prophecy.htm and commentary at https://thehill.com/changing-america/opinion/566362-the-hopi-prophecies-are-coming-true-heres-why-we-should-pay/. Concern for the predatory power of greed appears in many Indigenous wisdom stories from around the Americas (examples at https://www.native-languages.org/legends-fairness.htm). These tales are often humorous, but also deadly serious about the corrosive and destructive power of greed in the community.
2. The few exceptions are all short sayings: 12:1 (Mark 4:22); 12:8–9 (Mark 8:38); 12:10 (Mark 3:28–29); 12:11–12 (Mark 13:11); 13:18–21 (Mark 4:30–32); 13:30 (Mark 10:31); 14:27 (Mark 8:38); 14:34 (Mark 9:50); and 17:1–2 (Mark 9:42).
3. These Woes move beyond those directed to broad classes of people in the Sermon on the Plain (6:24–26), or cities (10:13), now singling out Pharisees and lawyers (three directed toward each group, 11:42–52).
4. On its literary unity, see A. J. Malherbe, "The Christianization of a Topos (Luke 12:13–34)," *Novum Testamentum* 38, no. 2 (1996): 123–135. Richard Lowery traces Sabbath principles threading through the sequence, "Sabbath and Survival: Abundance and Self-Restraint in a Culture of Excess," *Encounter* 54, no 2 (1993), 143–167.
5. The verb *merizō* means "to divide" or "separate" (from the noun *meris*, "part" or "portion"), but here in the middle voice means "to share." A similar scenario appears in the later Prodigal Son Parable (15:11–12). See Hanson and Oakman, "*Palestine*," 23, for ancient Middle Eastern inheritance laws. Jesus's response (12:14) rejects a role as *meristēs* ("divider" or "arbitrator," only here in the New Testament) or "judge" (*dikastēs*, used only by Luke). The rhetorical question "Who made you a judge over. . ." appears similarly in Acts 7:27, 35.
6. *Orate* (only here in Luke) connotes vigilance against serious danger in all seven appearances in the New Testament
7. Ulrich Duchrow and Franz Hinkelammert, *Property for People, Not for Profit: Alternatives to the Global Tyranny of Capital* (Windsor, ON: Zed Press, 2004), 6–7.
8. Herman Waetjen, "Imitation of the Year of Jubilee in the Parable of Workers in the Vineyard," in *Liberating Biblical Study,* Dykstra and Myers, 96. For further exploration on this economic background, see: Sean Freyne, *Galilee from Alexander the Great to Hadrian, 323 BCE to 135 CE: A Study of Second Temple Judaism* (Wilmington, DE: Glazier, 1980), 162–166; Michael Rostovtzeff, *Social and Economic History of the Roman Empire*, 2nd ed. (Oxford, UK: Clarendon, 1957),

I, 270, 663; Douglas Edwards, "The Socioeconomic and Cultural Ethos of the Lower Galilee in the First Century: Implications for the Nascent Jesus Movement," ed. Lee Levine, in *The Galilee in Late Antiquity* (New York: Jewish Theological Seminary of America, 1992), 55–65; Gerhard Lenski, *Power and Privilege: A Theory of Social Stratification* (New York: McGraw-Hill, 1966), 280–281; S. Safrai and M. Stern, ed., *The Jewish People in the First Century: Historical Geography, Political History, Social Cultural and Religious Life and Institution*, Vol 1. (Assen: Van Corcum, 1974), 259–261; and Schottroff and Stegemann, *Jesus and the Hope of the Poor*.

9. Hanson and Oakman, "*Palestine*," 106.
10. To "demand back" something on loan (*apaiteō*) appears only here and in 6:30 in the New Testament
11. Pilgrim's *Good News to the Poor* was an early work on Luke and economics. He argues that this teaching, grounded in traditional wisdom images, is not an eschatological warning about the end of the age but practical advice about the endemic danger of wealth in everyday life.
12. Luke 12:22–34 consists of mostly Q material (Matt 6:19–21, 25–34).
13. The noun *trophēs* (food or nourishment) appears only here in Luke, but seven times in Acts, including the celebration of communal meals in the house churches of Pentecost (Acts 2:46; epilogue, iii). Of particular interest is Paul's argument against the fetishizing of his healing ministry in Lystra by appealing to the Sabbath Economics witness of Creation: "You should turn from these vain things to a living God who made heaven and earth and the sea and all that is in them . . . and gave you rains and fruitful seasons from heaven, satisfying your hearts with food (*trophēs)* and gladness" (Acts 14:15–17).
14. See Rebecca Gould, "Book of Nature," in *Encyclopedia of Religion and Nature*, ed. Bron Taylor (New York: Continuum, 2005), 210–211, at http://www.religionandnature.com/ern/sample/Gould--BookNature.pdf.
15. Coined by Thomas More in the early sixteenth century, "utopia" is often used derisively in modernity for an ideal world that does not—indeed cannot—exist. More's book by that name was published a mere quarter century after Europeans' first encounter with Turtle Island, where the old cosmology of grace was still intact, but which colonization commenced destroying through extraction, enslavement, and genocide. For a discussion of the ambiguities in More's work see https://en.wikipedia.org/wiki/Utopia_(book).
16. Richard Dillon, "Ravens, Lilies, and the Kingdom of God (Matthew 6:25–33/ Luke 12:22–31)," *Catholic Biblical Quarterly* 53, no. 4 (1991): 605, 620.
17. Raven (*korax*) is only here in the New Testament. In the LXX, a raven is sent out by Noah (Gen 8:7); the species is included in a list of unclean birds (Deut 14:14); and in prophetic oracles, ravens are among the creatures who will reinhabit the decaying built environment of vanquished empire (Isa 34:11; Zep 2:14).
18. At https://en.wikipedia.org/wiki/Common_raven.
19. Working with an impressively broad range of media, Ted served for many years as resident artist for his United Methodist Iowa Conference and has often collaborated with us at conferences and in publications. I encourage you to learn

more about his spectacular work, and peruse many more images, at www.tedlyddonhatten.com.

20. Though this phrase with the genitive can be (and usually is) read through a lens of anthropocentric hierarchy, the verb is used elsewhere by Paul to connote difference, not superiority (see 1 Cor 15:41, Gal 2:6).
21. Two examples must suffice. Consuming the blood of *any* living thing, human or animal, was taboo in the Noahic covenant (Gen 9). Psalm 104 beautifully places humans alongside all other living things in a benevolent Creation. Our ecological crisis has animated long overdue theologies of creatureliness. An example is Richard Bauckham, *The Bible and Ecology: Rediscovering the Community of Creation* (Waco, TX: Baylor University Press, 2010). An engaging new offering is our friend Laurel Dykstra's *Wildlife Congregations: A Priest's Year of Gaggles, Colonies and Murders by the Salish Sea* (Surrey, BC: Hancock House, 2023): Laurel is in British Columbia (https://www.salalandcedar.com/) and works with the Wild Church movement (https://www.wildchurchnetwork.com/).
22. *Krinon* (Matt 6:28), only here in the New Testament. The word appears in three ways in the Hebrew Bible: as Temple decoration, as prophetic symbol of beauty and renewed life (Hos 14:6; Isa 35:1), and eight times in the flowery Song of Songs. Note the lily included on the back of this book cover as part of Lyddon Hatten's composition!
23. See https://www.worldwildlife.org/species/directory?direction=desc&sort=extinction_status.
24. On this, see the anthropological work of Sahlins, *Stone Age Economics*; Shepard, *Coming Home to the Pleistocene*; Gowdy, *Limited Wants, Unlimited Means*; and Scott, *Against the Grain*.
25. Significantly, the verb *eudokēsen* is used elsewhere in the gospels only in relation to God's delight in "the only Son" (e.g., Matt 3:17; 17:5; Mark 1:11 // Luke 3:22).
26. The verb *chrēzō* emphasizes necessity. In 11:8 it is used in the context of village mutual aid (see also Rom 16:2).
27. The phrase "little flock" (*to micron poimnion*) is a double diminutive, also used by Paul in Acts 20:28–29, and in 1 Pt 5:1–2. The image captured the extreme minority status of the early Jesus movement. Unlike women, males were socialized to compete publicly for honor and prestige. Catholic Worker writer and activist Jeff Dietrich brought to my attention the tension in Luke between earthly fathers and the "heavenly Father." Though the former can imperfectly mirror the divine gift-economy toward their children (11:11–13), family relationships are not reliable when it comes to discipleship (12:53, 14:26). The "fathers of the nation," meanwhile, are forever killing the prophets (11:47f, see 6:23, 26).
28. "Giving alms" (see Matt 6:2–4) appears also in the curious exhortation of Luke 11:41, but Zerwick and Grosvenor note "there is a possibility of a mistranslation, for the same Aramaic word may mean 'purify' as well as 'give alms' . . ." Thus the text would read "'purify that which is inside and . . .', as Matt 23:26 seems to have understood the saying" (Zerwick and Grosvenor, *Grammatical*, 226. In Acts almsgiving is a highly respected practice (9:36; 10:32–34; 10:31; 24:17). An episode

worth noting is the first apostolic healing, which comes on the heels of the first description of the Pentecostal community of goods (Acts 2:43–47). Peter says to a disabled beggar at the Temple: "I have no silver and gold, but I give you what I have; in the name of Jesus Christ of Nazareth, walk" (Acts 3:6).

29. "Does not fail" (*anakleiptos*) appears only here in the New Testament (compare Matt 6:19–21).
30. Jesus's brother James employs this very image in his diatribe against affluenza:

> Come now, you rich, weep and wail for the miseries that are coming to you. Your riches have rotted, and your clothes are moth-eaten. Your gold and silver have rusted, and their rust will be evidence against you, and it will eat your flesh like fire. You have laid up treasure (*ethēaurisate*) for the last days. Listen! The wages of the laborers who mowed your fields, which you kept back by fraud, cry out, and the cries of the harvesters have reached the ears of the Lord of hosts. You have lived on the earth in luxury and in pleasure; you have fattened your hearts on a day of slaughter (Jas 5:1–5).

31. See I Thessalonians 5:2–4; 2 Peter 3:10; Revelation 3:3; 16:15. Luke ends his Little Apocalypse with a similar call to vigilance (21:34-36 // Mark 13:34–37 // Matt 24:42–43). This story, so familiar to Jesus's audience of workers, is followed by similar scenario (12:42–48), which emphasizes the harshness of life for servants tasked with protecting the master's possessions (*huparchousin*, 12:44), who endure beatings *for acting like the master* (12:45). Luke seems to leave it to disciples to discern whether this "parable" is meant for us (12:41)!
32. Image at: www.researchgate.net/figure/Hazel-Hendersons-layer-cake-with-icing_fig1_29457315. See explication at: http://avery.wellesley.edu/Economics/jmatthaei/transformationcentral/valuingthedevalued/valuedevaluedcake.html. See Hazel Henderson, "Valuing Love Economies," (WSIM), 4 June 2021, at https://www.ethicalmarkets.com/valuing-love-economies-by-hazel-henderson. Learn more about Henderson's work and legacy at https://hazelhenderson.com/the-love-economy/.
33. See a summary of this practice at https://www.tenthacrefarm.com/what-do-you-see-how-to-use-the-power-of-observation-in-permaculture-site-design/.

CHAPTER NINE

1. Quoted in Plutarch's "On Love of Wealth," 524b, trans. Phillip H. De Lacy and Benedict Einarson; found at Michael Gilleland, "Avarice and Dropsy," https://laudatortemporisacti.blogspot.com/2004/09/avarice-and-dropsy.html.
2. The Greek noun comes from *kûros* ("supremacy"), from Proto-Indo-European ḱewh$_1$- ("to swell, spread out, be strong, prevail," https://en.wiktionary.org/wiki/κύριος). *Kurios* is first a sociological term in the New Testament; its transposition into a theological title was the early church's polemical renunciation of Caesar's moniker. Luke's term *oikodespotes* (usually translated "householder," e.g., 12:39; 13:35; 14:21) is generally synonymous.

3. Luke often "provides his readers with certain political notices pertaining to empire history" (Cassidy, *Politics and Society*, 14). This can be as broad as listing rulers during the time of John and Jesus (3:1–2); as notorious as Quirinius's census (2:1–3), which provoked a Judean rebellion (see Acts 5:37); as polemical as alluding to how Herod Antipas curried the favor of Tiberius (19:12); or as local as the two incidents noted in this passage. Pilate's massacre of Galileans—perhaps during a Passover pilgrimage, hence the reference to "their sacrifices" (13:1)—could refer to any number of skirmishes between Roman authorities and Judean dissidents during the first century CE, many of which were documented by Josephus. Urban construction accidents (13:4) were common, given the notorious working conditions and "code violations" in the many Herodian building projects. The two incidents might be connected if the Tower of Siloam was part of Roman aqueduct construction, since Josephus reports that Pilate killed a group of Jews protesting his seizure of Temple funds to pay for imperial waterworks projects in Jerusalem; see Yoder, *Politics of Jesus*, 43–47; 90–93. Jesus's emphatic refrain—"I tell you, unless you repent, you will all perish as they did" (13:3, 5)—implies that unless his listeners defected from this system, they too would "perish" (*apollumi*) from its oppressions (Luke uses this verb far more frequently than any other New Testament writer).
4. Hanson and Oakman, *Palestine*, 120. Malina and Rohrbaugh give more context: "In Roman law a magistrate could grant a creditor one of two choices: he could either force his debtor to work until the debt was paid off or have him put in prison for ransom, that is, to extort the debt payment. In the latter case, the expectation was that relatives would either sell his land to pay the debt or bail him out themselves. The 'cent' (*lepton)* was the smallest coin in use in first-century Palestine" (*Social Science*, 362).
5. "Division" (*diamerismos*, a generic mass noun of the verb *diamerizō*) appears only here in the New Testament. The verb is more important to Luke than to any other writer; as noted previously, he uses it to describe the sharing of the cup at the Last Supper (22:17) and the distribution of tongues *and property* at Pentecost (Acts 2:2, 45; see epilogue, i, iii).
6. The notion of a *kairos* moment is scattered throughout Luke's narrative: it is a time or season of believing or falling away (8:13b); of "visitation" (19:44); of being led astray (21:8); of divine promises fulfilled (1:20); and of the Gentiles (21:24). Its use in 12:56 sets up for 13:1: "At that very moment (*kairō*). . ."
7. Pieter Botha, "Health and Healing in New Testament Times: Historical Understanding and the Health Care Debate" *Health SA Gosondheid* 1, no. 2 (1996), 10.
8. For a detailed exploration of these issues, see John Pilch, "Understanding Biblical Healing: Selecting the Appropriate Model." *Biblical Theology Bulletin* 18, no. 2 (1988): 60–66.
9. The 2020 murder of George Floyd by Minneapolis police was a *kairos* moment for the US, forcing many to acknowledge for the first time how the political bodies of Black citizens are perceived and treated as "dangerous other" by a white majority body politic's policing culture. I recommend these orienting books: W. E. B. Du Bois, *The Souls of Black Folk: Essays and Sketches* (Chicago: A. G. McClurg, 1903); Eric Wolf, *Europe and the People without History* (Berkeley: University of

California Press, 1982); Toni Morrison, *The Origin of Others* (Cambridge, MA: Harvard University Press, 2017); Khalil Gibran Muhammad, *The Condemnation of Blackness: Race, Crime, and the Making of Modern Urban America* (Cambridge, MA: Harvard University Press, 2019).

10. See the final chapter of Fanon's classic work *The Wretched of the Earth* (New York: Grove Press, 1961).
11. Mary Douglas, *Natural Symbols: Explorations in Cosmology* (New York: Vintage Books, 1973), 112.
12. Douglas, *Natural Symbols*, 93.
13. "In symbiotic anatomy, a body part has its own relationship with other body parts, the person they are all attached to, and other entities in the world. . . . The Canaanites attributed disease and illness to the degradation of relationships. This network of relationships is navigated by a system of contracts and law codes as well as patronage. . . . If illness, disease, and trauma signal a break down in social relationships, then restoration of health allows a person and the anatomy to reintegrate with the human community" (Laura Zucconi, "Ancient Near Eastern and Mediterranean Medicine," *The Bible and Interpretation*, January 2020, at https://bibleinterp.arizona.edu/articles/ancient-near-eastern-and-mediterranean-medicine).
14. Botha, "Health and Healing," 5.
15. In both cases, Luke follows Mark's wording exactly: *mē katharisai* ("you can declare me clean," Mark 1:41 // Luke 5:12) and "your sins are forgiven" (Mark 2:5 // Luke 5:20). See my commentary on Mark's twinned episodes in the context of the prevailing purity and debt codes (Myers, *Strong Man*, 69–77; 143–155). Luke intensifies Mark's portrait of Jesus as unlicensed practitioner by placing this sequence right after the unauthorized large harvest of fish (5:1–11).
16. J. D. Derrett, "Positive Perspectives on Two Lucan Miracles," *Downside Review* 104, no. 357 (1986): 272.
17. Natalie Houghtby-Haddon, *Changed Imagination, Changed Obedience: Social Change, Social Imagination, and the Bent-Over Woman in the Gospel of Luke* (Eugene, OR: Pickwick Publications, 2011).
18. Oakman, *Peasants*, 217.
19. "You have been set free" (perfect passive) represents the "divine passive," used also in Jesus's pronouncement to the anointing woman (7:48). In Luke, *apoluo* can connote a legal pardon (6:37), divorce (16:18) or release from custody (23:16–25; particularly ubiquitous in his story of the early church, Acts 4:21, 23; 5:41; 16:35–36; 17:9; 23:22; 26:32; 28:18)! The same verb is also used in 14:4, the twinned healing.
20. Luke's other use of *anorthoō* refers to the raising of the destroyed Temple (Acts 15:13); it only appears elsewhere in Hebrews 12:12.
21. Lowery, *Sabbath and Jubilee*, 134–135.
22. The two verbs in 21:28 tell the tale: *anakuptōo* is also what the woman does here (13:11); *apolutrōosis* ("redemption," only here in the Gospels) means to buy back someone trapped in debt.
23. Willi Braun argues that 14:1–6 is "best understood as a *chreia* that has been expanded into a longer narrative episode" (*Feasting and Social Rhetoric in Luke 14*, Society for New Testament Studies Monograph Series 85, Cambridge: Cambridge

University Press, 1995), 158. A *chreia* is a "concise statement or action . . . [that is] the basis for an expanded argument" that follows (*Feasting*, 11).

24. Stuart Love, "The Man with Dropsy." *Leaven* 6, no. 3 (1998): 137. This phrase is an interesting use of both *aphietai* ("to be left," but also "forgiven" or "released") and *erēmos* ("desolate," but also "wilderness"). It anticipates Jesus's longer lament over Jerusalem in 19:41–44—right after people have chanted "Blessed the One coming in the name of the Lord" (19:38 = 13:35b).
25. See https://library.leeds.ac.uk/special-collections/collection/2156; the older medical text is found at https://www.piratesurgeon.com/pages/surgeon_pages/dropsy_scarification_and_trocar1.htm.
26. Michael Gilleland, "Avarice and Dropsy," (2004) at: https://laudatortemporis-acti.blogspot.com/2004/09/avarice-and-dropsy.html, which gives full references. Braun, *Feasting* also notes many of the same literary traditions.
27. These examples confirm a symbolic correlation between body and society. Love focuses on purity issues in reading this story, but agrees (following Braun) that "though Luke makes no explicit connection between dropsy and covetousness, the metaphorical meaning was so extensive in Greco-Roman literature that it is reasonable to assume 'that it was familiar both to the author and to the readers of Luke's gospel'" (Love, *Dropsy*, 140).
28. The RSV decided in favor of the variant reading "ass or an ox" (obviously under the influence of 13:15), while the NRSV changed it (back to the KJV) "child or an ox." The latter would be an escalation of the former's logic. Drowning in a well could be a symbolic allusion to the watery experience of dropsy.
29. Braun, *Feasting*, 42.
30. Braun (*Feasting*, 134) analyzes the banquet narrative as Luke's "performance of a traditional 'gist', that is, a Lukan textualization of a story he knew in general form from an older repertoire." A similar tale is found in the Gospel of Thomas 64 (see it and commentary at www.earlychristianwritings.com/thomas/gospelthomas64.html).
31. Neyrey, *Social World*, 365.
32. Braun, *Feasting*, 55. Pliny the Younger describes (disapprovingly) a Roman dinner at which he was guest, where three different types of food and drink were served to different guests based on social position (see Malina and Rohrbaugh, *Social Science*, 136, 191).
33. It is, however, a key New Testament conviction. Paul argues that Jesus modeled the notion that the world can renew only from the bottom up (Phl 2:3–7) and characterizes his apostolic rank as "least/last" (*eschatous*; 1 Cor 4:9).
34. In economic anthropology, this is called "balanced reciprocity." See basic definitions at https://anthropology4u.com/economic-anthropology-the-three-forms-of-economic-exchange/.
35. The only noun on this list not repeated elsewhere, and which occurs only here in the New Testament, is *anapeiros*, unfortunately translated as "maimed" or "crippled." It is unclear whether it is synonymous with the noun *chulōs*, which I have translated "disabled"; this term occurs more often, three times in Lukan Gospel "lists" as well as in three episodes in Acts that clearly describe physical disability (Acts 3:2; 8:7; 14:8).

36. Conversely, in Luke, some who Jesus liberates go on to exhibit dramatic agency in the discipleship community, Mary Magdalene being a notable example (see 8:2; 24:10).
37. The disability rights movement, in which I've been involved since college, taught me how the political body of someone in a wheelchair mirrors the discriminations of the body politic. Reading bodies as "maps" of social diseases is a strategy employed here precisely in order to mitigate the ableist bias that many Gospel healing accounts appear to perpetuate. This indicates one of many ways that ancient healing stories pose formidable challenges to hermeneutics, exegesis, and the ethics of reading for us moderns. Fortunately, recent disability-critical readings of Scripture are tackling these challenges (even if some do not take into sufficient account the differences between modern biomedical and ancient socio-symbolic anthropologies). See, e.g., the very different approaches to Luke of Kathy McReynolds, "The Gospel of Luke: A Framework for a Theology of Disability," *Christian Education Journal* (2016) 13, no. 1: 169–178; J. T. Carroll, "Disability and Dis-ease: Body, Restoration, and Ethics of Reading in Luke's Gospel," in *Anatomies of the Gospels and Beyond*, ed. M. Parsons, E.S. Malbon and P. Anderson (Leiden: Brill, 2018); James Metzger, "Disability and the Marginalisation of God in the Parable of the Snubbed Host (Luke 14.15–24)," *The Bible and Critical Theory* 6, no. 2 (2010): 23.1–23.15; Verity Link, *The Gospel of Puke: A Disabled Person's Response to Luke's Gospel* (London: Angry Dog, 2020). An evangelical contribution is Andrew Draper, Jody Michele, and Andrea Mae, *Disabling Leadership: A Practical Theology for the Broken Body of Christ* (Downers Grove, IL: InterVarsity Press, 2023).
38. *Antapodidomi* in both verbal and nominal form is used in the LXX and New Testament both in a positive sense, but also as divine vengeance or "consequences" (e.g., Rom 12:19; 2 Thes 1:6; Heb 10:30). The last two *makarioi* in Luke are uttered by misguided people: here in 14:15 and again in 23:29. "Resurrection of the just" is a unique phrase in the New Testament (though see Acts 24:15), again indicating Luke's interest in equity.
39. Bailey, *Poet and Peasant*, 92. See www.kennethbailey.net/ for helpful resources on Jesus's Mediterranean cultural context, including a series of informative videos.
40. According to Malina and Rohrbaugh, this also allowed guests to determine "who was coming and whether all had been done properly"—indicating the competitive nature of these scenarios (*Social Science*, 365).
41. Bailey, *Poet and Peasant*, 96.
42. Malina and Rohrbaugh, *Social Science*, 365.
43. A *plateia* was a town's main thoroughfare, which often served as a sort of public plaza; see 10:10; 13:26; Acts 5:15.
44. Braun, *Feasting*, 94. A *phragmos* was a hedge fence usually around a field (as in Matt 21:33; Mark 12:1), often providing shelter for unhoused people.
45. This verb is unfortunately still associated with evangelist C. H. Spurgeon's famous mid-nineteenth-century sermon that legitimated forced conversion (see it at https://www.spurgeon.org/resource-library/sermons/compel-them-to-come-in/#flipbook/). This logic of "anything to save a soul" was appropriated by European

missionaries for colonizing purposes, with genocidal results around the world (see Enns and Myers, *Haunted Histories*, 131–140).

46. Joachim Jeremias notes that a version of this parable in the Gospel of Thomas "ends with the sentence, 'Tradesman and merchants shall not enter the places of my Father. . .' convey[ing] the idea of a sharp attack on the rich. This attitude of class-consciousness is to some extent in line with that of Luke in this parable." See Jeremias, *The Parables of Jesus*, 2nd revised ed. (New York: Charles Scribner's Sons, 1972), 44–45.
47. Braun, *Feasting*, 174.
48. See the synopsis at https://www.blackpast.org/african-american-history/greensboro-sit-ins-1960/. This legacy inspired the first of our series of Word and World schools at the intersection between faith and justice in 2002, curated by a national collaborative of which I was part (see http://www.wordandworld.org/2001-greensboro.html). That week in Greensboro was an important pilgrimage for me, hosted by mentors Joyce and Nelson Johnson (learn about them at https://belovedcommunitycenter.org/).

CHAPTER TEN

1. Eugene Kamenka, "Gemeinschaft and Gesellschaft," *Political Science*, 17, no. 1 (1965), 3.
2. Ferdinand Tönnies, *Community and Society*, trans. Charles P. Loomis (Mineola, NY: Dover Publications, 2011).
3. Karl Polanyi, *The Great Transformation: The Political and Economic Origins of Our Times*, 2nd ed. (Boston: Beacon Press, 2001).
4. These ideas were briefly summarized in the introduction, v. See Berry, "Two Economies," and Henderson, https://hazelhenderson.com/the-love-economy/ (summarized in 8B). Daniel Kemmis parsed these ideas further by centering economic geography in *Community and the Politics of Place* (Norman: University of Oklahoma Press, 1992), contrasting a "totally placeless, abstract market" with a "place-centered market offering nurture and support for locally owned enterprises," 95.
5. See 1:71; 6:22, 27; 21:17. Once it refers to how citizens feel about their king (19:14).
6. In every other appearance in the New Testament, *apotassō* connotes "saying farewell" or "taking leave of" (Mark 6:46; Luke 9:61; 2 Cor 2:13). Especially when referring to *huparchonton* it means renouncing private control over (12B).
7. Luke is citing Mark (Mark 9:50); see my comments on salt symbolism in Myers, *Strong Man*, 264.
8. Jo Bailey Wells, "Squandering and Scattering," Sunday's Coming (*The Christian Century*) September 17, 2007, https://www.christiancentury.org/blogs/archive/2007-09/squandering-and-scattering.
9. This is similar to a later sequence which also features "two rich men and a beggar" (see chapter 12):

   18:18–30: ". . .for he was very rich" (18:23): Ruler's rejection of the call to discipleship

   18:31–34: Teaching on fate of the Human One

   18:35–43 Healing a blind beggar outside Jericho

   19:1–9: ". . .he was a chief tax collector and was rich" (19:2): Zacchaeus's embrace of discipleship

Both sequences are key to Luke's economic theology. This section is an edited version of Myers, "From Capital to Community: Discipleship as Defection in Jesus's Parable about a 'Manager of Injustice' (Luke 16:1–13)" in Zoe Bennett and David Gowler, *Radical Christian Voices & Practices: Essays in Honour of Christopher Rowland* (Oxford: Oxford University Press, 2012), 51–67.

10. Ben Witherington, *Conflict and Community in Corinth: A Socio-rhetorical Commentary on 1 and 2 Corinthians* (Grand Rapids, MI: Eerdmans, 1995), 22–24.
11. Hanson and Oakman, *Palestine*, 70–86.
12. Herzog, *Subversive Speech*, 240–241. Herzog has done substantial analysis of this parable, as well as assessment of its recent history of interpretation. He estimates the value of such amounts might range between one and three thousand *denarii*.
13. Bailey, *Poet and Peasant*, 92–93; Malina and Rohrbaugh, *Social Science*, 375.
14. Lenski, *Power*, 243–245.
15. Malina and Rohrbaugh, *Social Science*, 373–374.
16. Herzog, *Subversive Speech*, 244. For his concise overview of the retainer class in a great household, see p. 157.
17. W. Bauer, W. Arndt, and F. Gingrich, *A Greek-English Lexicon of the New Testament and Other Early Christian Literature* (Chicago, IL: University of Chicago Press, 1957), 180.
18. Herzog, *Subversive Speech*, 242.
19. The Greek *chreopheiletēs* (debtors) appears only here and in 7:41 in the New Testament That earlier story at Simon's also is the only other place in Luke where amounts owed are specified—in both cases large amounts. These resonances strengthen my thesis that these are keystone stories for Luke's overall theme.
20. Herzog, *Subversive Speech*, 240, 246.
21. The phrase *ton oikonomon tēs adikias* is normally translated "unjust steward," rendering the genitive noun as an adjective. However, in 13:27, *hoi ergatai tēs adkikias* (same construction) is translated "workers of iniquity," as in Acts 1:18; 8:23 and other places in the New Testament. So with Herzog, I believe "manager of injustice," like "mammon of injustice" in 16:9, is a better rendering, given the parable's assumption that it is the *system* that is unjust.
22. The adverb *phronimōs* appears only here in the New Testament, though it often appears as an adjective (*phronimos*). Luke may be comparing the master's commendation to Gen 41:33, 39, where Joseph is appointed by Pharaoh as a "shrewd" (LXX, *phronimos)* manager over all the financial dealings of imperial Egypt (after putting the idea in the ruler's head by interpreting his dream!) Luke refers to an *oikonomos ho phronimos* in 12:42, also in relation to a commendation by a master.
23. Herzog, *Subversive Speech*, 250–252.
24. Gestures of debt-amnesty by rulers or patrons were always a politically motivated strategy of securing loyalty from their clients; they were ritually followed by public praise from the beneficiaries. A wry contemporary analogy is narrated in a scene at the end of the film *Ocean's Thirteen* (dir. Steven Soderbergh, 2007), where master thief Danny Ocean refuses to deliver to casino owner Terry Benedict his cut of the loot because Benedict staked him to the job but then tried to double-cross him. Instead, Danny publicly donates Terry's cut to charity; in the next scene, Benedict is on the *Oprah Winfrey Show* receiving Oprah's praise for his amazing generosity.

25. *Phronimōteroi* is comparative. Canadian New Testament scholar William Richards translates it "are more astute," in his helpful and lively translation of all L material identified by Eusebius of Caesarea (*"To a Friend of God": The Special Material of Luke's Gospel,* Saskatoon, unpublished manuscript, 2015). Richards has been a great friend and support to this project over many years.
26. *Mamōnās,* only in the New Testament here and Matthew 6:24, does not appear in the Hebrew Bible, but does in later Jewish writings. Possibly an Aramaic term, in the Mishnah it connotes property, often as contrasted with life. In the Targum it is an epithet for "bad money": dishonest gain, profit made through exploitation, spoiling a neighbor's property, or even a bribe. "He destroys his house who gathers the mammon of injustice" (*Targ Prov* 15:27). For a technical discussion see Scott Callaham, "Mammon," video presentation, Daily Dose of Aramaic (Jan 5, 2024), Daily Dose Ministry, https://dailydoseofaramaic.com/?s=mammon.
27. The verb *ekleipō* (whence comes our word "eclipse") appears only here, in Luke 22:32 and Heb 1:12. The conclusion of Revelation envisions such an eternal *skēnē* (Rev 21:2), reiterated in the beautiful phrase "Look! God is tenting with humans" (*skēnoō*; see also John 1:14).
28. Gerhard Kittel and Gerhard Friedrich, *Theological Dictionary of the New Testament, IV* (Grand Rapids, MI: Eerdmans, 1967), 388–389, contends that *mamōnās* was "used in rabbinic writing as a term for a deposit or a 'safebox' in which personal or household treasures were held."
29. This quote is legendary among those who knew Jordan; I first heard it from my mentor Ladon Sheats, who was a disciple of Clarence's. Frustratingly, I cannot find it in print or online—though I can *hear* it in the telling!
30. Wendell Berry, *Home Economics* (San Francisco: Northpoint Press, 1987), 74.
31. It is with some trepidation that I allude here to the complicated philosophical discourse of "historical trialectics" (see, e.g., https://wiki.p2pfoundation.net/Trialectics), which has been defined by Mark Whitaker as "a novel synthesis for understanding the origins of social stratification, conflict, cooperation, inequality processes or equality processes historically worldwide" (in his talk at https://www.youtube.com/watch?v=D23aD5sIbxc).
32. Catholic Worker Brian Terrell gives context and history to this, Day's most famous tagline, emphasizing that she was lamenting specifically the *church's* acceptance of the status quo; see https://www.ncronline.org/news/people/dorothy-days-filthy-rotten-system-likely-wasnt-hers-all.
33. For a recent reflection on these issues that uses this parable as a springboard, see Miguel Escobar, *The Unjust Steward: Wealth, Poverty, and the Church Today* (Cincinnati, OH: Forward Movement, 2022).
34. For a compelling and instructive portrait of racist and displacing redevelopment in Charlotte, NC, over the span of a century, see Greg Jarrell, *Our Trespasses: White Churches and the Taking of American Neighborhoods* (Minneapolis, MN: Fortress Press, 2024).

CHAPTER ELEVEN

1. See an image of his 1929 article at https://babel.hathitrust.org/cgi/pt?id=mdp.39015020076041&seq=339.
2. Herzog, *Subversive Speech*, 114–130. Herzog critiques how an earlier generation of scholarship tended to treat Luke 16:19–31 as two relatively separate parts. He also laments how they gave precedence to the text's teaching about the importance of Torah and Nevi'im over its stark portrait of disparity, a typical bourgeois strategy of eclipsing sociology with theology. Herzog's excellent treatment of the tale replaces it in social context and restores its bite.
3. Stegemann and Schottroff believe this story comes from the earliest stratum of the Jesus tradition, and note Egyptian tales that exhibit interesting similarities (*Hope of the Poor*, 24–25).
4. See Walter Scheidel and Steven J. Friesen, "The Size of the Economy and the Distribution of Income in the Roman Empire," *The Journal of Roman Studies* 99 (2009), 61–91. Their work has been applied to first-century Galilee by Sakari Häkkinen, "Poverty in the First-century Galilee," *HTS Teologiese Studies/Theological Studies* 72, no. 4 (Sept 2016), http://www.scielo.org.za/scielo.php?script=sci_arttext&pid=S0259-94222016000400046.
5. For contemporary numbers see https://en.wikipedia.org/wiki/Wealth_inequality_in_the_United_States and https://www.statista.com/chart/19635/wealth-distribution-percentiles-in-the-us/.
6. Greg Jarrell's *Our Trespasses*, a social history of urban redevelopment in Charlotte, North Carolina, gives a compelling portrait of how this social architecture and its hauntings persist, and the complicity of white churches.
7. To see great examples of contemporary caricaturing, see Jeff MacNelly's political cartoons from the *Chicago Tribune*, archived at http://www.jeff-macnelly.com/jeff-macnelly-pulitzer.htm.
8. Latin *dives* means "rich man," related to *divus* ("divine"), originally meaning "favored by the gods"; a synonym was *opulentus*.
9. Herzog, *Subversive Speech*, 121.
10. Herzog, *Subversive Speech*, 118.
11. John Chow, "Patronage in Roman Corinth," in *Paul and Empire: Religion and Power in Roman Imperial Society*, edited by Richard Horsley (London: Bloomsbury Academic, 1997), 123. Chow notes how Roman writer Juvenal (roughly contemporary with Luke) ridicules such "generosity" in *Satires*, 1.127.146, at https://www.poetryintranslation.com/PITBR/Latin/JuvenalSatires1.php. See also https://penelope.uchicago.edu/Thayer/E/Roman/Texts/secondary/SMIGRA*/Sportula.html.
12. Part of the cartoon is the fact that, as Herzog says, "it is unlikely that Lazarus would have been allowed to camp out in the wealthy district of the city. He would most likely have been cleared out when the gates separating the elite quarter from other, poorer areas were closed. Once again the purpose of the codification is to bring together figures who were normally kept apart." Herzog, *Subversive Speech*, 120.

13. See a discussion of the origins of this phrase at https://en.wikipedia.org/wiki/Bosom_of_Abraham. Nineteenth-century enslaved African American people, who shared Lazarus's social degradation but embraced Gospel visions of redemption, preserved this beautiful vision in the venerable spiritual "Rocka My Soul" (https://en.wikipedia.org/wiki/Bosom_of_Abraham_(song)). See context and commentary in Cone, *Spirituals*, 53–96.
14. Herzog, *Subversive Speech*, 122. Though Luke uses the Greek vernacular *hadēs*, this portrait resembles more the Jewish tradition of Sheol. Alan E. Bernstein, *The Formation of Hell: Death and Retribution in the Ancient and Early Christian Worlds* (Ithaca, NY: Cornell University Press, 1993), 242, comments: "By stressing the finality of death, Abraham . . . emphasizes the authority and regularity of the Jewish tradition as compared to the more haphazard appearances of the dead in the larger Mediterranean culture." But the influence of Greek lessons about the afterlife are present here as well: "Plato allowed victims comfort on the banks of the Acherusian Lake and the authority to forgive or not to forgive their offenders" (Bernstein, *Formation*, 244).
15. The verb *ekballō* appears often in the Gospels with multiple connotations that in Luke include: spurning (4:29; 6:22; 20:12, 15), exorcism (9:40; 11:14–20), and driving moneychangers from the Temple (19:45).
16. *The Matrix*, dir. by the Wachowskis, 1999.
17. Herzog, *Subversive Parables*, 128.
18. See our definition of restorative justice in Enns and Myers, *Ambassadors II*, xiii, and Enns's profiles of practitioners there (45–149). We often wonder whether the traditional Catholic notion of purgatory needs reconsideration by Protestants as an alternative to the persistent idea of eternally retributive "fires of hell." A liminal, temporary state of afterlife *could* be understood as a period in which those implicated in oppression (which to different degrees includes all of us) must face the testimonies of those who were harmed—a process for making things right and healing both victims and offenders. If this has any credence, it might help make sense of the "flames" image in 16:24. Dives is in "agony," but *odunaō* (only used by Luke in the New Testament) is more associated with anxiety (2:48) or sorrow (Acts 20:38) than retribution, suggesting the pain of remorse. Elaine has worked with offenders in the criminal justice system who told her that facing their victims was "like walking through a fire, the hardest thing they've ever done." For an important sociological psychology of the "implicated subject" see Michael Rothberg, *The Implicated Subject: Beyond Victims and Perpetrators* (Palo Alto, CA: Stanford University Press, 2019).
19. Herzog, *Subversive Parables*, 126.
20. On this, see https://www.r2hub.org/library/emotional-labor-and-antiracism-work.
21. This is a rare place where I disagree with Herzog, who sets this verse aside as Lukan editorializing. We take different approaches: he comments on a hypothesized, reconstructed "original" parable, while I work with the canonical text as a literary whole. The verb *anistēmi* can mean many forms of rising up; in 8:55 and 9:8 it is used to mean rising from death, and in 9:22; 18:33; 24:7, 46 specifically Jesus's resurrection.

22. The verb *peithō* is key in Luke's narrative of Paul's evangelization in Acts, used more than a dozen times, especially regarding the apostle's arguments from "Moses and the prophets" (Acts 28:23).
23. Herzog, *Subversive Parables*, 130.
24. See two stunning examples: from the eleventh century (at https://artandtheology.org/2019/09/24/dives-and-lazarus-artful-devotion/; and the sixteenth century (https://www.museodelprado.es/en/the-collection/art-work/lazarus-and-dives/449efb74-3344-4d5d-97ff-e6fb985dedb9). Find dozens of other images at https://commons.wikimedia.org/wiki/Category:Paintings_of_Lazarus_and_Dives.

CHAPTER TWELVE

1. *Telling the Truth: The Gospel as Tragedy, Comedy, and Fairy Tale* (San Francisco: Harper & Row, 1977), 63.
2. As noted several times in this book, the verb to forgive (*aphiēmi*) is at the heart of the Jubilee semantics of "release" in Luke. "Be on your guard" is also a warning (as *prosechō* is also used in 12:1; 20:46; 21:34). These two verses abbreviate Matthew's longer teaching about an ecclesial restorative justice process; for extended commentary on that text see Myers and Enns, *Ambassadors of Reconciliation I,* 49–81.
3. The noun *pistis* is best rendered "trust." In Luke it often describes marginalized, outcast and diseased persons who embrace Jesus's healing (5:20; 7:9, 50; 8:48; 17:19; 18:42), whereas trust is what disciples are characterized as lacking (8:25; 22:32 and here). Though this is a Q tradition, the verb "be uprooted" (*ekrizoō*) isn't used by Matthew (see Matt 17:20); it does, however, appear in a related verse ("Every plant which my heavenly Father has not planted will be rooted up," Matt 15:13).
4. See Malina and Rohrbaugh, *Social Science*, 378–79. They also suggest that the verb *achreios* is better translated "We are slaves who are owed nothing" (17:10).
5. *Social Science*, 379.
6. Zerwick and Grosvenor, *Grammatical*, 251–252. *Entos* is only here and Matt 23:26 in the New Testament
7. The noun *aetos* here likely alludes to "the silver eagle mounted on a pole carried as a military standard... of the legion" (Hanson and Oakman, *Palestine*, 168).
8. Herzog, *Subversive Speech*, 221. Herzog overviews the politics of a typical Palestinian judiciary in the first century, which may have been either a local or regional court. He wonders why there was just the one judge for this case rather than three (as per Torah); and whether the widow had not gotten a hearing "because she did *not* bribe the judge" (220–24).
9. "Legal opponent" (*antidikos*) appears only three other times in the New Testament: once in 12:58 (// Matt 5:35), a vignette about the cruel court system of the day, the other referring to the Devil-as-Adversary (1 Pet 5:8).
10. Malina and Rohrbaugh, *Social Science*, 397.
11. The verb *ekdikēsō*, "to avenge" or "procure justice" appears just four other times outside of this passage, most pointedly in Rev 6:10, where martyrs cry for divine

vindication (realized in the vision of Rev 19:2). Such vindication is promised (e.g., 2 Cor 10:6), but "avenging oneself" is sharply prohibited in Romans 12:19.

12. Herzog, *Subversive Speech*, 225.
13. *Penichros* is only here in the New Testament, but appears in the LXX of Exodus 22:25: "If you lend money to my people, to those *poor* among you, you are not to act as a creditor; you shall not charge interest" (22:24 in the Masoretic text). See my comments on Mark's version of this sequence in Myers, *Strong Man*, 320–23.
14. Summarizing Herzog, *Subversive Speech*, 226–29.
15. Herzog, *Subversive Speech*, 230.
16. The verb to vindicate (*ekdikēsis*) is used by Luke only three times: here; in 21:22 (referring specifically to Luke's *ex eventu* prophecy of the Roman siege of Jerusalem); and Acts 7:24 (Moses's vengeance for the oppressed). Similarly, the noun "elect" (*eklektos*): only here, in 14:24 (those invited to the banquet), and 23:35 (the authorities' ridicule of Jesus on the Cross as "the Chosen One").
17. Zerwick and Grosvenor explain the use of *makrothumeō* ("to be long-suffering") here thus: "Though God is slow to show anger (with their oppressors) on their behalf. . .will God delay? . . .the answer is negative" (*Grammatical*, 253–254).
18. See image at https://en.wikipedia.org/wiki/Saint_Lucy_Before_the_Judge.
19. Herzog, *Subversive Speech,* 179. For my structural analysis of this "symbolic order," see Myers, *Strong Man*, 68–80.
20. Herzog, *Subversive Speech,* 180–181.
21. Herzog, *Subversive Speech,* 180. Herzog argues for a distinction between tax collectors (who worked directly with, and enjoyed the protection of, the Roman state) and toll collectors (*telōnēs*, as here) who "were visible and socially vulnerable. On them fell the full force of popular resentment toward the whole oppressive system in which they were but minor functionaries" (180; see sources there). While the evidence for a hard distinction is inconclusive (nor have I followed it consistently in this project), it *could* explain why Luke groups toll collectors with sinners and other marginalized persons responsive to John (3:12; 7:29) and Jesus (5:27–30; 7:34; 15:1).
22. Herzog, *Subversive Speech*, 186.
23. Bailey suggests he is specifically hoping that the atonement sacrifice offered in the Temple that day might apply to him (*Poet and Peasant*, 154). *Hilaskomai* in 18:13 (to receive mercy in the passive) has a cultic connotation of propitiation, as in Hebrews 2:17c, its only other appearance in the New Testament.
24. Herzog, *Subversive Speech*, 192.
25. Luke is the only Gospel to use the term *brephos*, which appears four times in his first two chapters (1:41, 44; 2:12, 16), and make a good case for the powerful role of infants in salvation history! The disciples' objection stems either from their disregard of the young or that the babies were not Jesus's kin. See my comments on Mark's version of this episode in Myers, *Strong Man*, 266–271.
26. Malina and Rohrbaugh, *Social Science*, 383.
27. Between 19:28 and 24:12 we find only a smattering of material unique to Luke: 19:1–10 (Zacchaeus) and 39–44 (Jesus's lament over Jerusalem); 21:22, 28

(fragments of apocalyptic discourse); 22:35–38 (Peter's two swords); 23:6–16 (Jesus before Herod), 27–32 (weeping daughters of Jerusalem); and 39–43 (promise to social bandit crucified next to him). There is only one passage of Q material (parable of the pounds/talents, 19:12–27 // Matt 25:14–30); this is unsurprising, since Q is postulated as a sayings source without a Passion narrative.

28. This section is edited and adapted from Myers, *Biblical Vision*, 30–37. For a recontextualized re-narration of the story as a call to reparations for Indigenous peoples, see Enns and Myers, *Haunted Histories*, 275–282.
29. Karl Marx, *A Contribution to the Critique of Political Economy* (1859); see the passage at https://sites.pitt.edu/~syd/marx.html.
30. Luke uses the verb *leipō* here, whereas Mark uses *hustereō.* The latter connotes that it is the rich man who is impoverished by his complicity with the destitute poverty (*husterēsis*) of people like the widow at the Temple treasury (Mark 12:44). Mark implies this further by Jesus's addition of the Levitical imperative "do not defraud" to his recital of the ethical commands Decalogue (Mark 10:19). Luke, however, omits that addition—another key edit—not to soften Mark's story, but perhaps because Jesus's critique of wealth is already so well-established.
31. The intensified verb *perilupos* appears in the Septuagint in the poignant refrain of the Psalmist "Why are you cast down, my soul, why are you disquieted. . .?" (Ps 42:5, 11; 43:5; [LXX 41:6, 12, 42:5]). Though only here in Luke, it is used by Mark and Matthew to describe Jesus's struggle in the Garden of Gethsemene. There he keeps walking toward Golgotha, but here the ruler turns away.
32. Luke changes Mark's future verb to present tense. The adjective *duskolōs* appears in the New Testament only here and its synoptic parallels (// Mark 10:23 // Matt 19:23). The same is true of *chrēma* in the gospels, though Luke uses it four times in Acts (4:37; 8:18–20; 24:26).
33. A similarly absurd contrastive pairing is found in Matthew 23:24, where Jesus accuses scribes and Pharisees of "straining out a gnat and swallowing a camel."
34. David King, *Reclaiming*, overviews the textual "volatility" of the camel/needle's eye saying, indicating that early on it was considered scandalous, and notes "we can detect the same discomfort in patristic writings" (136–137). The famous medieval assertion is that the "eye of the needle" imagined a certain small gate in ancient Jerusalem, through which camels could enter only on their knees! It is specious, yet remains one of the enduring ways preachers have devised to rob this metaphor of its class-critical power. Jesus's stinging sarcasm is more recognizable to moderns in Frederick Buechner's wry paraphrase cited at the top of this chapter. See the whole quote and learn more about Beuchner's work at https://www.frederickbuechner.com/quote-of-the-day/2021/4/28/catching-by-surprise.
35. The nominative neuter adjectives *adunatos* and *dunatos* are best translated "impossible/possible," though the word means powerless/empowered (as in the genitive in Rom 15:1).
36. *Social Science*, 384.
37. The adjective *pollaplasiōn*, only here in the New Testament, is a compound word—*polla* (many) + *plassō* (to make or create)—thus my translation "multiplied."

CHAPTER THIRTEEN

1. Sylvia Keesmaat and Brian Walsh "Outside of a Small Circle of Friends: Jesus and the Justice of God," in *Jesus, Paul, and the People of God: A Theological Dialogue with N. T. Wright*, ed. N. Perrin and R. Hays (Downers Grove, IL: InterVarsity Press, 2011), 82.
2. See 9:22 and 9:44–45; Luke follows Mark in these three "portents." However, he omits the dispute between the Zebedee brothers (Mark 10:35–40) and displaces the follow-on teaching about greatness and servanthood (Mark 10:41–45) to immediately following the Last Supper (Luke 22:24–30). Mark's sequence connects three consecutive episodes with a common setting on "the way" (Mark 10:17, 32, 46), in order to contrast the aspirations of the rich man, the disciples and Bartimaeus. Luke instead connects the blind beggar to Zacchaeus by their proximity to Jericho (Luke 18:35; 19:1), though with a similar contrastive purpose.
3. Mark's version is preferred by the lectionary, and is a story dear to me, having shaped my ministry for almost fifty years. We named our intentional community after Bartimaeus (1976–1986) and similarly our Cooperative (1998 to the present). See https://bcmonline.org/bcm-online/about-bcm/.
4. Only three times in Luke is Jesus referred to as the "Nazarene": near the beginning (4:34), here, and toward the end (24:19), though seven times in Acts. The verb *parerchomai* can mean "pass by" but also "neglect" (12:37; 15:29) or "pass away" (16:17; 21:32–33), a negative connotation that may explain the man's assertive urgency. Similarly, the verb *dierchomai* ("pass through") is used twice in the Zaccheaus episode (19:1, 4); at least twice earlier in Luke it means "to pass through a hostile territory" (4:30; 11:24).
5. The association with David is prominent in Luke 1–3, but will be problematized in 20:21–24 (following Mark; see Myers, *Strong Man*, 319–320).
6. "Leading" (*proagō*) is only here in Luke. The verb to rebuke is used for demons, natural forces or people. Only here in Luke is "to silence" pressed on someone else (see 9:26; 20:36); it may be that Luke has Amos 6:10 in mind ("Be silent! We must not mention the name of the Lord").
7. Map shows the two main routes: "skirting Samaria, the eastern route crosses the Jordan River, passes through the region of Perea, and then crosses back over the Jordan River near Jericho. It would have taken pilgrims five to seven days to traverse it... Because of the Jewish communities in Perea, this region was safer—and more hospitable—than Samaria for Galilean pilgrims" (map and citation found at https://www.biblicalarchaeology.org/daily/biblical-topics/new-testament/3-pilgrimage-paths-from-galilee-to-jerusalem/).
8. If it isn't lodged in your consciousness, hear it at https://www.youtube.com/watch?v=bkd-QFD7vMA.
9. See Luke 2:52; Luke 12:25 // Matt 6:27; Josh 9:21, 23; Eph 4:13; Heb 11:11. In the LXX and papyri as well the word connotes age, not stature.
10. As noted (11B), this bizarre image sought to remind his disciples of the fate of Pharaoh's army in Exodus 14. A similar image is conjured by John the Revelator in his vision of the demise of Rome's oppressive economy (Rev 18:9–21). There is

still debate about whether the *sukomorea* and *sukaminō* are the same tree, related, or entirely different. See the majority view at https://en.wikipedia.org/wiki/Sycamine. Some feel the sycamine is a kind of mulberry; see https://israel-tourguide.info/2012/09/11/what-tree-is-the-sycamine/ and https://www.biblicaltraining.org/library/sycamine. From a literary (rather than a horticultural) perspective, it seems best to consider them symbolically synonymous.

11. As inevitability: 9:22; 13:33; 17:25; 21:9; 22:37; 24:7, 26, 44 (see 1B). As "must needs" responsibility: 2:49; 4:43; 11:42; 12:12; 13:16; 15:32. Almost half of the appearances of this verb in the New Testament are in Luke-Acts.
12. The verb *hupodexomai* (see also 10:38) appears only once outside of Luke-Acts in the New Testament: a commendation of Rahab's hospitality to the Israelite spies infiltrating *Jericho* (Jas 2:25).
13. In the LXX this verb often describes the people's distrust in God's provision or each other (e.g., Exod 17:3; Num 14:2, 36; 16:11; Deut 1:27; Josh 9:18, Ps 105:25).
14. This verb (whence comes our word "sycophant") is used twice in Luke and nowhere else in the New Testament. It can refer variously to oppression or false accusation (3:14 and often in the LXX), or dealing falsely, fraud, or extortion (here and Lev 19:11).
15. See also Num 5:7. This litany of breaking faith frankly reads like a summary history of settler treaty-making and breaking with the Indigenous peoples of North America over the last five hundred years, for which conversations about reparations are only now beginning (see Enns and Myers, *Haunted Histories*, 296–304).
16. In the case of theft of an animal, a two-to-five-fold reparation was required (Exod 22:1–4; see also 2 Sam 12:6).
17. Keesmaat, *Fountain*, 2025.
18. Keesmaat sketches a compelling portrait of the reality of peasant impoverishment as the background to this story, comparing "the loss of land by peasants in first-century Judea with the loss of Indigenous land and lifeways" in North America today. To explain "the reasons for the animosity that the villagers displayed towards Zacchaeus," she suggests we need to acknowledge how "their experience paralleled the deep collective grief [and] trauma that Indigenous peoples feel over the loss of their land today. No wonder they responded with such disbelief when Jesus indicated his intention of eating with Zacchaeus. Was this not Jesus, who had previously acknowledged their trauma when he honored those who mourn, those who hunger and thirst for justice, those who are impoverished, and those who are persecuted? Was this not Jesus, who had repeatedly called those who followed him to sell all that they had and share with the poor?" (*Fountain*, 2025).
19. Zerwick and Grosvenor, *Grammatical*, 258.
20. An example of expository sleight of hand, moving seamlessly from "talent" as an ancient unit of money to "talent" as competence in modern English, can be seen at https://fee.org/articles/the-parable-of-the-talents-the-bible-and-entrepreneurs/. Stewardship Sunday in many churches is timed to correspond with the RCL's 25th Sunday of Pentecost in Year A (conveniently as the US approaches the Thanksgiving holiday).
21. Myers, *Biblical Vision*, 38–45.

22. Herzog begins his groundbreaking study of the tradition by pointing out that differences between Matthew and Luke "are significant enough to raise questions about whether they are different versions of a common source or distinctive variations on a common theme. Do we have one parable redacted by two evangelists or two oral performances using similar themes? . . . Not surprisingly, none of these variations has kept interpreters of the parable from settling on its theological meaning" (*Subversive Speech*, 150).
23. Brian Schultz, "Jesus as Archelaus in the Parable of the Pounds (Luke. 19:11–27)." *Novum Testamentum* 49, no. 2 (2007) http://www.jstor.org/stable/25442543; and E. Van Eck, "Do not question my honour: A social-scientific reading of the parable of the minas (Luke 19:12b–24, 27)." *HTS Teologiese Studies/Theological Studies,* 67, no. 3, Art. 977 (2011) https://doi.org/10.4102/hts.v67i3.977 review the evidence. Both offer a source-critical study of the parable, and argue for its setting in the thirties CE, two generations closer than Luke to the dramas of Herodian succession.
24. For Josephus's account see https://weekly.israelbiblecenter.com/rabbis-herods-golden-eagle. Herod had placed a golden eagle over the Temple entrance, which was perceived as blasphemous. It was chopped down with axes, for which two rabbis and some forty youths were arrested and immolated. For more background, see https://en.wikipedia.org/wiki/Herodian_tetrarchy and https://en.wikipedia.org/wiki/Herod_Archelaus.
25. Josephus, *Antiquities* 17.219–49, 299–30; *Jewish War* 2.1–38, 80–100.
26. At https://engediresourcecenter.com/2015/07/03/a-parable-of-a-king/.
27. Depictions of this parable are absent from Christian art until the beginnings of mercantilism in the fifteenth-century Europe (see this early image from that period: https://en.wikipedia.org/wiki/File:Parable_of_the_Talents.jpg). As capitalism developed across Europe, however, the theme became ubiquitous in both Catholic and Protestant art.
28. At https://faithandpubliclife.com/the-bible-and-economics-will-there-be-inequality-in-heaven/. Commentary that marries the Parable of the Talents with modern business practices is ubiquitous on the web. It is one of the most widely known New Testament stories in popular US culture; I've even seen it quoted by a local chamber of commerce!
29. Herzog, *Subversive Speech*, 157.
30. See https://testamentpress.com/ancient-money-calculator.html; also https://en.wikipedia.org/wiki/Mina_(unit).
31. The first slave's "ten cities" tempt one to think of the "Decapolis" (mentioned in Mark 7:31 and Matt 4:25, though not by Luke). This region, formed during the Hellenistic period, was not part of the tetrarchies (see map at https://www.biblestudy.org/maps/palestine-under-the-herods.html). These "cities on the eastern frontier of the Roman Empire. . . formed a group because of their language, culture, religion, location, and political status, with each functioning as an autonomous city-state dependent on Rome. . . in a region which was otherwise populated by Jews, Nabataeans and Arameans" (https://en.wikipedia.org/wiki/). Many imperial military veterans who

had helped colonize Palestine settled in the Decapolis, which may be why Mark 5:20 associates it with the exorcism of the "Legion" (see Myers, *Strong Man,* 190–191). Might Luke 19:17 then be a wry Lukan tweak of Herodian aspirations?

32. Malina and Rohrbaugh, *Social Science*, 390; they also summarize Eusebius's comments on a peasant version of this parable "found in the (now lost) Gospel of the Nazoreans," in which "the servant who preserved his master's money is the one who is accepted with joy—exactly the way a peasant would have understood the story" (391).
33. Herzog, *Subversive Speech*, 162.
34. *Tokos* is proscribed in Exod 22:25 [LXX 22:24]; Lev 25:35–36; and Deut 23:19 [LXX 23:20; see Ps 15:5 [LXX 14:5]).
35. *Ethics, 1122a.* Aristotle goes further in *Politics* (1258b): "Usury is most reasonably hated [form of wealth-getting], because its gain comes from money itself and not from that for the sake of which money was invented. For money was brought into existence for the purpose of exchange, but interest increases the amount of the money itself (and this is the actual origin of the Greek word: offspring resembles parent, and interest is money born of money), consequently this form of the business of getting wealth is of all forms the most contrary to nature."
36. Keesmaat, *Fountain*, 2025.
37. Herzog describes the process thus: "elites used their wealth to make loans to peasant farmers... at interest rates ranging from 60% to perhaps as high as 200%... The purpose... was not so much to make a large profit... but to accept land as collateral so that the elites would foreclose on their loans in [lean] years... By the early decades of the first century, owing to the effects of commercialization on the agrarian economy, elites were more interested in the control of land, not just of the peasants who lived on the land. [This resulted in efforts] to displace peasants from their patrimonial plots of land and to reduce their status to that of landless, dependent laborers. In this way, elites could control the typed of crops grown on land and could shift patterns of crops to maximize their yield or convert land usage to enterprises yielding harvests more easily monetized and exported... The retainers of the elites who implemented these policies...are the types who appear in this parable" Herzog, *Subversive Speech*, 161–162.
38. Keesmaat, *Fountain*, 2025.
39. Luke follows Mark with minor selectivity, mostly regarding episodes he has placed elsewhere. His few notable additions are as follows:

    - Jesus's heartbreaking lament over Jerusalem (19:39–44), which with a few other insertions into the Little Apocalypse (21:20, 24, 39) indicate that Luke is writing after the fact of Jerusalem's destruction in 70 CE;
    - The koan of 20:18;
    - His close to the Little Apocalypse calling disciples to "insomniac" faith (21:34–36);
    - Jesus comments at the Last Supper, shared with disciples who will both betray him and "reign" with him (22:21–23, 27–30);

- His renunciation of armed resistance (22:35–38; 51);
- Jesus before Herod (23:6–16), another political critique, portraying how imperial rivals became friends over the execution of a dissenter;
- Jesus's encounter with weeping women on the Via Crucis (23:27–32); and
- His conversation with those being crucified with him (23:39–43).
- Luke closes his narrative with his unique resurrection epilogue (24:13–53), with which this book opened (see chapter 1).

EPILOGUE

1. Anglican Eucharistic Prayer B. See variations and different traditions at https://en.wikipedia.org/wiki/Memorial_Acclamation.
2. Parts of this section have been adapted from a sermon I gave during the closing Eucharist at Greenbelt Festival in Cheltenham, England in August 2004. I was privileged to share this event with the wonderful former Archbishop of Canterbury Rowan Williams, and our dear colleague Richard Sewell, who today serves at Residentiary Canon at St. George's Cathedral in Jerusalem.
3. Luke follows Mark's description of an official covert operation to arrest and execute Jesus, including the infiltration of the discipleship community by a member who has "turned" (21:2–6; 21–23). It is countered by the disciples' underground movements, replete with special instructions for how to find a clandestine meeting place (21:7–13). For comments on Mark's version, see Myers *Strong Man,* 360–361.
4. See, e.g., Walzer, *Exodus and Revolution.*
5. See Silko epigraph, introduction.
6. The noun *epithumia* appears only two other times in the gospels, both with negative connotations: a lust for things associated with wealth (Mark 4:19) and the "desires of the Devil" (John 8:44). The verb *epithumeō* is used elsewhere in Luke to describe a desperate hunger that will settle for scraps experienced by both the Prodigal Son (15:16) and Lazarus (16:21)!
7. "In a rare transposition of the Markan order of events, Luke shifts the prediction of Judas's betrayal to the end of the Passover meal, where a group of Jesus's sayings are collected. Doing so intensifies the tragedy of the moment: betrayal comes from the very one who has participated in the Passover meal of the surrogate family" (Malina and Rohrbaugh, *Social Science*, 402).
8. The verb *philoneikia*, meaning literally (and ironically) "love of contentiousness," appears only here in the New Testament
9. The present tense of the verbs "lord over" (*kurieuō,* only here in Luke, but five times in Paul) and "exercise power over" (*exousiazō*) connotes ongoing behavior. The noun *euergetēs* (only here in the New Testament) "is the language of patronage" assumed by "wealthy citizens," and often in the Hellenistic world, "gods and kings. Both Caesar Augustus and Nero were so designated in inscriptions honoring their largesse" (Malina and Rohrbaugh, *Social Science,* 402).
10. The reference in 22:30b to "appointing them judges over the twelve tribes of Israel" seems to be a counterpoint to the Parable of the Minas, in which the corrupt king

rewards his cronies with "ten cities" (19:17). Against imperial colonization Jesus invokes the old non-hierarchical ethos of Israel's wilderness tribal confederacy.

11. This time the last verb is the compound *epididōmi*, used in Luke twice to connote giving of food (11:11–12 and later here in 24:42).
12. *Huperōon,* only here and Acts 9:37, 39; 20:8 in the New Testament. In Luke 22:12 it is *anagaion* (only there and Mark 14:15 in the New Testament). Both could imply a safehouse attic. Though the last line in Luke's gospel states that the disciples "returned to Jerusalem and were continually in the Temple blessing God" (Luke 24:53), this likely refers to *after* they had "gone public" at Pentecost (that scenario is repeated in Acts 2:46).
13. Noted by Tannehill, *Narrative Unity*. 26. The verb *sumplēroō* is used only by Luke in the New Testament (Luke 8:23; 9:51).
14. After the Hellenistic period and destruction of the Temple in 70 CE, the festival became a commemoration of the giving of Torah to Moses on Mount Sinai, which is how it is celebrated in synagogue today.
15. On this see Bill Wylie Kellermann, *Seasons of Faith and Conscience: Kairos, Confession, Liturgy* (Maryknoll, NY: Orbis Books, 1991), 198–206.
16. Fire-as-life is particularly meaningful here in the American Southwest, where periodic wildfires cleanse the landscape and allow new growth. It is an appropriate metaphor, therefore, for the renewal of religious traditions choked by generations of underbrush and overlay.
17. See also Isaiah 2:12–15. For a discussion of the cosmological meaning of the ziggurat and Babel, see Eisenberg, *Ecology*, 69-98). I explore these questions further in Myers, *Undocumented*, 17–36.
18. The verb *sungcheō* in 2:6 echoes the LXX of Gen 11:7 and 9, where the Creator "confuses" the monoculture of Babel. It is unique to Acts in the New Testament, its four other appearances similarly associated with social turmoil. For more on this Pentecost insurgency see my reflections at https://bcmonline.org/2005/09/01/articles-theology-culture-pentecost-part-i-cultural-insurgency-and-gospel-liberation-reflections-jaz/.
19. Kellermann, *Seasons*, 201.
20. The Hebrew verb *shaphak* in the prophets most often refers to God's *wrath* (e.g., Isa 42:5; Jer 6:11; Lam 4:11; Ezek 7:8; Hos 5:10; Zeph 3:8). Similarly, Joel's apocalyptic imagery of cosmic upheaval (Joel 2:10, 30–31) connotes divine intervention and reckoning (e.g., Isa 13:9f; 34:4; Ezek 32:7; Amos 8:9).
21. Peter's "blaming" of the nation (Acts 2:23, 36), which has been twisted to fuel two millennia of Christian antisemitism, can only be rightly understood as a Jewish lament over how their political leadership once again silenced rather than heeded a prophet, thereby forfeiting its legitimacy (see 3:22–26). Such collective self-critique is found throughout both Jesus and the prophets. Peter alludes in 2:40 to the ancient Song of Moses: "Save yourselves from this crooked generation" (Deut 32:5).
22. The verb *apodexomai* is used only by Luke in the New Testament. In the gospel it describes how crowds of poor folk gladly welcomed Jesus (Luke 8:40; 9:11), and in Acts how the apostolic movement practiced the Sabbath Economics ethos of radical hospitality (Acts 18:27; 21:17; 28:30) in the spirit of Jesus's missionary instructions (6A).

23. The noun *klasis* ("breaking") here is also used in the Emmaus eucharistic revelation (Luke 24:35; its only two appearances in the New Testament). In Acts 2:36 the verb *klaō* is used, as in Matthew's Last Supper (Matt 26:26) and Luke's Emmaus meal (Luke 24:30). This links the third sacred meal firmly with the first two.
24. The phrase *semeia... kai terata* ("signs and wonders") first appears in Acts in Peter's citation of Joel (Acts 2:19). Both nouns are used frequently in the plagues narrative of Exodus 3–13 (LXX, *semeia* sixteen times, *teras* five times; on the plagues as resistance to empire, see Myers, *Nature against Empire*). Luke's use of that phrase eight other times in Acts (including 7:36, which refers specifically to the Exodus story) likely connotes his conviction that the early church was engaged in an analogous struggle with empire.
25. The meals of 2:42 and 46 are not the last time sacramental bread is broken in Acts. Paul presides over such a ritual in Troas (in *another* upper room, 20:7–8, 11), and toward the end of Luke's second volume, does so again aboard a sinking ship. There he "takes bread, gives thanks (*eucharisteō*) and breaks it," sharing with exhausted sailors in the promise that all will be saved (27:33–36)—the penultimate scene before Paul reaches Rome.
26. See more on this at Myers, *Biblical Vision*, 52–50.
27 See, e.g., Bob Utley's comment on Acts 2:44: "This early experiment in 'community' was not successful (cf. 4:32–5:11). It was not meant to be a universal principle, but an attempt at a loving, mutually supportive community or faith. This is a good example that not everything recorded in the Bible is meant to be universally implemented!" in *Luke the Historian: Acts, Study Guide Commentary Series, New Testament, Vol. 3B*, 2013, published online at https://bible.org/book/export/html/21323. Similar logic is used to dismiss the Sermon on the Mount's command to love enemies as a "counsel to perfection" or "impossible ethic"; its function is not parenetic, but soteriological, showing us why we fall short and need redemption. On this see Myers and Enns, *Ambassadors I*, 54–56.
28. For further reflections on Acts 4:32–5:11 see https://bcmonline.org/2005/09/01/articles-sabbath-economics-pentecost-part-ii-church-power-spirit-reflections-socio-economic-redistri/.
29. For an overview of issues pertaining to their theorized relationship, see https://en.wikipedia.org/wiki/Luke_the_Evangelist; and Paul Barnett, "Luke's Acts as a Historical Source for Paul" blog at https://paulbarnett.info/2012/12/lukes-acts-as-a-historical-source-for-paul/.
30. Steven Charleston, *We Survived the End of the World: Lessons from Native America on Apocalypse and Hope* (Minneapolis, MN: Broadleaf Books, 2023).
31. Charleston, *We Survived*, 61–62,
32. McCarraher, *Enchantments*, 679.

APPENDIX I

1. Alyce McKenzie, "Lectionary or Series?" Nov 10, 2016, Perkins Center for Preaching Excellence blog, at https://pcpe.smu.edu/blog/lectionary-or-series.

2. See, e.g., https://www.workingpreacher.org/columnist/lectionary-pros-and-cons; https://wels.net/ptw-lectionary-can-cover-what-matters/; https://www.preaching.com/articles/preaching-by-lectionary/.
3. Find RCL weekly texts at https://lectionary.library.vanderbilt.edu/.
4. See https://www.workingpreacher.org/narrative-faq). Unfortunately, I find the NL's Year 3 Luke schedule (see https://www.workingpreacher.org/wp-content/uploads/2023/09/WP-Narrative-Lectionary-2024-25-Luke.pdf) only marginally more suitable than the RCL's Year C for correlating with the textual choices of my Luke study.

APPENDIX II

1. McMullen, "Radical Orthodox Economics," *Christian Scholars Review,* July 15, 2015, at https://christianscholars.com/radical-orthodox-economics/.
2. This model, developed by BCM staff and partners, was published in Colwell, *Household Practices,* 2007, pp. 11–15), a sequel to Myers, *Biblical Vision*. See more at https://bcmonline.org/sabbath-economics/.
3. See an overview at https://www.investopedia.com/terms/s/sri.asp, and some history from one of the longest running firms advocating and capacitating SRI at https://www.calvert.com/.
4. See for example "credit card condoms" at https://www.moneysense.ca/columns/get-a-credit-card-condom/. For more basic suggestions see: https://www.tiaa.org/public/learn/retirement-planning-and-beyond/managing-your-money/seven-steps-to-more-effectively-manage-and-reduce-your-debt.
5. See, e.g., https://debtcollective.org/about-us/history-and-victories/; https://cooperatewnc.org/about-community-savings-pools; https://braid.co/mutual-aid-money-pool.
6. Find a calculator at https://forterra.org/carbon-calculator-individuals/?gad_source=1&gclid=EAIaIQobChMI25DZ7vnlhQMVHTfUAR1qfQn-PEAAYAiAAEgI51PD_BwE. See Christine Platt's "Afro Minimalism" at https://www.youtube.com/watch?v=tm8pvacsC_8.
7. Excerpted from: "Covenanting for Justice in the Economy and the Earth," World Alliance of Reformed Churches 24th General Council, Accra, Ghana, July 30-Aug 13, 2004. See whole text at https://reformedjournal.com/covenanting-for-justice-in-the-economy-and-the-earth/.
8. See full text at https://www.vatican.va/contenthttps://www.iccr.org//francesco/en/letters/2019/documents/papa-francesco_20190501_giovani-imprenditori.html. See further Anna Madsen's 2013 list of denominational statements at https://omgcenter.com/2013/01/16/religious-social-statements-on-economic-justice-and-poverty/.
9. Exceptions include the United Church of Christ's Economic Justice Movement and EJ Covenant Program (https://www.ucc.org/what-we-do/justice-local-church-ministries/efam/economic-justice/economic-justice-covenant-program/); the Episcopal Network for Economic Justice (http://www.enej.org/);

and the Evangelical Lutheran Church in America's Justice Portal (https://www.elca.org/Our-Work/Publicly-Engaged-Church/Justice-Portal)–*none* of which are well-resourced. Stalwart traditions of justice advocacy continue, such as Mennonite Central Committee (https://mcc.org/what-we-do/initiatives/justice-equity), the American Friends Service Committee (https://afsc.org/issue/economic-justice), and groups rooted in Catholic social teaching (https://www.usccb.org/resources/catholics-living-economic-justice). Yet more than a decade ago, a resource site for study and action listed more than eighty key national and regional economic justice organizations in the US; only *two* identified as faith-based (one has since folded; see https://www.startguide.org/orgs/orgs04.html). For a (rather optimistic) overview of rising concern for economic justice among evangelicals, see Marcia Pally, "The Theology of Economic Justice and Creation Care: New Evangelicals," 2020; at https://marciapally.com/the-theology-of-economic-justice-creation-care-new-evangelicals/. Three recent publications are good practical resources: Brian Humphreys, *The Wages of Peace: How to Confront Economic Inequality and Love Your Neighbor Well* (Harrisonburg, VA: Herald Press, 2024); Adam Gustine and Jose Humphreys, *Ecosystems of Jubilee: Economic Ethics for the Neighborhood* (Grand Rapids: Zondervan, 2023); and Sheryl Johnson, *Serving Money, Serving God: Aligning Radical Justice, Christian Practice, and Church Life* (Minneapolis, MN: Fortress Press, 2023).

BIBLIOGRAPHY

Anderson, Kat. *Tending the Wild: Native American Knowledge and the Management of California's Natural Resources*. Berkeley: University of California Press, 2005.

Bailey, Kenneth. *Poet and Peasant and through Peasant Eyes: A Literary-Cultural Approach to the Parables in Luke*. Combined edition, Grand Rapids, MI: Eerdmans, 1983.

Balch, Oliver. "The Relevance of Gandhi in the Capitalism Debate." *The Guardian*, January 28, 2013. https://www.theguardian.com/sustainable-business/blog/relevance-gandhi-capitalism-debate-rajni-bakshi.

Bartchy, Scott. "The Sibling Secret (Revealed)." *Leaven* 9, no. 1, Article 5 (2001). https://digitalcommons.pepperdine.edu/leaven/vol9/iss1/5.

———. "Who Should Be Called Father? Paul of Tarsus between the Jesus Tradition and Patria Potestas." *Biblical Theology Bulletin* 33, no. 4 (Nov 2003): 135–147.

Bauckham, Richard. *Gospel Women: Studies of the Named Women in the Gospels*. Grand Rapids, MI: Eerdmans, 2002.

———. *The Bible and Ecology: Rediscovering the Community of Creation*. Waco, TX: Baylor University Press, 2010.

Bauer, W., W. Arndt, and F. Gingrich. *A Greek-English Lexicon of the New Testament and Other Early Christian Literature*. Chicago: University of Chicago Press, 1957.

Bennett, Zoe and David Gowler. *Radical Christian Voices and Practices: Essays in Honour of Christopher Rowland*. Oxford: Oxford University Press, 2012.

Bernstein, Alan E. *The Formation of Hell: Death and Retribution in the Ancient and Early Christian Worlds*. Ithaca, NY: Cornell University Press, 1993.

Berry, Wendell. "Two Economies." *Review and Expositor* 81 no. 2 (May 1984): 209–223.

———. *Home Economics*. Berkeley, CA: Northpoint Press, 1987.

———. *What Are People For? Essays*. Berkeley: Northpoint Press, 1990.

Biery, Brian. "A Tribute to Dorothea Bradley, Who Represented the 'Power of One.'" *Pasadena Now*, May 13, 2020. https://www.pasadenanow.com/main/dorothea-bradley-representing-the-power-of-one.

Bivin, David. "Farewell to Emmaus Road," *Jerusalem Perspective*, January 13, 2017. https://www.jerusalemperspective.com/16208/.

Boorstein, Michelle. "Rebel Pastor Gordon Cosby Left Lasting Mark on Mainstream Christianity." *The Washington Post*, April 5, 2013. www.washingtonpost.com/local/rebel-pastor-gordon-cosby-left-lasting-mark-on-mainstream-christianity/2013/04/04/6e478f1c-9a7f-11e2-9a79-eb5280c81c63_story.html.

Botha, Pieter. "Health and Healing in New Testament Times: Historical Understanding and the Health Care Debate." *Health SA Gosondheid* 1, no. 2 (1996): 3–11.

Braun, Willi. *Feasting and Social Rhetoric in Luke 14*. Society for New Testament Studies Monograph Series 85. Cambridge: Cambridge University Press, 1995.

Brawley, Robert. *Luke: A Social Identity Commentary*. London: T&T Clark, 2020.

Brenes, Michael. "How the Philippines Were Crucial to the Making of American Empire." Review of *Bound by War: How the United States and the Philippines Built America's First Pacific Century*, by Christopher Capozzola. *Jacobin*, August 13, 2021. https://jacobin.com/2021/08/philippines-filipinos-us-empire-military-bases-colonialism-christopher-capozzola-bound-by-war-review.

Broshi, Magen. "The Population of Western Palestine in the Roman-Byzantine Period." *Bulletin of the American Schools of Oriental Research* 236 (Autumn 1979): 1–10.

Brown, Pamela. "Reimagining Jubilee: A Political Horizon for Our Times." *Tikkun* 30, no. 1 (2015) 26–27.

Buechner, Frederick. *Telling the Truth: The Gospel as Tragedy, Comedy, and Fairy Tale*. San Francisco: Harper & Row, 1977.

Buffa, Cristina. "The Magnificat and the Song of Hannah: Comparing Social Conditions." *Revue des Sciences Religieuses* 92, no. 3 (July 2018) 377–392.

Callahan, Mat. *Songs of Slavery and Emancipation*. Jackson, MS: University Press of Mississippi, 2022.

Canadian Ecumenical Jubilee Initiative. *A New Beginning: A Call for Jubilee: The Vision of the Canadian Ecumenical Jubilee Initiative*. Toronto: Canadian Ecumenical Jubilee Initiative, 1998.

Carnahan, Kevin. "Jesus Did Not Teach Nonviolent Resistance in the Sermon on the Mount." *Political Theology Network*, October 14, 2021. https://politicaltheology.com/jesus-did-not-teach-nonviolent-resistance-in-the-sermon-on-the-mount/.

Carroll, J. T. "Disability and Dis-ease: Body, Restoration, and Ethics of Reading in Luke's Gospel." In *Anatomies of the Gospels and Beyond*, edited by Mikeal Parsons, Elizabeth Struthers Malbon, and Paul Anderson. Leiden, Netherlands: Brill, 2018.

Carroll, John. *Luke: A Commentary*. Louisville, KY: Westminster John Knox Press, 2012.

Carter, Warren. *Matthew and the Margins: A Sociopolitical and Religious Reading*. Maryknoll, NY: Orbis Books, 2000.

Cassidy, Richard and Philip Scharper, eds. *Political Issues in Luke-Acts*. Maryknoll, NY: Orbis Books, 1983.

Cassidy, Richard. *Jesus, Politics, and Society: A Study of Luke's Gospel*. Maryknoll, NY: Orbis Books, 1978.

Charleston, Steven. *The Four Vision Quests of Jesus*. Harrisburg, PA: Morehouse, 2015.

———. *We Survived the End of the World: Lessons from Native America on Apocalypse and Hope*. Minneapolis, MN: Broadleaf Books, 2023.

Chase, Malcolm. "From Millennium to Anniversary: The Concept of Jubilee in Late Eighteenth- and Nineteenth-Century England." *Past & Present: A Journal of Historical Studies* 129 (Nov 1990): 132–147.

Chow, John. "Patronage in Roman Corinth." In *Paul and Empire: Religion and Power in Roman Imperial Society*, edited by Richard Horsley, 104–125. London: Bloomsbury Academic, 1997.

Cobb, John and Herman Daly. *For The Common Good: Redirecting the Economy toward Community, the Environment, and a Sustainable Future*. Second updated edition, Boston: Beacon Press, 1994.

Collins, Chuck, Felice Yeskel and United for a Fair Economy. *Economic Apartheid in America: A Primer on Economic Inequality and Insecurity*. New York: The New Press, 2005.

Colwell, Matthew. *Sabbath Economics: Household Practices*. Washington, DC: Tell the Word Press, 2007.

Cone, James. *The Spirituals and the Blues*. Maryknoll, NY: Orbis Books, 1991.

Conn, Jim. "Plantation Capitalism." *Capital and Main: Investigating Power, Money, and Society*, June 25, 2013. https://capitalandmain.com/plantation-capitalism.

Coomber, Matthew, ed. *Economics and Empire in the Ancient Near East: Guide to the Bible and Economics 1*. Center and Library for the Bible and Social Justice Series. Eugene, OR: Cascade Books, 2023.

Coomber, Matthew and Ludwig Noya, eds. *Class and Intersectionality in the Hebrew Bible: Engaged Biblical Studies in the Academy and on the Streets*. Center and Library for the Bible and Social Justice Series. Eugene, OR: Cascade Books, 2024.

Corley, K. E. "The Anointing of Jesus in the Synoptic Tradition: An Argument for Authenticity." *Journal for the Study of the Historical Jesus* 1, no.1 (2003): 61–72.

Crossan, John Dominic. *God and Empire: Jesus against Rome, Then and Now*. San Francisco: HarperOne, 2007.

Culpepper, R. Alan. *The People of the Parables: Galilee in the Time of Jesus*. Louisville, KY: Westminster John Knox Press, 2024.

Czech, Brian. *Supply Shock: Economic Growth at the Crossroads and the Steady State Solution*. Washington, DC: Steady State Press, 2021.

Davenport, Gene. *Into the Darkness: Discipleship in the Sermon on the Mount*. Eugene, OR: Wipf & Stock, 1988.

Davis, Ellen. *Scripture, Culture, and Agriculture: An Agrarian Reading of the Bible*. Cambridge: Cambridge University Press, 2008.

———. *Opening Israel's Scriptures*. Oxford: Oxford University Press, 2019.

Davis, Murphy. *Surely Goodness and Mercy: A Journey into Illness and Solidarity*. Atlanta, GA: Open Door Community Press, 2020.

De Graaf, John, David Wann, and Thomas Naylor. *Affluenza: How Overconsumption Is Killing Us—and How to Fight Back*. 3rd ed. Oakland, CA: Berrett-Koehler Publishers, 2014.

Derrett, J. D. "Positive Perspectives on Two Lucan Miracles," *Downside Review* 104, no. 357 (1986): 272–287.

Desmond, Matthew. "In Order to Understand the Brutality of American Capitalism, You Have to Start on the Plantation." *The New York Times Magazine—The 1619 Project*, August 14, 2019. https://www.nytimes.com/interactive/2019/08/14/magazine/slavery-capitalism.html.

———. *Poverty, by America*. New York: Crown Publishing, 2023.

Destro, Adriana, and Mauro Pesce. "Fathers and Householders in the Jesus Movement: The Perspective of the Gospel of Luke." *Biblical Interpretation* 11, no. 2 (2003): 211–238.

Dicken, Frank. "Composite 'Herod' in Luke-Acts." *The Bible and Interpretation* (June 2015). https://bibleinterp.arizona.edu/articles/2015/06/dic398023.

———. Frank. *Reading Luke.* Eugene, OR: Cascade Books, 2023.

Dillon, R. J. "Ravens, Lilies, and the Kingdom of God (Matthew 6:253–3/Luke 12:223–1)." *Catholic Biblical Quarterly* 53, no. 4 (1991): 605–627.

Douglas, Mary. *Natural Symbols: Explorations in Cosmology.* New York: Vintage Books, 1973.

Draper, Andrew, Jody Michele, and Andrea Mae. *Disabling Leadership: A Practical Theology for the Broken Body of Christ.* Downers Grove, IL: InterVarsity Press, 2023.

Du Bois, W. E. B. *The Souls of Black Folk: Essays and Sketches.* Chicago: A. G. McClurg, 1903.

Duchrow, Ulrich and Franz Hinkelammert. *Property for People, Not for Profit: Alternatives to the Global Tyranny of Capital.* Windsor, ON: Zed Press, 2004.

Duchrow, Ulrich. *Global Economy: A Confessional Issue for the Churches?* Translated by David Lewis. Geneva: WCC Publications, 1987.

———. *Alternatives to Global Capitalism: Drawn from Biblical History, Designed for Political Action.* Heidelberg: International Books/Kairos Europa, 1995.

Dykstra, Laurel. *Wildlife Congregations: A Priest's Year of Gaggles, Colonies, and Murders by the Salish Sea.* Surrey, BC: Hancock House, 2023.

Dykstra, Laurel and Ched Myers, editors *Liberating Biblical Study: Scholarship, Art, and Action in Honor of the Center and Library for the Bible and Social Justice. Eugene.* OR: Cascade Books, 2011.

Edwards, Douglas. "The Socioeconomic and Cultural Ethos of the Lower Galilee in the First Century: Implications for the Nascent Jesus Movement." In *The Galilee in Late Antiquity* edited by Lee Levine, 53–73. New York: Jewish Theological Seminary of American, 1992.

Eisenberg, Evan. *The Ecology of Eden: An Inquiry into the Dream of Paradise and a New Vision of Our Role in Nature.* New York: Vintage Books, 1998.

Elliott, John H. "From Social Description to Social-Science Criticism." *Biblical Theology Bulletin,* 38 no. 1 (Spring 2008): 26–36.

Ellul, Jacques. *Anarchy and Christianity.* Translated by Geoffrey Bromiley. Grand Rapids, MI: Eerdmans, 1988. https://theanarchistlibrary.org/library/jacques-ellul-anarchy-christianity-en.

Enns, Elaine and Ched Myers. *Ambassadors of Reconciliation II: Diverse Christian Practices of Restorative Justice and Peacemaking.* Maryknoll, NY: Orbis Books, 2009.

Enns, Elaine and Ched Myers. *Healing Haunted Histories: A Settler Discipleship of Decolonization.* Eugene, OR: Cascade Books, 2021.

Epp, Roger. *We Are All Treaty People: Prairie Essays.* Edmonton: University of Alberta Press, 2008.

Escobar, Miguel. *The Unjust Steward: Wealth, Poverty, and the Church Today.* Cincinnati: Forward Movement, 2022.

Evers-Hillstrom, Karl. "Majority of Lawmakers in 116th Congress Are Millionaires." April 23, 2020. www.opensecrets.org/news/2020/04/majority-of-lawmakers-millionaires/.

Fanon, Frantz. *The Wretched of the Earth.* New York: Grove Press, 1961.

Felder, Cain Hope and Charles Herbert Smith. *The Jubilee Legacy Bible.* Nashville: Townsend Press, 1999.

Fiensy, David. "The Galilean Economy in the Time of Jesus: Can You Dig It?" *The Bible and Interpretation* (2013) https://bibleinterp.arizona.edu/articles/2013/07/fie378015.

———. *Christian Origins and the Ancient Economy.* Eugene, OR: Cascade Books, 2014.

———. *The Realia Jesus: An Archaeological Commentary on the Gospel of Luke.* Eugene, OR: Cascade Books, 2024.

Formisano, Ronald. *Plutocracy in America: How Increasing Inequality Destroys the Middle Class and Exploits the Poor.* Baltimore: Johns Hopkins University Press, 2015.

Fowl, Stephen and Gregory Jones. *Reading in Communion: Scripture and Ethics in Christian Life.* Grand Rapids, MI: Eerdmans, 1991.

Fox, Nickolas. *The Hermeneutics of Social Identity in Luke-Acts.* Eugene, OR: Pickwick Publications, 2021.

Freeland, Chrystia. *Plutocrats: The Rise of the New Global Super-Rich and the Fall of Everyone Else.* New York: Penguin Press, 2012.

Freyne, Sean. *Galilee from Alexander the Great to Hadrian, 323 BCE to 135 CE: A Study of Second Temple Judaism.* Wilmington, DE: Glazier, 1980.

Gambo, F. X. *From Feral to Family: Coming Home to Casa Anna.* Ventura, CA: BCM Press, 2021.

Gans, Herbert. *The War Against the Poor: The Underclass and Antipoverty Policy.* New York: Basic Books, 1995.

Goff, Stan. *Mammon's Ecology: Metaphysic of the Empty Sign.* Eugene, OR: Cascade Books, 2018.

Gordon, Avery. *Ghostly Matters: Haunting and the Sociological Imagination.* Minneapolis: University of Minnesota Press, 1997.

Gottwald, Norman. *The Tribes of Yahweh: A Sociology of the Religion of Liberated Israel, 1250–1050 BCE.* Maryknoll, NY: Orbis Books, 1979.

———. *The Hebrew Bible: A Brief Socio-Literary Introduction.* Minneapolis, MN: Fortress Press, 2009.

Gould, Rebecca. "Book of Nature." In *Encyclopedia of Religion and Nature,* edited by Bron Taylor, 210–211. New York: Continuum, 2005. http://www.religionandnature.com/ern/sample/Gould—BookNature.pdf.

Gowdy, John. *Limited Wants, Unlimited Means: A Reader on Hunter-Gatherer Economics and the Environment.* Washington, DC: Island Press, 1998.

Graeber, David. *Debt: The First 5,000 Years.* New York: Melville House Publishing, 2011.

Gustine, Adam and Jose Humphreys. *Ecosystems of Jubilee: Economic Ethics for the Neighborhood.* Grand Rapids, MI: Zondervan, 2023.

Häkkinen, Sakari. "Poverty in the First-century Galilee." *HTS Teologiese Studies/Theological Studies* 72, no. 4 (Sept 2016). http://www.scielo.org.za/scielo.php?script=sci_arttext&pid=S02599-4222016000400046.

Hanson, K. C. "BTB Readers Guide: Kinship." *Biblical Theology Bulletin* 24 (1994): 183–194.

———. "The Galilean Fishing Economy and the Jesus Tradition," *Biblical Theology Bulletin* 27, no. 3 (August 1997): 99–111.

Hanson, K.C. and Douglas Oakman. *Palestine in the Time of Jesus: Social Structures and Social Conflicts*. Minneapolis, MN: Fortress Press, 1998.

Haraway, Donna. *Staying with the Trouble: Making Kin in the Chthulucene (Experimental Futures)*. Durham, NC: Duke University Press, 2016.

Haughey, John C. *Virtue and Affluence: The Challenge of Wealth*. New York, NY: Sheed & Ward, 1997.

Hendricks Jr., Obery M. "Guerilla Exegesis: 'Struggle' As a Scholarly Vocation." In *Liberating Biblical Study: Scholarship, Art, and Action in Honor of the Center and Library for the Bible and Social Justice*, edited by Laurel Dykstra and Ched Myers, 119–137. Eugene, OR: Cascade Books, 2011.

Hertig, Paul. "The Jubilee Mission of Jesus in the Gospel of Luke: Reversals of Fortunes." *Missiology* 26, no. 2 (1998): 167–179.

Herzog, William. *Parables as Subversive Speech: Jesus as Pedagogue of the Oppressed*. Louisville, KY: Westminster John Knox Press, 1994.

Higdon, Nolan. "Elon Musk and the Oligarchs of the 'Second Gilded Age' Can Not Only Sway the Public—They Can Exploit Their Data, Too." *The Conversation*, April 27, 2022. https://theconversation.com/elon-musk-and-the-oligarchs-of-the-second-gilded-age-can-not-only-sway-the-public-they-can-exploit-their-data-too-181936.

Horsley, Richard. *Covenant Economics: A Biblical Vision of Justice for All*. Philadelphia, PA: Westminster, 2009.

———. *You Shall Not Bow Down and Serve Them: The Political Economic Projects of Jesus and Paul*. Eugene, OR: Cascade Books, 2021.

Horsley, Richard and Neil Asher Silberman. *The Message and the Kingdom: How Jesus and Paul Ignited a Revolution and Transformed the Ancient World*. London: Penguin Publishing Group, 1997.

Houghtby-Haddon, Natalie. *Changed Imagination, Changed Obedience: Social Change, Social Imagination, and the Bent-Over Woman in the Gospel of Luke*. Eugene, OR: Pickwick Publications, 2011.

House, Anna Swartwood. "The Long History of How Jesus Came to Resemble a White European." Posted July 17, 2020. https://theconversation.com/the-long-history-of-how-jesus-came-to-resemble-a-white-european-142130.

Howard-Brook, Wes, and Anthony Gwyther. *Unveiling Empire: Reading Revelation Then and Now*. Maryknoll, NY: Orbis Books, 1999.

Hudson, Michael. . . *.And Forgive Them Their Debts: Lending, Foreclosure and Redemption From Bronze Age Finance to the Jubilee Year*. Dresden, Germany: ISLET-Verlag, 2018.

———. *The Lost Tradition of Biblical Debt Cancellations*. New York: Social Science Forum of the Henry George School, 1993. https://michael-hudson.com/wp-content/uploads/2010/03/HudsonLostTradition.pdf.

———. "Proclaim Liberty Throughout the Land: The economic roots of the Jubilee," *Bible Review* 15, no. 1 (February 1999). https://library.biblicalarchaeology.org/article/proclaim-liberty-throughout-the-land.

Humphreys, Brian. *The Wages of Peace: How to Confront Economic Inequality and Love Your Neighbor Well.* Harrisonburg, IN: Herald Press, 2024.

Huyssen, David. "We Won't Get Out of the Second Gilded Age the Way We Got Out of the First." *Vox*, April 1, 2019. https://www.vox.com/first-person/2019/4/1/18286084/gilded-age-income-inequality-robber-baron.

Hyde, Lewis. *The Gift: Imagination and the Erotic Life of Property.* New York: Vintage Books, 1983.

James, Oliver. *The Selfish Capitalist: Origins of Affluenza*. London: Vermilion, 2008.

Jarrell, Greg. *Our Trespasses: White Churches and the Taking of American Neighborhoods.* Minneapolis, MN: Fortress Press, 2024.

Jeremias, Joachim. *The Parables of Jesus*. 2nd revised ed. New York: Charles Scribner's Sons, 1972.

Johnson, Elizabeth. "Mary, Mary, Quite Contrary: How Can the Image of Mary Be Construed as a Source of Blessing Rather Than a Blight for Women's Lives in Both Religion and Politics?" *U.S. Catholic* 68, no. 12 (Dec 2003):12.

Johnson, Sheryl. *Serving Money, Serving God: Aligning Radical Justice, Christian Practice, and Church Life.* Minneapolis, MN: Fortress Press, 2023.

Jones, Arthur. *Wade in The Water: The Wisdom of the Spirituals.* Maryknoll, NY: Orbis Books, 1993.

Joseph, Simon. "A Social Identity Approach to the Rhetoric of Apocalyptic Violence in the Sayings Gospel Q." *History of Religions*, 57, no. 1, University of Chicago Press Journals (2017). https://www.journals.uchicago.edu/doi/full/10.1086/692316#.

Josephus, Flavius. *War of the Jews.* https://penelope.uchicago.edu/josephus/war-7.html.

Kamenka, Eugene. "Gemeinschaft and Gesellschaft." *Political Science* 17, no. 1 (1965): 3–12.

Keddie, Anthony. *Class and Power in Roman Palestine: The Socioeconomic Setting of Judaism and Christian Origins.* Cambridge: Cambridge University Press, 2019.

Keesmaat, Sylvia. *A Fountain of Tears: Ecological Grief in the Biblical Story.* Center and Library for the Bible and Social Justice Series, Eugene, OR: Wipf & Stock, 2025.

Keesmaat, Sylvia and Brian Walsh. "Outside of a Small Circle of Friends: Jesus and the Justice of God." In *Jesus, Paul and the People of God: A Theological Dialogue with N.T. Wrigh*t, edited by N. Perrin and R. Hays, 66–89. Downers Grove: InterVarsity Press, 2011.

Kellermann, Bill Wylie. *Seasons of Faith and Conscience: Kairos, Confession, Liturgy.* Maryknoll, NY: Orbis Books, 1991.

Kemmis, Daniel. *Community and the Politics of Place.* Norman: University of Oklahoma Press, 1992.

Ker, Donald. "Family Finances: 'Kinship' and the Collection." *Irish Biblical Studies* 25, no. 1 (2003): 2–30.

King, David D. M. *Reclaiming the Radical Economic Message of Luke.* Eugene, OR: Pickwick Press, 2022.

King, Martin Luther. *Why We Can't Wait.* Signet Classic ed. New York: Harper & Row, 1963.

———"Beyond Vietnam: A Time to Break Silence." Delivered April 4, 1967. https://www.americanrhetoric.com/speeches/mlkatimetobreaksilence.htm.

Kinsler, Ross and Gloria Kinsler, eds. *God's Economy: Biblical Studies from Latin America.* Maryknoll, NY: Orbis Books, 2005.

———. *The Biblical Jubilee and the Struggle for Life: An Invitation to Personal Ecclesial and Social Transformation.* Maryknoll, NY: Orbis Books, 1999.

Kittel, Gerhard and Gerhard Friedrich. *Theological Dictionary of the New Testament, IV.* Grand Rapids, MI: Eerdmans, 1967.

Knight, Jonathan. *Luke's Gospel.* New York: Routledge, 1998.

Knohl, Israel. "YHWH: The Original Arabic Meaning of the Name." TheTorah.com, posted on April 23, 2023. https://www.thetorah.com/article/yhwh-the-original-arabic-meaning-of-the-name/.

Kohler, Kauffmann and E. Schreiber. "Catechisms." In *Jewish Encyclopedia* New York: Funk & Wagnalls, 1901–1906. https://www.jewishencyclopedia.com/articles/4149-catechisms

Lapide, Pinchas. *The Sermon on the Mount: Utopia or Program for Action?* Maryknoll, NY: Orbis Books, 1986.

Lehmann, Gunnar. "Ancient Israel's Social Structure(s)." In *The Ancient Israelite World,* edited by Kyle Keimer and George Pierce, 209–223. London: Taylor and Francis, 2022.

Lenski, Gerhard. *Power and Privilege: A Theory of Social Stratification.* New York: McGraw Hill, 1966.

Linebaugh, Peter and Marcus Rediker. *The Many-Headed Hydra: Sailors, Slaves, Commoners, and the Hidden History of the Revolutionary Atlantic.* Boston: Beacon Press, 2013. https://freeuniverseity.files.wordpress.com/2012/12/mhh-9.pdf.

Linebaugh, Peter. "Jubilating; Or, How the Atlantic Working Class Used the Biblical Jubilee against Capitalism, with Some Success." *Radical History Review* 1991, no. 50 (May 1, 1991):143–180.

Link, Verity. *The Gospel of Puke: A Disabled Person's Response to Luke's Gospel.* London: Angry Dog, 2020.

Love, Stuart. "The Man with Dropsy." *Leaven* 6, no. 3 (1998): 136–141.

Lowery, Richard. "Sabbath and Survival: Abundance and Self-Restraint in a Culture of Excess." *Encounter,* 54, no. 2 (1993): 143–167.

———. *Sabbath and Jubilee.* St. Louis, MO: Chalice Press, 2000.

Luthy, Christopher James, and Keith Dyer. *Rethinking the Acceptable Year: The Jubilee and the Basileia in Luke 4 and Beyond.* Eugene, OR: Wipf & Stock, 2019.

Mace, Sam. "Book Review: Limitarianism: The Case against Extreme Wealth." Review of *Limitarianism: The Case Against Extreme Wealth* by Ingrid Robeyns, *Theory Matters* (Substack), March 17, 2024. https://theorymatters.substack.com/p/book-review-limitarianism-the-case.

Malherbe, A. J. "The Christianization of a Topos (Luke 12:133–4)." *Novum Testamentum* 38, no. 2 (1996): 123–135.

Malina, Bruce. *The Social World of Jesus and the Gospels*. London: Routledge, 1996.

Malina, Bruce and Richard Rohrbaugh. *Social Science Commentary on the Synoptic Gospels*. Minneapolis, MN: Fortress, 1992.

Marx, Karl. *Capital: A Critique of Political Economy*. Edited by Frederick Engels. Translated by Samuel Moore and Edward Aveling. Online version (Marx/Engels Internet Archive). See esp. Volume One, Chapter 24, Section 3, https://www.marxists.org/archive/marx/works/1867-c1/ch24.htm#S3.

May, Gerald. *Addiction and Grace: Love and Spirituality in the Healing of Addictions*. Annotated edition. San Francisco: HarperOne, 2007.

McCarraher, Eugene. *The Enchantments of Mammon: How Capitalism Became the Religion of Modernity*. Cambridge, MA: Harvard University Press, 2019.

McKenzie, Alyce. "Lectionary or Series?" Nov 10, 2016, Perkins Center for Preaching Excellence blog. https://pcpe.smu.edu/blog/lectionary-or-series.

McMullen, Steven. "Radical Orthodox Economics." *Christian Scholars Review*, July 15, 2015. https://christianscholars.com/radical-orthodox-economics/.

McReynolds, Kathy. "The Gospel of Luke: A Framework for a Theology of Disability." *Christian Education Journal* 13, no. 1 (2016): 169–178.

Meeks, M. Douglas. *God the Economist: The Doctrine of God and Political Economy*. Minneapolis, MN: Fortress Press, 1989.

Meier, John. *A Marginal Jew: Rethinking the Historical Jesus, Volume II: Mentor, Message, and Miracles*. The Anchor Bible Reference Library, New Haven: Yale University Press, 1994.

Mendels, Doron. *The Rise and Fall of Jewish Nationalism: Jewish and Christian Ethnicity in Ancient Palestine*. New York: Doubleday, 1992.

Merton, Thomas. *The Seven Storey Mountain*. San Diego, CA: Harcourt Brace, 1948.

Metzger, James. "Disability and the Marginalisation of God in the Parable of the Snubbed Host (Luke 14.15–24)." *The Bible and Critical Theory* 6, no. 2 (2010): 23.1–23.15.

Miranda, José Porfirio. *Communism in the Bible*. Translated by Robert R. Barr. Maryknoll, NY: Orbis Books, 1982.

Moe-Lobeda, Cynthia. *Building a Moral Economy: Pathways for People of Courage*. Minneapolis, MN: Fortress Press, 2024.

Monbiot, George. "For the Sake of Life on Earth, We Must Put a Limit on Wealth." *The Guardian*, Sep 19, 2019. https://www.theguardian.com/commentisfree/2019/sep/19/life-earth-wealth-megarich-spending-power-environmental-damage.

Moore, Jason, ed. *Anthropocene or Capitalocene? Nature, History, and the Crisis of Capitalism*. Oakland, CA: PM Press, 2016.

Morrison, Toni. *The Origin of Others*. Cambridge, MA: Harvard University Press, 2017.

Moxnes, Halvor. *The Economy of the Kingdom: Social Conflict and Economic Relations in Luke's Gospel*. Eugene, OR: Wipf & Stock, 2004.

——— "Social-scientific Readings of the Bible." In *The New Cambridge History of the Bible*, edited by John Riches, 160–171. Cambridge: Cambridge University Press, 2015.

Muhammad, Khalil Gibran. *The Condemnation of Blackness: Race, Crime, and the Making of Modern Urban America.* Cambridge, MA: Harvard University Press, 2019.

Myers, Ched. *Binding the Strong Man: A Political Reading of Mark's Story of Jesus.* Maryknoll, NY: Orbis Books, 1988.

———. "Beyond the 'Addict's Excuse': Public Addiction and Ecclesial Recovery." In *The Other Side of Sin: Woundedness from the Perspective of the Sinned-Against*, edited by Susan Nelson and Andrew Sung Park, 77–108. New York: SUNY Press, 2001.

———. "Food Politics in the Practice of Jesus." *Priests and People* (February 2004): 45–49.

———. "Jesus's Risen, Mutilated Body." *The Christian Century*, September 3, 2019. https://www.christiancentury.org/article/critical-essay/jesus-risen-mutilated-body.

———. "Nature against Empire: Exodus Plagues, Climate Crisis and Hard Heartedness." *Direction* 49, no. 1 (Spring 2020): 5–17.

———. "Neither Authoritarian Nor Diffident: Conversing about Biblical Differences." *Uniting Church Studies* 4, no. 2 Melbourne: Australia (August 1998), at https://bcmonline.org/1998/08/01/articles-biblical-interpretation-neither-authoritarian-nor-diffident-conversing-about-biblical-diffe/.

———. "Reconnecting Seminary, Sanctuary, Streets and Soil: Curating Alternative Spaces for Theological Education." In *Let Your Light Shine: Mobilizing for Justice with Children and Youth,* edited by Reginald Blount and Virginia Lee, 59–74. New York: Friendship Press, 2019.

———. *The Biblical Vision of Sabbath Economics.* Washington, DC: Tell the Word, 2001.

———. "The Wilderness Temptations and the American Journey: Resistance and Contemplation in a Quincentennial Perspective." In *Richard Rohr: Illuminations of His Life and Work*, edited by Andreas Ebert and Patricia Brockman, 143–157. New York: Crossroads, 1993.

———, ed. *Watershed Discipleship: Reinhabiting Bioregional Faith and Practice.* Eugene, OR: Cascade Books, 2016.

———. *Who Will Roll Away the Stone? Discipleship Queries for First World Christians.* Maryknoll, NY: Orbis Books, 1994.

Myers, Ched, and Elaine Enns. *Ambassadors of Reconciliation I: New Testament Reflections on Restorative Justice and Peacemaking.* Maryknoll, NY: Orbis Books, 2009.

Myers, Ched, and Matthew Colwell. *Our God is Undocumented: Biblical Faith and Immigrant Rights.* Maryknoll, NY: Orbis Books, 2012.

Myers, Ched, Stuart Taylor, Cindy Moe-Lobeda, Joseph Nangle, and Marie Dennis. *"Say to This Mountain": Mark's Story of Discipleship.* Maryknoll, NY: Orbis Books, 1996.

Nam, Roger. "Israelite and Judean Society and Economy." In *The Oxford Handbook of the Historical Books of the Hebrew Bible*, edited by Brad Kelle and Brent Strawn. Oxford: Oxford University Press, 2020. https://digitalcommons.georgefox.edu/gfes/164/.

Narayan, Deepa. "Poverty Is Powerlessness and Voicelessness." *Finance & Development*, International Monetary Fund Quarterly, 37, no. 4 (Dec 2000). https://www.imf.org/external/pubs/ft/fandd/2000/12/narayan.htm.

Nelson, Stanley, director. *The Murder of Emmett Till: Emmett Till's Mother Speaks* (clip). American Experience: PBS, 2003. https://www.pbs.org/wgbh/americanexperience/features/emmett-till-sacrificial-lamb.

Neyrey, Jerome, ed. *The Social World of Luke-Acts: Models for Interpretation.* Peabody, MA: Hendrickson Publishers, 1991.

Nikondeha, Kelly. *The First Advent in Palestine: Reversals, Resistance, and the Ongoing Complexity of Hope.* Minneapolis, MN: Broadleaf Books, 2022.

Nodjimbadem, Katie. "Emmett Till's Open Casket Funeral Reignited the Civil Rights Movement." *Smithsonian Magazine,* September 2, 2015. https://www.smithsonianmag.com/smithsonian-institution/emmett-tills-open-casket-funeral-reignited-the-civil-rights-movement-180956483/.

North, Robert, *Biblical Jubilee after Fifty Years.* Rome, Italy: Gregorian & Biblical Press, 2000.

O'Connor, Sean. "Aristotle's Thinking Hack." Medium, November 13, 2016. https://medium.com/stoicsunday/stoic-sunday-aristotles-thinking-hack-50114e529f44.

Oakman, Douglas. *Jesus and the Peasants.* Eugene, OR: Cascade Books, 2008.

——— "The Shape of Power and Political Economy in Herodian Galilee." In *Liberating Biblical Study,* edited by Laurel Dykstra and Ched Myers, 147–161. Center and Library for the Bible and Social Justice Series. Eugene, OR: Cascade Books, 2011.

Pack, Justin. *Money and Thoughtlessness: A Genealogy and Defense of the Traditional Suspicions of Money and Merchants.* New York: Palgrave Macmillan, 2023.

Paeth, Scott. "Walter Wink, the Powers, and the Sermon on the Mount." *Political Theology Network,* October 28, 2021. https://politicaltheology.com/walter-wink-the-powers-and-the-sermon-on-the-mount/.

Pally, Marcia. "The Theology of Economic Justice and Creation Care: New Evangelicals," 2020. https://marciapally.com/the-theology-of-economic-justice-creation-care-new-evangelicals/.

Parten, Bennett. "Blow Ye Trumpet, Blow: The Idea of Slavery and Freedom." *Journal of the Civil War Era* 10, no. 3 (Sept 2020):298–318.

Patterson, Stephen. "Didache 11–13: The Legacy of Radical Itinerancy in Early Christianity." In *The Didache in Context: Essays on Its Text, History, and Transmission,* edited by Clayton Jefford. Novum Testamentum Supplements 77 (1994): 313–339.

Paulson, Dave. "The Trials and Triumph of the Fisk Jubilee Singers, One of America's Great Musical Institutions." *Nashville Tennessean,* February 1, 2021. https://www.tennessean.com/in-depth/entertainment/music/2021/02/01/how-fisk-jubilee-singers-became-american-musical-institution/3730118001/.

Pepper, William. *The Plot to Kill King: The Truth Behind the Assassination of Martin Luther King Jr.* New York: Skyhorse Publishing, 2018.

Pesonen, A. "The Weeping Sinner: A Short Story by Luke?" *Neotestamentica* 34 no.1 (2000), 87–102.

Petersen, Anne Helen. "The Beginnings of Student Debt Jubilee." *Anne Helen* (Substack), August 24, 2022. https://annehelen.substack.com/p/the-beginnings-of-student-debt-jubilee.

Pettifor, Ann. "The Jubilee 2000 Campaign: A Brief Overview." In *Sovereign Debt at the Crossroads: Challenges and Proposals for Resolving the Third World Debt Crisis*, edited by Chris Jochnick and Fraser Preston, 297–318. Oxford: Oxford University Press, 2006.

Pilch, John. "Understanding Biblical Healing: Selecting the Appropriate Model." *Biblical Theology Bulletin* 18 no. 2 (1988): 60–66.

Pilgrim, Walter. *Good News to the Poor: Wealth and Poverty in Luke-Acts.* Minneapolis, MN: Augsburg, 1981.

Polanyi, Karl. *The Great Transformation: The Political and Economic Origins of Our Times* (1944). 2nd ed. Boston: Beacon Press, 2001.

Pressley, Sue Anne. "Memphis Jury Finds Conspiracy Led to King Assassination." *The Washington Post*, Dec 8, 1999, online at https://www.washingtonpost.com/archive/politics/1999/12/09/memphis-jury-finds-conspiracy-led-to-king-assassination/318b25c1-e5cd-44f48522-231c7a54f880.

Prior, Michael. *Jesus the Liberator: Nazareth Liberation Theology, Luke 4:16–30.* Sheffield, UK: Sheffield Academic Press, 1995.

Reid, B. E. "'Do You See This Woman?' Luke 7:36–50 as a Paradigm for Feminist Hermeneutics." *Biblical Research* 40 (1995): 37–49.

Resseguie, J. L. "Automatization and Defamiliarization in Luke 7:36–50." *Journal of Literature and Theology* 5, no. 2 (1991): 137–150.

Rhoads, David. *Israel in Revolution, 6–74 CE: A Political History Based on the Writings of Josephus.* Minneapolis, MN: Fortress Press, 1976.

———"Children of Abraham, Children of God: Metaphorical Kinship in Paul's Letter to the Galatians." *Currents in Theology and Mission* 31, no. 4 (August 2004): 282.

Richards, William. *"To a Friend of God": The Special Material of Luke's Gospel.* Saskatoon, unpublished manuscript, 2015.

Richter, Sandra. *The Epic of Eden: A Christian Entry into the Old Testament.* Downers Grove, IL: InterVarsity Press, 2008.

Ricoeur, Paul. *Freud and Philosophy.* New Haven, CT: Yale University Press, 1970.

———. "The Model of the Text: Meaningful Action Considered as a Text." In *Understanding and Social Inquiry*, edited by F. Dallmayr and T. McCarthy. South Bend, IN: University of Notre Dame Press, 1977.

Ringe, Sharon. *Jesus, Liberation, and the Biblical Jubilee: Images for Ethics and Christology.* Minneapolis, MN: Fortress Press, 1985.

Robeyns, Ingrid. "What, if Anything, Is Wrong with Extreme Wealth?" *Journal of Human Development and Capabilities*, 20, no. 3 (2019): 251 266. https://doi.org/10.1080/19452829.2019.1633734.

——— *Limitarianism: The Case against Extreme Wealth.* New York: Astra House, 2024.

Rostovtzeff, Michael. *Social and Economic History of the Roman Empire.* 2nd ed. Oxford: Clarendon, 1957.

Rothberg, Michael. *The Implicated Subject: Beyond Victims and Perpetrators.* Redwood City, CA: Stanford University Press, 2019.

Safrai, S., and M. Stern, eds. *The Jewish People in the First Century: Historical Geography, Political History, Social Cultural and Religious Life and Institution* 1. Assen: Van Corcum, 1974.

Sahlins, Marshall. *Stone Age Economics*. New York: Aldine de Gruyter, 1972.

Sanders, J. A. "Extravagant Love." *New Blackfriars* 68, no. 806 (1987): 278–284.

Scheidel, Walter, and Steven J. Friesen. "The Size of the Economy and the Distribution of Income in the Roman Empire." *The Journal of Roman Studies* 99 (2009) 61–91.

Schluter, Michael, John Ashcroft, and James Jones, eds. *Jubilee Manifesto: A Framework, Agenda & Strategy for Christian Social Reform*. Downers Grove, IL: InterVarsity Press, 2005.

Schottroff, Luise, and Wolfgang Stegemann. *Jesus and the Hope of the Poor*. Translated by M. O'Connell. Maryknoll, NY: Orbis, 1986.

Schultz, Brian. "Jesus as Archelaus in the Parable of the Pounds (Lk. 19:112–7)." *Novum Testamentum* 49, no. 2 (2007): 105–127. http://www.jstor.org/stable/25442543.

Scott, Brandon. *Hear Then the Parable*. Minneapolis, MN: Fortress Press, 1989.

Scott, James C. *Against the Grain: A Deep History of the Earliest States*. New Haven, CT: Yale University Press, 2017.

Seo, Pyung Soo. *Luke's Jesus in the Roman Empire and the Emperor in the Gospel of Luke*. Eugene, OR: Pickwick Publications, 2015.

Shepard, Paul. *The Only World We've Got*. San Francisco: Sierra Club Books, 1996.

——— *Coming Home to the Pleistocene*. Washington, DC: Island Press, 1998.

Silko, Leslie Marmon. *Ceremony*. New York: Viking Press, 1977.

Sloan, Robert B. *The Favorable Year of the Lord: A Study of Jubilary Theology in the Gospel of Luke*. Austin, TX: Schola Press, 1977.

Smiley, Tavis, and Cornel West. *The Rich and the Rest of Us: A Poverty Manifesto*. New York: Smiley Books, 2012.

Song, C. S. *Third-Eye Theology: Theology in Formation in Asian Settings*. Maryknoll, NY: Orbis Books, 1979.

Sorek, Susan. *Jews against Rome: War in Palestine AD 66–73*. New York: Continuum, 2008.

Stegemann, Ekkehard and Wolfgang Stegemann. *The Jesus Movement: A Social History of its First Century*. Translated by O. C. Dean. Minneapolis, MN: Fortress Press, 1999.

Streett, R. Alan. *Songs of Resistance: Challenging Caesar and Empire*. Eugene, OR: Cascade Books, 2022.

Talbert, Charles. *Reading Luke: A Literary and Theological Commentary on the Third Gospel*. New York: Crossroad, 1992.

Támez, Elsa. *Bible of the Oppressed*. Translated by Matthew O'Connell. Eugene, OR: Wipf & Stock, 2006.

Tannehill, Robert. *The Narrative Unity of Luke-Acts: A Literary Interpretation I*. Minneapolis, MN: Fortress Press, 1986.

Thomaskutty, Johnson. "A Sociolinguistic Reading of *ptōchos* in Luke's Gospel, Part I." *New Testament Scholarship Worldwide*. October 15, 2013. https://ntscholarship.wordpress.com/2013/10/15/a-sociolinguistic-reading-of-ptochos-in-lukes-gospel-part-i-2/.

Tönnies, Ferdinand. *Community and Society* (1887). Translated by Charles P. Loomis. Mineola, NY: Dover Publications, 2011.

Trocmé, André. *Jesus and the Nonviolent Revolution*. Maryknoll, NY: Orbis Books, 2003.

Tuck, Eve and C. Ree. "A Glossary of Haunting." In *Handbook of Autoethnography*, edited by S. Jones, T. Adams and C. Ellis, 639–658. Philadelphia, PA: Routledge, 2018.

Tudge, Colin. *The Time before History: 5 Million Years of Human Impact.* New York: Simon & Schuster, 1996.

Utley, Bob. "Luke the Historian: Acts." *Study Guide Commentary Series, New Testament* 3B. Published online, 2013, https://bible.org/book/export/html/21323.

Van Eck, E. "Do Not Question My Honour: A Social-scientific Reading of the Parable of the Minas (Lk 19:12b–24, 27)." *HTS Teologiese Studies/Theological Studies* 67, no. 3, Art. #977 (2011) https://doi.org/10.4102/hts.v67i3.977.

Vecsey, Christopher. *Imagine Ourselves Richly: Mythic Narratives of North American Indians.* San Francisco: Harper & Row, 1991.

Wachtel, Paul. *The Poverty of Affluence: A Psychological Portrait of the American Way of Life*. Santa Cruz, CA: New Society Publishers, 1989.

Waetjen, Herman. "Imitation of the Year of Jubilee in the Parable of Workers in the Vineyard." In *Liberating Biblical Study*, edited by Laurel Dykstra and Ched Myers, 93–104. Eugene, OR: Cascade Books, 2011.

Wagner, Donald. *Glory to God in the Lowest: Journeys to an Unholy Land.* Olive Branch Press, 2022.

Walzer, Michael. *Exodus and Revolution*. Revised edition. New York: Basic Books, 1986.

Waskow, Arthur. "And the Earth Is Filled with the Breath of Life." In *Torah of the Earth: Exploring 4,000 Years of Ecological Thought in Judaism II*, edited by Arthur Waskow, 261–286. Woodstock, VT: Jewish Lights Publishing, 2000.

Waskow, Arthur. *Dancing in God's Earthquake: The Coming Transformation of Religion*. Maryknoll, NY: Orbis, 2020.

Watts, James W. "Leviticus 25's History of Inspiring Freedom as a Moral Challenge to Literary-Historical Interpretation." *Biblical Interpretation 14, no. 2*. Syracuse: Syracuse University, 2023. Online 2022 doi:10.1163/15685152-20221703.

Wells, Jo Bailey. "Squandering and Scattering." *The Christian Century*. September 17, 2007. https://www.christiancentury.org/blogs/archive/2007-09/squandering-and-scattering.

Wink, Walter. *Engaging the Powers: Discernment and Resistance in a World of Domination*. Minneapolis, MN: Augsburg Fortress, 1992.

Winn, Christian T. Collins. *Jesus, Jubilee, and the Politics of God's Reign*. Grand Rapids, MI: Eerdmans, 2023.

Witherington, B. *Conflict and Community in Corinth: A socio-rhetorical commentary on 1 and 2 Corinthians*. Grand Rapids, MI: Eerdmans and Paternoster, 1995.

Wolf, Eric. *Europe and the People without History*. Berkeley: University of California Press, 1982.

Wolfe, Patrick. "Settler Colonialism and the Elimination of the Native." *Journal of Genocide Research* 8, no. 4 (December 2006): 387–409.

Yoder, John Howard. *The Politics of Jesus*. Grand Rapids, MI: Eerdmans, 1972.

York, John. *The Last Shall Be First: The Rhetoric of Reversal in Luke*. Journal for the Study of the New Testament, Supplement Series 46. Sheffield, UK: JSOT Press, 1991.

Zank, Michael. "Apocalyptic Literature." *Michael Zank*, October 25, 2019. https://blogs.bu.edu/mzank/2019/10/25/apocalyptic-literature/.

Zerwick, Max, and Mary Grosvenor. *A Grammatical Analysis of the Greek New Testament.* Revised ed. Rome, Italy: Biblical Institute Press, 1981.

Zucconi, Laura. "Ancient Near Eastern and Mediterranean Medicine." *The Bible and Interpretation*, January 2020. https://bibleinterp.arizona.edu/articles/ancient-near-eastern-and-mediterranean-medicine.

NAMES INDEX

SUBJECT INDEX

SCRIPTURE INDEX

Leviticus

Numbers

Deuteronomy

Joshua

Judges

1 Samuel

2 Samuel

1 Kings

2 Kings

2 Chronicles

Nehemiah

Esther

Job

Psalms

Proverbs

Isaiah

Jeremiah

Lamentations

Ezekiel

Daniel

Hosea

Joel

Mark

Luke

John

Acts

Romans

1 Corinthians

2 Corinthians